Makers of
History

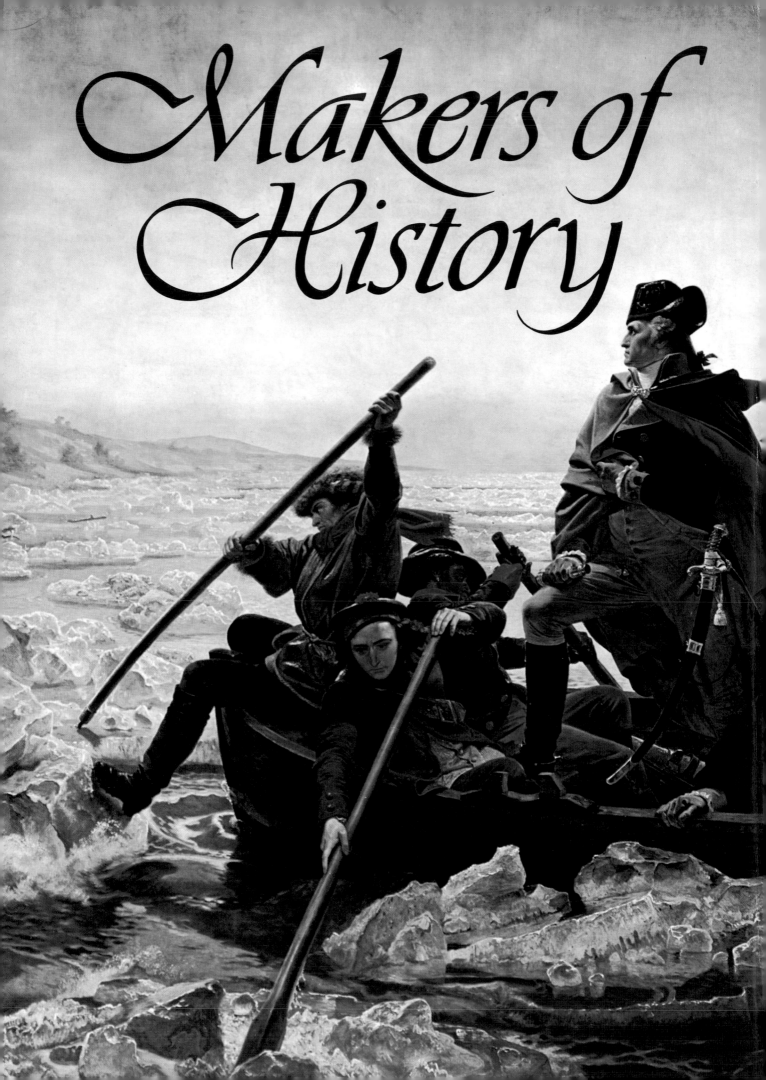

Makers of History

Elizabeth Floyd and
Geoffrey Hindley

Bloomsbury Books
London

Editorial Coordinator: John Mason
Art Editor: Grahame Dudley
Design: Juanita Grout
Editor: Paul Hutchinson
Research: Marian Pullen,
Frances Vargo, Sarah Waters

©J.G. Ferguson Publishing Company U.S.A.

This edition published 1989 by
Bloomsbury Books an imprint of
Godfrey Cave Associates Limited
42 Bloomsbury Street, London WC1B 3QJ
Printed in Hong Kong by Regent Publishing Services Ltd.
ISBN 1 870630 18 1

Frontispiece: "Washington Crossing the
Delaware" by Emmanuel Leutzé. George
Washington, who led a five-year war against almost
impossible odds and achieved independence for the
United States, is among the great makers of
American history.

Introduction

This book covers world history from the earliest times to the present in a novel and exciting way – by concentrating upon men and women whose deeds or ideas have, in fact, made history. Here are the lives of over 150 kings, statesmen, soldiers, patriots, revolutionaries, and religious leaders who directed the course of history. From men like Abraham and Julius Caesar who dominated the ancient world, it spans the Middle Ages, the Renaissance, the American and French revolutions, the 19th century, and our own tumultuous century. Here the figures range from leaders of World War I such as Kaiser William II and Clemenceau, President Wilson and Lloyd George to great patriots such as Sun Yat-Sen and Kemal Ataturk. With Hitler, Mussolini, Roosevelt, Churchill, De Gaulle, and Stalin, World War II is fully covered. The post-war years provide a wealth of names whose memories are still fresh, from Khruschev to Kennedy, from Mao Tse-Tung to Ben Gurion. A complete index to the history-makers included in the book may be found on page 318. The result is a fascinating introduction to the whole study of history for student and browsing reader alike.

Abraham

c1800 BC

An obscure shepherd tended his flock near Ur at the head of the Persian Gulf. He was Abraham, then called Abram, and the history of two peoples and three religions based on the belief in one god begins with him in about 1800 BC. The Old Testament states that he was chosen by God to travel to a new land, Canaan. There, through his son, Isaac, the Jewish people, Judaism, and Christianity are said to have been born. Through his son Ishmael, the Arab people and Islam came to be.

Ur was one of many cities in the fertile plain between the Tigris and Euphrates rivers in present day Iraq. Known then as Mesopotamia, it was one of the two areas in the Middle East where people first settled down, farmed, and founded civilizations. Egypt, in the Nile valley, was the other. The arc of watered land connecting them was called the fertile crescent.

Most of the people of Mesopotamia were Sumerians, but Abraham was an Aramaean. The Aramaeans were nomadic herders. They prob-

Above: mosaic of agrarian life in Sumeria as Abraham would have seen it.

Left: portrait of Abraham by the 17th-century Bolognese painter Guercino. No authoritative records exist to show what Abraham really looked like, so Guercino is clearly drawing on his own imagination.

Above: this pen and ink drawing by Rembrandt shows Sarai complaining to Abraham of their Egyptian maid Hagar. Hagar had borne Abraham's son Ishmael, as Sarai was barren.

ably came originally from the Arabian peninsula and had migrated to irrigated areas around the cities to obtain food and water for their flocks of sheep.

Nobody knows why Abraham's father Terah, the head of the family, decided to leave Ur and move north to Heran. He was probably looking for better grazing land and chose Heran because it was a friendly town whose people worshipped the same gods as the people in Ur.

Terah died in Heran, and Abraham became head of the family. At about the same time, it is said that a new god, unknown to anyone before then, spoke to Abraham and told him to take his wife, Sahai, and his nephew Lot, and travel to a new land. This was the God of the scriptures, and Abraham apparently obeyed His commands, and went with Sarai and Lot along the fertile crescent until he came to Canaan, a hilly area west of the Jordan river. Here, God appeared again, saying, "Unto thy descendents I will give this land." Abraham pitched his tent, built an alter to God and turned his sheep loose to graze. For years to come, he continued to wander as far afield as Egypt, but always returned to Canaan, the land God had promised his descendants.

Abraham still had a problem – no children. Sarai was barren. She suggested that Abraham have a child by a woman of her choosing, her Egyptian maid Hagar. This was quite in keeping with the custom of the time. Hagar conceived a child by Abraham. But Sarai responded by driving her out into the desert. God appeared to Hagar. He told her that she would bear a son to be called Ishmael, who would father a nation.

Hagar returned to Abraham's household, and duly bore a son. Later she was again driven out into the desert where God looked after her and her child. Her son, Ishmael, grew up, and married an Egyptian, who bore him 12 sons. These sons, their father, and their grandfather, Abraham, are regarded by Arabs as the founders of their nation.

Ishmael was not to be Abraham's only son. According to legend, God appeared again – this time with a list of commands and revelations. He ordered Abraham to change his name from Abram to Abraham, "father of nations," and Sarai's name to Sarah, "princess." God revealed that Sarah would give birth to a son, whose name would be Isaac. Both Abraham and Sarah laughed when they heard this news, for Sarah was 90 years old and Abraham 100. Sarah bore a son within a year.

The Old Testament tells of the sadness Abraham felt when he received word from God that he was to sacrifice 12-year old Isaac as a burnt offering. Still, he prepared to follow God's word. He piled firewood on his son's shoulders. Together they climbed Mount Moriah where the sacrifice was to take place. Abraham bound Isaac, and placed him on top of the wood. As he was about to drive his knife into the boy, God stopped him. Abraham had proved his faith. A ram appeared on the scene, and was slaughtered instead.

Isaac's salvation seemed to assure Abraham of descendants, but his work was not yet done. A wife had to be found for Isaac. He did not want his son to marry a Canaanite. The bride would not believe in his God, so he sent his most trusted servant back to Heran to find a woman from among his own people. The servant found Rebekah, granddaughter of Abraham's brother, Nahor. Rebekah, like Sarah, seemed to be barren, but she eventually gave birth to twin sons, Esau and Jacob. Esau, the firstborn, sold his birthright to Jacob for food when he was starving. Jacob's 12 sons are said to have given birth

Above: this miniature from a 15th-century manuscript depicts Abraham praying to God.

Below: the 19th-century French illustrator Gustave Dore, one of the most prolific book artists of his time, depicts Abraham's journey into Canaan in this engraving. This fertile land was the home of Judaism and occupied territory now claimed by the state of Israel. This area of the Middle East has been a major region for sheep farming for thousands of years.

to the origins of the 12 tribes of the Children of Israel.

Hundreds of years were to pass before Abraham's descendants through Jacob would become a nation and rule Canaan as their homeland. They did not rule it for long before they were dispersed. But they would never forget Abraham and God's promise to him. They would return more than 2000 years later to found the modern state of Israel in the land where Abraham once grazed his sheep, and would live in still unresolved conflict with their Arab neighbors.

Moses

c1450-1300 BC

Moses seemed an unpromising choice as the man to lead the Israelites from bondage in Egypt to the promised land. His stammer was not calculated to inspire. He had also murdered in his time – to save a fellow Hebrew from the brutal attentions of an Egyptian taskmaster. The Old Testament says that God (Yahweh) appeared before Moses in a burning bush that was not consumed, and told him to save his people. "Who am I?" Moses protested. God persisted, and Moses finally agreed.

After a harrowing escape from Egypt, the Israelites wandered for 40 years in the Sinai desert. Not surprisingly, their morale suffered badly. They complained, blamed Moses for everything, and even pleaded to return to Egypt. Moses got angry and discouraged too, but with God as his constant companion, he instilled discipline and a sense of destiny into his people. They reached the promised land safely at last, and went on to conquer it and build a nation there.

The Israelites Moses delivered to Canaan had been sustained and inspired by laws handed down from God to Moses and taught them during their 40-year exodus. Moses is said to have been told many of these laws in their third month in southern Sinai. God called upon Moses to climb Mount Sinai. There He spelled out the civil, criminal, and religious laws by which the Israelites were to live and to worship. Moses carried back two stone tablets upon which God had written the most important of his laws, the Ten Commandments. These became the foundation of the moral beliefs both of Jews and Christians.

Moses did not go on with his people to the promised land. His job was done. He climbed to the top of Mount Pisgah to catch a glimpse of

Above: this Gustave Dore engraving illustrates the famous Old Testament legend of Moses being placed in the bull rushes. The Pharaoh, Ramses II, had ordered the murder of all the Israelites' newborn boys. So that her son could escape this fate, Moses' mother hid him in the bull rushes on the banks of the Nile river. The child was eventually discovered by Ramses' daughter, who adopted him. He was brought up in the Egyptian royal household and only learnt of his people's sufferings when he was a grown man.

Left: there is no historical data to indicate what Moses looked like, but many artists have attempted to portray him. The Italian artist Michaelangelo's statue of Moses is one of the best known examples. This 16th-century work can still be seen in the Church of St. Peter in Chains, Rome.

Canaan, but he never set foot there. He died as he was born, in a foreign land.

The exact details of Moses' death and burial are not known, but his birth is better documented. He was probably born in Egypt in the late 14th century BC. The Israelites had fled a famine in Canaan, and settled in Egypt about 400 years earlier. For most of that time they had lived there in peace and prosperity. Their numbers had grown until the Pharaoh (Ramses II) began to be wary of their potential power. To protect himself, he enslaved the Israelites and put them to work building cities for him under Egyptian taskmasters. When enslavement did not cut down their numbers, he ordered that all their new born male children should be slaughtered.

Moses survived infancy only because his mother hid him soon after his birth. When he was a few months old, she put him in a basket in the rushes near the bank of the Nile. He was found by none other than the Pharaoh's daughter. She adopted him and brought him up as part of the royal household.

As an adult, Moses found out about the plight of his people and tried to help them, but the Pharaoh heard about it and threatened to have him killed. Moses fled into exile. He settled in Midian territory in northwestern Arabia. Here, he met and married the daughter of Jethro, the leader of a Midian tribe. Moses tended Jethro's flocks and wandered far and wide in search of grazing land. One day, near Mount Sinai, God spoke to him from a bush that burned but was

to get away. Egyptian troops chased them and almost trapped them at the Sea of Reeds in northeastern Egypt. A wind came up and blew the water aside permitting them to cross in safety. The Egyptians rushed after them, but the wind shifted and they were drowned.

According to the Old Testament, God arranged the Israelites' miraculous escape from Egypt. He continued to watch over them and help them through all the trials and tribulations that followed. But it was Moses who acted as His go-between. It was Moses who explained, reassured, and sustained the people. He berated them for their weakness; and it was Moses who interceded with God for their forgiveness. Through Moses, the Israelites learned of their role as chosen people and their mission to return to the promised land. Largely because of him, they carried it out. Today, Christians and Jews alike regard Moses as the greatest of the early Hebrew leaders – the man most responsible for shaping the Jewish nation and its religious beliefs.

Left: this full-page illumination from the 9th-century Grandval Bible depicts Moses being given the tablets of Law by God (Yahweh), and showing them to the Israelites. The most important of God's laws were the Ten Commandments, which form the moral basis of both Judaism and Christianity.

Right: Moses in Egypt. This painting, by the early Renaissance artist Pinturicchio, is in the Sistine Chapel in Rome.

Below: Moses' name lives on in the Middle East. This is a 19th-century photograph of an oasis called Moses' Well.

not consumed, and assigned him his life's work. Whatever interpretation can be put on the burning bush story there is little doubt that Moses believed himself confronted with Deity.

A reluctant Moses returned to Egypt where he set about convincing his people that God had spoken to him and would help him lead them out of Egypt. His better spoken brother, Aaron, helped him in this considerable task. The Pharaoh was not so easily impressed. He was not about to accept the commands of an unknown god nor to let a large chunk of his workforce walk out on him. He had second thoughts after a series of plagues visited themselves upon Egypt. It is said that the Nile's water turned to blood, and frogs, lice, flies, locusts, and other pests infested the land. Finally, the first born child of every Egyptian family died.

The Israelites were spared. God had instructed them to kill a lamb and smear its blood on the doors of their homes so they would be passed over. The Pharaoh relented. He was in despair at the loss of his own son, and the spectacle his ravaged land presented. The Israelites were able

Solomon
c1015-977BC

Many of the hills, pools, springs, and other physical features of the land of modern Israel would be familiar to the ancient Israelites. Archeologists have also uncovered cities, fortresses and houses that existed in Biblical times. The most sacred to Israelis of all these remains is a stone wall in the Old City of Jerusalem (the Wailing Wall). It borders the rocky hill where King Solomon built his magnificent temple in the 10th century BC. Under Solomon's rule, ancient Israel reached its peak of power.

Solomon succeeded to the throne of his father, David. David began life as a shepherd and ended as king, ruling an empire stretching from Egypt to the Euphrates river. Solomon was not David's eldest son, but his mother, Bathsheba, persuaded David to annoint him as king while David still lived so there would be no argument over the succession. After David's death, Solomon had his rivals and enemies murdered as extra insurance against any challenge to his authority.

Solomon took no chances on losing his empire either. Alliances were formed with vassal states and neighbors through marriage. According to the Old Testament he had 700 wives and 300 concubines. Solomon had built garrison cities at strategic points and stationed troops, horses, and chariots in them. Colonies of Israelites were planted in outlying areas to protect administrative and commercial interests.

Israel was divided into 12 administrative districts, the lines cutting across the old tribal lines to prevent conspiracies. Each district had to supply food for the royal household of about 5000 people for one month a year.

Right: this wall painting, completed in the 3rd century AD in a Mesopotamian synagogue, is an impression of the lavish temple Solomon had built in Jerusalem. This imposing structure had been the Jews' most important place of worship from as early as the 10th century BC.

Bottom right: The famous "Wailing Wall" in the heart of the old city of Jerusalem is visited by devout Jews from all over the world. It skirts the base of the hill on which Solomon built his synagogue. The Wall is apparently part of the western side of King Herod's temple. Though modern Israel vociferously champions sexual equality, the ancient wall is still provided with a "women's sector."

The empire was primarily a commercial one. It took full advantage of its strategic location at the crossroads of trade routes between Africa, Asia, and the Mediterranean. Solomon taxed caravans passing through his territory. He sold them supplies, and bought their goods to sell elsewhere at a profit. He also traded Israeli goods such as copper for the much needed wares of others.

The Queen of Sheba might have traded with Solomon. Sheba lay along the Red Sea, either in

Left: Solomon and Sheba as depicted by the 15th-century Italian painter Piero della Francesca. Solomon and Sheba have been favorite subjects for artists over the centuries, even though there is little historical data showing a likeness of Solomon or Sheba. In this example, Solomon is shown wearing the headgear typical of semitic men in 15th-century Europe.

southern Arabia or in eastern Africa. The queen controlled the sea routes to the east and traded in such sought after products as gold, spices, and precious stones. Legend has it that Solomon and the queen were lovers, and they bore a son who founded the royal house of Ethiopia. The Bible says only that the queen heard of Solomon's wisdom and wealth. Her curiosity aroused, she paid him a royal visit, tested him with questions, and exchanged lavish gifts with him before returning to Sheba.

Right: a section of the Assyrian relief sculpture the "Black Obelisk' completed at Nimrud between 858 and 828 BC. It depicts Jews bringing tribute from Jehu to the Assyrians. The work clearly shows how Jews in the ancient Middle East looked. Such men would have been completely familiar to Solomon. Indeed, this work gives us a pretty clear indication as to what Solomon looked like himself. The "Black Obelisk" is housed in the British Museum, London.

Solomon used the spoils of trade to finance a vast building program that included cities, fortresses, quarters for some of his wives and for foreign traders and envoys. But most of the money went to build a palace, the famous Wailing Wall, and a magnificent temple in Israel's capital city, Jerusalem.

The temple took seven years to build and was lavishly decorated with carved cedar wood covered and inlaid in gold and precious stones. King Hiram of Tyre, an ally of Solomon, supplied the gold and cedar, as well as designers and craftsmen. Some of the workforce were Canaanites. But with more than 100,000 workers needed, Israelites also had to work as builders. Solomon forced them to put in one month in three as laborers.

When the temple was completed, the ark of the covenant containing the stone tablets bearing the Ten Commandments was placed inside. Solomon dedicated the temple. Thousands of sheep and oxen were slaughtered in sacrifice. A great feast lasting seven days was attended by people from all over the empire.

Solomon's huge building program and his royal life style eventually took its toll. The people resented the heavy taxes and forced labor, and grew restless. Old tribal rivalries surfaced. Solo-

mon was accused of forsaking his God for the gods of his foreign wives. Even the vassal states caused trouble.

Solomon held the empire together for the rest of his life. But his son, Rehoboam, who succeeded him, was not as strong or able as his father. The 10 northern tribes of Israel seceded from the country dividing it into two quarrelsome rivals, Israel and Judah. Both were eventually conquered by outsiders.

Solomon's temple stood for almost 400 years. It made Jerusalem the spiritual, if not the political, capital of the Children of Israel. Destroyed by the Babylonians in 580 BC, it was rebuilt 65 years later and enlarged and restored by the Roman ruler Herod, beginning in 20 BC. The Roman emperor Titus destroyed Herod's temple in 70 AD. It was never rebuilt, but the west wall of the platform supporting it remained. It continued to inspire latter-day Israelites and to pull them back to Jerusalem to restore it once more to the central place it held in the lives of the ancient Israelites in the days of Solomon.

Thutmose III
c1490-1436 BC

Thutmose III became Pharaoh of Egypt as a boy of about 10. But he had no real power for more than 20 years. His shrewd and ambitious stepmother, Queen Hatshepsut, had declared herself "king" in his stead. She permitted him to retain the title of co-regent and to be trained in such royal skills as archery and horsemanship,

but then she sent him off to spend his time with the army while she exercised the pharaoh's prerogatives. Not until Hatshepsut died did Thutmose attain the power due to a pharaoh. He was ready to use it by then. Taking full advantage of his military skills, he built a vast Egyptian empire. He became an able administrator, statesman, builder, even a patron of the arts. He is considered by many to have been Egypt's greatest pharaoh.

Thutmose achieved power at a critical moment in Egyptian history. His grandfather, Thutmose I, conquered much of Syria during his reign and impressed Egyptian authority there. But Egyptian influence waned through inattention during Hatshepsut's reign. A coalition of enemies was threatening to take power in the area. Thutmose III, acting as his own strategist and commander in chief, led his troops along the least expected route. Taking the enemy by surprise, he defeated them at Megiddo. The victory placed nearly all of Syria under Egyptian rule.

In a second military success, Thutmose III vanquished the Kingdom of the Mitanni, a Mesopotamian empire centered on the east bank of the Euphrates river. He built pontoon boats,

Above left: a portrait of Thutmose III. Under his reign, ancient Egypt reached a peak of power and prestige, culturally as well as militarily. Although Egypt remained a force to be reckoned with for centuries to come, it was never again to achieve the degree of influence it enjoyed under Thutmose III.

Above: Thutmose III had this obelisk built. It is the famous "Cleopatra's Needle', and is now placed on the Embankment, London, England.

Right: this detail from another obelisk shows Queen Hatsheput – Thutmose's stepmother. While she was alive effective power rested with her. Thutmose was pharaoh in name only. He was in this unhappy position for 20 years. Then Hatsheput died and he at last wielded power. Thutmose III is regarded by many historians as having the greatest influence on the development of ancient Egypt of any of the pharaohs.

and carried them overland by oxcart to the river bank. In the ensuing battle on the east bank of the river, the Mitanni were beaten and the King fled, abandoning much of his harem and his army. Thutmose set up a marker, showing the easternmost point of his advance, next to one placed there by his grandfather. He returned in triumph to Thebes, his capital on the Nile. Here he dedicated his prisoners and his booty to the state god, Amun.

Thutmose fought 17 campaigns to win and make safe an empire stretching from the east bank of the Euphrates to the Mediterranean and from northern Syria and present-day Lebanon to Nubia along the Nile in what is now Sudan. He held it together with a clever administrative system. He allowed the local ruler of each area to remain in power, but the son and heir was carted off to Egypt as a hostage. These hostages were brought up and educated at the Egyptian court. Egyptian ideas and methods were thoroughly instilled in them and then they were returned to their own countries when the time came for them to assume power. Fortresses and garrison cities were built at key points in the empire just in case. Local rulers were bound by oath to keep the peace and pay tribute.

Tribute from Egypt's many vassal states and gifts from independent neighbors anxious to keep on good terms such as Crete, Cyprus, Assyria, Babylonia, and the Hittite Kingdom swelled Egypt's coffers. Thutmose used much of the wealth to patronize arts and crafts and to build massive temples along the banks of the Nile. He added many buildings to the temple complex at Karnak near Thebes and decorated them with elaborate carvings. Two obelisks

Above: this magnificent temple at Deir el Bahri was built for Queen Hatsheput when she was at the height of her power. Built mainly by forced labor, the work on the temple claimed hundreds of lives before it was completed. It stood as a monument to Hatsheput's vanity.

Left: Thutmose III took after his stepmother in a taste for grandiosity. He ordered the building of the Temple of Amon at Karnak. Picture shows the three naves viewed from the north in the ceremonial temple of Thutmosis.

Right: this Egyptian tomb painting depicts guests at a banquet at around Thutmose' time. The people shown are typical of the social strata a pharaoh would be familiar with. The tomb painting can still be viewed at the British Museum, London.

added by Thutmose to the Temple complex are now in Rome and Istanbul. Obelisks Thutmose had built at Heliopolis are now in London and New York.

The closing years of Thutmose' reign saw the start of the most glorious period in Egyptian history. It was a time of peace, prosperity and splendor marked by the highest achievement in Egyptian art and architecture. Thutmose' son, Amenhotop II who succeeded him, and his grandson Thutmose IV ruled for most of this period. A decline began during the reign of his great grandson Amenhotop III and his son Ikhnaton. Ikhnaton was a reformer who introduced a new religion based on the worship of the sun as the one god. He moved the capital to Akhetaton (now Tel El Amarna) and introduced a more relaxed style of art. These changes were not accepted by the people. And the empire, now taken for granted and neglected, gradually crumbled. Ikhnaton's son Tutankhamen inherited a still rich but much smaller Egypt. It was an Egypt that would never again approach the glories of the past.

Assurbanipal
669-640 BC

Left: Assurbanipal hunting lions. Hunting was one of the favorite leisure pursuits of the Assyrian nobility. This illustration is part of a contemporary Assyrian relief.

As a boy, Assurbanipal had two tutors, a general and a scholar. Partly as a result of their instruction, he became the greatest of a long line of Assyrian rulers. The general taught him the harsh military tactics his ancestors used to build the Assyrian empire – siege warfare, sacking defeated cities, and exchanging populations to prevent uprisings. Assurbanipal was to use these techniques to hold on to and subjugate the vast territory he inherited. The scholar interested him in art, literature, and history. As king, Assurbanipal filled his capital at Nineveh on the Tigris river with huge temples and palaces decorated with magnificent bas-relief carvings. He built the world's first great library and filled it with catalogued cuneiform tablets covering such subjects as science, language, history, fables, and epics. Much of what we know about the ancient world comes from that source.

The Assyrian empire began with Assyria itself in northern Mesopotamia – successor to the earlier Mesopotamian civilizations of Sumer and Akkad. It gradually grew from the 13th century BC onwards under a succession of Assyrian kings including Tiglathpileser I and III, Ashurnasirpal II, Shalmaneser III and V, Sargon, Sennacherib, and Esar-Haddon.

When Assurbanipal became king, his father,

Esar-Haddon, was far away in Assyria's latest acquisition – Egypt. The old Assyrian king died there, and this encouraged the deposed Egyptian ruler to try to regain his throne. Assurbanipal was forced to take on Egypt as his first serious military opponent. Two campaigns were necessary for the seizure of one ancient Egyptian capital, Memphis, and the sacking of another, Thebes, before Assurbanipal restored control.

A far greater challenge to his authority came from Babylonia, south of Assyria. Assurbanipal's younger brother, Shamash-shum-ukin, ruled Babylonia. He had been given the job by their father. The younger brother ruled under the watchful eye of the government in Nineveh for 16 years. But eventually Shamash-shum-ukin was infected by the nationalist feelings of the Babylonians as well as other subject peoples like the Arabs and the Elamites. In 652 BC, he rebelled against Assyrian rule. Assurbanipal countered the rebellion by laying siege to Babylon and simply waiting for its people to starve. Two years after the siege began, Shamash-shum-ukin killed himself by leaping into the flames burning his palace. The city held for another two years before giving in. Assurbanipal looted Babylon,

Right: the rebuilding of Nineveh is recorded on this cuneiform tablet. This tablet is shaped as an octagonal prism and describes the 15 gates leading into the city, as well as the laying out of a park. Assurbanipal was a prominent scholar of his time, and he ordered the building of a magnificent library at Nineveh. This cuneiform and many other tablets on a whole range of subjects was stored there. Assurbanipal built Nineveh into the most beautiful city of the ancient world, and the Assyrian empire into a force to be reckoned with.

but rather than complete its destruction, he had it rebuilt, and named a Babylonian as its local ruler.

Babylonia's allies, the Arabs and the Elamites, refused to surrender after Babylon fell, and fought on in their own lands. Assurbanipal had little trouble routing the Arabs, but the Elamites proved more difficult. The war with them was waged for nine years until the Assyrians finally captured and sacked the Elamite capital, Susa, in 639 BC.

To mark the end of the Elamite war, Assurbanipal staged a victory parade. His chariot was pulled by four kings, and he boasted that he ruled the world. But while he had been fighting in the east, Egypt had rebelled yet again and had taken itself out of the Assyrian empire. The Egyptians were later to become allies and trading partners, but their departure signalled the decline of the Assyrian empire.

Little is known about the last 12 years of Assurbanipal's reign. Most of the empire held

Above: a reconstruction of Assurbanipal's capital at Nineveh. The illustration shows the palaces of Nimrud on the banks of the Tigris river shortly after they were completed. The skill and effort involved in building these magnificent structures with only the most primitive tools to hand can only be imagined. First published in London in 1853, this picture was included in Austin Layard's book *The Monuments of Nineveh.*

Below: Assurbanipal was a superb military strategist as well as a scholar. This Assyrian palace relief shows Assurbanipal leading his men in the capture of an enemy. The Assyrian war machine was formidable. While engineers undermine the city's walls, an enormous battering ram is employed for good measure.

together and was prosperous and well run by provincial governors with Assyrian garrisons standing by. The king probably did the same as his father, and named two of his sons to succeed him. But Assurbanipal's successors were unable to cope with the problems he left behind. The endless battles to preserve the empire had taken a huge toll in manpower, to such an extent that later kings were dependent upon foreign soldiers. Assurbanipal's building program and his court's luxurious life had drained the royal coffers. In 612 BC an alliance of Babylonians and Medians, using Assyrian tactics, captured and sacked Nineveh. The Assyrians fought on, but they were soon vanquished. Most of them, especially the craftsmen, were carted off into slavery.

Unlike many ancient peoples, the Assyrians were completely absorbed into other cultures. No trace of them can be found today. Only the ruins of Assyrian cities and the great library remain to tell the story of the once mighty Assyrian empire and its last great leader, Assurbanipal.

Nebuchadnezzar II
died 562 BC

Left: this 16th-century Dutch stained glass work depicts three children before Nebuchadnezzar. It was Nebuchadnezzar who finally defeated the mighty Assyrian empire and established Babylonia as the dominant power of the ancient world. The three children in this picture are from Judah. Nebuchadnezzar forced the surrender of its capital Jerusalem in 586 after a two-year siege. Most of Judah's population were taken into captivity in Babylon.

Below: the gates and walls of Nebuchadnezzar's rebuilt Babylon were adorned with ceramic representations of various animals. Ishtar gate was the most important in all Babylon. It surmounted a broad road, along which processions of lavish pomp were staged by Nebuchadnezzar at the height of his rule. The bull against a ceramic brick blue background was one of many that decorated the most impressive of all Babylon's many gates.

At the time of Nebuchadnezzar's birth, his country, Babylonia, was a subservient province in the mighty Assyrian empire. When he died 68 years later, he ruled a powerful Babylonian empire, which had swallowed not only Assyria but most of its provinces as well. He controlled this huge territory from a splendid palace topped by hanging gardens in Babylon. The Children of Israel, whom he had deported from Judah and taken into captivity, were numbered among his subjects.

Nebuchadnezzar and his father, Nabopolassar, brought about this startling change. Nabopolassar had been governor of the southern part of the Babylonian province under Assyrian rule. As soon as he saw that Assyrian power was declining, he led a revolt which freed Babylonia and then he went on to join the Median king in defeating the Assyrians and destroying their capital, Nineveh. Nebuchadnezzar began his military career alongside his father, fighting in mopping-up operations after the fall of Nineveh. He showed such skill that his father left him in charge and returned to Babylon.

Nebuchadnezzar won what was probably his greatest victory while still a crown prince – in a battle against the Egyptians at Carchemish on the Euphrates river in 606 BC. The Egyptians had marched through Syria and Palestine filling the vacuum left by the departing Assyrians and were endeavoring to save their old allies from final defeat. Even the Egyptians could not save Assyria. Soundly defeated by Nebuchadnezzar, they turned tail for home, leaving the whole area open to Babylonian takeover. Nebuchadnezzar chased them all the way to the Egyptian border before he was called home to take the throne upon the death of his father.

In the years that followed, Nebuchadnezzar made frequent forays into Syria and Palestine to expand and consolidate his empire, put down rebellions – many inspired by the Egyptians, and to collect tribute.

Judah was one of the most troublesome of his vassal states. This Hebrew state in Palestine had Jerusalem as its capital city. Judah rebelled against Babylonian rule in 600 BC, after Nebuchadnezzar had suffered heavy losses in a clash with the Egyptians and had gone home to Babylon to repair his chariots, and have a strategic rethink. He returned to Palestine in 598 BC. In 597 he attacked Judah, occupied Jerusalem, and deported the king to Babylon. Judah rebelled again, in 588. This time Nebuchadnezzar laid siege to Jerusalem. It surrendered in 586. Nebuchadnezzar looted and destroyed the city, including Solomon's temple. Most of its citizens were packed off to Babylon where they remained in captivity for 60 years.

The city the Hebrews found themselves in was the most splendid in the world at that time. Nebuchadnezzar was as interested in building his capital as he was in building his empire. Under his direction, a wide moat and two huge walls were built around the city. A Processional Way paved with limestone entered the city through the Ashtar Gate and led past the royal palace and all the important temples to the Euphrates river. Many of the gates and walls

Left: this print from a 14th-century French bible depicts Nebuchadnezzar eating grass. The book of Daniel tells us that the king "was driven from men and did eat grass like oxen" apparently as a punishment for his idolatry. Nebuchadnezzar comes in for a lot of criticism in the Old Testament, mostly unjustified as he was an able ruler.

Right: the dream of Nebuchadnezzar. According to Daniel, the king dreamed that he saw a huge tree reaching to heaven. A holy one came from heaven and ordered the tree felled. Daniel predicted that the king would be deposed and ordered to eat grass like oxen "for seven times" until he recognized that God ruled the kingdom of men. None of this actually came to pass.

were covered with glazed tiles bearing pictures of animals. Nebuchadnezzar built his palace around a series of open courtyards and roofed part of it with a terraced garden. This was later acclaimed by Greek travellers as one of the seven wonders of the ancient world. The king is said to have built the gardens for his wife, a Median princess, homesick for the hills and trees of her homeland.

Nebuchadnezzar withdrew from the splendor and luxury of Babylon to take on the Egyptians for the last time in 567 BC. It is known that he fought them in or near Egypt. The outcome of the battle, however, remains obscure. There are few records detailing the last years of his reign. In the Old Testament, it says he went mad in

Right: *The People Mourning over the Ruins of Jerusalem*, an engraving by Gustave Dore. Judah was the biggest nuisance of all Nebuchadnezzar's vassal states. It revolted against Babylonian rule in 600 BC, and again in 588 BC. This time Nebuchadnezzar sacked Judah's capital Jerusalem and took most of its citizens into captivity.

Below: perhaps the most famous representation of the Babylonian ruler, the *Madness of Nebuchadnezzar* by the English painter, poet, and visionary William Blake. Nebuchadnezzar's madness was probably a myth. Most historians believe that he remained an effective ruler until his death.

these years, but historians have found no evidence to support this. They think it more likely that he remained an effective administrator of his far-flung domain until his death.

The empire Nebuchadnezzar fought so hard to build and hold did not long survive him. His successors were weak and could not withstand the growing power of the Persians to the east. Within a few years, Babylon was again a subject to foreign rule – this time as part of the mighty Persian empire.

Darius I
584-486BC

Historians differ over which of the Achaemenian rulers of the Persian empire was the most significant. Many support Cyrus II. He built the huge empire, the largest the world had seen to that time. A fierce fighter but a modest and humane man, he was beloved by his people. But other historians insist that Cyrus' successor, Darius I, has a greater claim to greatness. He extended the empire into Europe and India, and organized it so efficiently that it survived almost 200 years and succumbed only to Alexander the Great.

Darius, the son of a noble Persian family, became king in 522 BC after the death of Cyrus and his two sons. Most likely to deter doubts about his claim to the throne, Darius had the story of his accession inscribed on a huge rock near the village of Behistun in present-day Iran. Most historians believe it is true. According to Darius, Cyrus left his throne to his eldest son, Cambyses, with an added provision that his younger son, Bardiya, should rule some of the eastern provinces. But the harsh Cambyses was jealous of his popular young brother, and when he became king, he had Bardiya killed secretly before leaving for Egypt to carry out his father's plan of conquest there. Cambyses succeeded in adding Egypt to the empire. But on the way home he heard that a usurper, bearing a strong likeness to Bardiya, had seized power and was attracting widespread support. Cambyses killed himself in despair, leaving the throne vacant.

Darius, then a member of Cambyses' bodyguard, and six other young nobles, suspected the usurper, managed to get into the royal palace, and killed him. Darius was a member of a branch of Cyrus' Achaemenian family. He considered himself the rightful heir to the throne and the empire, so he took power.

Not all of the vassal states agreed that Darius

Above: this gold buckle was worn by Darius I. It is but a small manifestation of the massive wealth of the Persian empire under Darius. The empire's prosperity persisted until it was defeated by the armies of Alexander the Great in 331 BC.

Left: Darius is shown giving audience to a priest in this relief from Persepolis. The sculpture was executed at the height of Darius' reign. His successor, Xerxes, is pictured standing behind the throne.

had a right to the throne. Many took advantage of his questionable position to rebel against Persian rule. The most serious of these revolts was in Babylonia. Darius laid a siege. At the same time he and his generals took on and defeated rebels in Susiana, Media, and many other provinces. According to Darius' account, he fought 19 battles in all to defeat nine rebel leaders. By 518 BC he had won control of the empire and established himself as both soldier and leader.

As a precaution against further internal disorder, Darius reorganized the administration of his empire. Under the old system, inherited from the Assyrians, a provincial governor or satrap ruled in each vassal state or province with little supervision or control from the palace. This loose arrangement made rebellion easier. Darius solved the problem by putting three officials in charge of each province – a satrap, a general, and a secretary of state. Each was independent of the other and reported directly to the king. Inspectors also visited each province at irregular intervals. Darius stationed garrisons of loyal troops in important centers to further discourage revolt.

Darius promoted centralization by improving transportation and trade within the empire. He built a royal road that ran from Susa in Persia to Sardis in Asia Minor. Weights and measures

Above: hunting was a favorite pastime of the Persian ruling class, and lions were a favorite prey. Here, Darius is shown chasing lions by chariot. This cylinder seal impression was made in about 500 BC. The inscription at the left of the picture gives Darius' name in three languages.

Left: Darius I is honored in this memorial on the Behistun Rock. The cuneiform inscription on the memorial is in three languages – Elamite, Babylonian, and Old Persian. The Behistun Rock is near the ruined town of the same name in modern-day western Iran.

were standardized. His gold coins were of such purity that they were soon accepted almost universally for currency.

Like Cyrus, Darius encouraged local peoples within the empire to maintain their customs, languages, and religions. In Egypt, for example, he restored the temple to the god Amon and ordered the Satrap there to cooperate with local priests to codify Egyptian laws. The Greek cities of Asia Minor, then under Persian rule, were given special privileges as religious sanctuaries. In Jerusalem, he allowed the Hebrews, who had returned to their homeland under Cyrus' rule, to rebuild their temple. Darius was probably responsible for making Zoroastrianism the state religion in Persia itself.

Darius drew on the ideas and skills of the many diverse people under his rule to build two new capital cities – an administrative capital at Susa and a new royal residence at Persepolis. Both were characterized by a new style of art and architecture created by merging the best of foreign influences and local ideas.

One of the few failures Darius experienced in his highly successful reign came near the end of his life. It was inflicted by the Greeks. The Greek city-states of Athens and Eretrea had supported uprisings in Persian controlled Greek cities in Asia Minor. Darius sent his fleet to punish the two city states in 492 BC, but it sank in a storm off Mount Athos. Two years later, a Persian land force defeated Eretrea but lost to an Athenian military force in the battle of Marathon. While Darius prepared for a third assault, Egypt rebelled drawing his attention away from Greece. He died before he could launch the attack. His son, Xerxes, picked up where he left off, but he too lost to the Greeks at the battle of Salamis.

Although a decline set in after Darius' death the Persian empire survived largely intact until it finally fell to Alexander in 331 BC. After Alexander's death, Persia came under a succession of rulers – the Selucids, the Parthians, and in 224 AD, the Sassanids, native Persians who revived the Achaemenian tradition. They built a new empire that extended to Egypt, established a smooth running administration. A splendid new capital was by then at Ctesiphon. They also revived Zoroastrianism as the state religion, and produced a wealth of new art. Conquered once again in 637 AD by the Arabs, Persia adopted Islam and produced some of the world's most beautiful Islamic art and architecture. The Arabs, along with the Achaemenids, and the other rulers of Persia together laid the foundation for what is today the modern state of Iran.

Solon
c638-559BC

Solon was an Athenian poet who used his art to put over his politics. He believed that the state took precedence over any group or individual in it, that government should be moral and humane, and that moderation should be exercised in all things. Elected archon, the head of the Athenian government, in 594 BC, he set reforms in train which ended aristocratic rule, eased poverty, humanized the law, and laid the foundations for Athenian democracy.

A noble, and a member of the ruling class by birth, Solon rose to power at a time of crisis in Athens. Growing unrest in all sections of society threatened revolution. Many farmers were hopelessly in debt. Some had put themselves up as security for loans, and had become slaves when they failed to repay. Others had become virtual serfs. They had made agreements with larger landowners whereby they had to hand over part of the produce of their land each year to pay off their debt. Rich landowners traded their crops in foreign countries for exotic luxuries rather than feed the growing city population. The middle class farmers, merchants, and craftsmen resented the monopoly on political power enjoyed by the nobility.

Solon put right most of Athens' economic problems with a few brave measures. He freed all those enslaved for debt, redeemed all mortgaged land, and made it an offence for anyone to offer his person as security for a loan. The export of any food products, except olive oil which was plentiful, was forbidden. Citizenship was granted to foreign craftsmen living in Athens, and they were encouraged to produce goods for export.

The political problems took a little longer to solve. Solon tackled them by writing a new constitution which allotted political power on the basis of wealth rather than birth. The population was divided into four groups based on the value

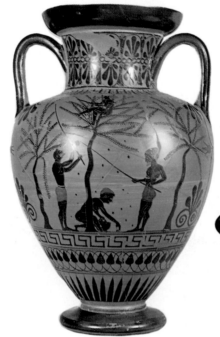

of the goods they produced. All citizens were granted some political power, but the richest groups received the most. All free citizens could sit in the Assembly which passed laws, elected officials, and heard appeals from the courts. A Council of Four Hundred, open to the top three economic groups, was created to prepare the agenda for the Assembly. Only members of the two wealthiest groups could be archon, or hold other senior government posts.

A new code of laws guided the rule of the new government. The old laws, codified by a former archon named Draco, were so harsh that the adjective "Draconian" was coined. Solon threw out almost all Draco's laws and put a more moderate and humane set in their place. The laws were inscribed on wooden tablets and posted in public. Every citizen had to swear that he

Above: in the Athens of Solon's time, household utensils often told a little story in their decorations. This water pitcher shows an olive tree being shaken to bring the fruit to the ground, where it is gathered up by an assistant.

Above right: depictions of battle were a favorite pottery decoration. The painting on the inside of this cup shows an injured Spartan being carried to safety by his comrades. Spartans were the toughest and most disciplined of Greek warriors.

Left: the great Athenian poet and statesman, Solon. He is still regarded by many as the "father of democracy."

Right: an ox draws a primitive plow. Ancient Greek agriculture only cultivated half the fields each year. The other half were left fallow to recover fertility. Under Solon, peasants like the man shown here were freed from the threat of enslavement for debt.

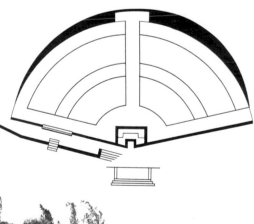

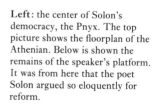

Above: Athenian foot soldiers (hoplites) pictured going into battle on this Chigi vase. Impressively equipped soldiers like this preserved the security and increased the power of Athens. Meanwhile, the Athenian citizen enjoyed a period of unprecedented political and cultural advance during Solon's reign.

Left: the center of Solon's democracy, the Pnyx. The top picture shows the floorplan of the Athenian. Below is shown the remains of the speaker's platform. It was from here that the poet Solon argued so eloquently for reform.

would uphold and obey them. Solon's code of laws remained in force until about 400 BC and parts of it were retained in the new code which took its place.

Solon used poetry to explain and justify his reforms, just as he had used it to urge change before he gained power. But many Athenians were dissatisfied by his moderate approach. Farmers complained because he had not redistributed the land. Nobles were put out because they had to share power with ordinary citizens. To give Athenians time to try out, and get used to his reforms, Solon left Athens, and travelled for 10 years. On his return, he found the people divided, and moving steadily towards tyranny. He warned them of the danger through his poetry, but they dismissed the old man as mad.

A series of tyrants began to come to power at about the time of Solon's death, but democracy was restored some 50 years later in 511 BC. During the golden age of Athenian democracy which followed, Greek thinkers made lists of the sages of the previous century whose ideas had influenced them most. Solon was included on every list. Even today, this Athenian statesman and poet is sometimes called the "father of democracy".

Pericles
c490-429 BC

Pericles was apparently not easy to get on with. Aloof, unemotional, and arrogant, he had few friends, and spent most of his time working. But the Athenians repeatedly elected him to be one of their top government officials for 30 years. They knew he believed deeply in their democratic government, and the freedom it gave them to think, learn, and create. As a result, Pericles presided over a golden age of Athenian culture. The city achieved a peak of political power as a result of his spreading Athenian ideas.

Pericles was the son of a wealthy and prominent Athenian family. He first came to public attention as one of a group of radicals trying to add even more reforms to Athens' already democratic constitution. As a means of extending the democratic rights of the poor, this group succeeded in having all members of the government from top officials to members of the popular assembly, and juries paid for their services. Shortly after these reforms were accepted, in about 461 BC, Pericles was elected one of Athens' 10 strategi, or generals. He continued to be re-

Right: many theaters like this were built for Pericles as he developed Athens. This one has one of the world's first stages, and can seat 14,000 people: Its acoustics are excellent.

elected annually almost until the end of his life. In theory, the Assembly held supreme power, but in fact it usually gave Pericles what he wanted.

When Pericles began to serve in the government, Athens, an independent city-state, was a member with other Greek city-states in the

Right: similar to the later Olympic games, the Panathenaic games were held annually in Athens in Pericles' time as part of the ceremonies in honor of the goddess Athena.

Left: a Roman copy of a Greek portrait bust of Pericles. One of Pericles' main concerns while in power was to open the government of Athens so that the common man could have a say in its running. His greatest ambition was to make Athens the political and cultural leader of the Greek states. In this, Pericles amply succeeded.

Delian League. The League had been formed to harass the neighboring Persian Empire and to protect Greeks from Persian attacks. Athens was virtually the only Greek city-state with a navy, so it did most of the fighting, while other League members paid money to a treasury on the centrally located island of Delos. Athens, gradually, and not surprisingly, came to dominate the League. Other members were treated more like vassal states than allies. Athens told them how much they must pay, and in some cases, forced Athenian style governments on them. When some members tried to resign, military force was used to discourage them.

Pericles wanted to make Athens the political and cultural leader of the Greek states. With the League, it had political dominance. To help achieve cultural supremacy, he embarked on a massive building program. The temples that the Persians destroyed when they sacked the city in 480 BC were replaced. Most important of the building sites was the Acropolis. There was an elaborate gate, the Proplaea; a magnificent temple to the goddess Athena (later called the Parthenon), and a smaller temple to victory. To pay for these, and other costly buildings, the Athenians moved the League's treasury from Delos to Athens. Understandably, some League members protested at Athens' use of their war fund for temples. Athens took no notice, and the new temples gradually took shape. Sparta, Athens' powerful neighbor to the south, proved more troublesome.

Sparta had once been as powerful as Athens, but it fell behind after the Persian attacks in 490 and 480 BC because it lacked a navy with which to continue the fight. It resented Athens' growing power, refused to join the Delian League, and gave no money for the temples. Instead it formed its own group of allies made up mostly of the city-states located around Sparta on the Peloponnesus. When Athens attempted to extend its influence in this area, the two clashed. After some fighting among the two camps, Athens and Sparta reached an agreement in 445 BC. Athens' empire was to be confined largely to the islands, and overseas Greek cities, while Sparta's would include the mainland cities, especially those in the Peloponnesus.

Thirteen years of peace followed this agreement – the only peace Athens had had during Pericles' lifetime. Athenians were free to enjoy one of the most creative, and intellectually

Above: the Acropolis which Pericles had built still stands overlooking the modern city of Athens. Dominating the Acropolis is the huge but elegant bulk of the Parthenon – a temple built in honor of the goddess Athena. The Erechtheum temple – dedicated to Erechtheus, supposed founder of Athens – is on the left of the Parthenon. To the extreme left of the picture is the Propylaea (gatehouse).

Below: when built, the Parthenon was lavishly decorated and adorned in a manner befitting a temple dedicated to the goddess Athena. No effort was spared. Phidias sculptured this frieze. It depicts Athenian riders preparing to form a procession.

stimulating periods in all history. Phidias, and his assistants carved the friezes and pediments for the Parthenon, and the huge 40-foot-high ivory and gold statue of Athena to go inside, while poets such as Aeschylus, Sophocles, and Euripides wrote plays that were performed in open air theaters, and attended by Greeks from every strata of society. Philosophers like Socrates led discussions among students, and intellectuals.

Athenian cultural progress continued apace into the next century, but peace did not. Friction between Athens, and Sparta resulted in fighting, and by 431 BC, the two rivals were embroiled in the bitter and disastrous Peloponnesian War. Athens' navy was vastly superior, so Pericles decided to fight the war at sea. He called all Athenians into the city for protection against Sparta's land army. Plague killed many Athenians. Pericles himself died soon afterwards. The war dragged on for 28 years. In the end, Sparta triumphed. Athens regained its power briefly in the 4th century BC, but finally fell along with the rest of Greece before the advancing armies of Philip of Macedon in 338 BC.

Other nations have lasted longer and been richer and more powerful than Pericles' Athens. But all that remains of most are a few crumbling ruins, and fragments of art, and records. Much more remains of Athens. It lives on through the influence it still has on governments around the world. The reason may be that Athens was the first nation to be ruled by its people, and that idea was too powerful to be destroyed.

Alexander the Great
356-323 BC

Alexander the Great died of a fever when he was only 33. He left behind him more than 70 new cities scattered from present-day Egypt through Persia, Afghanistan, and central Asia to India. These cities, all called Alexandria, marked the route this remarkable young Macedonian king took as he swept across Asia, conquering everything in his path, and taking it into his empire. More important, they marked centers of Greek culture and influence in all parts of the known world. They would provide a common ground upon which diverse peoples could meet, communicate, and trade for centuries to come.

Alexander gained his interest in Greece from both his birth and his education. The son of King Philip II of Macedon, and his Greek queen, Olympias, the boy was taught by the Greek philosopher Aristotle who introduced him to philosophy, science, and history. Alexander read of Greek heroes, and imagined himself as their successor. He learned of Persian attacks on Greece 150 years earlier, and plotted with his father for Macedonian revenge.

Philip was assassinated in 336 BC. Alexander became king at the age of 20. Part of his empire was Greece, and he quickly made it clear that he intended to hold on to it. While fighting to en-

force his control in the northern and eastern parts of his domain, he was brought news that the Greek city-state of Thebes had rebelled. Rushing back to Greece, he razed Thebes, killed thousands of its people, and sold the rest into slavery. The Greeks did not resist Alexander any further. Indeed, they even appointed him to command a combined Macedonian–Greek army in the invasion of the Persian empire, originally planned by his father.

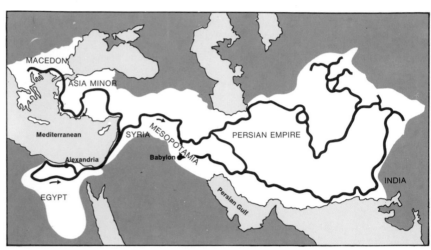

Above: the empire that Alexander built in 12 years (white). His route is shown by the black lines.
Below: a 15th-century French miniature depicts part of Alexander's war fleet. A superb military tactician, Alexander was adept at combining sea and land forces for maximum effect.
Below left: Alexander the Great pictured in this Roman copy of a Greek head by Lysippus.

Alexander proved to be a brilliant general from the start. Clever, flexible, and imaginative, he adjusted his tactics to the terrain, the enemy, and the weapons to hand. Probing for enemy weaknesses, he took full advantage of their mistakes. He personally led the cavalry, which spearheaded most attacks, sustaining many wounds but winning the unqualified admiration and loyalty of his troops. Unlike many military leaders, Alexander was a brave fighter himself.

In less than four years since the time he crossed the Dardanelles into Asia in 334 BC, Alexander had conquered Asia Minor and freed the Greek cities there. He had breached the almost impregnable defenses of the island city of Tyre; been hailed as pharaoh after he marched into Egypt, and established the first Alexandria there; and crushed the Persian army at Gaugamela, and taken control of Babylonia, Elam, Media, and Persia itself.

Above: a Persian coin bearing the profile of Alexander the Great. He avenged Greece for Persian attacks 150 years earlier.

Left: Alexander is one of history's most successful conquerors. In this illustration, a talking tree warns him that he too will be conquered – by death. Alexander was taken ill after a heavy drinking session, and died of a fever 10 days later on June 13, 323 BC. Painted to accompany an heroic poem written in the 900s, this picture dates from about 1425.

With Persia at his feet in 330 BC, Alexander had accomplished what he set out to do, but he continued to wage a more personal war. Marching east he conquered Bactria (now Afghanistan) and Sogdiana (in central Asia) where he fought a kind of guerrilla war. Here, he married Roxanne, the daughter of a local chieftain. In 327 BC, he marched on India, where he defeated the kings Taxala and Porus, and prepared for the next battle against the Nanda King of Magadha. But his troops refused to continue. Alexander accepted their decision. He turned south and followed the Indua river to its delta. Here, he split his force, sending half of them back by sea and taking the other half overland through Baluchistan. Survivors of these two rugged journeys met in southern Persia, and marched back to Susa. They did not arrive until 324 BC.

Alexander found much to challenge his mind as well as his military skills on his travels. He regarded his journeys as one of exploration as well as conquest. Geographers and scientists were included in his court to study, record their findings, and send them back to Greece. He also found much to admire in many of the people he conquered, and often left local rulers in charge of their own territory – Macedonian garrisons being stationed nearby as a precaution.

Alexander liked and admired the Persians in particular. He gradually came to regard them more as partners than subjects. He placed Persians in top administrative posts, recruited them into all branches of the army including the elite royal cavalry bodyguard. Eighty of his officers and 10,000 of their men took Persian wives with Alexander's encouragement. He adopted Persian dress, and even demanded that his people prostrate themselves before him as the Persians had done for their ruler. His attempts to fuse the Macedonians and Persians into one people caused increasing unrest among his Macedonian troops, which finally led to open revolt. This rebellion collapsed when Alexander dismissed all his Macedonian troops and replaced them with Persians. A great banquet was held to celebrate the reconciliation. The officers' resentment of Alexander's growing tendency toward autocracy brought a different response. Those he did not trust were killed, but his demand for prostration was withdrawn. When Alexander later came to believe he was a god, they agreed with him.

Ambassadors, suitably attired in wreaths of flowers out of respect for Alexander's new divinity, began to arrive from as far afield as Libya and Italy to pay their respects. Between ceremonial duties, Alexander busied himself with plans to explore the Caspian Sea, settle the shores of the Persian Gulf, and open sea communications with India. But Alexander fell ill after a prolonged drinking bout. He died of a fever 10 days later, on June 13, 323 BC. His body was taken to Alexandria in Egypt, and eventually placed in a golden coffin in a mausoleum there.

Above: a side panel from Alexander the Great's sarcophagus (tomb). It can be seen in what is now Istanbul.

Alexander had become a legend in his lifetime. Tales of his exploits travelled from one end of his empire to the other, and the legends continue to the present. But historians remember him for a different reason. Alexander was the first European to rule the known world, and by spreading Greek language and culture, he provided a foundation upon which Rome later built and consolidated its empire.

Ptolemy I
died 283 BC

A military career brought unprecedented rewards to Ptolemy I, son of an obscure Macedonian noble family. Serving as a general under Alexander the Great, he traveled as far as India, was praised and decorated for his military skills, married a Persian woman, and finished up as King of Egypt in 323 BC. He proved to be an able diplomat and administrator as well as a soldier in Egypt, built a dazzling center of Greek culture, was named an Egyptian God, and founded a dynasty that ruled Egypt for almost 300 years.

Ptolemy gained power in Egypt when Alexander's generals got together after his death and parcelled out his empire among themselves. The empire theoretically continued to exist and the generals served as regional administrators. But in fact, most of them fought from the beginning to achieve hegemony and succeed Alexander as absolute ruler.

Ptolemy steered a careful course through these struggles for power. He concentrated on holding Egypt and preserving and consolidating his position there. But he did not hesitate to acquire new territory when he thought it would help him keep what he already had. At various times he ruled, as well as Egypt, Cyprus, parts of present-day Libya, and Saudi Arabia, Syria, and Palestine, eastern Asia Minor, and some Greek cities. The citizens of Rhodes gave him the title Soter (Saviour) after he had helped them in a struggle against Antigonus, another of Alexander's generals.

Ptolemy also strengthened his hold on Egypt

Below: after Ptolemy established his rule in Egypt in 323 BC, he was followed by a long line of descendants – all named Ptolemy.
Below left: a contemporary portrait of Ptolemy I. His considerable military skill was demonstrated as a general under Alexander the Great. He displayed equal abilities as King of Egypt.

through alliance, and marriages. In 321 BC, he married Eurydice, daughter of the Macedonian ruler of Europe. He took another wife in 317, Berenice, granddaughter of Cassander who eventually became the ruler of Macedonia and Greece. In 305 BC the squabbling generals abandoned all pretense of belonging to a common empire and named themselves kings in their own domains. Ptolemy made Berenice his queen, and their younger son to succeed him as Ptolemy II.

Throughout his reign, Ptolemy depended on Greek soldiers to form the mainstay of his army. He maintained their loyalty by giving them land and special privileges in Egypt. Other Greeks were encouraged to settle in Egypt as well, and many of them were placed in administrative positions all over the country. At Alexandria, the city founded by Alexander in 332 BC, Ptolemy laid out a new capital and built a musum and library

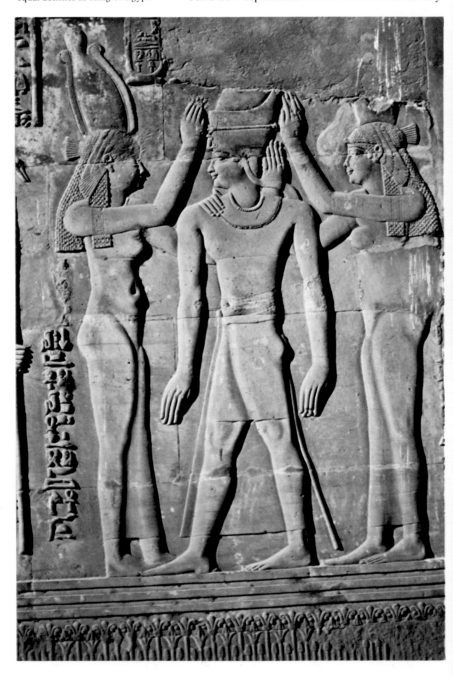

which attracted many of the leading Greek philosophers, scholars, writers, and artists of the day. The city also became a center for science and trade, and the lighthouse in its harbor was named one of the wonders of the ancient world. Here, Ptolemy lived in splendor surrounded by a Greek court amidst a growing population of privileged immigrants that soon came to include not only Greeks but also Jews, Syrians, and Anatolians.

The old Egyptian culture continued to live alongside the new Greek civilization in Egypt. Although Egyptians no longer held much power and they had to share the land with Greeks, they kept their language, customs, and religion. Ptolemy won them over by restoring temples destroyed by previous invaders, by offering gifts to Egyptian gods, and by supporting their ancient priesthood. He also established at Memphis, the old Egyptian capital, a new religious cult based on the worship of a combined Greco-Egyptian god called Sarapis. Ptolemy was named as a god by the Egyptians after his death.

Ptolemy was followed by a long line of successors, all named Ptolemy. The last of the line was Cleopatra. She ruled in Egypt after it had become a vassal state in the rising Roman empire. She bore a child by one Roman general and politician, Julius Caesar. Later she married another, Marc Antony, perhaps in the hope of regaining complete Egyptian independence. But the Roman people hated and feared Cleopatra, and in

Above: Ptolemy I ordering the building of the museum at Alexandria. Under the rule of the Ptolomies Alexandria became a center for learning without equal in the ancient world. It was to remain so for centuries to come.

Above: the right profile of Ptolemy I as depicted on a coin minted during his reign. Under Ptolemy, Egypt was made a self-reliant power with a strong currency.
Above right: Cleopatra was the last of the illustrious line of the Ptolemies. By her time coins had been fully accepted as a means of exchange in Egypt.

31 BC Rome sent a fleet to Alexandria. Antony and Cleopatra resisted, but when they saw they could not win, they both committed suicide, thus ending Ptolemaic rule in Egypt, and opening the way for a complete Roman takeover in Egypt in 30 BC.

Through their long rule, the Ptolemies preserved, strengthened and spread Greek culture. More important, they established at Alexandria a center for learning that influenced and enriched the ancient world and continued to attract scholars and thinkers up to modern times.

Chandragupta Maurya
c321-297BC

ruler in the eastern part of the empire, tried to regain the Indian territories. Chandragupta met him in battle, drove him back, and forced him to hand over much of Afghanistan in return for a few elephants in a peace treaty signed in 303 BC.

With the west firmly in his grip, Chandragupta pushed his empire east to Bengal and south to the Vindhya Mountains and perhaps beyond. He built a magnificent palace at Pataliputra (near present-day Patna).

The origins and early life of Chandragupta Maurya are shrouded in mystery. One legend has it that he was a slave, another that he was the illegitimate son of a king, and a third that he was a mercenary soldier. His later life is much better known. Chandragupta seized the Magadha Kingdom in east-central India, built it into ancient India's largest and greatest empire, and founded the Mauryan dynasty.

In earlier times, the founders of Buddhism and Jainism had lived in Magadha – an Aryan kingdom. A member of the Nanda family overthrew the original line of rulers, and took power in Aryan in about 363 BC. Nanda and his sons were efficient but oppressive kings, who grew rich from heavy taxes and spent their money building a huge army. Chandragupta apparently challenged Nanda rule when it was weak because of a dispute over succession. He was probably helped by Canakya – a clever but ruthless Brahman. Canakya taught him military tactics, helped him raise a mercenary army, and encouraged the Nanda king's subjects to rise up against him. Victorious in bloody battle with the Nandas in about 325 BC, Chandragupta wiped out all his opponents and established a tightly controlled administration, borrowing many of the methods of Darius I of Persia.

Alexander the Great's death shortly after his conquest of northwestern India helped Chandragupta turn his kingdom into an empire. Alexander had left his own representatives in India. They withdrew soon after their leader's death and Chandragupta took control. Later, Seleucus, one of Alexander's generals and his successor as

Above: excavations reveal the foundations of Chandragupta Maurya's palace at Pataliputra. It was from here that Chandragupta administered his sprawling empire. The palace was one of the wonders of the ancient world.

Right: Asoka, Chandragupta's grandson, extended and consolidated the Mauryan empire. As a young man he was a conqueror, but later rejected violence and became a Buddhist. It was then that he ordered the building of the Great Stupa at Sanchi in central India. The Stupa's shape represents the cosmos – the dome being heaven, and the central shaft the axis of the earth. This is one of the world's oldest surviving Buddhist monuments.

Towards the end of his 24-year reign, Chandragupta began being influenced by a Jainist sage who predicted a 12-year famine. When the famine came and Chandragupta could do nothing to alleviate his people's suffering, he withdrew to a Jainist monastery in southwest India,

Left: the Mauryan empire under Asoka. Its capital Pataliputra is modern-day Patna. The rock edicts and stone pillars shown on the map were erected on Asoka's instruction in honor of Buddha.

Left: detail from the east gate of the Stupa at Sanchi. It depicts the conversion of the Kasyapas to Buddhism. The Mauryan empire lavished a great deal of its considerable wealth on monuments to Buddha after its ruler Asoka, Chandragupta's grandson, had converted.

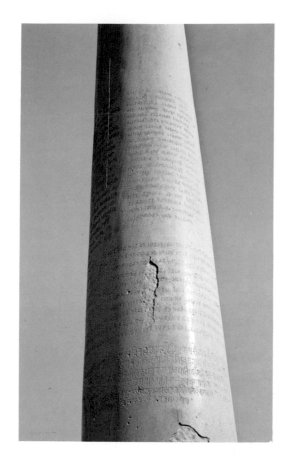

Right: a close-up of one of the many pillars Asoka had built in homage to Buddha. Shown is the lettering of the edict carved in the side to spread the Buddhist gospel.

Left: the pillar at Lauriya Nandangarh erected while Asoka ruled the Mauryan empire. Surmounted by Asoka's lions – the Mauryan empire's symbol of authority – this pillar was only one of 10 built around the empire in honor of Buddha. No less than 17 rock edicts were also completed. A number of pillars and rock edicts can still be seen today.

Below: this modern Indian 20-rupee note still displays the lion symbol first adopted during the Mauryan dynasty more than 2000 years ago. The lions are printed on the note. By holding it to the light they can also be seen in the watermark.

and fasted to death. The empire passed to his son, Bindusara. He extended it to the south, maintained its efficient administrative system, and in turn passed it on to his own son, Asoka, the greatest of the Mauryan rulers.

Asoka began as a conquerer and brought almost all of India into the empire giving him a domain that stretched from the Himalayas in the north to the Indian Ocean in the south, and from the borders of Persia to the Bay of Bengal. But after a particularly bloody battle, Asoka suffered deep remorse for the deaths he had caused. He abandoned war. He became a Buddhist, denounced violence, built monasteries and stupas, and sent Buddhist missionaries as far afield as Syria, Egypt, and Greece as well as to Sri Lanka and southeast Asia. Under Asoka's rule, India prospered, and Buddhism gradually became an international religion.

After Asoka's death in 232 BC, the Mauryan empire declined rapidly and India entered a dark period of disintegration, invasion, and fighting. Not until the 4th century AD was ordered restored under the Gupta kings. They established a Hindu empire and presided over a golden age of art and literature from the old Mauryan capital at Pataliputra. Most ancient ruins in India today date from the Gupta period. Only the edict pillars Asoka built across India to proclaim his Buddhist beliefs remain from Mauryan times. Standing 50 feet high, and topped with capitals of animals and flowers, these pillars are monuments to the ancient Mauryan rulers and their once-great empire.

Hannibal
247-182 BC

The story of the Carthaginian general Hannibal struggling across the Alps with his army and his elephants is familiar to almost everyone, but few remember where he was going, or why. Hannibal is better known for his brilliant tactics than for his many victories. In the end, his victories came to little. Even Hannibal was unable to protect Carthage from the rising power, and imperial ambitions, of the Romans.

Carthage was a Phoenician city-state located in what is now Tunisia. It had been established in the 8th century BC – about the same time as the city-state of Rome – and had grown into an important trading center. Carthage had gradually expanded to absorb territory in the western Mediterranean, while Rome was swallowing much of the Italian peninsula. The two cities collided, and did battle. In the first of these Punic (from the Roman word for Phoenician) Wars, Hannibal's father, Hamilcar Barca, lost Sicily to the Romans. But afterwards he invaded and took Spain for Carthage. Carthage's control of Spain sparked off the second Punic War, and gave Hannibal his first clash with the Romans.

Legend has it that Hannibal's father forced him to swear eternal hostility to Rome as a boy. Hannibal spent his entire life fighting the Ro-

mans. Beginning as a right hand man to his brother-in-law, Hasdrubal, who succeeded Hamilcar in Spain, Hannibal proved himself a skilled commander. After Hasdrubal's death, he was acclaimed by the army as their leader.

Hannibal knew only too well that Rome's territorial ambitions knew no bounds, and he was determined to prevent further expansion. Perhaps to provoke a confrontation, he laid siege to the Spanish town of Saguntum. Although well within the agreed area of Carthaginian influence, Saguntum was friendly to Rome. He captured it in 219 BC. Rome declared war on Carthage, and

Above: Hannibal and his army's famous crossing of the Italian Alps to confront the Roman forces under the command of Scipio Africanus. Hannibal's men, elephants, and pack horses were badly depleted by exhaustion after this gruelling expedition.

Left: Hannibal (left) and his Roman adversary Scipio Africanus. A threat to Rome for 14 years, Hannibal was finally defeated by Scipio's forces at Zama in 202 BC.

Right: this detail from an 18th-century engraving shows Hannibal's elephants being ferried across the Rhone river prior to crossing the Italian Alps. The rafts were covered in earth in an attempt to avoid frightening the elephants, but they were terrified all the same.

Hannibal set off with his armies of mercenaries, horses, baggage trains, and elephants to confront the Romans on their own ground. He followed the little-used overland route through the Pyrenees and Gaul to the Rhone river. After floating the terrified elephants across the river on rafts, Hannibal marched his army up the Rhone valley to avoid coming up against the waiting Romans. He wished instead to catch them off guard in a more exposed position by going over the Italian Alps, and descending into the Po Valley.

In the early days of the war, which now began in earnest, Hannibal won all the battles. This was in spite of the exhaustion of his depleted forces and the lack of support and supplies from Carthage. Using clever tactics, he outmaneuvered, and virtually wiped out two Roman armies. He advanced as far as Rome itself, but his army was not strong enough to take the city. The Romans finally worked out a strategy that avoided outright battles, but threatened limited action in a wide area. This forced Hannibal to spread his

Above: Scipio's Roman forces storming the city of Carthage. Scipio's methods of assaulting the walled city were to be copied for centuries to come. Hannibal had unwittingly revealed to Scipio various effective techniques of warfare in their earlier confrontations.

Left: a silver shekel bearing Hannibal's profile. It was struck in Carthage in about 220 BC.

meager forces, and switch from the offensive to the defensive. The Roman General Scipio Africanus had, meanwhile, crossed the sea to Spain and was fighting and defeating the Carthaginian force Hannibal had left behind to defend his territory there. When Scipio crossed the sea again to North Africa and approached Carthage itself in 203 BC, Hannibal rushed home to defend the city. The details of the battle in which the two generals met are sketchy, but Scipio apparently used tactics learned from Hannibal to defeat the Carthaginians. Carthage was forced to give up Spain as part of the terms of the resulting peace treaty.

The war was not the end of Hannibal's struggle with Rome. Appointed an official in Carthage's government, he forced through reforms that deprived the nobles of much of their power. In retaliation, they reported to the Romans that he was plotting against them. Hannibal fled first to Ephesus, and later to Bithynia (both in present-day Turkey). He helped the rulers there in their struggles against Rome until the Romans demanded that he be turned over to them. Rather than give himself up, he poisoned himself and died at the age of 64 in Bithynia.

The Romans met their greatest obstacle on the road to conquest in Hannibal. His struggle with them, and his near victory against overwhelming odds, assured him a place in history. Through his defeat, the Romans secured for themselves a sprawling empire that was to profoundly affect the development of the western world.

Julius Caesar
c100-44 BC

Julius Caesar was one of the greatest soldiers and statesmen of ancient Rome. He spent much of his life in danger. As a young man, he was forced to flee to save his life when he sided with reformers against conservative members of the Senate, and their powerful leader, Sulla. Later, on his way to study public speaking in Rhodes, he was taken prisoner by pirates. Later still, as a

general in Gaul, he led troops against barbarian tribesmen, and brought most of Europe under the Roman heel. With vast energy, imagination, and skill, he escaped death repeatedly until he was nearly 60. Then he was murdered in the one place he should have been safe, the Roman Senate. There on the Ides of March he was stabbed to death by friends and associates, angered by his assumption of dictatorial powers.

Caesar, a member of an undistinguished patrician family in Rome, decided early in life to make his way in politics. He made known his reformist point of view at about 18 when he married the daughter of a reformist leader. But his start was delayed when Sulla drove him into exile for refusing to get a divorce. Returning to Rome in 78 BC after Sulla's death, he began climbing the political ladder. By 62 BC, he had been elected a

Left: a bust of Julius Caesar. Caesar was a brilliant soldier and politician who made a number of dangerous enemies during his career. It was only when he took dictatorial powers upon himself that he upset his friends too. He was murdered in the Senate on the Ides of March.

Below: at 13 x 12 inches this Sardonyx cameo is the second largest known to exist. It shows Julius Caesar in heaven, attended by Drusus and Augustus. A pegasus is being led to heaven by Cupid. Tiberius and Livia are seated before Germanicus, whose wife Agrippina and the young Caligula are in attendance as well. The young Drusus and Julia Livilla are shown too. The whole work depicts the family of the Caesars in heaven.

praetor, the second highest office in the Roman government. The following year, he was made the governor of Farther Spain (Andalusia and Portugal) and used the position, as most Roman governors did, to make military forays and win loot. These spoils made it possible for him to run for and win a consulship in 59 BC.

In this post, Caesar won the allegiance of Pompey, a popular and successful general, and once a Sulla supporter, by forcing the Senate to

give land to Pompey's retired soldiers. Caesar then persuaded Crassus to join the alliance, making it a triumvirate. Crassus, an old opponent of Pompey, was a leading statesman, and the richest man in Rome. When Caesar's one year term as consul ended, he entrusted his political affairs in Rome to his two associates, and left for Gaul to take up appointment as proconsul there.

Gaul provided Caesar with the chance to build an army, and use it to win glory and financial rewards through conquest. He took full advantage of it. By 50 BC, he had conquered all of Gaul from the Italian frontier to the Rhine, pacified it, and placed it firmly under Roman control. His victories were partly due to the loyalty of his army who respected his courage and skill, partly to his decisiveness and inspired tactics which often caught the enemy off-guard, and partly to the lack of unity among the Gallic tribes. He also raided Germany and Britain, but did not have enough troops to add them to the empire.

Caesar's Gallic triumphs impressed the Romans, but frightened his ally Pompey who saw Caesar's power and prestige growing at the expense of his own. Crassus was getting restless under the arrangement as well. But Caesar patched up the differences among the three, and kept the triumvirate intact until he had finished his wars in Gaul. Crassus had been killed fighting the Parthians in the East by then. Pompey and Caesar were left as the two major contenders.

Left: this relief illustrates a battle between Roman troops and a Germanic tribe. Julius Caesar's military skill was put to the test in a campaign to subdue the increasingly restive peoples of Europe. He succeeded in bringing large tracts of western Europe under the heel of Rome.

Below: the famous Forum that Julius Caesar ordered to be built. It is the only building of which any traces remain, built in the years when Julius Caesar held sway in Rome.

Both Caesar and Pompey had armies. Each feared giving up unless the other did as well. When the Senate decided to back Pompey, and ordered Caesar to turn over his command, he refused. Declaring "the die is cast," he led his troops across the Rubicon, a small river marking the border between Gaul, and Italy proper, and marched toward Rome. This sparked off a civil war between Romans who supported him as ruler, and those who supported the republican form of government under the power of the corrupt and inefficient Senate.

Troops supporting the Senate, under Pompey's command, fell back, and finally fled from Italy to Greece as Caesar advanced. Caesar followed. In their first clash in Greece, he was routed. But Caesar regrouped his forces in a strategic spot near Pharsala. When Pompey's forces attacked, they were crushed. Pompey fled again, this time to Egypt where he was killed, but his troops marched on to Tunisia. Caesar, in pursuit, got as far as Egypt where he met Cleopatra, and decided to rest before returning home by way of Syria and Pontus (Turkey), where he put down rebellions. He described his victory in Pontus in three words, "Veni, Vidi, Vici" ("I came, I saw, I conquered").

Caesar returned to Rome in 47 BC. Now a dictator, he set to work drawing up plans, some of them later used by his successor, for securing the empire and reorganizing its administration. But he was called away twice to put down challenges from Pompey's followers in Africa, and Spain. He had less than a year in all for administration. In 44 BC, as he was planning a campaign against Parthia which might have added more eastern territory to the empire, a group of 60 opponents carried out a plot to kill him. His growing arrogance, and dictatorial ways worried them.

No-one knows for certain why Caesar has become one of history's most famous men. It may be his books. These are regarded not only as the best source of information available on the Gallic and Civil Wars, but have considerable literary merit as well. Or it may have been his military genius, his magnanimity toward some of his enemies, or the skill with which he achieved, and used political office. Most likely, his fame stems from the effect he has had on the course of history in Europe. By conquering Gaul, he brought Europe under the civilizing influence of both Greece and Rome. By destroying the crumbling republican government, he opened the way for the emperor and made possible the creation and survival of the Roman empire.

Augustus
63 BC-14 AD

Rome was plunged into civil war when Julius Caesar destroyed the old republican government and declared himself dictator. But he also provided the solution to the problem he caused. He named his grandnephew Gaius Octavius, later called Augustus or Caesar Augustus as his successor. Augustus not only ended the war, and created a new and stronger government, but he reorganized the empire so efficiently that it lasted 300 years, and changed the lives of most of those who lived in it. He was the first and the greatest of a long line of Roman emperors.

The transfer of power from Caesar to Augustus was not as smooth as Caesar might have wished, for the boy was only 18 when his uncle was killed. He heard of Caesar's death, and of the will which named him as successor as well as heir, and adoptive son, while he was away at school in Apollonia (now Albania). Against his family's advice, he decided to return to Rome, and make good the will by challenging Marc Antony, Caesar's chief lieutenant, who had taken power. Thinking it could use Augustus to

Above: the Forum is one of the most impressive surviving monuments to Augustus' Rome. It is one of the finest pieces of architecture still partially standing from the ancient world. Used as meeting places and centers of trade, forums, though less imposing than the one in Rome, were built in cities and settlements throughout the Roman empire.

regain its authority, the Senate made him a senator, and Caesar's loyal army, siding with the boy, demanded that he be made a consul. With the army's support, Augustus was able to persude Antony to make up a triumvirate with him and Lepidus, chief priest under Caesar. In 43 BC, when Augustus was 20, the Senate gave the triumvirate dictatorial powers to rebuild the government, and reestablish its control over the empire.

Marc Antony dominated the trio at first. A talented general, he defeated Brutus and Cassius, Caesar's murderers, who had fled to the eastern part of the empire and seized power there. Augustus meanwhile, never a brilliant military leader, suffered a disastrous defeat in his efforts to gain control of Sicily. But in 32 BC, things began to go Augustus' way. He finally won in Sicily with the help of his old friend, Agrippa, and using ships supplied by Antony. When Lepidus challenged Augustus' growing power, he was disarmed, removed from the triumvirate, and retired. Augustus then increased his edge over Antony by starting, and winning wars in Illyricum and Dalmatia (both in present-day Yugoslavia) to protect the northeast approaches to Rome. But supreme power was not to be his until Antony made the mistake of falling in love with Cleopatra, ruler with her brother-husband of Egypt.

Rome began to turn against Antony when he gave Cleopatra gifts of Roman territory in the eastern part of the empire. Augustus, taking full advantage of the situation, declared war on the Egyptian queen. With Agrippa commanding his fleet, he attacked and defeated the combined

Left: this contemporary sculpture portrays the Emperor Augustus as a young man. Many Roman sculptures were originally colored to give a lifelike impression of their subjects. The paint has worn off over the centuries.

naval forces of Antony and Cleopatra. The two lovers committed suicide, and in 30 BC, Augustus took control of Egypt and its bulging treasury. Augustus' victory in Egypt made him sole Roman ruler, gave him complete control of all the territory around the Mediterranean, and provided the resources to pay his troops, and begin the work of reorganizing the empire.

Augustus tackled the job of reorganization with patience, and good sense. Moving slowly, he tested each step before going on to the next. He tried out different ideas until he found the solution to a problem. His cautious approach led to changes and innovations that worked, were accepted, and endured. They included: a comprehensive network of roads linking all parts of the empire; an overhaul of the administration of the provinces both at the center, and at the local level, and a rudimentary new civil service to run the system; periodic censuses of the population; a local government, police, and fire forces for Rome; a fleet to keep order in the Mediterranean, and a smaller and more efficient and reliable army to protect the border areas, and add new territory to the empire. A military treasury was set up to assure soldiers of retirement benefits.

Like his uncle, Augustus had supreme power, but he was clever enough to cloak it in the familiar institutions of the republican government. He ruled as a consul for many years, but also controlled the provinces in which the bulk of the army was stationed. The Senate remained the chief legislative and administrative body, but it was reduced in size and filled with compliant followers of Augustus. War-weary Romans

Above: cameos were popular pieces of decorative art in ancient Rome. This one shows the Emperor Augustus being crowned a god. In the bottom half of the cameo, soldiers can be seen dragging in newly captured slaves. Augustus was worshipped as a god by his subjects during his reign.

accepted his supremacy because it wasn't too obvious, and it provided much-needed peace and stability.

Romans were particularly pleased when Augustus returned to many old Italian beliefs and customs. He restored old temples, reintroduced the ancient secular games, took a title, Augustus, with ancient religious overtones, and encouraged writers such as Vergil, Livy, and Horace to glorify the past. Because of his attachment to ancient Italian culture, the empire remained essentially western even though most of its people spoke Greek, and Greek influence remained strong.

Augustus ruled for more than 40 years despite constant, and severe illness. He was beloved, admired, and even worshipped in his own lifetime. His long rule gave his changes time to root, and the empire endured for three centuries very much as he shaped. Its stability and its superb communication system allowed classical ideas, both Greek and Roman, and Christianity, born during his reign, to flourish, spread, and be passed on. Whatever the benefits the Roman empire conferred on succeeding generations, they have to be attributed in large part to Caesar's successor, Augustus.

Right: Romans set great store in the signs of the zodiac and the predictions of astrologers. Their opinions were eagerly sought, especially on the eve of battle or on the birth of a child. Augustus was born under the sign of Capricorn. This Roman coin was minted in Spain in his honour.

Diocletian
284-305

ency of the local administration. As no single man could be in all the provinces at once, or even visit them frequently, Diocletian chose a co-emperor, Maximian, to help him maintain order in the west, while he looked after the east. Like further control, Diocletian appointed two assistants with the title of caesar – Galerius for the east and Constantius for the west. The two

When Diocletian was growing up in a village in what is now Yugoslavia, the aging Roman empire was crumbling. Barbarians in Europe threatened its northern provinces, while Persia menaced it from the east. Generals who were supposed to protect outlying areas often seized political power there and declared themselves local rulers. Would-be emperors, most of them military men, fought each other for power.

At first, the young Diocletian appeared to be cast in the same mould. Rising through the army, he was declared emperor by his troops and fought the existing emperor, Carinus, for power until Carinus was assassinated. But Diocletian wanted more than power; he wished to restore the empire to its former greatness. By the time he retired in 305, he had pacified the borders, revamped the army and removed it from politics, and reorganized the internal administration of the empire as well. He had also begun the last great persecution of Christians in the Roman Empire, and instituted an administrative system that would eventually split the empire in two.

Diocletian appreciated that the empire was too big to be held together and administered by one man sitting in Rome. The emperor, he believed, should travel to the distant provinces to ensure the loyalty of his troops, and lead them in battle if necessary, and to check up on the effici-

Above: the four rulers of the Roman empire. Diocletian and his caesar Galerius maintained order in the eastern half of the empire, while co-emperor Maximian and his caesar Constantius looked after the west.
Left: a bust of the Emperor Diocletian sculpted during his reign. It can be seen today in the Capitoline Museum, Rome.

caesars were attached to their augusti through marriage – Galerius to Diocletian's daughter, Valeria, and Constantius, to Maximian's step-daughter, Theodora. So was the empire divided into four zones, each with its own imperial head ruling from his own capital.

The system worked well. Eventually, the four imperial heads were able to drive out the invaders and reestablish control throughout the empire.

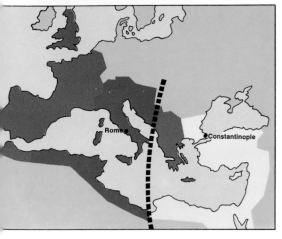

Above: the Roman empire experienced a huge expansion in building and various public works under Diocletian and Maximian. Twenty miles south of Tunis an impressive aqueduct was built across the valley of Oued Miliana – part of which is shown here. Diocletian's rule saw a tremendous expansion in road building to strengthen communications and security within the far-flung empire.

Left: Diocletian's divided empire. He ruled from Constantinople, while Maximian's capital was Rome.

Christians in his court, and possibly even in his family. The reasons for his change in attitude are not clear. Many believe he was encouraged by his caesar, Galerius, or by anti-Christian intellectuals in his court. Others say he feared disunity among his people that the Christians with their bitter doctrinal disputes might cause. Whatever the motive behind them, the edicts led to violent persecution throughout the empire, but especially in the East. But the persecution failed to stamp out Christianity. On the contrary, it strengthened it by producing martyrs.

In 305, an aged and ill Diocletian decided to abdicate as emperor and persuaded his fellow Augustus, Maximian, to retire with him. They

Diocletian, meanwhile, concentrated on the empire's internal problems. He began by reorganizing the structure of the central government in such a way that he held all the strings of power and could take prompt action whenever necessary. Many of the institutions and offices of the old Roman government remained, but some, such as the Senate, had no powers and others, such as the office of praetorian prefect, changed function – from military leadership to financial administration. The central administration of the empire was split into separate functions and put in the hands of specialists, operating on the basis of rules and regulations. The basis for all the bureaucracies of the future was established. In outlying areas, provinces were divided into smaller units to diminish the power of governors and bring local government closer to the people.

The economy like the political administration of the empire was in ruins after years of war. Diocletian tried to restore it by encouraging agriculture and launching a building program. To encourage trade, he restored a sound currency based on gold and silver coins, and issued new small coins to ease everyday transactions. Property owners were encouraged with new laws protecting private property, creditors' rights, and contracts. Less popular economic reforms included taxes on cultivable land, and on individuals and the famous Edict of Diocletian of 301, controlling wages and prices. The edict was intended to slow inflation and prevent exploitation of consumers, but it proved to be ruinous for farmers and merchants.

Toward the end of his reign, in 303–4, Diocletian issued four edicts designed to suppress Christianity. Until then he had been tolerant of

Above: Diocletian's magnificent palace at Split on the Adriatic coast of modern-day Yugoslavia. This is a view of the Peristylum of the palace drawn by the famous 18th-century English architect Robert Adam.

handed their posts over to their two caesars, who now became augusti and were replaced by two new caesars. Diocletian then retired to his magnificent palace at Salona (in present-day Split, Yugoslavia), and took up gardening. There he died, almost unnoticed, eight years later.

Through his reforms and reorganization, Diocletian probably kept the Roman empire alive for an extra 100 years. But by dividing the empire into eastern and western sections for administration, he opened a crack that would later split the empire in two and lead to the destruction of the western half, including Rome itself.

Constantine I
c274-337

As Constantine the Great led his army towards Rome in 313, he is said to have seen a cross of light against the sun. The words "In this sign conquer" were written in the sky. Overwhelmed by what he took to be a message from the Christians' God, he ordered his troops to paint the sign on their shields. In the following battle of Milvian Bridge, they won against overwhelming odds. The victory gave Constantine control of the western half of the Roman empire, and brought him a giant step closer to the supreme power he later achieved. It was also a turning point for Christianity, and its relations with Rome. Constantine became the first Christian emperor of the Roman empire, and he actively encouraged the organization, and spread of his new-found religion.

Constantine arrived at Milvian Bridge via a long and tortuous route of infighting among the emperor Diocletian's co-emperors, and their heirs. The son of Constantius, one of Diocletian's caesars, Constantine was brought up in Diocletian's court at Nicomedia after his mother, Helena, was cast aside so his father could make a politically expedient marriage. Constantius became a co-emperor after Diocletian's abdication. He ruled the western half of the empire, and sent for his son to help him fight in Britain. Constantius died there in 306, and his army proclaimed Constantine as his successor. But the young leader could not take power until some other claimants to the post had eliminated each other and Constantine himself had eliminated, and defeated the forces of the survivor at Milvian

Bridge. Meanwhile, another ruler, Licinius, seized power in the eastern half of the empire, and soon tried to extend his rule to the west. His first attack on Constantine failed, and the two ruled as co-emperors in an uneasy truce for nine years. Lincinius attacked again in 324; Constantine decisively defeated him, and became absolute ruler of the whole Roman empire.

While Constantine and Licinius were jointly ruling the empire, they issued the Edict of Milan

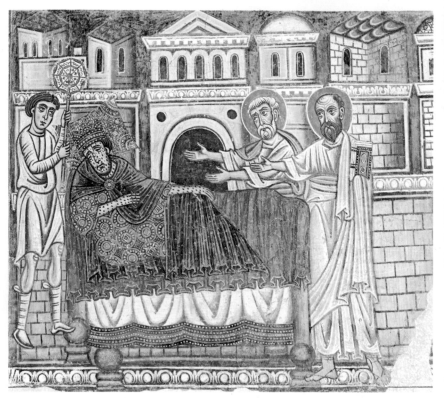

Above: Constantine I was the first Roman emperor to convert to Christianity, and he ended 300 years of Roman persecution of Christians. This illustration shows Saints Peter and Paul appearing before Constantine in a dream, where he also sees a cross inscribed "By this sign shall you conquer." Another version has it that Constantine was leading his army toward Rome when he saw a cross of light against the sun, with the words "In this sign conquer" written in the sky.

in 313. This brought the persecution of the Christians, begun by Diocletian to an end, and proclaimed toleration for all religions. But Constantine went far beyond this, both as ruler of the west, and later as emperor of the whole empire. Seeing himself as the 13th apostle, he encouraged the spread of Christianity in any way he could. Laws were passed, enforcing such Christian practices as the observance of Sunday as a day of rest, and gave special privileges to the Church and the clergy. He wrote a prayer for his troops, and commissioned new Bibles to be copied for the growing Christian community. Imperial land in Rome was donated for the building of a cathedral, Basilica Constantiniana (now called St. John Lateran). He also began the original St. Peter's Church. Directly or indirectly, Constantine was also involved in the building of churches in Alexandria, Nicomedia, Antioch, Trier, and many other cities while his mother, Helena, travelled to the holy land, found the sites of the manger in Bethlehem, and the cave where Jesus was buried in Jerusalem. She built churches there. Constantine became embroiled in several of the doctrinal disputes dividing the early Christians. He tried to resolve one

Right: this Sardonyx cameo shows Constantine and his family in a chariot drawn by centaurs (mythical creatures, half man and half horse).

argument over the nature of the Trinity by convening the Council of Nicea. The dispute was not settled, but the Council became a model for future Ecumenical councils.

Constantine was less imaginative when it came to civil matters, but he continued, and improved on the administrative, legal, military, and economic reforms initiated by Diocletian. Like his predecessor, too, he ruled from the East, where he had been born, and which provided easier

Right: the Council of Nicea, convened by Constantine to try to settle a dispute over the nature of the Holy Trinity that divided early Christendom.
Below: the Triumphal Arch built for Constantine in Rome in AD 312.
Below right: an edict of Constantine ending the exemption of Cologne's Jews from public office.

access to all parts of the vast empire than Rome itself did. On the site of old Byzantium, he began to build Constantinople in 330. Although Constantinople was called "a second Rome", and decorated with spoils looted from Greek temples, it was a Christian city that numbered churches among its most beautiful and important buildings.

In Constantine's day, Constantinople was the capital of the whole Roman empire. When the empire split in 395, it became the capital of a new East Roman or Byzantine empire. Unlike the old Roman empire, the Byzantine empire was dominated by a Christian ruling class, formed originally by Constantine. It included religious as well as civil authorities, and it fostered the growth of a new Christian culture side by side with the old classical one. The Byzantine empire continued to flourish long after the West Roman empire fell to the barbarians. It preserved and encouraged culture, and passed it on to the West in the Middle Ages.

Justinian I
c482-565

Above: Justinian's monogram – a sort of stylized signature.

Byzantine emperor Justinian the Great shared an advantage with other great leaders. He was fortunate in his aides. Two great generals, Belisarius and Narses, helped him preserve and enlarge his empire. Tribonian, a gifted advocate, helped him codify his laws. Two skilled administrators, John of Cappadocia and Peter Barsymes, moulded his rule into a fair and efficient one. Justinian's wife, Theodora, bolstered him up when opponents tried to overthrow him. But the emperor himself, with his sharp mind, sense of natural justice, energy, and vision played the most important role in making his long reign a golden age in the Byzantine era.

Justinian began his career as a valued aide to his uncle, emperor Justin I. Born of peasant stock in a village in what is now Yugoslavia, Justinian held an important military post. When Justin became emperor in 518, he legally adopted his nephew, and gave him several important government positions. Justinian became an influential adviser, and was responsible for many of his uncle's policies. In 527, he was made co-emperor with his uncle. When Justin I died later that year, he became sole ruler.

Justinian inherited a war with Persia, along with his throne. This was the first of several threats to his territory. The war continued off and on until about 561 when a 50-year truce was negotiated. It returned almost all conquered land to the Byzantines. In return, they had to pay a tribute of 30,000 gold coins a year.

Justinian was less successful in maintaining his borders against barbarian invaders from the Balkan peninsula. At one point, his loyal general

Above left: a portrait of Justinian I on a coin minted during his reign. His lasting contribution to history was the codification of Roman law.

Belisarius stopped their advance just outside Constantinople by rallying the civilian population to battle. Some of these invaders were eventually driven out of the empire, while others settled in Byzantine territory, and even joined the army to resist further invasions.

Justinian also met with mixed results in his efforts to push his empire westwards. He considered it his duty as emperor to regain control of the western provinces of the old Roman empire. Carefully timed attacks on North Africa and Italy were mounted in an attempt to topple barbarian rulers there. Belisarius easily defeated the Vandal ruler in North Africa, and restored his territory to the empire. But Italy proved more difficult. The Byzantines captured Ravenna, and the surrounding area from the Ostragoths in 540. But their advance was halted by the able Ostragoth leader, Totila, until 552. Then he was defeated and killed in battle by a huge Byzantine force under the command of Narses. Narses went on to take Rome. By 562, the Byzantines held all of Italy. But Italy was so devastated by war that normal economic and political life could not be restored. Shortly after Justinian's death, the Byzantines lost Italy again when the Lombards invaded and conquered much of it.

Justinian spent much of his time on internal

Right: the peak of Byzantine splendor, the Hagia Sophia in Constantinople (Istanbul). Otherwise known as the Church of the Holy Wisdom, it was the brainchild of Justinian. The church became a mosque when the Turks captured Constantinople in 1453. The large discs shown in the picture bear the names of Allah, Mohammed, and the first Caliphs and Imams. Another sign of Islamic influence is the Sultan's box on the left of the picture. Also shown is the prayer niche (mihrab) pointed toward Mecca, and the pulpit (minher). Hagia Sophia is used as a museum today.

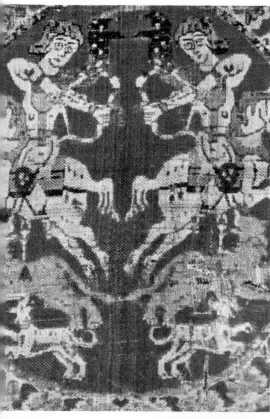

Left: this hunting scene is woven in silk in the Byzantine tradition. It was made by either Syrian or Egyptian craftsmen in the 8th century. Court etiquette required the use of intricate figure silks. Indeed, this regulation is laid down in Justinian's comprehensive codification of Roman law – a feat for which he is most remembered today.

Below: Justinian's wife, the Empress Theodora and her train pictured in 6th-century mosaic from San Vitale, Ravenna. Theodora was perhaps a tougher personality than her husband. In 532, Justinian hunted down tax evaders, and cut public expenditure – including the popular spectacles. Rich and poor alike were angered, and violent mobs appointed a new emperor. Theodora persuaded Justinian to resist. The revolt was quelled when thousands of the rioters were slaughtered by Justinian's loyal troops and generals.

reform, while the generals fought his wars. He was especially interested in rooting out corruption and privilege for special interest groups, and in providing his subjects with easy access to justice. Partly in pursuit of justice, he formed a commission headed by Tribonian to codify all his own laws, as well as all Roman laws. He also tightened up financial administration, and rooted out tax evaders. Public expenditures, including the popular spectacles, were cut.

Justinian's financial reforms led to widespread discontent among both rich and poor. They were partly responsible for a severe riot in Constantinople in 532. The other cause was unrest due to a Christian doctrinal dispute. A rampaging mob appointed a new emperor, but Justinian's wife, Theodora, persuaded him to resist while loyal generals put down the unrest by killing thousands of the rioters.

Despite almost constant war and dissention, Justinian ruled over a flowering of Byzantine literature, art, and architecture. The most beautiful building, a church called Hagia Sophia in Constantinople, was the brainchild of the emperor himself. Designed by mathematicians as well as architects, it incorporated vast spaces under a series of huge domes that gave the illusion of floating unsupported. Justinian was also responsible for many other buildings ranging from forts to monasteries – including two superb churches in Ravenna. But Hagia Sophia is considered the masterpiece of Byzantine architecture.

A lot of what Justinian accomplished was lost under his successors, but two monuments remain. The Hagia Sophia, now a museum, still stands much as he built it, and impresses visitors with the splendor of the Byzantine empire under Justinian's rule. Even more important, Justinian's legal code preserved Roman law for later generations, and forms the basis for much of the law under which Europeans now live.

Attila the Hun
c406~453

A small, broad-shouldered man with a big head, flat nose, and a thin beard, Attila, King of the Huns, swept out of Eastern Europe in 441. For a few years, he terrorized both the East and West Roman empires. This most famous, and perhaps the most powerful of the barbarian leaders, died peacefully in his sleep. He left little behind but devastation, and a name that to Europeans is synonymous with cruelty in battle.

But Attila was not as evil as all that. His nickname, "The Scourge of God," was unjust. The Mongols, for example, were much more destructive. Attila respected law, and he often showed mercy to his enemies. His goal was not so much to conquer the Romans as to frighten and weaken them so they would not threaten him. A just ruler of his own people, he provided order, and protection. Many Romans settled in his territory. Even learned Romans attended his court, despite the fact that the king himself was illiterate.

Attila and his elder brother Bleda inherited their empire from their uncle, Rua, in 435. It was centered in Hungary and extended from the Alps in the west to the Caspian Sea in the east. Rua had built the empire by bringing many separate Hun tribes under his authority, and then extending his control to alien barbarians as well. Probably by threatening invasion, he had forced his neighbor to the south, the East Roman or Byzantine Empire, to sign a treaty pledging to pay 700 pounds of gold a year to the Huns.

Soon after Attila and Bleda came to power,

they announced that the Byzantine Emperor, Theodosius II, was in arrears with his payments. In 441 they crossed the Danube, and sacked Singidinum (Belgrade), and a number of other cities. A truce temporarily stopped the fighting. But in 443 the Huns attacked again, this time pushing all the way to Constantinople, before veering off to defeat the Byzantine army at Gallipoli. In the peace treaty ending the war, the Byzantines had to pay all their back debts (set at 6000 pounds of gold by Attila), as well as 2100 a year from then on, three times their former tribute bill. The treaty also forbade Byzantines to harbor exiles from Hun territory, or to co-operate with any other barbarian people in fighting the Huns. The Byzantines were financially ruined by this treaty. They were also prevented from strengthening their depleted army by recruiting barbarians.

Perhaps on the pretext that the Byzantines were harboring fugitives, Attila again crossed the Danube in 447. He had killed his brother two years earlier, and was now sole ruler. This time, the Huns devastated much of the northern Balkan peninsula and got all the way to Thermopylae before being stopped. The treaty ending this war took three years to negotiate, and gave the Huns a strip of land south of the Danube as well as tribute.

With the Byzantine empire reeling, Attila turned to the west and announced as his target the Visigoth territory around Tolosa (Toulouse) in Gaul. But when the West Roman emperor's sister, Honaria, sent him a ring and asked him to free her from an arranged marriage, he claimed she had proposed and demanded half the West Roman Empire as a dowry. The Romans, and the Visigoths hurriedly allied themselves, and

Bottom left: a profile of Attila on a coin. History has labeled Attila as a cruel barbarian. In fact, he had a respect for law and was merciful to his defeated enemies – although he was ruthless in battle.

Below: the image of Attila and his marauding band of Huns has inspired artists and writers over the centuries. The 19th-century painter Checa portrays Attila and his followers in typically warlike fashion attacking the Visigoths in an attempt to wrest their territory around Tolosa (Toulouse) from them.

Above: this is a detail from a Vatican fresco by Raphael. It shows Pope Leo I repulsing Attila. Attila was advancing south through Italy, conquering all before them. Pope Leo I pleaded with Attila to spare Rome. Attila took heed and turned back, though it is likely that shortage of food and disease among his men weighed more with Attila than any papal eloquence.

rushed to Orleans to head off Attila, and his 500,000-strong army marching through Gaul. The two forces finally clashed at Maunica, and after heavy fighting, and losses on both sides, Attila withdrew. It was his first and only defeat. A year later, he invaded Italy and marched south sacking such cities as Medialanum (Milan), Patavium (Padua), and Verona along the way. But disease, shortage of food, and the pleas of Pope Leo I to spare Rome finally persuaded him to turn back.

Attila was preparing another attack on the Byzantine empire where a new emperor, Marcian, was refusing to pay tribute when he died at his palace in Hungary. His empire passed to his sons, but it disintegrated soon afterwards.

While Attila himself may have left little but fear as his legacy, the Huns as a people left much more. It was the Huns sweeping out of Asia astride their swift horses who displaced the barbarians, and set off the waves of migration into Europe. Among these refugees from the Huns were the Goths who eventually conquered Italy, and many others who helped change the course of European history.

Gregory the Great
c540-604

In the year 590, with Italy overrun by destructive and land-hungry Lombards, the Roman Empire was based upon faraway Constantinople. Even the supremacy of the Church was threatened by rival bishops or "patriarchs" in Constantinople, Alexandria, and Antioch. Any man elected to be Pope had his work cut out, and would need to be outstanding. Gregory the Great was such a man. Civilized government was crumbling all over the known world. But at the head of the Church of Rome was a Pope whose courage, administrative skills, piety, and missionary zeal have led many historians to call Gregory the "architect of the medieval papacy."

Born in Rome of a wealthy family, Gregory received a good education, though, surprisingly, he never learned Greek, the language of the Eastern Roman Empire. He began his public life as Prefect, or civil administrator, of Rome at the remarkably young age of 30. On the death of his father, he became a monk, devoting his considerable fortune to charitable works. These included the establishment of six new monasteries in Sicily. Later he became a priest. The Pope sent him to Constantinople as papal envoy in 579. He had the vital task of rallying military support from the Emperor Tiberius II against the invading Lombards. In 584, Gregory returned empty-handed to Rome. There, on the death of Pope Pelagius II, both priests and lay leaders persuaded a reluctant Gregory to succeed to the papacy in 590.

His first job, with the Lombards occupying most of northern Italy, was to provide for the refugees who were streaming into Rome, where

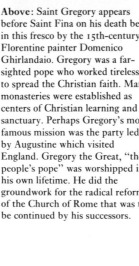

Above: Saint Gregory appears before Saint Fina on his death bed in this fresco by the 15th-century Florentine painter Domenico Ghirlandaio. Gregory was a far-sighted pope who worked tirelessly to spread the Christian faith. Many monasteries were established as centers of Christian learning and sanctuary. Perhaps Gregory's most famous mission was the party led by Augustine which visited England. Gregory the Great, "the people's pope" was worshipped in his own lifetime. He did the groundwork for the radical reform of the Church of Rome that was to be continued by his successors.

plague was already a danger, and to secure a peace with the invaders. He imported grain from the papal lands in Sicily to feed the refugees, who included some 3000 nuns. His efforts to achieve even a truce with the Lombards were less successful, partly because the new emperor, Maurice, supported the continuation of the war. It was not until 598 that a temporary peace was made between the Pope and the Lombard King Agilulf. As Gregory explained to the Emperor, it was a peace made "amid the swords of the Lombards." The situation forced Gregory to become a secular ruler and statesman. It was he who first consolidated the papal lands in Sicily, France, and Italy, the so-called Patrimony of Peter, into a whole – the Papal States. He believed that the wealth from these lands should be used by both the Church and the poor. But he was well aware of the dangers offered by a rich, and even corrupt Church: "We do not want the treasury of the Church defiled by disreputable gain."

Gregory took a farsighted and fruitful attitude to the pagan invaders of Europe. He realized that they had come to settle, and that to survive, and prosper, the Church of Rome must do all in its power to convert and civilize them. He be-

Left: portrait of Gregory the Great.

44

Left: Diptych of Saint Gregory the Great. Gregory once described himself as "the servant of God's servants." This title is still used by the modern papacy. Probably his greatest achievement as pope was a reform of the mass from which came the famous Gregorian chant. Catholics have looked upon Gregory as a doctor (teacher) of the Church since the 8th century.

Below: a marble relief by the 15th-century Italian sculptor Luigi da Milano depicts scenes from the life of Saint Gregory the Great – possibly the Catholic Church's most significant pope.

worked tirelessly for the spread of the monasteries as oases of Christian faith and learning in a Europe where civilized government was often non-existent.

As an administrator, Gregory's achievement was the centralization of the Church. He claimed the right to supervise and put right all bishops at a time when many disputed his authority. "I know of no bishop who is not subject to the Apostolic See (that is, to Rome) when a fault has been committed". He did not hesitate to remove offenders from office, and to correct abuses in the monasteries. His most important written work is the *Regula Pastoralis*, which unequivocally spells out the duties of a bishop. He wrote over 800 letters to bishops all over Christendom, instructing, correcting, and encouraging them. He encouraged a reform of the liturgy from which came the Gregorian chant.

A few years after becoming Pope, Gregory wrote: "Everywhere we observe strife; everywhere we hear groans. Cities are destroyed, fortresses are turned over, fields are depopulated, the land has returned to solitude . . . See what has befallen Rome, once mistress of the world." A lesser man would have given way to such pessimism. But Gregory, known and loved by his Church as "the people's pope", gave to his successors a practical program of action that was to enable the Church of Rome both to inspire and outlive the dark decades of the Middle Ages.

friended Theodolinda, Christian wife of Agilulf. After Gregory's death, her son Adaloald was to become a Christian. Gregory sent a missionary party to England led by St. Augustine. This not only won important converts, but organized them under Roman leadership. In this way, he prepared western Europe, by a program of conversion and "romanization," for what he saw as the inevitable split between the Eastern Church and the Church of Rome. At the same time, he

Charlemagne
742-814

"If I had known the Pope's intention, I would never have set foot in the church", Charlemagne, king of the Franks, is reported to have said after a Christmas mass in Rome in 800 at which the Pope crowned him emperor of the West. But

Above: although Charlemagne was not himself an "educated" man he had a thirst for knowledge. He ordered Alcuin of York, abbot of Saint Martin's abbey Tours, to revise the text of the bible. Alcuin completed the revision between AD 796 and 801. The decorated initial shown here is from the completed Alcuin Bible. Monks at the abbey took 25 years (AD 825–850) to finish the work.

Left: Charlemagne mounted, wearing his emperor's crown and dress armor.

Right: Charlemagne being crowned emperor of the West by Pope Leo III at his coronation in about AD 800.

Charlemagne was probably pleased. In the eyes of his people at least, the ceremony made him the successor to the cultured, and powerful Roman emperors, dating back to Augustus. It also broke the tie that made the Pope subordinate to the Byzantine emperors in the East, and irretrievably linked the Church of Rome with Europe.

The Franks had come a long way. At the height of Roman power they had been just a barbarian tribe living in the Rhine Valley, just outside the borders of the empire. As the empire's power declined, the Franks expanded their domain. Clovis, the first Frankish king defeated the Roman legions at Soissons, and ended Roman rule over most of Gaul in 486. Clovis took the Christian faith, and converted his people to his new religion. He also founded the Merovingian dynasty, which was to rule the Frankish empire for more than 250 years. Towards the end of the dynasty, the Merovingians only held the royal title. Real power was in the hands of the

"mayors", or administrators in various regions of the empire. Charles Martell was one of these mayors. He earned a lasting place in history with his defeat of the Arabs at Tours, which halted their advance into Europe. His son, and heir, Pepin the Short, deposed the Merovingians and declared himself king in 751. He won the Pope's approval at the time when the Pope needed his help to defeat the Lombards, another barbarian people, who held territory in Italy, and were threatening to expand their domain to include Papal land. Pepin died in 768. He left his empire, including most of present-day Germany, France, the Netherlands, Belgium, Switzerland, and Austria, to his two sons, Charlemagne and Carloman. Charlemagne's brother died in 771 leaving him sole ruler.

Pepin's work was carried on by Charlemagne. He added the Lombard Kingdom in northern Italy, Bavaria, and Saxony to his empire, and took sovereignty of the Avars and the Slavs. The Saxons proved most difficult to conquer. As early as 777, they had signed a declaration of allegiance to Charlemagne, and had been converted to Christianity in a mass baptism. But they continued to rebel. Charlemagne considered these rebellions treason against church as well as king. He punished them savagely, beheading 4500 people. In all, Charlemagne fought 18 battles, over 32 years, before he finally subdued the Saxons.

In an unsuccessful attempt to add Spain to their holdings, the Franks attacked Saragossa in 788. They failed to conquer it, and withdrew. While crossing the Pyrenees on the way home, they were attacked by Basques, and their commander, Roland, was killed. Roland was later immortalized in the epic poem, the *Song of Roland*.

While Charlemagne was planning his frequent battles, raising troops to fight them, and often leading them himself, he was also administering

Above: the cathedral at Charlemagne's capital, Aachen, with the chapel attached to his palace.

Right: Charlemagne's coronation as emperor of the West and of the Romans in AD 800. Picture shows Saint Peter (center) conferring power on Charlemagne (right) and Pope Leo III (left). Charlemagne became Holy Roman Emperor, a title that was to be coveted by prominent European monarchy for centuries to come.

his growing empire almost alone. Unlike the well organized Romans, Charlemagne had no civil service, no provinces, no roads to aid communication, and no common law. The central government consisted of Charlemagne's court. This was made up of his family, and a small group of secular and religious officials. Local areas kept their own laws, and were administered by a local noble, and a bishop. They received their instructions from a pair of royal messengers, one civil, and one religious. About once a year, Charlemagne and his court met with local officials in a general assembly. This discussed not only civil, but also religious and military affairs.

Although Charlemagne was rough-mannered, and not very well-educated, he had a thirst for knowledge. He filled his court at Aachen with scholars from all over his empire and beyond. To encourage learning throughout the empire, and improve religious practice, he supported education – especially of the clergy through monastic, and cathedral schools. These efforts

led to a carolingian renaissance that included not only a new interest in learning, but new forms of art, and architecture as well.

The size of Charlemagne's empire, and the inclusion in it of part of the old West Roman empire, made it the rival of the Byzantine empire, successor to the old East Roman empire. Byzantium still held sway over some territory in Italy, though most was under barbarian control, and they claimed jurisdiction over the Pope and

his lands. But the Popes favored the Franks. Partly because they were better protectors, and partly because the Western Church disagreed with certain doctrines accepted by Eastern bishops. In 799, Pope Leo III fled to Charlemagne's court to escape his enemies. Charlemagne returned him safely to Rome, and followed him there the next year, receiving an imperial welcome when he arrived, and the emperor's crown during the Christmas mass. After a lengthy struggle, the Byzantines acknowledged Charlemagne as emperor in 812 and gave up their claim to rule Rome, and the Pope.

Charlemagne's empire survived him by only one generation, before breaking up into smaller units. But it had a profound effect on medieval and modern Europe. For Charlemagne gave Europeans a common heritage based on Roman, Christian, and barbarian foundations. He introduced the idea of a combined secular and religious authority, and he provided the political tradition for what would become Germany and France.

Otto I
936-974

Otto I was regarded by contemporaries as the champion of Christian Europe. He was King of Germany from 936 AD and western emperor from 962. The state he founded was the continent's greatest power for two centuries. His coronation as emperor revived memories of Charlemagne. The German Holy Roman Empire, founded by Otto, lasted until 1806.

He was the son of Henry, Duke of Saxony – Germany's northeast province, on the frontier of the still pagan Slavs. Elected German king in 919, Henry laid the foundation of his son's success. He had won the cooperation of the other great German dukes – of Franconia, Lotharingia, Bavaria and Swabia – only by allowing them great independence. The first years of Otto's reign were plagued with rebellion.

The young king, already a hardened campaigner in his father's wars against the Slavs, combined a strong nerve with shrewd political judgement. He was ruthless towards his enemies. The duke of Bavaria was deposed and outlawed, the duke of Franconia killed in battle. But Otto's own brother, after several pardons, was finally reconciled, and given Bavaria. By 947 all the duchies were held by members of the king's family.

On the northeastern frontiers, two loyal counts, Gero and Hermann Billung were waging

Bottom left: profile of Otto I. A clever military tactician, Otto became a seasoned warrior in his father's wars against the Slavs.

Right: a coin from the reign of Otto I. It took Otto 15 years to pacify the German Duchies, and so unite his empire after he was crowned king in AD 936.

Below right: Otto I's empire. It was strengthened by political harmony between the two great kingdoms of Italy and Germany. Princes ruled sub-sections as semi-independent states.

Below: in a probably mythical scene, Otto I throws a spear in Jutland in the North Sea. It is said that where the spear landed would mark the northern boundary of his empire.

a merciless war of conquest and conversion against the pagan Slavs. Otto himself forced Boleslav I of Bohemia to submit. An Italian bishop considered Otto "truthful, guileless, merciful when right, severe when necessary, truly humble and generous." To the Slavs, he was regarded as a true servant of the "German god," the Sword. Otto once said, "I believe that the protection of the empire is bound up with the rising fortunes of the Christian worship."

He was again harrassed by rebellion in the 950s. This time, it involved his son by his first wife, who had died in 946. At the same time the nomad Magyars, the scourge of Europe for 50 years past, were raiding in southern Germany. On 10 August 955, after a long and bloody battle on the Lechfeld near Augsburg, Otto totally

routed them. His troops hailed him as emperor, and Europe honored him as its protector. The Magyars were henceforth confined to the plains of Hungary.

But Otto faced problems in the south. In 951 Adelaide, the widow queen of Italy, appealed to him for help against an ambitious marquis, Berengar. Otto's relations, the dukes of Bavaria and Swabia, went to her aid. Otto, fearing a new power block, marched against Berengar himself, married Adelaide, and was crowned King of Lombardy. Ten years later Berengar's power was again increasing and, at the behest of Pope John XII, Otto marched to Rome. There, on 2 February 962, the pope crowned him emperor. The two signed the *Privilegium Ottonianum*. This confirmed papal privileges, and, as Otto believed, gave the empire certain supervisory rights in papal affairs. But the wily pope was plotting against his now unwanted protector within a year. Furious, Otto deposed him.

The emperors at Constantinople, heirs of Constantine, wielded immense power in the Eastern Church, and John, pope since he was 17, was a notorious debauchee. But the Romans considered the papacy their political preserve, and Otto had to put down successive rebellions. He then marched into southern Italy, a province of the Eastern empire. Wiser than many of his successors, he soon realized that the conquest would be an expensive business, so he resorted to diplomacy. In 972 his 16-year-old son Otto

(later emperor as Otto II) was betrothed to a Byzantine princess. The following Easter, the emperor presided over a glittering council at Quedlinburg, attended by King Boleslav II of Bohemia and envoys from Kiev, Denmark, Poland, Magyar Hungary, and imperial Constantinople.

Once regarded as a barbarian usurper by the eastern emperors, Otto was now recognised by them. The Slavs were eager for his favors. The see of Magdeburg had been founded as the base for German imperial, and Christian expansion in the east. In Germany, bishops were the willing servants of government (many were related to the emperor). They conducted the secular administration in return for generous endowments, but still recognized the ultimate authority of the emperor.

This emperor, unable to read until he was 30, and with only a smattering of the Slav and Romance languages, had built a state extending from Rome to the Baltic, from the Rhone to the Elbe, had deposed a pope, and installed his own nominee. To contemporaries, it seemed that the future of Latin Christendom lay in German hands. Yet the imperial dream led to Italian adventures which distracted Germany's rulers, and sapped her strength. When, in the reign of Henry IV, church cooperation turned to antagonism, the tensions in the tightly meshed civil–church administration came close to destroying the system.

■ Kingdom of Germany
■ Kingdom of Italy

49

King Canute
994-1035

Canute was "a man of great good luck in every-thing to do with power," or so said a contemporary. When his father, the great Sweyn Forkbeard, king of Denmark died, the ancestral kingdom went to Canute's elder brother Harold. Canute was left merely with the chance of making good his father's claim to the crown of England. But by the time he died, Canute was lord of England, Denmark and Norway, a friend of popes, and emperors.

He had come to England in his early teens as a warrior. "Never did prince younger than thou set out on war," ran the *saga*, "thou who made red the enemy's armour before the walls of Norwich and won renown on Thames' side." Sweyn Forkbeard was recognized as king of England in 1013, but died the year after. His son

regained the title only after two years of bitter fighting against the young English hero, Edmund Ironside, son of the old king Æthelred the Rede-less ("Lacking in Council").

England, at the time, was divided between Anglo-Saxons in the West and the eastern "Danelaw," settled by Viking raiders in the ninth century. Defeated by the English king, Alfred the Great, they had been held in check by his successors until the weak rule of Æthelred opened the country to renewed Danish invasions. Canute's reign brought peace, and strengthened the sophisticated administrative system of the 10th-century English kings. The system provided the basis for the state of William the Conqueror.

Canute became undisputed king of England

Below left: a portrait of King Canute taken from an English manuscript of the mid-13th century.

Right: a likeness of Canute forms part of the decorated initial on a page from a 14th-century manuscript concerning the history of England. The page shown here is taken from a section detailing the laws of Canute.

Below: Canute shown duelling with Edmund Ironside – his predecessor on the throne of England. This illustration comes from *Historia Major*. One of the earliest historical works ever completed in Europe, it was certainly written before 1253. It can be seen today at Corpus Christi College, Cambridge.

only when Edmund Ironside, barely older than himself, died in November 1016. Tall, strong, fairhaired, and keen eyed, Canute's good looks were a little marred by a long bent nose. He was also shrewd. Confident in delegating power, Canute divided England into four great earldoms – Mercia, Northumbria, Wessex and East Anglia – to be administered by Danes and loyal English. Thus, when his brother died unexpectedly in 1018 he was free to leave England to assert his rights as king of Denmark. Ten years later, he waged further wars, which bought him the kingdom of Norway.

A fervent convert to Christianity, Canute respected the English tradition of strong co-operation between king and church. Advised by the saintly Wulfstan, archbishop of York, he introduced church reforms, and used them to

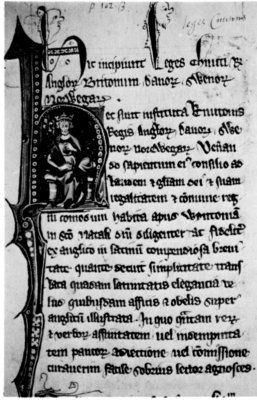

Left: this full-page drawing from the *Liber Vitae*, the Register and Martyrology of Newminster and Hyde Abbey, depicts King Canute and Queen Aelfgifu placing a cross on the altar of the abbey. Written in both Latin and Anglo-Saxon, the register was completed in about 1020.

Right: a coin struck during Canute's reign shows him in left profile.

Right: this 19th-century print depicts the scene for which Canute is best remembered. Popular mythology has it that Canute was an arrogant man, and believed that he had the power to command the waves to retreat. In fact, the reverse is the case. Canute set up this demonstration before the incoming tide to impress upon his more sycophantic courtiers that he was merely mortal, and not all powerful.

further his aim of uniting the English and Danes in England. He supported monasteries destroyed by earlier Danish raiders. Bury St. Edmunds is a notable example. It was dedicated to a martyred English warrior king, much admired by Danish converts. Canute encouraged the cult of the 10th-century English saint, Dunstan. In two famous letters to his English subjects he promised to observe God's laws, condemned paganism and promised to forsake the "sins of my youth."

Perhaps he had in mind his English concubine, Aelfgifu of Northampton, by whom he had two sons, and whom he seemed to honor as wife even after his marriage to Emma, widow of king Æthelred. At their marriage she had agreed that her sons by Canute should take precedence over Æthelred's heirs Alfred and Edward, living in

exile at the court of her brother Duke Richard of Normandy.

Canute kept on good terms with the duke, while his friendship with the emperor Conrad II yielded practical results. Present at the emperor's coronation in Rome in 1027, Canute won concessions for English and Danish pilgrims passing through the emperor's dominions. Later he persuaded Canute to return Schleswig to Denmark. He also won concessions for the English church from the pope.

Canute's English subjects long honored the memory of his piety with one of history's most famous legends. To teach his flattering courtiers a lesson, we are told, he went down to the beach one day and commanded the rising tide to go back. When the sea was "disrespectfully" lapping at his feet the great king turned to his courtiers with the words: "Know that none is worthy of the name of king, save only he whose nod the heavens, earth and sea obey."

His great empire disintegrated at his death. Yet it has been said that Canute's completion of the Danish conquest of England had more important results than the Norman one. One of England's greatest law givers, he brought English England and the Danelaw under one system.

William the Conqueror
1027-1087

William, duke of Normandy, was one of a race of conquerors which changed the map of Europe in the 11th century. The Normans were descended from Vikings, who had founded the duchy early in the 10th century. By 1100, they had conquered southern Italy from its former Lombard and Byzantine rulers and were already beginning to carve out new states in Syria and Palestine in the wake of the First Crusade.

These hard, and warlike men had a genius for government. At the battle of Hastings in 1066, William became master of one of Europe's best governed kingdoms. He built well on this solid foundation, and died leaving what was, for those days, a uniquely centralized state.

William was the bastard son of Duke Robert I, and Herleva, daughter of a wealthy citizen of Falaise. Duke Robert died when his son was only eight. Violence, and intrigue immediately closed in about the boy. Three of his advisers were murdered, and he was nearly assassinated himself.

He faced a full-scale rebellion when he was only 16. His military skill was already apparent, but victory was assured by the army of King Henry I of France. Over the next five years, William emerged as an able ruler. Henry faced a powerful neighbor, instead of a grateful and pliable vassal. His attempts to dismember the Norman state failed, and after the king's death in 1060 William enlarged his territory by annexing the neighboring southern county of Maine. He had proved himself a master in the most tur-

bulent region of France. The English adventure opened before him.

England was ruled by the childless Edward the Confessor. During the reign of Canute, Edward had lived as an exile in Normandy. As king he brought in Norman advisers. In 1051 he formally designated William his successor, and in 1053 William married Matilda, who was descended from Alfred the Great of England. But developments in England brought Harold God-

winson to the fore. By the 1060s he had the chance to win the succession by election. Then, in 1064 he was shipwrecked off the French coast. Taken as a "guest" to the court of William, he seems to have been tricked into an oath to support William's claim to the English crown. King Edward died, and in January 1066 Harold was duly elected king.

Despite the opposition of his own council, Duke William began massive preparations for the invasion of England. He built a fleet of transport ships, and recruited mercenaries from Brittany, Flanders, and elsewhere. Papal blessing was forthcoming for his war against a "perjured Usurper." A contrary wind kept his forces in Normandy throughout the late summer of 1066.

Meanwhile Harold had posted men and ships all along the Channel coast of England. But in September he disbanded the fleet. Immediately, news reached him that Norwegian forces had landed in the north. He marched at such speed that he took the Norwegians, and their allies by surprise, and routed them at the battle of Stamford Bridge on 25 September. But in the south, the wind had changed. William landed at Pevensey unopposed.

Harold and his household troops raced back

Above: the Charter of Waleran FitzRanulf bearing the *signas* of William I, Queen Matilda, and John, Archbishop of Rouen. This charter granted the church of Bures Saint Mary, near Sudbury, Suffolk, and a house in London to Saint Stephen's Abbey, Caen, France. Like nearly all people of the time, rich or poor, William was illiterate, and so adopted a *signa*, or mark. Scribes were employed to draft documents and write the names of the signatories.

Left: a portrait of William the Conqueror with horsemen taken from a 14th-century manuscript miniature.

Right: a section of the famous Bayeux tapestry shows the Norman invaders on their way to the south coast of England prior to the Battle of Hastings. After the defeat of the English, and Harold's death at Hastings, William's forces cut a swathe of destruction and death across southern England before finally entering London. The Bayeux tapestry was probably woven at the end of the 11th century by English needlewomen on the orders of Odo, Bishop of Bayeux, and half-brother of William.

to London. By 13 October, they were drawn up atop a hill near the modern town of Battle. They had only to rest and await reinforcements to be confident of defeating the invader. But Harold decided to give battle at about nine the following morning, before his men were properly rested, or any reinforcements had arrived. The English held their ground throughout the day. As the autumn evening approached, William's force, close to defeat twice already, feigned flight. The English left their ranks to give chase but were scattered as the enemy regrouped. Harold was killed.

The 40-year-old victor was brutal, avaricious, ruthless and consumed by ambition. He was also a courageous and resourceful leader, and was to be one of England's greatest kings. From Hastings, he marched on London leaving a trail of destruction and death across the southern counties. He was crowned king in Westminster Abbey on Christmas Day 1066. Rebellions followed in 1069, 1072 and 1075. All were crushed. The midlands, and the north were so devastated by the conqueror that the country was barely restored 50 years later.

William distributed the lands of the defeated English nobility among his followers. But the new Norman magnates were awarded fragmen-

Above: probably the best remembered achievement of William the Conqueror's reign, the *Domesday Book*. This "social survey" listed all the estates in England as well as the numbers of serfs working on them. It came in useful when settling disputes over land, and was a form of census as well. Even estimates of livestock were included. The book was written in Latin on vellum, and was compiled in 1086 on the orders of William. "Dom" was the Anglo-Saxon word for "judgement."

Right: a left profile portrait of William the Conqueror on a silver penny. Probably struck in 1068, the design is attributed to Theodoric.

tary fiefs to make it difficult for any one family to develop a concentration of power. The castles, erected to hold down the hostile country, were built with royal licence. The greatest among them were the king's own at Windsor, and the Tower of London. At the end of the reign he ordered a survey of the country known to the English as Domesday Book. A massive and unique document, it would have been impossible without the sophisticated administration he inherited from his English predecessors. The famous Bayeux Tapestry which recorded the invasion is also probably the work of English needlewomen.

William died while fighting enemies in Normandy. His reign had set a new pattern for English society. It also began English involvement in France, which spawned countless foreign wars throughout the middle ages. "This king excelled in wisdom. He was tall, of great dignity and so strong that no man might draw his bow. He was sparing in wine, fluent of speech, harsh of voice and stern of countenance." So he impressed his contemporaries. A modern historian has said of him: "William had an undaunted mastery . . . in both fighting and ruling unapproached in creative power by any other medieval ruler after Charlemagne."

King John
1167-1216

According to legend, King John of England was the caricature of a bad king. In fact, he was an able administrator, who suffered numerous misfortunes. He inherited a divided kingdom, fought and lost a number of expensive foreign wars, and was eventually defeated by an armed rebellion of barons and churchmen, who resented his powers as a feudal monarch. These setbacks have obscured his considerable administrative achievements. Ironically, the one political event of John's reign that is remembered, Magna Carta (from the Latin for Great Charter), he was forced

to sign. He died before he could succeed in revoking it.

Henry II, king of England and half of France, had three sons: Geoffrey, Richard, and John. There was intense jealousy among the brothers. That Henry appeared to favor John, the youngest, made matters worse. Geoffrey the eldest died young. But Richard, better known as the Lionheart for his bravery in battle, fought a civil war against his father in 1189. Henry died the same year, and Richard succeeded him. He set off on a crusade in 1190. Before leaving, he made John promise to stay out of England during his absence. Later in the year, Richard recognized Arthur, son of his dead brother Geoffrey, as his heir. Understandably resentful, John returned to England, and made an unsuccessful bid to take the throne in 1193. When Richard returned John was at first exiled. But the brothers were reconciled in 1196. Richard recognized John as his heir.

Richard died in 1199. John became king of

Above: the document that King John's reign is best remembered for, and one that he did not willingly sign, the Magna Carta. Signed in 1215 at Runnymede on the banks of the Thames river, the Magna Carta guaranteed the feudal rights of the barons, and immunity from royal interference for the church. It is still regarded as a constitutional landmark.

Above left: King John depicted in a miniature from a 13th-century English manuscript.

Right: before the signing of the Magna Carta, King John had stubbornly refused to grant any of the list of rights drawn up by the feudal barons and the church. The barons raised an army in an attempt to force him to change his mind. This 19th-century painting by Ernest Nuimond portrays the barons presenting their demands to the king.

England, and, like all English kings since William, duke of Normandy. But King Philip II of France supported the claim of Arthur, who was raised at the French court. A disastrous war with the French resulted. French superiority, and the strained resources of the English brought a series of defeats. By 1206, England had lost Normandy, Anjou, Maine, and parts of Poitou. These losses forced John to raise money for another war to win back England's French possessions. He tackled this problem by imposing a ruthlessly efficient financial administration, a series of enquiries into the enormous power and wealth of his barons, and a severe exploitation of his own feudal rights and privileges. None of this would have been possible without the centralized system of government built up by William the Conqueror. John gained a reputation for tyranny, which has endured over the centuries. He was excommunicated from 1209 to 1213, because he clashed with the pope over the king's traditional right to appoint the Archbishop of Canterbury. This infuriated churchmen, including the monks. Their chronicles provide the most detailed contemporary account of his reign. For them, John became not only a cruel despot, but sacrilegious.

But it was the powerful English barons who most resented John, and who gave him the most trouble. John pushed to the limit his feudal right to demand their military support, or its money equivalent. Another unsuccessful campaign in France in 1214 gave added cause for grievance. Barons, and churchmen had already met in 1213 to prepare a list of rights to be demanded from the king. Twice the king refused to sign. The third time, in 1215, the barons raised an army to force him to submit to their demands.

On June 15, John signed Magna Carta on a Thameside meadow called Runnymede. Today, this is the world's best-known constitutional document. It has become the model for all who demanded democratic rights and individual liberties. In fact, the charter of 1215 contained 65 articles, most of which benefited the barons, and church leaders. Feudal rights were guaranteed, as was freedom for the church to ignore royal interference. But what John granted unwillingly to the barons in 1215 – the final say in matters of taxation – later became the right of the English parliament to restrict the king's right to impose taxes. Other articles laid the foundations for modern justice. One states, for example, that no freeman of England should be punished for any crime without first being tried by his peers (equals), or by the law of the land. The whole concept of due process of law, including trial by jury, developed from this.

John was not prepared to accept the Magna

Above left: not long after the signing of the Magna Carta, the agreement broke down. King John had never willingly assented to its terms, and did his best to frustrate it. Civil war ensued. This 19th-century engraving shows the famous defeat of John's army at the Wash in eastern England. John died in 1216, while the war still raged.

Above right: King John out hunting. Hunting was a popular pastime with the nobility of the period, and had a role to play in the feudal economy. The most common prey were deer and wild boar.

Below: The effigy of King John – still to be seen in Worcester Cathedral.

Carta, any more than he had been willing to accept the loss of England's French possessions. He raised an army, and, with the blessing of the pope was campaigning against the barons in 1216, when he died. Cruel, suspicious, vengeful – John was however a king who took a keen personal interest in the administration of his realm. He extended the activities of the royal courts of justice, methods of taxation and military organization were improved, and numerous towns were granted charters. The concept of town councils had its origins in arrangements John made for London. The loss of English land in France led to the Hundred Years War. Magna Carta, modified in 1225 under Henry III, was the lasting, if unwilling, achievement of John's unhappy reign. It was the first attempt by Englishmen to lay down in legal form the principles they regarded as the basis of good government. To that extent Magna Carta is a milestone in constitutional history.

Pope Gregory VII
c1020-1085

greatest of them, Leo IX (1049-54), appointed reforming cardinals and brought Hildebrand, still only an archdeacon, into the papal administration. Leo held yearly councils in Rome, their decrees being enforced through provincial synods throughout Europe. He also tried to extend Rome's authority into southern Italy. Here, Norman adventurers were carving new states from territories once held by Constantinople, now claimed by the Holy Roman Empire.

Hildebrand Bonizo became Pope Gregory VII after 30 years at the center of major reforms in the papacy. One of the truly dramatic figures of history, he raised the office to a prestige it had never known. Europe's greatest ruler was brought to his knees at the historic encounter at Canossa. Gregory established the papacy as the unquestioned authority in the church. But he died in exile, his life's work seemingly in ruins.

The son of a poor Lombard carpenter, Hildebrand had risen to become chaplain to Pope Gregory VI by the time he was 30. The prestige of the papacy was at a low ebb. Elected by "the clergy and people of Rome," popes were often clever Roman politicians, rather than loyal churchmen. The church needed reform. Priests and bishops often bought their livings – the sin of simony. Many were married, or lived openly with concubines, in defiance of the laws of chastity. There had been a number of regional attempts at reform. But improvements in the papacy itself began only when the great emperor Henry III undertook its reform.

Emperors had vague, but recognized, rights as final arbiters in papal elections. A sincere man, Gregory VI had bought his election hoping to begin reform. But he was clearly guilty of simony, and Henry ordered him deposed in 1046. The emperor installed four reforming popes. The

Above: Pope Gregory VII surrounded by angels and cherubs in a fresco by Raphael, which can be seen in the Vatican. A power within the Church for 30 years before becoming pope, Gregory VII raised the standing of the papacy. The pope could now challenge the might of kings successfully.

Left: a contemporary portrait of Gregory VII.

In 1059, Pope Nicholas II, in return for their promise of military protection, invested the Normans with their conquests, lands which feudal law accorded to the empire. In the same year, with advice from archdeacon Hildebrand, Nicholas instituted the system of papal election by the college of cardinals. Rome's politicians were excluded and the emperor's role as arbiter ended. The popes had rejected their imperial patrons in just 10 years.

But the reforming movement had enemies. The death of Henry III in 1056, while it freed the pope's hands in Italy, deprived them of support in Germany. Alexander II (1061-73) sought reform by diplomacy rather than confrontation.

Hildebrand chafed. When the old pope died, he was acclaimed pope by the Roman people, and elected by the conclave.

Pope Gregory was "short, fat, swarthy and exceptionally ugly." He was also exceptionally able, and energetic. Pope Leo's system of Roman councils, and provincial synods was restored and stricter decrees against simony, and clerical marriage were passed. Then, in 1075, Gregory threatened excommunication to any

Left: the first page of the *Dictatus Papae*. This document was written by Gregory VII in 1075. Its 27 propositions uncompromisingly asserted the overriding authority of the papacy in conflicts between the Roman Catholic Church and the state. Secular interests were to be subordinated to those of the Church.

Below: illustrations from the 12th-century chronicle of Otto of Freising. The top pictures show Henry IV and his choice as pope, Clement II, expelling Gregory VII from Rome. Gregory's death at Salerno in 1085 is depicted at the bottom.

layman who invested a priest with the insignia of his office. It was a challenge to the German king.

Bishops played a central role in the German administration (Otto I). They were also great landholders. At their inauguration, they received a ring and staff from the emperor as token of their feudal loyalty. Moreover, the 25-year-old Henry IV, hoping to reassert German authority in Italy, had installed a new archbishop of Milan. In response to the pope's threat of excommunication, he convened the Synod of Worms which proclaimed Gregory "no more pope." Gregory excommunicated Henry in reply, and declared him deposed, and his subjects released from their obedience. German rebels asked the pope to choose a new king.

In January 1077, the pope was resting at Canossa on his journey north. Henry came to him as penitent. It was clear to Gregory that to absolve the king would weaken his own political position in Germany. He also saw that he could not betray his priestly duty to show mercy to a repentant sinner. The excommunication was lifted, and the king returned to fight the rebels. Gregory ordered both sides to accept his arbi-

tration. When Henry refused, he was again deposed. He proclaimed the archbishop of Ravenna pope as Clement III in 1080.

Three years later Henry marched into Rome, installed Clement in St Peter's, and was crowned emperor by him. Gregory took refuge in the Castle of Sant Angelo. Humiliated, he appealed for help to the Norman leader Robert Guiscard, even though he too had been excommunicated – for annexing papal lands. The Norman army rescued the pope. It also subjected Rome to a terrible sack. The Romans, loyal for so long, turned against their pope. Gregory had to leave with his Norman "protectors." He died in Salerno in 1080 with the words: "I have loved righteousness and hated iniquity – therefore I die in exile."

It was a bitter death but Gregory's turbulent, and arrogant rule founded the greatness of the medieval papacy. "The pope can be judged by none; he alone can depose and restore bishops; he can depose emperors; he can absolve subjects from their allegiance." These are some of the famous Papal Dictates (*dictatus papee*) in which Gregory VII spelled out his program. Canossa became a symbol of church authority which Christian Europe never forgot. Gregory VII's reign raised the papacy to new position of respect in Europe, and did much to put right its past.

Henry IV
1030-1106

Henry IV is best remembered for his barefoot penance at Canossa in January 1077, when this German King and Western Emperor begged forgiveness from Pope Gregory VII. At odds with the Church for most of his long reign, Henry, like Gregory, died a broken man. He had tried to restore the glories of his father Henry III, who had deposed and installed popes at will, and mastered his nobles. His failure was fateful for Germany.

Henry was only six when his father died. The regency government, led by the pious but incompetent Empress Agness, floundered in a sea of crisis. Revolt broke out in Saxony. Duke Godfrey of Lorraine quickly established a North Italian power base in the lands of his wife, Beatrice Countess of Tuscany. He thereby threatened the central German government on two fronts. The papacy, reformed and strengthened by Henry III, usurped imperial rights in southern Italy. At home, the archbishops of Cologne and Bremen contested the regency with the empress, and all three dispensed crown lands and revenues liberally to win support. Declared of age in 1065, Henry inherited a profoundly weakened monarchy.

With a reputation for dissipation and headstrong arrogance, the youth nevertheless showed courage, and skill. Putting down revolts in Sax-

Right: Henry IV with his wife and child standing barefoot at the gates of Canossa. For three days and three nights, Henry stood in the cold, and begged Gregory VII's forgiveness for challenging his authority. In the face of such abject pleading, it would have been unchristian not to yield. Pope Gregory VII had no choice but to lift Henry's excommunication. The vigil at the gates of Canossa was a shrewd piece of political tactics on Henry's part.

Below: Pope Gregory VII being expelled from Rome in 1084. Gregory had excommunicated Henry a second time, but this time Henry picked a pope of his own in Bishop Guilbert of Ravenna. Gregory was forced to flee Rome, and Bishop Guilbert became Pope Clement III. He can be seen seated at Henry's left, while Gregory is pictured being removed from their presence at the right of the picture.

Below left: an engraving of Henry IV.

ony and Bavaria, and restoring much of the monarchy's authority, in the 1070s he turned to the problems of Italy, and the growing power of the church. In 1075, Henry challenged the pope by investing a new archbishop of Milan. Gregory VII threatened immediate excommunication. But the pope's arrogant ways had made him unpopular. German church leaders renounced their allegiance to him at the Synod of Worms, convened by Henry. Pope Gregory thundered the

bull of excommunication of the king, and declared him deposed.

Rudolph of Swabia, and other German nobles, worried by the reviving royal power, now found rebellion to be their Christian duty. Demanding that Henry be reconciled with the pope by February 1077, or else face a rival king, they placed guards in the Alpine passes and invited Gregory to Germany.

The pope wintered at Canossa in the northern

Above: Henry IV in Saint Nicholas' Chapel at Canossa. He is asking Matilda of Tuscany and the Abbot of Cluny to intercede for him with Gregory VII to persuade the pope to lift his excommunication. This illustration is from a contemporary chronicle of the Life of Matilda.

Below: Henry IV cowers on the ground of the castle yard at Canossa in 1077, and beseeches Pope Gregory VII to forgive him and lift his excommunication. A haughty and arrogant man, Gregory appears in this picture to be enjoying Henry's discomfiture. But Henry's public display of humility forced Gregory to relent and lift the excommunication if he was to be thought a just pope. A popular subject with artists, this version was painted by J. A. Cluysenaar in about 1880.

Appenines as guest of Matilda, the new countess of Tuscany. With a scanty retinue, Henry evaded his enemies to reach Canossa. There, "standing before the castle gate, barefoot and coarsely clad, for three days he begged with many tears for apostolic help and comfort." This impressive act of self abasement was brilliantly calculated. Before such penitence the pope had no choice but to exercise Christian compassion, and lift the excommunication. The German rebels no longer had papal blessing.

They nevertheless elected Rudolph as king. But, after three years of civil war, Henry felt strong enough to defy the pope once again. He suffered a second excommunication for his pains. But, this time he proclaimed his own pope, "Clement III," and in 1084 was crowned emperor by him in St Peter's, Rome.

Gregory's successors, notably Pope Urban II, were to prove too powerful for the emperor. While even imperialist bishops deserted the cause, Henry remained loyal to Clement, and maintained his own right to invest bishops. Matilda of Tuscany married the duke of Bavaria, and Henry, campaigning in Italy, was often cut off from Germany. His power there was eroded by opponents enjoying papal approval. Even his own son, Henry V, joined the rebels. In 1105, after a despicable pretence of reconciliation, he imprisoned his father. The broken emperor escaped to die a few months later.

Henry showed many qualities of greatness. He salvaged much from the turmoil of the regency. At Canossa he won a tactical victory over the century's greatest pope, and he ensured the succession of his son. But his struggle with the church over investiture shattered his authority, and side-tracked his energies. In his reign the powerful centrifugal forces of medieval Germany finally asserted themselves.

Genghis Khan
c1162-1227

Mongol conqueror Temujin, whose adopted name Genghis Khan may be translated as "Universal Ruler", came close to fullfilling that ambitious dream. At his death, he ruled an Asian empire, stretching from Peking to Samarkand. His successors built on this massive foundation, and pushed the boundaries of Mongol control east to the China Sea, and west to the frontiers of Sweden, Poland, Hungary, and the Byzantine empire. The "pax Mongolica" made Asia safe for travellers and merchants for a hundred years, and opened the way for the first faltering contacts between Europe and China.

Genghis Khan was a subject of the Kerait chief, who was treated by the north Chinese Chin empire as the leading figure among the warring Mongol tribes on their northern frontier. After a series of bloody battles, he made himself master of the Kerait and was soon recognized as a leader capable of uniting the warring tribes. His simple barbaric doctrine was summed up in memorable words: "A man's greatest pleasure is to defeat his enemies, to drive them before him, to take from them that which they possessed, to see those whom they cherished in tears, to ride their horses, to hold their wives and daughters in his arms." The nomads who terrorized Asia for the next 50 years needed no encouragement to put these sentiments into practice. But Genghis Khan possessed greater qualities of leadership than those of a mere brigand.

In 1206 a *kuriltai*, or general assembly, of Mongol chieftains elected him their leader. It

Above: a Chinese town falling to the Mongol army of Genghis Khan, or "Great Khan." China was conquered by the Mongols under Khan in the early 1200s. The Chinese people were kept in subjugation by employing the methods of massacre and terror for the next 150 years, but it was the superb military tactics of Genghis Khan's army that defeated them in the first place.

Left: Genghis Khan as portrayed in a detail from a Persian miniature painted in 1397.

was here that he took the name Genghis Khan. At the same time, the people were mobilized in an organization which exploited the strengths of tribal society, and took its weaknesses into account. The fighting men were divided into units of 10, 100, 1000, and 10,000. They and their families were under the command of their officers in peace as in war. The chief commanders were to be personal friends of Genghis Khan, and their senior subordinates were generally their own kinsmen. Later, an elite imperial guard was recruited from the whole army. Its privates outranked the commander of 1000 men.

The Mongols lived as they fought. Men rode horseback, bow in hand either to hunt or to fight. The women and children lived in tents, or in the great wagons when the camp was seeking new grazing. These nomad hunter warriors now had an organization suited for conquest. China was divided between the states of Hsi Hsia, Chin, with its capital of Peking, and the Southern Sung with its capital at Hangchow. These last two were at war.

Renegade Chinese officers urged Genghis Khan to attack Chin without delay, but first he forced Hsi Hsia to submit. Plundering campaigns against Chin followed. In 1212, these

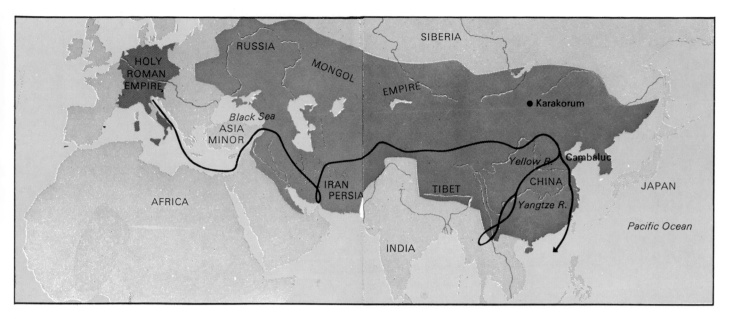

Above: the extent of Genghis Khan's empire is shown in orange. The route of Marco Polo's first expedition (1271–1295) is also shown.
Left: this Mongol warrior wears a golden helmet lined and trimmed with fur, and a Chinese-patterned cloak held in place with an ornate belt.
Below: the funeral of Genghis Khan in 1227. He died during a campaign against neighboring Tanggut. A hunting fall hastened his death.

the military, political, and economic position of his enemies before attacking them.

Among his own people Genghis Khan was revered as a ruler of justice and good sense. He was loyal to his friends if merciless to his enemies. His *yasa*, or legal code, codified traditional practice, promulgated new laws, and formed moral precepts. In a lightning career of conquest, he not only unified the Turco-Mongol peoples of Asia, but moved from being a tribal raider to an imperial ruler.

precipitated a palace revolution, and forced the new emperor to move his capital to the southern city of Kaifeng. The Mongols sacked Peking, and slaughtered its people. But Chin was to hold out for another 15 years.

Meanwhile, Genghis Khan ranged westward to the Pamir mountains and the Oxus river. The huge kingdom of Kara-khitai fell to him, and then the Khwarazmin empire, reaching to the shores of the Caspian Sea. His armies won victories in Georgia, the Crimea, and the Ukraine. The great Islamic cultural capitals of Bokhara and Samarkand became provincial cities in his empire. Three thousand miles distant, on its eastern wing, Manchuria and Korea had been absorbed. The conqueror died, aged about 60, on campaign.

The success of the Mongol armies over so vast an area of the earth's surface in so short a time is one of the marvels of history. The entire Mongol population of approximately 1,000,000 barely exceeded that of the Chinese city of Hangchow. The Mongols' systematic use of massacre and terror no doubt weakened their opponents' will to resist. More important was the brilliant horsemanship and coordinated battle tactics of Genghis Khan's army, and the thorough reports on

Kubilai Khan
1215-1294

Great Khan at his residence of Shangtu. But his younger brother, who by Mongol tradition had inherited the Mongol homeland, proclaimed himself at Karakorum. There followed four years of civil war before Kubilai could turn his attention to the war against the Sung. In 1271, he made Peking his winter capital, and adopted the Chinese dynastic title Yuan – meaning "Origin." Sung resistance was finally crushed eight years later.

Right: a Mongol ruler receives an embassy in his court. The visitors are seated at the left of the picture, while Mongol courtiers congregate on the right. This picture shows the lavishness of dress expected in the Mongol court when the empire was at the height of its prestige. Painted in Tabriz in 1307, this miniature is taken from the *Jami Al-tawarikh* (Universal History) of Rashid al-Din.

Left: a portrait of Kubilai Khan painted in 1291. This is the official Chinese portrait of the great Mongol ruler.

As Great Khan of the Mongol empire founded by Genghis Khan and emperor of China, Kubilai Khan was nominal sovereign of a larger population than had ever before acknowledged one man's rule. He was a man of good stature, and well proportioned. His complexion was "fair and ruddy like a rose, the eyes black and handsome, the nose shapely and set squarely in the face." This description comes from the *Travels* of Marco Polo, the famous Venetian. He was one of the many foreigners to serve the cosmopolitan administration of Kubilai Khan which laid the foundations of the later imperial state.

Genghis Khan was succeeded by his youngest son Tolui. But in 1229, a *kuriltai*, or assembly, transferred the rule to Ogödei, an older son. Ogödei built the Mongol capital city at Karakorum, the residence of Genghis Khan. He carried on with campaigns against the Chinese Southern Sung empire and made conquests in Korea and Southern Russia. In the late 1240s the succession passed back to Tolui's line in the person of Möngke, the brother of Kubilai, who was made governor of the occupied regions of China.

Campaigning against the Sung, Kubilai's forces occupied a large region outside the western frontier of China, and incorporated it into the state to become the province of Yunnan. When Möngke died in 1259, Kubilai immediately made a truce with the Sung, and marched north to secure his succession. He had himself proclaimed

A number of leading Mongol chiefs considered Kubilai's shift of capital from Karakorum a betrayal, and his wise, conciliatory policies in China contemptible compromises. He was harassed throughout his reign by revolt in the western Mongol territories. But he never relinquished his position as lord of the vast, cosmopolitan empire.

All the world's major religions were contained within its borders. Even in China, Buddhism, Taoism, and Confucianism stood side by side with Christian, Moslem, and Jewish communities. Möngke had been the son and husband of Nestorian Christian princesses. A Nestorian was chief minister. Like Möngke, Kubilai preferred to use Mongols or foreigners in the higher ranks of the administration. He legislated to keep the Mongol elite distinct from the mass of the

Below: Kubilai Khan hands the Polos the gold tablet of safe conduct and help (*paizah*). This is a European impression of what Kubilai Khan looked like from Marco Polo's story of his travels. The picture is a miniature from the 14th-century French manuscript *Le Livre des Merveilles*, in which the Adventures of Marco Polo is included.

population, but he abolished the special powers still retained by the Mongol nobility and restored much of the ancient Chinese administrative system. As a result, once the Sung armies were defeated, Kubilai met little opposition to his regime.

But, as Marco Polo noted, the Mongols distrusted the Chinese Confucian establishment. Kubilai abolished the traditional examinations in the Confucian classics for the mandarin civil

service, which became hereditary in reliable families. He favored Buddhism as the state religion, and even created a special government department for the Nestorian Christians who had their own Archbishop of Peking from 1275.

Two years after the fall of the Sung, Kubilai, always mindful of his responsibility as Great Khan to extend the empire, tried to invade Japan. An army of 140,000 men was to be shipped in the largest seaborne invasion the world had seen. But the fleet was scattered and thousands drowned by a typhoon remembered by the Japanese to this day as "*kamikaze*," or "divine wind."

Above: Mongol religious demons. Under Kubilai Khan's reign most Mongols worshipped the spirit forces in winds, forests, and mountains. These were presented as demons – half beast, half man.

Below: this miniature shows the awesome appearance of the Great Khan's warriors. It comes from the Universal History of Rashid al-Din and shows Mahmud ibn Sebuktegin defeating his opponent Baktuzun.

In China itself, the Great Khan laid the foundations of a new order. The 12 great provinces, the basis of China's administration into the late 19th century, were established. Agriculture was revived, and the distribution of grain surpluses from the Lower Yangtze river to Peking was secured by the building of the Grand Canal. This impressive feat of engineering made it possible to travel by water direct from Hangchow to Peking, a distance of 1100 miles. Kubilai built a new city at Peking, known in the West as Cambaluc. It became one of the wonders of the world. The Mongol conquest had reunited China, and laid the foundations for the glories of the Ming native dynasty 100 years later.

Philip the Good
1396-1467

Today's Belgium and the Netherlands have their origins in the reign of Philip the Good, duke of Burgundy. Before him territories such as Holland, Zeeland, Brabant, and Flanders constituted an area of many common interests, but divided between rival dynastic rulers. Philip united them by a steady policy of marriage, conquest, and purchase. It seemed possible that a new state might emerge between the Rhine, the Seine, and and the Rhone rivers. This prospect died with Philip's son, Charles the Bold, at the battle of Nancy in 1477. But the Burgundian territories in the Low Countries, inherited by Charles's daughter Mary, were of central importance in subsequent European history.

The Burgundian state, and its involvement in the Low Countries, had started with Philip's grandfather, Duke Philip the Bold (d. 1404), of the French royal house of Valois, duke of Burgundy, and, count of Flanders by marriage. He was also a commanding figure in French politics. His son, Duke John the Fearless, continued the tradition. He disputed control of the mad king Charles VI with the supporters of the Dauphin. Northern France was opened up to English conquest by Henry V's great victory at Agincourt in 1415. A meeting was finally arranged between Dauphinists and Burgundians at Montereux on

10 September, 1419. But instead of a reconciliation, Duke John the Fearless was treacherously murdered. Philip the Good entered an alliance with England, and recognized Henry V's claims to the French crown.

The English paid Philip a generous pension, and "granted" him various French territories, such as Macon and Ponthieu. His sister, Anne, married Duke John of Bedford, the English regent in Normandy. A Burgundian garrison

Right: *The Madonna of Chancellor Rolin*, painted in about 1415 by Jan van Eyck. Rolin was Philip the Good's closest adviser. A patron of the arts, Philip appointed van Eyck painter to his court and *varlet de chambre* on May 19, 1425, and paid him a salary of 100 livres. On more than one occasion, Philip intervened personally to ensure that "our excellent painter and beloved friend," van Eyck, was duly paid his salary.

surrendered Joan of Arc to the English authorities. But Joan had inspired a reawakening of French patriotism. France was also developing contacts with German rulers on Philip's eastern frontiers. A contemporary observed that "as time went on the more anxious Duke Philip became to display his French heart." The Congress of Arras convened in 1435 to reconcile England and France. Philip dramatically switched alliances at this. Nevertheless, he retained the lands

Below: a letter from Philip to Charles, Duke of Orleans. Philip has signed the postscript.

Below left: a portrait of Philip the Good, now housed in the museum at Dijon, east-central France.

granted him by the English and extensive frontier territories along the Somme river.

Burgundian connections in the south hinged upon an understanding between Philip and Duke Amadeus VIII of Savoy, and with the duke of Bourbon. He looked for Burgundian advantage in the troubled politics of Charles VII's France, supporting the noble opposition, or Praguerie, for a time, and offering asylum to the king's rebellious son, the future Louis XI. But his most important achievement was the consolidation of Burgundian power in the Low Countries.

The Treaty of Delft of 1428 recognized his claim to the succession in Holland, Hainault, and Zeeland. In 1430, the estates of Brabant accepted him as duke. Namur was purchased, and Luxembourg conquered. He acquired Friesland, Limburg, and Cambrai, and extended his family's influence in the bishoprics of Liege and Utrecht. In spite of these solid territorial gains, however, Philip failed to solve the political problems posed by the powerful towns, on whose wealth Burgundian power depended.

Revolts flared up in Bruges, Amsterdam, Rotterdam, and Leiden. Then, in 1447, a government demand for a salt tax sparked off a protracted crisis in Ghent. This, "the most powerful town in the duke's territories," had been foremost in the Flemish opposition to Philip's grandfather, crushed at the battle of Roosebeek in 1382. The city and its council, the *collatie*, exercised considerable power in the surrounding countryside. Their hold reinforced through nonresident burgesses – the *hagepoorters*. But in the conflict with the ducal government a revolutionary government took control. It was defeated at the battle of Gavere in July 1453, after a struggle which threatened the Burgundian state, and gravely disrupted the Flanders economy.

Above: the *Chroniques de Hainault* being presented to Philip the Good. His closest adviser Rolin, and Charles, the Count of Charolais are present, along with other courtiers.

Left: *The Just Judges and Knights of the Faith*, a section of the Ghent altarpiece painted by Jan van Eyck between 1426 and 1432. The splendor of Philip the Good's court was the envy of monarchs throughout 15th-century Europe. Even the Sun King, Louis XIV of France, was influenced by its ceremonials. Philip's court actively encouraged the arts. Apart from Jan van Eyck, the painter Rogier van der Weyden, and the musicians Guillaume Dufay, Gilles Binchois, and Johannes Ockeghem were among the many artists to receive support. European culture flourished.

The diverse traditions of the duke's territories were reflected in the system of government. Taxation was channeled through such regional centers as The Hague, Brussels, Lille, and Dijon. The *stadtholders* (provincial executives) tended to become a permanent institution, provincial estates evolved, and regional institutions, inherited from the past, continued in existence. Administrative coherence was provided by common administrative practices, rather than by one centralized bureaucracy. The ducal council, the *groote raade*, supervised and intervened, but did not take over all the functions of government. It was presided over by the duke, ably helped by his wife Isabella and Chancellor Rolin. His reluctance to involve his son Charles in the government caused serious estrangements between them. To Philip's contemporaries, it seemed that this great state was doomed to collapse when his guiding hand was finally removed by death.

Financed by the immense wealth of the Dutch and Flemish towns, Philip's court was the most brilliant of his age, influencing courtly ceremonial even in the France of Louis XIV. The duke's chivalric Order of the Golden Fleece was second only to the Order of the Garter. Painters Jan van Eyck and Rogier van der Weyden, and musicians Guillaume Dufay, Gilles Binchois, and Johannes Ockeghem were among the great artists active in the Low Countries during his reign. It was a golden age for European culture.

Henry the Navigator
1394-1460

Regarded by many as the father of European Atlantic and coastal African exploration, Prince Henry financed a series of voyages. These succeeded in discovering and colonizing the Azores, Madeira, and the Cape Verde Islands. They reached as far south as Sierre Leone – 1500 miles beyond the then known limit of African navigation.

Henry was a younger son of King John I of Portugal and his English wife, Philippa, daughter of John, duke of Lancaster. He distinguished himself at the capture of the Moroccan town of Ceuta, on the straits of Gibraltar, when he was only 19. According to Diogo Gomes, one of his captains in later years, prisoners' tales of fabulous gold mines south of the Sahara fired his imagination, and he "determined to reach them by sea so as to trade with them to sustain the nobles of his household."

Ceuta was a terminal of the trans-Saharan gold routes from mines on the Upper Volta, Niger, and Senegal rivers. But it was crusading zeal and chivalrous ideals, rather than crude commercial gain that inspired the expedition. Henry later took part in other expeditions against the infidel. Many people believed the real motive behind his explorations was to circumnavigate Moslem Africa, and so join forces against Islam with "Prester John," the fabled ruler of a Christian empire somewhere in "the Indies."

Right: the marriage in 1387 of King John I of Portugal to Philippa, eldest daughter of John of Gaunt of England. Ties between the two countries were strengthened, and the marriage helped to cement what is still referred to in Britain as the "oldest alliance." Philippa gave birth to Prince Henry seven years after the wedding, in 1394. He was the younger son of the marriage.

Above: a ship of the type which undertook the voyages which Henry financed. It had square-rigged sails and was of lateen construction – a long yard suspending the sails from the mast. Henry's passion for exploration laid the foundations for Portugal's future imperial power.

Left: a tall, suntanned, strongly built young man – Prince Henry the Navigator in adulthood.

There were other factors to arouse his interest. His father had come to the throne with the strong support of Portugal's merchant classes, while the country, excluded from the Mediterranean trade by Aragonese and Italian interests, naturally looked westward.

The Prince was "tall, big-boned and brawny, with a dark, sun-tanned complexion. His look was stern but he was loved by all for he did good to all and showed respect even to the least distinguished. He did not drink and was never known to sleep with a woman; he was driven by ambition to do great things." He certainly subjected himself to an appallingly heavy work load. He established an observatory at his home at Sagris on the Algarve in 1419, and assembled mathematicians, astronomers, and navigation experts.

The best maps were Catalan, Majorcan, and Arab, the simple instruments – mariners' compass, astrolabe, and quadrant were learned from the East. Cape Bojador was the southern limit of African Coastal navigation. It was about 200 miles south of the Canary Isles. Stormy and wreathed in fogs, it shielded the way to the "Green Sea of Darkness" from which, it was popularly believed, return was impossible. Prince Henry dispatched expeditions annually. Manned by Portuguese, Italians, and Flemings they finally forced the passage in 1434. This was the breakthrough. Advance down the African coast was steady thereafter.

As the venturers sailed past the Senegal river and on to Sierre Leone, they began to show profits in spices, gold dust, and slaves. The first Portuguese trading factory in Africa was established in 1445. Lisbon merchants and nobles, for 20 years contemptuous of the prince's fruitless ventures, jostled for shares, and licenses to trade. The revenue was welcome. Henry had a large income from monopolies, and the lands of the Order of Christ of which he was the Master. But

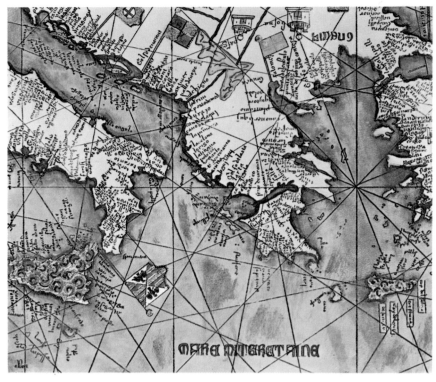

Above: Henry and his scholars would have used maps similar to this Catalan map of 1375. Areas already discovered and well explored would be marked fairly accurately. But off the beaten track, the maps became largely guesswork.

Below: this 19th-century print depicts the early days of the African slave trade. Captives were brought back from 1441. Henry was interested in learning of their homelands, and tried to convert them to Christianity. Others regarded the slaves less sentimentally – as a handy source of profit.

the financing of the long years of pioneering and colonizing had been enormously costly. His efforts earned Portugal a papal bull which, in 1455, guaranteed the country's monopoly of future conquests round the coast of Africa – as far as the Indies.

Africa was probably circumnavigated, and the Atlantic penetrated, in antiquity. But Henry was the first man to conduct a systematic program of maritime exploration. His shipwrights evolved the lateen rigged caravel, Europe's most efficient ship, and his sailing masters laid the foundations of oceanic navigation. Henry inaugurated the momentous epoch of the European colonial empires.

Mohammed II
1430-1481

Below: Mohammed II's army lays siege to Constantinople. The siege started in April, and the city fell on May 29, 1453. This illustration is a miniature from Bertrandon de la Broquiere, *Voyage d'Outremer*. It was produced two years after the siege.

Below left: a portrait of Mohammed II, painted by Sinan Bey.

the Hungarian, Janos Hunyadi, at the Battle of Varna. Murad was Mohammed II's father.

Mohammed's education was intensive. He was a more cultured ruler than many a Renaissance prince. Well read in Greek, as well as Islamic literature, he was fluent in Arabic, Greek, Latin, Persian, and Hebrew. He was well informed in the contemporary sciences. After Varna, Murad retired. The empire was left in the charge of his ministers of state and his 12-

The Turkish sultan, Mohammed II captured Constantinople in 1453. So ended the epoch of the Christian Byzantine empire, the medieval continuation of the ancient Roman empire. In Turkey itself, Mohammed's reign rounded off the Ottoman occupation of the region that is now modern Turkey, and began the golden age of Ottoman art.

The Ottoman Turks traced their descent through Osman, a warrior chief of the early 1300s. For 300 years, nomad *ghazis*, or "warriors for Islam," had been pushing back the Byzantine frontiers in Anatolia. By 1300, the region was divided between the large Karaman sultanate of Konya, and a group of lesser emirates. Osman's lands bordered the narrow Christian territory on the southern coast of the Sea of Marmora. Ghazis from all over the Moslem world flocked to this last frontier territory. By 1400, the early Ottoman sultans, helped by this restless force, had conquered much of Anatolia and the Balkans, from their capital at Adrianople.

Tamburlaine smashed the growing empire at the battle of Ankara in 1402. The sultan Bayezit was taken captive. Karaman and the lesser emirates were reestablished. But Bayezit's successors quickly recovered their lost position. Constantinople again became an island in a dangerously Turkish sea. In 1444 Murad, Bayezit's grandson, defeated a Christian army under

year-old heir. But the self-opinionated conduct of the boy caused such upheavals at court that Murad resumed the government until he died in 1451.

The haughty young sultan was impressively and strongly built. A pair of piercing eyes under arched eyebrows dominated his face, and a thin hooked nose that curved under full red lips completed the picture. He was a secretive, strong-willed young man, and as capable as he was

Left: Mohammed being crowned sultan after his father Murad's death in 1451. Murad had retired after the Battle of Varna in 1444, but was forced to take control again because of his son's impulsive and arrogant behavior.

Right: after becoming sultan, Mohammed II's first priority was the capture of Constantinople. To guard the Bosphorous Straits, he had the Rumeli Hisar fortress built. It was completed in just four months – April to August 1452. This remains an astonishing feat, and it can only be imagined what expense of labor was involved. With only the most primitive building tools to hand, nearly all of the most gruelling toil was achieved by the muscle power of thousands of slaves – many of whom died in the process. When Constantinople fell to Mohammed's forces in May 1453, the power of the Christian Byzantine empire was smashed.

energetic. The conquest of Constantinople was his first objective.

Between April and August 1452, the Rumeli Hissar fortress was built to control the Bosphorous Straits. Next April, Mohammed led his army to the siege. Constantinople, Christian for 1000 years, fell on May 29, after an epic defense. Its last emperor, heir to Constantine and the Caesars, died fighting on the walls. A bloody three-day sack followed. On the afternoon of June 1 the 21-year-old conqueror entered the city. The procession headed for the Church of the Holy Wisdom. A Turkish *ulema* climbed the pulpit and proclaimed, "There is no God but Allah." Christendom's most venerable temple became a mosque. But Mohammed allowed his Christian subjects the right of a self-governing religious community under its own patriarch within the empire. Like emperors before him, Mohammed invested the patriarch with his insignia, including a pectoral cross, paid for by the sultan himself.

Above: Gentile Bellini painted this portrait of Mohammed II in the last year of the Turkish sultan's life. Mohammed captured Constantinople 27 years earlier, in 1453, when he was only 21 years old.

The Greek city of Trebizond, at the far end of the Black Sea fell in 1461. Southern Greece and many Aegean islands surrendered before the end of the reign. In the Balkans, although defeated before Belgrade in 1456 by a Hungarian army led by Janos Hunyadi, the sultan's armies occupied the rest of Serbia and, for a time, the Hungarian province of Bosnia. Wallachia (now southern Romania), long a client state, was absorbed into the Ottoman state in the 1460s.

Albania followed after the death of the heroic Skanderbeg. The khan of the Crimea became a mere vassal. Most important of all, the revived emirate of Karaman was finally conquered in 1466, and incorporated into Ottoman Anatolia.

Mohammed consolidated the heartlands of the Turkish state and restored Constantinople as a capital worthy of its name. In 1453, it was a shadow of its former glories. By the end of the century, its population once again reached the 500,000 mark. Mohammed's architects raised many mosques still intact today. The vast Fatih ("Victor's") Mosque with its domed complex of baths, travelers' hospice, market, and university, rose on a superb hill site above the city. A new palace dominated Seraglio Point. Court painters, like Sinan Bay, and admiring European artists like Gentile Bellini have left vibrant portraits of him. Mohammed the "Conqueror" had overthrown the Eastern Christians' 1000-year empire and established a Turkish empire which was to harrass the West for the next two centuries.

Hernando Cortes
1485-1547

prophecies that Quetzalcoatl, god of the winds, of goodness, and of light, would return one day to destroy the empire. To many, Cortes, with his winged canoes and their voices of thunder (cannon), was the prophesied god. He built a fortified camp near Cempoalla, naming it Vera Cruz, and sent a ship back to Spain with despatches, trophies of conquest, and a painted book recounting the legend of Quetzalcoatl.

In August 1519, accompanied by 400 of his

"A man of noble bearing and lordly demeanor," Hernando Cortes was born into a family of the Castilian lesser nobility. Like his contemporary Francisco Pizarro (1475-1541), he came from the impoverished Spanish province of Estremadura. With a handful of men and a determination bordering on the reckless, Cortes conquered the Aztec empire of Mexico in a brilliant cam-

Right: the Aztec capital of Tenochtitlan on the site of modern-day Mexico City. This 1601 engraving by Hoefnagel from *Orbis Terrarum* is based on a sketch drawn by Cortes himself. His forces captured the city after a three-month siege. At the center of the capital was the temple area. Buildings were grouped around it. These were intersected by canals. The whole was surrounded by a lake.

Left: a portrait of Hernando Cortes on horseback from a Tlaxcalan Indian manuscript about his conquest of Mexico. The Indian artist pictured Cortes with a hat like that worn by their god Quetzalcoatl. Cortes' appearance was strange to the Indians, and reinforced their belief that he was their god returning from exile.

paign. It set the pattern for Pizarro's victory against the Incas in Peru.

Cortes fought in the conquest of Cuba, and became a leading and ambitious member of its new colonial society when he was only 19. In 1517, Governor Velazquez commissioned him to sail west to investigate reports of new lands. The governor regretted appointing the ambitious young soldier almost immediately. But Cortes had mobilized his force quickly, and had sailed before the recall order could reach him. His expedition was made up of 500 men, with 16 horses, 10 small cannons, and 48 hand guns. Reaching the coast of Yucatan, they were welcomed with presents by the local Mayan population – slave women among them. One of these spoke an Aztec language. She and a Spanish sailor, who had been a slave to the Mayas and spoke their language, were to be Cortes' interpreters. He landed at Cempoalla on the Mexican coast in April 1519.

Barely 100 years before, the Aztecs had launched a series of savage wars, and had forced tribute, slaves, and human sacrifices from their neighbors. Among the conquered, there were

Below: Cortes with the Indian princess Malinche, who became his interpreter. She is translating the words of an Aztec for Cortes' benefit. Malinche was known as Dona Marina by the Spaniards.

troops, thousands of Totonac porters, and seven cannon, he marched inland to meet the Tlaxcala, a mountain people at war with the Aztecs. The great capital city of Tenochtitlan, with a population of nearly a million, stood on islands in a lake surrounded by mountains and volcanoes.

Having failed to stop Cortes' approach, or to assassinate him, the Aztec emperor, Montezuma, gave him a palace within the walls.

Meanwhile, the Cuban governor, jealous of Cortes' success, had sent an expedition to Vera Cruz to arrest him. Cortes quickly returned to the coast, defeated his enemies, and persuaded the survivors to join him. The garrison left at Tenochtitlan, fearing to be overrun, had massacred a number of the citizens.

On Cortes' return, the Aztecs laid siege to him and his men. Montezuma was killed in the fighting, but the Spaniards were forced to take to flight. Many were dragged into the lake as they crossed the causeway, the rest headed back for the Tlaxcala. Although overwhelmingly outnumbered, they defeated a massive Aztec army at Otumba. On August 13, 1521, in alliance with the Tlaxcalans and thousands of other Aztecs rebels, they took Tenochtitlan after a three month siege. Hardly a building was left standing.

Cortes' soldiers were guilty of dreadful atrocities. Such behavior was not in keeping with their leader's undoubted religiosity. But it must be remembered that the Inquisition conducted in Cortes' homeland was hardly less brutal. And Aztec priests tore the hearts from living prisoners. Just how 500 Conquistadors, with a handful of guns, were able to overthrow an empire of several million people, remains a puzzle. One theory has it that the Europeans brought new diseases which spread epidemically. It is also true that the Aztec

Above: a mural by the Mexican painter Diego Rivera (1886–1957) depicts one aspect of the violence used by the Spaniards in their conquest of Mexico.

empire was riddled with rebellious discontent. Bernal Diaz, who served with Cortes, said of him: "Above all he possessed courage and spirit, which matters most of all."

Above: the Tlaxcalan Indians sue for peace. They were relieved of vast quantities of gold, which was shipped back to Spain. The Indians defeat was a disaster for them. Those who survived of this once proud people were turned into slaves and beasts of burden for the Spanish colonists who followed Cortes to the New World.

He extended the conquests through most of Mexico and into northern central America. But while the Spanish government gave him the title of "Marquis of Valle des Oaxaca," it refused to make him governor of the new province. He was constantly opposed by the colonial government or *audiencia*, and quarrelled with the viceroy. Madrid ignored his protests, and he died an embittered man.

71

Ferdinand V of Castile
1452-1516

A calm and affable man, Ferdinand V of Castile was apparently possessed of a strong will and powerful passions. He was, in Macchiavelli's view, a classic example of the calculating and ruthless princes who dominated Renaissance Europe. From his father he inherited the kingdom of Aragon with Valencia and Catalonia, the Balearic Islands, Sardinia, and the kingdom of Sicily. By the time of his death, all Spain was effectively under a single ruler. Southern Italy was under its control, as was a growing empire in the Americas. One of Ferdinand's daughters, Catherine of Aragon, was queen of England. The other had married into the mighty house of Hapsburg. He was to be succeeded by his grandson, Charles of Hapsburg (Emperor Charles V), ruler and heir of vast territories in Germany, Austria, and the Low Countries. Ferdinand's reign was a decisive period in European history.

In the 1450s, Spain was divided between the Christian kingdoms of Aragon, Castile, and Navarre, and the Moorish realm of Granada to the south. When, in 1469, John II of Aragon married off his heir to Princess Isabelle of Castile, a move towards unity was made. It was not the first tactical marriage in Spanish politics, but the

Ferdinand was increasingly absorbed in the affairs of Castile, no attempt was made to integrate the constitutions and administrations. Aragon, Valencia, Catalonia, and Sicily continued to be ruled through viceroys who reported to the royal council. Much of Ferdinand's success lay in the skill with which he filled these vital appointments.

In Castile, government had the co-operation of the brother-hoods, or friendly societies, of the towns. The restless nobility were also restrained, and a new source of finance acquired when, in 1476, Isabella claimed the right to appoint the grandmasters of the three rich and powerful military orders. Two of them went to Ferdinand. Crown lands taken over by powerful nobles during the troubled years before Isabella's accession were recovered through an Act of Resumption, and the royal council of Castile was reorganized to lessen their power.

Any remaining Castilian opposition to the dynastic settlement was discredited when the two Christian sovereigns initiated a united campaign against the Islamic kingdom of Granada. Its conquest 10 years later made a greater impact on Europe than the Castilian-financed voyage of the Genoese, Cristoforo Columbo, in the same year. After nearly 800 years Islam had been driven from its last foothold on Catholic soil. The brutal expulsion of the Spanish Jews followed immediately. This prosperous and talented community had been increasingly persecuted since the 1470s. In 1478 the Inquisition of Castile was founded to investigate the sincerity of the *Conversos*, Jews who had converted to Christianity. A government not a church agency, the Inquisition of Castile was active throughout

Below left: Ferdinand V and his queen Isabella as pictured in two details, the painting *Adoration of the Virgin by Kings*, from the School of Castile.

Below: the Alhambra palace, Granada. This was the sumptuous home of the Islamic rulers of Granada. The armies of Ferdinand and Isabella drove them out in 1486. Islam had already been forced to flee Cordoba for Granada, and after nearly 800 years were at last driven from Catholic soil. The collapse of Islamic influence had a profound effect on the course of European history.

political skill and mutual respect between the dynastic partners, as well as their long life, produced permanent results.

Isabella was immediately faced with civil war when she became queen of Castile in 1474. The rebels were defeated, with Ferdinand's help, in 1479. He succeeded to the throne of Aragon the same year. Isabella died in 1504, leaving Castile to her mad daughter Joan, and her husband Philip of Hapsburg. When Philip also died two years later, Ferdinand administered the kingdom as regent, not as king. To start with, though

Left: this 17th-century engraving shows Ferdinand and Isabella waving off an expedition bound for the Indies. Under Ferdinand's reign, a Spanish age of exploration was born, with expeditions financed by the royal purse.

Right: Cristoforo Columbo (Christopher Columbus) depicted in a 19th-century print being welcomed home by Ferdinand and Isabella. Columbo's exploration opened up territories in the Americas to Spain. Discoveries in the New World were shared between Spain and Portugal after the 1493 treaty of Tordesillas. Spain's New World territories brought it immense wealth – at the expense of the indigenous peoples.

Below left: the Monastery of San Juan de Los Reyes, built in 1476 in Isabeline style. The Inquisition of Castile investigated supposed heretics and dissidents to Catholic orthodoxy. It employed some of the most brutal methods in recorded history. Ferdinand and Isabella supervised and encouraged its work. The pope granted them the the title "the Catholic monarchs" as a reward.

Below: the site of the Monastery of San Juan de Los Reyes in Toledo. Apart from the 16th-century Alcazar this view of Toledo is much the same as it was in Ferdinand's time.

Spanish territories, investigating all heretics and suspected dissidents. It was to become Europe's most feared secret police, and plumbed new depths of brutality in the course of its investigations. The pope granted Ferdinand and Isabella the title of "the Catholic monarchs."

The Spanish army emerged from the wars against Granada as a superb fighting force. It was next launched against Ferdinand's Christian opponents. Between 1495 and 1504, years of turncoat diplomacy and military successes, the kingdom of Naples, which under a junior line of the Aragonese royal family governed southern Italy, was wrested from France.

When she died, Ferdinand said of Isabella "No monarch could have wished for a more worthy queen." But the maneuvers of diplomacy had to continue. In 1506 he married the heiress to Navarre, and in 1512 annexed most of the kingdom. A unified Spanish government was prepared.

By the treaty of Tordesillas in 1493, discoveries in the New World were partitioned between Spain and Portugal under papal auspices. Ferdinand's policies prepared the way for much that was to follow in the New World. The marriage of his daughter into the Hapsburg family shaped the political geography of Europe for 200 years.

Maximilian I
1459-1519

Emperor Maximilian presided over one of the decisive periods of European history. The first explosive reports of the Reformation were sounded in Wittenburg, in 1517, when Martin Luther nailed up his historic theses. The emperor's dynastic policy dictated the political geography of Europe for 400 years.

Maximilian was the son of Frederick III, the Hapsburg Holy Roman Emperor, and self-styled archduke of Austria. Frederick did little during his 53-year reign, but he guarded the ancestral rights of the Hapsburgs, secured his son's succession, and arranged his marriage to Mary of Burgundy (1457–1482), heiress of the lands of Charles the Bold the son of Philip the Good. With this marriage, the destinies of Aus-

Below left: Maximilian I as portrayed in a detail from the Torgau altarpiece by the artist Lucas Cranach. A weak ruler, Maximilian is largely remembered for the Diet of Worms in 1495.

Right: Maximilian in procession with his son Philip of Burgundy, and Philip's wife Joanna.

Below: this section of a stained glass window in Saint Catherine's Church, Hoogstraten, Belgium depicts four prominent rulers from the Hapsburg family. They are, from left to right, Philip the Good, Maximilian I, Philip the Fair, and Charles V. Philip the Good was Duke of Burgundy, and his son became Emperor Charles V.

Charles, duke of Burgundy, was killed at the battle of Nancy in January 1477. The French king, Louis XI, immediately occupied the duchy of Burgundy and the territory of Picardy, and prepared for further annexations. But Mary won support in the Low Countries by restoring traditional liberties with the Great Privilege, granted at Ghent in February. She married Maximilian in May 1477. After two years fighting, he defeated Louis, thus keeping the Burgundian

tria and the Netherlands were linked. Maximilian's children's marriages linked Austria and the Netherlands to the fortunes of Spain, and north Italy. By a treaty of 1515, Maximilian arranged a marriage for his grandson, Ferdinand, which established the Hapsburg claims to Hungaria and Bohemia. "Let others wage war; though, happy Austria, marry." So ran the saying. But the Hapsburgs waged war from the start too.

Netherlands independent of France. But the Low Countries had only grudgingly accepted him as the husband of their duchess. When she died in 1482, the Treaty of Arras was agreed with Louis of France. This stipulated that the infant Margaret of Austria, Mary's daughter by Maximilian, should marry the dauphin (later King Charles VIII of France). Margaret's dowry would be Artois and the free county of Burgundy. Meanwhile, four-year-old Philip, titular duke of Burgundy, was to do homage to France. Louis occupied the dower lands.

In 1490 he attempted to threaten France's northwestern frontier by a proxy marriage with Anne, duchess of Brittany. But Charles VIII, king since 1483, forced Anne to renounce the proxy marriage and marry him instead. Maximilian did recover Artois and the Free County, and also regained custody of Philip, who had been held for years as a virtual prisoner in Ghent. Then, in 1496, he brought off a spectacular double marriage treaty with Ferdinand II of Aragon, and Isabella of Castile. Margaret of Austria married their heir Don Juan, while Philip of Burgundy married their daughter Joanna.

Margaret's husband died the year after their marriage. A son, Charles, was born to Joanna and Philip in 1500. He became heir to the Spanish kingdoms and, when Maximilian himself died, emperor as Charles V.

Maximilian was an ineffectual ruler. The German lands of the empire were rapidly becoming an array of small, virtually independent duchies. He attempted reforms. The Diet of Worms of 1495 proclaimed a Perpetual Land

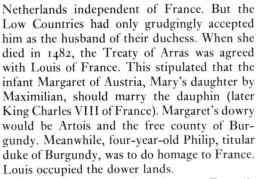

Above: Russian envoys present themselves to Maximilian I. As Hapsburg emperor, Maximilian maintained friendly relations with Russia. This enabled the empire to trade with its neighbor, and helped protect its eastern frontiers from attack. In this contemporary print, Maximilian can be seen receiving his guests in the full regalia of a Hapsburg emperor. The Hapsburg empire was extremely long-lived. It did not finally crumble until after World War I.

Above right: a full-page illustration from a Tyrolese hunting book depicts Maximilian chasing deer on a hunt. Hunting was a popular sport with European nobility, and remains so in the 20th century. Over the years the notion that a landowner owns every living thing on his land grew up. This led naturally to the "crime" of poaching being born.

Peace, and levied a land tax to finance a central government. The Swiss cantons refused to pay up, and won their virtual independence in 1499. The Aulic Council was established at Vienna under Maximilian's direct control, and a group of Circles, or administrative districts, was set up. Cities grew in influence during the reign, and the powerful Swabian League of Towns tended to support the emperor.

But Maximilian was quite unable to mobilize such backing against the centrifugal tendencies of the nobles, and was distracted by involved diplomacy and wars in Italy. No solid gains resulted, and his meager exchequer was soon exhausted. His dreams of leading a crusade against the Turks came to nothing.

But contemporaries liked this feckless idealist, "full of ideas and plans yet powerless to execute them." His jousting abilities won him the nickname "the last of the knights." But, as Macchiavelli observed, although he was a fine general, able to bear the fatigues of a campaign with the most hardened of his soldiers, brave in danger and just in governing, gracious and patient in audience and the pattern of many princely virtues, anyone could cheat him without his knowing it. Louis XII of France commented tartly, "what this king says at night, he does not hold to next morning."

But Maximilian created central institutions for the family lands in the provinces of Austria, Styria, and Corinthia, and, in so doing, inaugurated the modern history of Austria. He did well by his family, integrating its territories, and launching its career as one of the great names in the history of Europe.

75

Matthias Corvinus
c1443-1490

Matthias I, king of Hungary, died with an illustrious reputation. His deeds were even more impressive than those of his father, Janos Hunyadi, who had been hailed as Christendom's champion against the Turks. A heroic general and outstanding diplomat, Matthias held Hungary's

Left: a right profile portrait of Matthias Corvinus. Hungarian culture reached its peak under Matthias' reign. He and his wife, Beatrice of Aragon, ruled over the first Renaissance court outside Italy – at Buda.

Right: this 16th-century Turkish miniature depicts the army of Sultan Mohammed II laying siege to Belgrade. The sultan's army was soundly defeated by the forces of Matthias' father, Janos Hunyadi, in 1456. Matthias took part in the battle and was knighted there. Janos Hunyadi died later in the same year.

the leaders of the popular Hungarian faction opposed to the young Ladislas, dominated by Bohemian advisers. Laszlo was executed and Matthias put in jail. Then Ladislas himself died. The Bohemian regent, later king, George Podiebrad released Matthias immediately. At a meeting of Hungarian nobles on the ice of the frozen Danube near Buda, he was elected king in January 1458.

His future was uncertain. Janos Hunyadi had

southern frontiers against the warlike Turkish empire and extended her territory, and influence in central Europe. He was well read in classical learning, a patron of scholars and humanists, a collector of illuminated manuscripts, and one of the most brilliant early Renaissance princes.

He was born when the days of Hungary's glory seemed long past. Since the death of Louis the Great, 60 years earlier, a succession of weak kings had given the magnates scope to break the central power. The Turks won major victories, one of the greatest being at Varna when Matthias was four years old. His father, regent in Hungary for the youthful King Ladislas of Hungary and Bohemia, led a national revival.

It was not long before Matthias was deeply involved in politics and war. He was knighted at the battle of Belgrade in 1456, where his father smashed the army of the Turkish sultan, Mehmet II. Janos Hunyadi died the same year, and Matthias and his elder brother Laszlo became

won the title of *gubernator* or "governor of the state," but the family had no hereditary claim to the throne. Also, Matthias had not been crowned with the crown of St Stephen, the mystic talisman of Hungarian kingship which alone conferred true royalty. Indeed, the crown was in the possession of the Hapsburg claimant to Hungary, Frederick III, the Holy Roman Emperor. After four years of fighting, Matthias forced the emperor to recognize him as king and hand over the sacred crown. His coronation was held in 1464. But this triumph and year was darkened by the death in childbirth of his young wife Catharine, daughter of Podiebrad. Matthias married again, but left no legitimate heir.

Matthias kept the Turkish threat in the Balkans under control, and even recaptured Bosnia. He gained the reputation of a crusader, but his main concern was to reassert Hungary's power in central Europe. In 1466 he was persuaded by Pope Pius II to declare war on Bohemia, and its

now excommunicated king, George Podiebrad. King George allied himself with Poland, and recognized a Polish prince as his heir. By 1474, Matthias had won the provinces of Moravia and Silesia, but was forced to recognize the Polish succession to the Bohemian crown.

Next, he turned his attention to the Austrian lands of the Hapsburg emperor, conquering Styria, Carniola, and Carinthia. In 1485, he occupied Vienna which became his capital. When he died, Corvinus was the greatest figure on the stage of central Europe. But his conquests were lost, and Hungary went to the Polish king of Bohemia. It was parcelled out, 50 years later, between the old enemies, Turkey and the Hapsburgs.

Nevertheless, the reign of Matthias Corvinus was the heyday of Hungarian humanist culture. Fittingly for a Hungarian monarch, a gipsy band played at his wedding to Beatrice of Aragon in Buda in 1476. At his great palace there he pre-

Above: detail taken from a frieze above a mantel-piece in Matthias' magnificent palace at Buda. This relief was probably completed in the second half of the 15th century.

Right: a Majolica dish of Faenza. Made between 1485 and 1490, the dish formed part of Matthias Corvinus' table set.

Right: this relief on the wall of the Miklos Tower at Buda is an impression of Matthias Corvinus. It is a copy of a relief of Matthias at Bautzen.

Left: Matthias Corvinus acquired a vast collection of books and manuscripts during his lifetime. This is the title page of just one of his collection, *Trapezuntius: Rhetorica*. The initial "C" and the arms of Matthias Corvinus can be seen.

sided over the first true Renaissance court outside Italy. His magnificent book collection formed the basis of the internationally renowned Library Corvina. He established Buda's first printing press, and founded the university of Pozsnony.

Matthias' astonishing energy led admiring contemporaries to compare him to Alexander the Great. His power, resting on the support of the lesser nobility, was strengthened by a centralized government. He was ruthless with powerful rebels, but his reforms and codification of the laws were gratefully welcomed by gentry and peasantry. Later generations remembered the proverb "King Matthias is dead; justice has perished."

Henry VIII
1491-1547

Left: a portrait of Henry VIII at the age of 30 by an unknown artist. Henry is usually portrayed as a richly dressed obese character, but his ample figure only developed later in life. In this picture, Henry looks very much like his brother Prince Arthur.

Below: Henry met Francis I of France at the Field of the Cloth of Gold in 1520. Francis and Charles V of Spain challenged each other for European dominance. England held the balance of power. The Field with a special pavilion was set up for the meeting on the French frontier half way between Boulogne and English-held Calais. Henry and his Archbishop of Canterbury, Cardinal Wolsey, can be seen arriving for the meeting in procession.

Henry VIII's reign was dramatic and also formative for British history. It opened England to the revolutionary religious thinking in Reformation Europe. The state Church of England was born, and a massive redistribution of wealth from the monasteries to the aristocracy took place. Wales was formally integrated with England, and Henry became the first English king to assume the added title King of Ireland.

His father, Henry VII (Henry Tudor), had founded the Tudor dynasty in 1485 when he defeated the Plantagenet Richard III, and usurped the crown. Worries about the succession dogged Henry VIII. He became heir apparent on the death of his brother Arthur in 1502. Pope Julius II granted a dispensation for him to marry Arthur's widow, Catherine of Aragon, which he did soon after his accession in 1509.

Guided by his brilliant chief minister Thomas Wolsey (later Cardinal Wolsey), the handsome and talented young monarch entered eagerly into the complex currents of European diplomacy, joining the pope, Spain, and Venice in the Holy League against France. Henry inherited a full treasury from his father, and in 1513 invaded France where he captured two towns. During his absence, an English army easily defeated a Scottish invasion attempt at the battle of Flodden. James IV of Scotland died with many of his nobles. Meanwhile, Henry continued his maneuvers in Europe.

Wolsey arranged a treaty with France in 1518, and Henry met the brilliant new French king, Francis I, near Calais in an extravagant pageant known as the Field of the Cloth of Gold. Next, Henry allied himself with the emperor Charles V against France. But when he reaped no benefit from Charles' massive victory over France at Pavia in 1525, he once more made terms with France.

At home, Henry, partly because of his infatuation with the vivacious but wily Anne Boleyn, and partly because his wife had failed to give him a male heir, determined on divorce. In 1527, Cardinal Wolsey was made head of a commission, reluctantly appointed by pope Clement VII to investigate Henry's claim that his marriage to Catherine was invalid. But Catherine refused to recognize the commission. In 1529 it was summoned to Rome. Wolsey was dismissed by Henry and died shortly after in disgrace. His place was taken by Thomas Cromwell, who masterminded the religious revolution in England.

In 1532 the convocation of the English clergy made submission to the crown. The following year Thomas Cranmer, archbishop of Canterbury, declared the marriage to Catherine invalid. Henry married Anne. The pope excommunicated Henry. In 1534 Parliament stopped payment to Rome, and transferred papal powers to the king. The religious revolution had been effected without reference to doctrine. Yet Henry, named "Defender of the Faith" by the

pope in 1521 for a tract he wrote against Luther, vehemently resisted all radical theology.

Criticism of the corruption within the later medieval church was widespread, but it is doubtful that mass public opinion supported the king's revolutionary actions. Thomas Cromwell supervised the dissolution of the monasteries, but Sir Thomas More was beheaded because he refused to take the oath of supremacy to Henry as supreme head of the Church in England. In any case the upheaval did not produce the desired result. Henry was still not presented with a son. Catharine had given him his first daughter, later Queen Mary I. Anne Boleyn presented him with the future Elizabeth I. She was found guilty of adultery and incest in 1536, and executed. Her successor Jane Seymour, died giving birth to the future Edward VI. But the long-awaited heir seemed unlikely to survive to manhood. The king's marriages continued.

The German princess, Anne of Cleves, was briefly queen in 1540 as part of an alliance with Protestant Germany. Henry thought Anne as plain as a "Flanders mare," and on the wedding day protested to Cromwell: "My lord, if it were not to satisfy the world and my realm, I would not do that I must do this day for none earthly thing!" His lawyers soon found plausible grounds for a divorce.

Later that year Cromwell was executed, and Henry lost "perhaps the most accomplished servant any English monarch enjoyed." Cromwell

Right: the gold seal of Henry VIII. Wax impressions were made from the seal. Any document had to bear a wax impression of the seal before it was accepted as having been issued with royal authority.

Right: in 1534, the English parliament stopped payments to the Church of Rome, and conferred papal powers on the king. Henry was promptly excommunicated by the pope. This is the title page of the Great Bible, which was written and printed on Henry's instructions after his break with Rome. The Great Bible was to form the basis of the Anglican faith.

had been out-maneuvered by the duke of Norfolk's faction at court. Norfolk's nice, the young and sensual Catherine Howard, now became Henry's fifth wife. She too was executed shortly after, on a self-confessed charge of treasonable adultery, and Henry married the sober and virtuous Catherine Parr who outlived him.

Henry was often tyrannical, notably against the popular rising known as the Pilgrimage of Grace. He appointed some of the most talented men ever seen in English government, but was a harsh and arbitrary master. A humble contemporary grumbled: "Our king wants only an apple and a fair wench to dally with," and Henry is still popularly remembered for his remarkable career as a husband. But England was spared the horrors of the religious wars which plagued Europe, and was able to build a Reformed Church on the foundations laid in his reign.

Suleiman the Magnificent
1494-1566

Known as the Codifier of the Laws by his own subjects, Sultan Suleiman II liked to be known as a Second Solomon. To the West he has always been "Suleiman the Magnificent". During his reign, the Ottoman empire, consolidated by Mohammed II the Conqueror, was extended still further. Istanbul and the great cities of Islam – Mecca, Damascus, and Baghdad – were beautified with mosques, bridges, and acqueducts by the great architect Sinan (1489-1588). Suleiman proved one of the most remarkable of that quite outstanding line of rulers, the early Ottoman sultans.

In the early 1500s, the empire had been faced by the powerful new Safawid regime of Persia. Adherents of the extreme doctrinal version of Islam, Shi'i, the Safawids posed a religious threat to the orthodox sultan. They also intervened in the frontier lands between southern Turkey and Syria, which was then controlled by the Mamluk regime of Egypt. In 1514 Suleiman's father Selim won a victory which halted

Safawid expansion in Anatolia. Three years later he had driven the Mamluks from Syria, capturing Aleppo, Damascus, and Jerusalem, and finally Cairo. Suleiman sent his grand vizier, Ibrahim, to establish a firm Ottoman administration in Egypt in 1525.

Suleiman's accession had been welcomed in the West, where it appeared that the terrible Selim, "the angry lion", had left as successor "a mild lamb, young, inexperienced and gentle

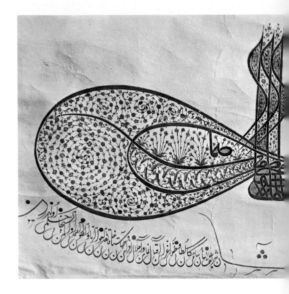

by nature." These wistful illusions were shattered within a year. In 1521, Suleiman captured Belgrade after a brilliantly fought campaign against the Hungarian armies. He expelled the Knights of St John from their island fortress of Rhodes the next year. In 1526 Hungary went down in ruin at the disastrous battle of Mohacs. By a treaty of 1516, the crown passed to Archduke Ferdinand of Austria, brother of the emperor Charles V. But Ferdinand was challenged by John Zapolya, the Hungarian *voivode* (ruler) of Transylvania. Zapolya did not scruple to call on Turkish aid, and Suleiman did not hesitate to give it.

He led his army against Vienna itself in 1529. Bad weather and faulty logistics brought the army to its objective late in the campaigning season, and a stubborn Christian defense forced the lifting of the siege. A second campaign three years later faltered against an epic defense at the little Austrian fortress of Guns. Austria was saved, but Zapolya remained a Turkish puppet at Buda. When he died in 1540, Suleiman forced the partition of the country.

Turkish Hungary constituted one frontier province in a chain which included Bosnia, Wallachia, Moldavia, and the khanate of the Crimea. In Asia, Suleiman occupied the regions around Erzerum and Lake Van, and took Iraq from the heretic Safawids of Persia. He was now lord of Baghdad, the ancient seat of the caliphate, of the holy cities of Jerusalem, Mecca, and Medina, and the acknowledged leader of orthodox Islam. Prestige brought heavy responsi-

Left: a 16th-century portrait of Suleiman by the painter Nigari. Besides being an effective ruler, Suleiman had a passionate interest in the arts and architecture. During his reign, magnificent mosques, bridges, and aqueducts were built – designed by the architect Sinan. Literature and painting flourished. Suleiman was a talented poet himself.

feated a Venetian and Spanish fleet and Venice surrendered her last strongholds on the Greek coast. Suleiman's next high admiral, "Dragut" the corsair leader of Tripoli, repelled a Spanish attack at Djerba in 1560. But in 1565, despite a four-month siege, a Turkish combined fleet and army failed to take Malta. The sultan died the following year while on campaign.

Bitter rivalry between his sons was evident in the last years of his reign. Rumor claimed that Khurren, the sultan's favorite wife, known in the West as Roxelana, was intriguing against Mustafa, his eldest son by another wife. But Mustafa was a focus for political unrest, and was executed in 1553. After Khurrem's death, one of her sons was also to be executed as a rebel. Selim, her favorite, took the throne without opposition on his father's death.

Suleiman had been brilliantly served by many outstanding men, notably the viziers Ibrahim and Mehmed Sokollu. An Austrian diplomat recorded in amazement, "No distinction is attached to birth among the Turks; it is by merit that men rise in the service of this state." The result was a superb administrative system. But it all rested on the sultan. Under Suleiman the Codifier that system had functioned to superb effect. He ruled wisely and brought order to the Turks.

bilities. With Portuguese expansion in the Indian ocean came a call for help from the distant Moslem state of Gujarrat in India. A naval expedition led by the governor of Egypt failed to take the Portuguese colony of Diu, but did capture the port of Aden and thus secured the approaches to the Red Sea.

In the western Mediterranean, the Knights of St John were securely based on the island of Malta, and the Spaniards in their north African bases at Oran and La Goletta. Suleiman appointed as his admiral the Algerian corsair, Khayr al-Din, "Barbarossa". In 1538 he de-

Martin Luther
1483-1546

Every thinking man in the Western Church was crying out for its reform in the early 1500s. Martin Luther answered that cry, and at the same time broke the unchallenged power of the Roman Church. His appeal to individual conscience, his claim that the word of God in Scripture was the ultimate authority, and that "justification by faith" was fundamental – these, together with his passionate belief in the early Christian teachers, made Luther the initiator of the European Reformation.

Luther was born a peasant in Eisleben, near Leipzig in present-day East Germany. He studied philosophy, became a monk, and, in 1507 a priest. In May 1517 he wrote to a friend "I am quite sure that the Church will never be reformed unless we get rid of canon law, scholastic theology, and logic as they are studied today and put something else in their place." He added action to words in October the same year by nailing a list of 95 Articles to the castle door at

Above: the differences between the Catholic Church and the Protestant supporters of Luther did not stop at disagreements over doctrine. Each side abused the other in the most vehement terms. This Protestant cartoon insultingly depicts the pope as a donkey playing the bagpipes. Catholic attacks on Luther and his supporters were often equally scurrilous.

Left: a portrait of Martin Luther from a 17th-century German engraving. Luther challenged the power of the Roman Catholic Church, which even the most devout and loyal knew was ripe for reform. A bitter doctrinal feud developed between Luther and the papacy. Luther was called upon to recant several times, and each time refused. Luther's greatest heresy, as far as the Catholic Church was concerned, was to attack the supremacy of the pope.

Wittenberg. These Articles attacked the sale of *Indulgences* – special dispensations from Rome which would allegedly provide remission of the pains of purgatory. They were sold largely to pay for the building of St Peter's in Rome. Luther's objections were social and nationalistic as much as religious: "The pope has wealth far beyond all other men – why does he not build St Peter's Church with his own money instead of the money of poor Christians?" The Articles

received immediate publicity. Within two weeks, they had been circulated throughout the numerous states that made up 16th-century Germany. Germany strongly resented the Italian power of the Roman Church in any case. Luther was acclaimed as a national hero.

Three years of controversy followed. Pope Leo X hesitated at first. Then, in August 1518 he summoned Luther to Rome to answer charges of attacking the sale of Indulgences, and, more serious, the supremacy of the pope. But Luther had powerful German friends who argued that he should be judged in Germany rather than Rome. The pope gave in, and in September 1518 Luther traveled to Augsburg to defend himself in public debate with Cardinal Cajetan. The debate was inconclusive. Luther refused to recant, or withdraw his previous statements. Cajetan finally lost his temper: "Go and do not return unless you are ready to recant." Luther went back to Wittenberg. He was challenged to another debate the following year, this time in Leipzig against Dr Eck of Ingolstadt. The debate was again inconclusive. Luther again refused to recant. In June 1520, the pope issued a papal edict denouncing Luther's writings as "heretical or scandalous or offensive to pious ears." In December Luther himself burned the edict in public at Wittenberg, declaring: "Because you have condemned the truth of God, He also condemns you today at the fire."

One last attempt was made to force Luther, by now a German hero with a European reputation, to recant his "heresies." He was called before the Emperor Charles V at Worms in 1521. The result was no different. "Unless I am proved wrong by the Scriptures or by evident reason, then . . . I cannot retract and I will not retract. God help me. Amen." Charles was equally adamant: "I will proceed against him as a notorious heretic." But Luther left Worms under safe conduct, going first to the castle of Wartburg, where he translated the New Testament into German, and then on to Wittenberg, and safety.

During the next three years, Lutheranism spread widely, with numerous German princes

Left: Luther attacked the established Catholic Church for, among other things, its corruption and greed for earthly riches. He lambasted it for building lavish churches and cathedrals, while neglecting to succour the poor among its flock. This picture shows Pope Leo X demanding that Luther recants his "heresy."

Below: Luther was an inspiring speaker. This painting by his friend Lucas Cranach depicts Luther preaching to newly converted Protestants.

many. Luther, though a peasant by birth, strongly opposed violent attacks upon property. In a bitter tract, *Against the Murdering, Thieving Hordes of Peasants*, he called upon the princes to put down the revolt by force. It was a kind of watershed. Luther the religious reformer had no intention of becoming Luther the revolutionary leader. It lost him some of his popular following, but it established him as an ally of the princes. By 1524, in fact, Luther was invincible. Only force or civil war could have crushed him.

In 1529, at Speyer, a minority of German princes delivered a "Protest" against the conduct of the Emperor Charles V and the Catholic princes. It is from this "Protest" that the word "Protestant" is derived. Two years later the Protestant princes formed the Schmalkaldic League. They included the princes of Prussia, Brandenburg, Saxony, Hesse, and 14 cities of the Empire. Then, in 1530, at Augsburg, the Protestant princes presented the Emperor with the *Augsburg Confession*, setting out the official statement of Lutheran doctrine. The Emperor reluctantly accepted what he could not destroy. Luther's achievement was secure.

adopting it. Luther wrote prolifically. In 1520 he wrote what are now seen as the three great Reformation treatises: *To the Christian Nobility of the German Nation*; *The Babylonish Captivity of the Church*; and *Of the Liberty of Christian Man*. As he explained: "I am hot-blooded by temperament and my pen gets irritated easily." Printing, a comparatively recent innovation, helped the spread of his ideas. An estimated 300,000 copies of his works had been published by 1520. Students crowded to Wittenberg to study under him, and Wittenberg remained the spiritual capital of the Lutheran movement. What happened there – the rejection of the Mass, the closing of monasteries and nunneries – was imitated all over Germany. Luther had become the leader of a great religious movement.

In 1524 a Peasant's Revolt broke out in Ger-

Luther had alone created a reformed Christian Church which resisted all attempts of the Roman Church to stamp it out, and which quickly spread through most of Germany, and the kingdoms of Sweden, Norway, and Denmark. Reform led to independence, helped by nationalism, anti-clericalism, and anti-Imperialism, and by Luther's own clear-eyed approach to the basic teachings of Christ. He insisted upon the importance of "justification by faith." This represented a major shift from external acts of communal religion, from ritual and ceremony, to the minds and hearts of people and to individual worship. It was a mighty achievement, one that only a man of Luther's courage and force of personality could have brought about. Luther had his critics, but he did succeed in bringing Christianity closer to its believers.

John Calvin
1509-1564

Luther's great achievement was to successfully challenge the authority of the Church of Rome, and to demonstrate that the Pope had no monopoly over Christian affairs in Europe. But the Lutheran Reformation had one weakness. By overthrowing the authority of Rome, it had left the authority of Christian priests vague and uncertain. Religious authority in general was dependent upon individual princes and city magistrates. How then was the vacuum to be filled? The vital example was provided by one extraordinary man in one small city. He was the Frenchman, John Calvin, who lived in Geneva, in French-speaking Switzerland. Calvin's contribution to the Reformation was complex and often controversial, but he is unquestionably the intellectual giant of the Protestant movement.

Calvin was born at Noyon, northeast of Paris. He studied Latin and theology at Paris, and law at Orleans. Here he absorbed Lutheran opinions from German fellow students. His conversion was sudden and complete: "As if by a sudden ray of light I recognized into what an abyss of errors I had hitherto been plunged. Now therefore, O Lord, I did what was my duty and fearlessly I followed in thy footsteps."

Right: this 16th-century engraving pictures the "heroes" of European Protestantism. The most prominent are indicated in the key below.
1, John Wycliffe of England;
2, John Huss of Bohemia;
3, Huldreich Zwingli of Switzerland; 4, Martin Luther of Germany; 5, John Calvin of Geneva; and 6, John Knox of Scotland. By the mid-16th century Protestantism had become the dominant religion in northern Europe.

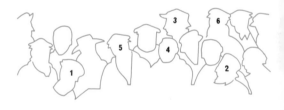

city as a teacher of Scripture. He presented the city council with a program of reform four months later. This was based largely upon the New Testament, and the teachings of the early Christian Church. But the people of Geneva were not impressed and in 1538 exiled both Calvin and Farel from Geneva. They were recalled in 1541, and Calvin's program, set out in a series of regulations called the *Ecclesiastical Ordinances*, was finally accepted. From then

until his death Calvin was the intellectual force behind the city republic of Geneva. It was as an experiment in applied Christianity that was to have a profound influence upon Protestants and Protestantism, both in Europe, and beyond.

Calvin's constitution rested on the assumption that every citizen was an orthodox member of the Church. The question of religious toleration simply did not arise. Moreover, that Church was to be quite independent and self-controlled. It alone decided its form of government, its form of service, its moral code, and how that code was to be enforced. A brilliant administrator, Calvin devised a constitution whereby priests or pastors selected priests though the city council could reject their choice. Lay "elders", or disciplinary officials, were made responsible for the moral behavior of the people, and reported to the "Venerable Company" of pastors. Every hursday, elders and pastors met together to decide whether there was any problem that required action. If the Church found a "sinner", he or she was handed over to the civil power for punishment. In 1550, the pastors were fully empowered to enter and inspect the home of each citizen once a year.

Left: a portrait of John Calvin. Calvin did not recognize the concept of religious freedom. To him every citizen was an orthodox believer in the Church, and therefore dissidence did not arise. But Calvin did not always get his own way in his zealous interpretations of "orthodoxy."

Catholic persecution in France drove him first to Strasbourg in 1534, then to Basle, where in 1536 he published a handbook of Protestant theology, *The Institutes of Christian Religion*. Another French Lutheran, William Farel, was then engaged in reforming the city of Geneva. After some hesitation, Calvin accepted Farel's invitation to help him, and settled in the lakeside

Calvin was powerful, but he was no dictator. In fact, many of his statutes were compromises. For example, the city council won its wish to be involved in the selection of pastors. Similarly, Calvin attempted to have all taverns closed down and replaced with cafes. But the citizens would not allow it. In 1546, he introduced an act to prohibit the use of non-Biblical Christian names, but the citizens of Geneva ignored it. Calvin himself was austere, ruthless, grave, and devout.

Right: John Calvin as sketched by one of his students. Calvin's radical views forced him to flee Catholic France. Settling in Geneva, he set about establishing an austere religious dictatorship, where even a citizen's home could be searched for signs of "unorthodoxy."

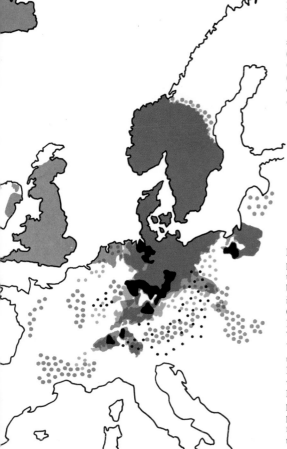

Left: the spread of Protestantism in 16th-century Europe. Before 1529 the religion was strong in only a few areas in central Germany (black). It dominated most of Germany and Scandinavia by 1555 (brown). Protestantism had established its northern European domain by 1600 (gray).

He was never a popular leader like Luther. Men either followed him or hated him. He had disciples, or opponents – there was little room for compromise. But he made Geneva the Rome of Protestant Europe. French refugees from Catholic persecution in France poured into Geneva, providing Calvin with support, and even becoming pastors. From Italy, the Netherlands, Spain, England, and Scotland came Protestants of all kinds to swell the Calvinist ranks. It was a refugee from Scotland, John Knox, who called Geneva "the most perfect school of Christ that ever was on earth since the days of the Apostles."

Calvin's theology was different from that of Luther in its concentration upon the idea of predestination. This was not a new concept – even the early Christian theologians like St Augustine and St Thomas Aquinas had seen it as a vital element of Christian belief. Calvin made it central to his doctrine. Christ, he argued, died on the cross not for all mankind but only for the elect. The seven sacraments of the Roman Church were cut to two – baptism and communion – and these were regarded as purely symbolic. Calvin's followers were, like himself, austere, fearless, devout men of the Bible. For 100 years they were to be the most powerful religious force in Protestant Europe and, through English Puritanism, they were to spread the new word of God into the new world of North America.

Right: austerity and simplicity was preached by Calvin as central to a truly Christian life. The lavish buildings and robes, as well as the idolatry of the Roman Catholic Church was condemned. This Protestant church in Port Washington, Long Island, New York, has been built with no unnecessary trimmings added. Protestantism stresses freedom of worship within the teachings of the Bible. Many a poor community provided themselves with utilitarian places of worship. The concept of freedom of worship also encouraged the foundation of numerous sects within Protestantism today.

Pope Paul III
1468-1549

By the middle of the 16th century, the full weight of the Reformation was hurling itself against the established order of the Roman Catholic Church. Already weakened by internal corruption, the Church reeled under the attack. But it soon began to retaliate with a great spiritual revival of its own – the Counter Reformation. The man who instigated the reforms and militancy that provided a foundation for this movement was a worldly, art-loving man, Pope Paul III. The last of the Renaissance popes, he did more than any other man to enable the Roman Catholic Church to come to terms with the Reformation.

Alessandro Farnese was born in Tuscany of noble parents, and was educated in Rome, and at Florence at the court of Lorenzo the Magnificent. Although a layman, he was made a cardinal in 1493 and became the bishop of Parma in 1509. In keeping with the customs of the time, the

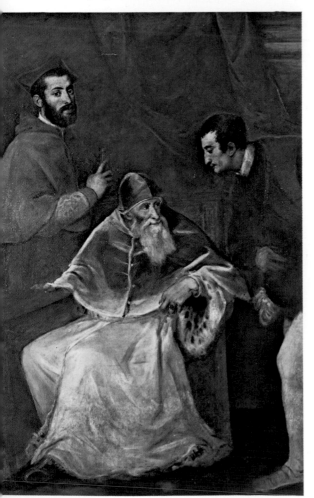

Left: a portrait of Pope Paul III with his nephews by Titian. If the Roman Catholic Church was to survive the onslaught of the Reformation, it had first to set its own house in order. Paul III was the first pope to attempt to eradicate the internal corruption of the Church, and win back the confidence of the laity.

future pope behaved like any Italian prince. He took as his mistress a well-born Roman, who bore him four children. But he seems to have undergone a spiritual change while a bishop. In 1513, he set aside his mistress and concentrated on Church matters from then on. He was ordained as a priest in June 1519, and from that point on the reform of the Church became the dominant ambition of his life. Upon his election as pope in October 1534, however, he made two

Left: Pope Paul III well knew that many of the Protestants' accusations against the Roman Catholic Church were well-founded. In an attempt to end the abuses within the Catholic Church and to heal the rift with the Protestants, Paul summoned the Council of Trent in 1545. Wars permitting, the Council met over a period of 20 years, and its deliberations spanned the reigns of five popes. It eventually announced important reforms in the internal affairs of the Catholic Church. These made Protestant accusations of corruption much more difficult to sustain. Nevertheless the two Churches remain split. Arguments about Christian unity persist to this day.

Below: under Paul III's reign a new militancy grew up within the Catholic Church. In 1540, the Society of Jesus (Jesuits) were formed to fight for the ideals of the Church wherever the pope might send them. Ignatius Loyola, son of a Spanish nobleman, became the Jesuits first general in 1541. This is is a painting of him by Rubens.

Two major problems faced the Church. One was how to end the quarrel that had split Europe between Rome, and the Protestant churches. The second was how to stamp out virulent corruption within the Church. It was to deal with both these that Pope Paul III, after many false starts and disappointments, finally called the Assembly in 1545, at Trent, in northern Italy. Known as the Council of Trent, this assembly met, unless war prevented it doing so, over a period of 20 years. Paul III presided over the important early sessions.

It was not until 1563, after much heated debate and under another pope, that the Council announced its decisions in a series of decrees. These included a restatement of Catholic doctrine, a radical revision of Church appointing methods, and wide reforms of clerical duties and disciplines. But one of the greatest controversies that raged in the meetings of the Council was whether the Church should attempt to win back Protestant support, or acquiesce in the split between the Protestant and Catholic Churches. It was largely due to the preference expressed by Paul III that the second course was eventually accepted.

Reforms alone would not have brought about the spiritual revival of the Counter Reformation. Pope Paul was also directly responsible for a new militancy within the Church. One of the great figures of this movement was a Spaniard, Itnatius Loyola (1491-1556). The son of a nobleman, Loyola gave up a military career to study theology at the University of Paris. There he collected a group of like-minded friends. They also shared his strength of character, his learning, and above all his determination to fight for the Roman Church. Loyola's Zeal and dedication greatly impressed Paul III when he visited Rome in 1539. There, he put forward his plan for a new religious order within the Church. Its members vowed to go as missionaries to any country to which the pope might send them. The next year Paul III approved the rule of the Society of Jesus, which in 1541 elected Loyola as its first general.

The Jesuits, as its members came to be known, provided the Church with a militantly evangelical order, organized on almost military lines. Fired with intense enthusiasm, and rigorously disciplined, the Jesuits set out to win new converts for Catholicism. Many, like Francis Xavier (1506-1552), followed in the footsteps of the explorers, and converted thousands of Asians and American Indians to the Catholic faith.

Pope Paul III was remembered by his contemporaries as a man "good-hearted, obliging, and supremely intelligent . . . worthy to be described as magnanimous." With the hindsight of history, it is also possible to see him as the pope who found the Church decadent and corrupt, but who left it well equipped to overcome and outlive the traumatic change and challenge of the Protestant Reformation.

of his teenage grandsons cardinals. This blatant piece of nepotism, together with his background, and love of fine things of life might have given the impression that he was to be simply another in a long line of worldly, and ineffectual popes. But it quickly became apparent that this was not the case. For, also in October 1534, he announced his intention of calling a general council of the Church, and of promoting a series of radical reforms.

Charles V
1500-1558

Charles of Hapsburg paid 1,000,000 gold florins to become Holy Roman Emperor. As the grandson of Maximilian I, the seven Electors – heads of the important German states – might have chosen him anyway. But there was a possibility they might elect Francis I, king of France. This was a worrying prospect for Charles, whose richest domains, the Netherlands, would lie uncomfortably between two Valois-controlled powers.

Charles' largesse to the Electors paid off. He was already Duke of Burgundy, King of Spain, Sicily, Sardinia and Naples, and heir to the Hapsburg lands in central Europe. He became Holy Roman Emperor and the most powerful monarch in Europe at the age of 19. But his

power was challenged on every side. Francis I was virtually surrounded by Hapsburg lands, and was determined to check the Emperor's ambitions in Italy. The Turks who, having captured Constantinople, continually threatened Eastern Europe and the Mediterranean. Charles was also threatened by some of the German princes. Their Lutheranism struck at such unity as the Empire possessed. The Reformation was the greatest issue of Charles' reign. He worked strenuously to bring the Protestants back into the Roman Catholic fold.

Charles agreed with Luther that the Church had been corrupted, and he spent a lot of his reign trying to force the papacy to reform it. But

Right: completed in 1537, this detail from a stained glass window in Brussels Cathedral depicts a scene from the coronation of Charles V. Charles is pictured with his wife, Isabella of Portugal.

Left: a portrait of the Hapsburg emperor Charles V, taken from a family portrait by the painter Bernard Striegel. The picture was painted when Charles was a teenager. He became Holy Roman Emperor at the age of 19. The Hapsburg family dominated central Europe for nearly 600 years.

Above: the magnificent shield of Charles V. Designed by the artist Raphael, the relief represents "a battle outside Carthage."

he could not accept Luther's new doctrines. But many of his subject princes not only adopted Lutheranism themselves, but insisted on their right to decide the form of religion within their own states as well. Without success, one Diet after another wrestled with the religious question. By the time Charles found a pope – Paul III – willing to call a council, the Protestant line had hardened. In 1546, the Protestant states, aided by Francis I, and the Catholic state, led by Charles with help from Paul III, went to war with each other. Fighting continued until 1555. The Peace of Augsburg established the right of a ruler to decide on the religion of his subjects.

While battling with the religious issue, Charles was continually engaged in wars with the French and the Turks. Influenced by his Italian Chancellor Gattinara, Charles embarked on a policy of forming alliances – often through marriage – with the ruling Italian families, so bringing most of Italy under Hapsburg domination. But, some of the popes were committed to achieving a balance of power and supported the French, who also had designs on Italy. War broke out between Charles and Francis in 1521, mainly over Milan, then a French possession. It continued off and on for years. But Charles at last succeeded in forming a federation of North Italian states loyal to the Empire. This was to last for 300 years.

Taking advantage of hostilities between the Christian powers, the Turks pushed into Hungary. In 1532, having almost reached Vienna, they were forced back by Charles' army. An uneasy peace was established in Hungary. Turkish domination of the North African coast received

a setback in 1535, when Charles conquered Tunis. Sometimes, Charles managed to rally support against the Turks from his rebellious German princes. Even the French backed him occasionally. But the Turks continued to menace the Mediterranean throughout Charles' reign, and after it.

Until money began pouring in from Spain's possessions in America Charles' main source of wealth was the Low Countries. Their industry and commerce had flourished for centuries. As Duke of Burgundy, Charles claimed the allegiance of these provinces and the right to call on them for funds (considered grants-in-aid, not taxes). His wars placed a crippling financial burden on them – about which he received repeated warnings from his Mary, the Regent. The people of Ghent overthrew the authorities who had complied with Charles' demands in 1539. Charles put down the uprising ruthlessly.

Charles was nevertheless popular in the Netherlands. He was born and bred there, and understood the people. Their territory in the north had increased during his reign and the southern provinces of Flanders and Artois had been freed from the threat of being re-absorbed by France.

Not surprisingly, Charles was exhausted by the time he was in his 50s. The strain of coping with challenges and crises on all sides, plus the

Above: a scene from the battle of Pavia of 1525, in which Francis I of France was decisively defeated by forces loyal to the pope with the forces of Charles V, Holy Roman Emperor. This defeat was a major setback to Francis' territorial ambitions in northern Italy.

Right: this color engraving, completed in the early 17th century, portrays Charles V abdicating his powers to his son Philip, husband of Mary Tudor of England, in 1555.

debilitating effects of his frequent attacks of gout, had turned him into an old man. His energy temporarily revived, when he engineered the match between Mary Tudor and his son Philip, which was designed to create an Anglo-Netherlandisch rival power to France.

In 1555, Charles began abdicating his various crowns to Philip and to his brother Ferdinand, who became Emperor. He retired to a small house attached to a monastery in Spain. Here he spent the last three years of his life holding court and indulging his fondness for hunting, music, and the rich food that undermined his health. He could not claim that he had succeeded in all his endeavors. But he had, for 40 years, shouldered immense and complex responsibilities.

Ivan the Terrible
1530-1584

came ingrained in Ivan's character. By the time he was 14, he was an able practitioner of the politics of terror. Siding with one faction, the Glinskys, he ordered the execution of their rivals, the Shuiskys. Their bodies were to be seen strung up along the road from Moscow to Novgorod.

Inspired by the grandeur of the Byzantine Empire, Ivan had himself crowned Czar, or "caesar," of what was to be a new Eastern,

After winning his first battle against the Tartars in 1551, Czar Ivan IV was taking stock of the supplies left behind by his foes with satisfaction. Among them were some exotic animals Ivan had never before seen – camels. He ordered one to kneel down so that he could ride it. The camel either refused to kneel or did not understand. Ivan killed it.

This is one of the milder episodes in the reign of a man justly known as "the Terrible". Ivan's atrocities are legendary. But he was not only a psychopath. He made Russia into a power to be reckoned with, and established trading and cultural links with the West.

Violence was endemic in the society which Ivan was born into. As a boy he played vicious games with his companions. His father, Grand Duke of the country then known as Muscovy, died when the boy was three years old, and his mother died a few years later. He was left in the middle of a powerful struggle among the *boyars*, the Russian aristocracy. Fear and suspicion be-

Above: a portrait of Ivan from a Russian icon. Many of the Czars were harsh rulers, but Ivan was the most bloodthirsty of them all.
Below: the magnificent ivory throne on which Ivan was crowned.

Orthodox empire. In the same year, 1547, he married his first wife Anastasia. A sweet-tempered, virtuous woman, she was the one person capable of calming his rages, and was probably the only person he ever loved.

Until Anastasia died in 1560, Ivan's reign might almost be regarded as constructive. His victories over the Tartars in the south and east (including part of what is now Siberia) expanded his nation's boundaries, and won him the adulation of the Russian people. He established the first Russian printing press. One of his nobler qualities was a thirst for learning. In 1553, he welcomed a party of English merchants to Moscow. He gave them a trading monopoly in the White Sea area, along with other trading advantages. A lifelong admirer of the English, Ivan corresponded with Elizabeth I for 25 years, and tried, in vain, to conclude a military alliance with her.

He was determined to extend his nation westward to the Baltic Sea. In 1557, he invaded Livonia, held by the Teutonic Order of knights. Russian expansion was opposed not only by the Germans, the Poles, and the Swedes, but also by Ivan's own advisers. They wanted him to move eastward. Ivan would tolerate no opposition. He announced his decision to abdicate in 1564. It was a gamble, but it worked. A delegation of boyars and clergy, fearing the wrath of the people if their beloved "Little Father" were replaced, begged Ivan to change his mind. Having named his terms, Ivan returned to the Kremlin as dictator.

For most of the remainder of his life, Ivan dedicated himself to two objectives: reaching

Above: Monomakh's Cap, decorated with jewels, cross, and sable edging.

descended on and destroyed Moscow in 1571. Ivan dispatched the Oprichniki as he had dispatched so many of the boyars. Once again the boyar class was at the center of power. But now they served an absolute monarch.

Ivan appeared more pathetic than terrible in his last years. Ill and wrapped in self-pity, he feared divine retribution for his sins. He sent a request to a monastery to pray for the souls of 3470 of his victims – many listed by name. But

the Baltic, and crushing the boyars. The Baltic undertaking was finally laid to rest by a treaty signed in 1582. His second project was more successful.

Since the death of Anastasia, Ivan had become increasingly paranoid and violent. He set about crushing the boyars by creating a kind of state-within-a-state, the Oprichnina. He appropriated vast holdings of the boyars, as well as parts of Moscow, and whole cities. Their inhabitants were resettled elsewhere. These areas were peopled by Ivan's hand-picked followers, called Oprichniki, whom he gave *carte blanche* to stamp out supposed treason. They set about this task with savage cruelty. In the winter of 1570, Ivan led an army to Novgorod, a proud and prosperous city whose independent spirit infuriated him. On the pretext of punishing it for harboring traitors, Ivan had his Oprichniki torture and kill thousands of its people (some records claim as many as 60,000). The Oprichniki also destroyed or stole everything they could get their hands on. Novgorod never recovered from the attack.

Now even the Oprichniki were suspect to Ivan. They were well and truly discredited by their cowardice in the face of a Tartar army, who

Above: Ivan's forces capturing Kazan in 1552. This was Ivan's first major victory over the Mongols, and is presented here as a triumph of the cross over the crescent.

Below: this painting by Repin shows him with the eldest son he struck and accidentally killed.

these were only a tiny fraction of those that had suffered from his violence. Then one day, in a fit of rage, he struck and accidentally killed his eldest son. He was overcome with grief. The death of the Czarevitch, his only capable heir, was more than a personal loss for the Czar. After his own death a few years later, it was to result in another bitter struggle for power.

Philip II
1527-1598

Philip II of Spain was, like his father Charles V, the most powerful monarch of his day. Although the crown of the Holy Roman Empire has passed to his uncle Ferdinand's family, Philip still had a handsome inheritance. The several kingdoms of Spain, Spanish possessions in the New World, the 17 provinces of the Netherlands, the Free County of Burgundy, Naples, and assorted other Mediterranean possessions were all in his domain. He temporarily became titular king of England through his second marriage – to Mary Tudor. In 1578 he inherited Portugal and its

empire. Philip's military ventures against the Turks, the French, the Dutch, and the English were financed with wealth from the New World. If he failed to achieve his overriding objective, the reestablishment of Roman Catholicism throughout Europe, it was not for lack of trying.

In spite of his position as an international figure, Philip viewed the world from a narrow Spanish perspective. He had no aptitude for foreign languages, and, unlike his father, avoided traveling abroad. Austere, pious, and abstemious, he lacked his father's natural rapport with the convivial Netherlanders. He failed to grasp the fact, well understood by Charles, that they would resist being governed by Spaniards.

Left: a portrait of Philip II.

Below: the Protestants of the Netherlands were treated with dreadful savagery by Spanish troops under the command of Philip's governor-general, the Duke of Alva. The Inquisition was imposed with particular brutality in the Netherlands.

Obedient to his father's wishes, Philip – a widower at the age of 27 – married the Queen of England, Mary Tudor in 1554. She was 11 years his senior. The marriage was not a success. Mary failed to give birth to the heir that would link England and the Netherlands. Twice she believed herself pregnant. In fact, the symptoms were those of dropsy.

Philip did not involve himself in "Bloody Mary's" persecutions of the Protestants, being pledged not to intervene in English matters. He had also promised not to drag England into Spain's wars, but in 1557 he became embroiled in a war with France and prevailed on Mary and her Privy Council to grant him men and money. Philip's army inflicted a crushing defeat on the French at St Quentin, in northern France. But the French captured the ill-defended port of Calais, which had belonged to England for 200 years. The loss of Calais because of Philip's war did not endear him to the English.

Mary's death in 1558 was followed by the accession of Elizabeth I. She would later prove a formidable opponent. But, meanwhile, Philip's main worry was the Netherlands. Although these provinces were independent of each other, they were beginning to develop a sense of unity. Their noble families resented the foreign junta sent by Philip to rule them. In 1566, a group of Protestant and Catholic nobles petitioned Philip not to introduce the Spanish Inquisition into the provinces. He turned down their appeal. Mobs of furious Calvinists desecrated Catholic churches. In response, Philip sent not only the Inquisition to the Netherlands, but also several thousand Spanish troops under the Duke of Alva, the new governor-general. Alva dealt with the rebels with dreadful cruelty ("pruning the king's vine-

yard" as he called it). The spirit of rebellion was rekindled, and long and bitter war began.

A later governor-general, the Prince of Parma, succeeded in winning over the southern provinces, but in 1581 the northern provinces declared their independence. These United Provinces received aid from the English, who were also harrying Spanish shipping, and stealing Spanish treasure.

Philip was not known for his decisiveness. ("Your Majesty spends so long considering your undertakings," wrote Pope Pius V, "that when the moment to perform them comes, the occasion has passed . . ."). But he now determined to teach the English a lesson, push the heretic Elizabeth off the throne, and take possession of the country for the Catholic faith. He ordered the construction of a fleet of 130 ships, the largest navy the world had ever seen. Carrying 30,000 men, the Armada sailed north in July 1588. The plan was to escort Parma's army from the Netherlands to the coast of England. But Parma's forces were hemmed in by a blockade, while in the Channel, the English navy pursued and outmaneuvered the Spanish ships, inflicting heavy

Above: the formidable Spanish Armada was repulsed by English maritime and fighting skill, helped along by some terrible weather. This defeat by the English in 1588 ended Spain's supremacy at sea. Below: the Armada Jewel was made in celebration of England's victory – probably by Nicholas Hilliard. Made in enamelled gold, and set with diamonds and rubies, it bears a left profile of Elizabeth I. It was given by the queen to Sir Thomas Heneage.

damages. A fierce wind then drove the crippled Armada into the North Sea. After a harrowing journey around the coast of Britain, only half of the Armada's ships and one third of its men returned to Spain.

In his own country, Philip had the disappointment of seeing its greatest asset, the rich empire overseas, produce the seeds of decline. To be sure, the pride and wealth of Spain stimulated a cultural "golden age", distinguished by Cervantes, El Greco, and other great writers and artists. But the influx of gold from the Americas unleashed severe inflation, which neither Philip nor his advisors could control. Meanwhile, the riches to be had abroad lured away a large part of the population. Industry languished. In the Escorial, the vast, rather forbidding palace he had built for himself, the king, now old and ill, withdrew more and more into the spiritual life, which offered him some respite from the frustrations of an intractable world. Philip's Inquisition to enforce conformity with Catholic orthodoxy was conducted with barbaric cruelty. Thousands died, and many more were tortured. It is for this that he is chiefly remembered.

Elizabeth I
1533-1603

In Henry VIII's time, it was considered vital for a king to have a male heir. Princesses came in handy only to secure alliances through marriage. So it is ironic that Henry – who stopped at nothing to sire a son – should father a daughter, Elizabeth, who turned out to be one of the most significant monarchs in England's history.

Intelligent and accomplished (she mastered seven foreign languages), Elizabeth also possessed a crucial talent for one in her position – a talent for survival. Early in the reign of her half-sister Mary, Elizabeth was implicated in an abortive rebellion led by a man named Wyatt, and was briefly locked up in the Tower of London. The 21-year-old princess composedly faced

Below: a portrait of Elizabeth I. It was painted in 1585 when the queen was 52 years old. The painter, Nicholas Hilliard, was probably also responsible for the Armada Jewel of 1588. Elizabeth is shown at the height of her power. England had emerged as a world power by the end of the "virgin queen's" long reign.

Below right: Robert Cecil, Earl of Salisbury. He and his father William (Lord Burghley) were prominent members of Elizabeth's court, and sworn enemies of Sir Walter Raleigh.

her interrogators and deflected their accusations. His circumspect behavior kept her alive during the next few dangerous years. Perhaps even "Bloody Mary" was reluctant to go so far as having her own half-sister killed. More danger awaited Elizabeth after she became Queen in 1558. But she was fortunate in her choice of ministers. Their farsightedness and loyalty shielded her from her enemies.

Chief of these ministers was William Cecil, her Lord Treasurer, later Lord Burghley. As cautious as Elizabeth herself, Cecil shared her conviction that the country's prosperity must be achieved through a careful financial policy and the avoidance of war. ("No war, my lords!" the Queen would declare when some of her Council showed aggressive leanings.) So England prospered. Her sagging credit was gradually restored. Industry profited from the influx of skilled immigrants fleeing the Continent's religious wars. Elizabeth opened the Royal Exchange in 1571. It was built by the financier Sir Thomas Gresham. The opening ceremony was one of the glittering affairs that she and her devoted subjects so enjoyed.

The year before, Elizabeth, a Protestant, had been formally excommunicated by Pope Pius V. The papal Bull not only freed English Catholics from allegiance to their Queen, but ordered them to disobey her (a clause revoked 10 years later). From then on all Catholics – about half the population – were potential traitors as far as the government was concerned. Elizabeth's relatively tolerant policy, which had allowed Catholics to worship in private, was replaced by tougher laws. When Jesuit missionaries began secretly entering the country in 1580, Elizabeth's government ruthlessly ran them to earth, and executed them.

The greatest threat to the Queen was the presence in her realm of her cousin Mary Stuart. Forced to abdicate the throne of Scotland by her rebellious nobles, Mary had impetuously fled to England for help. She continued to importune Elizabeth to name her as her successor, at the

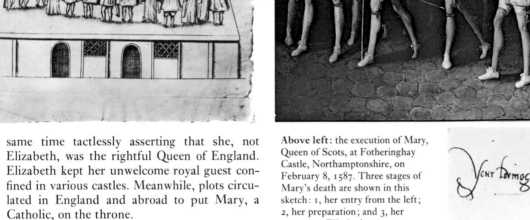

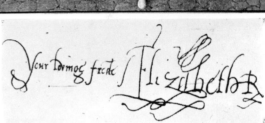

same time tactlessly asserting that she, not Elizabeth, was the rightful Queen of England. Elizabeth kept her unwelcome royal guest confined in various castles. Meanwhile, plots circulated in England and abroad to put Mary, a Catholic, on the throne.

A number of these plots were exposed and the plotters executed. Elizabeth's ministers begged her to get rid of Mary herself. Her complicity in some of the plots was evident. Elizabeth shied away from executing a crowned queen, but when she was shown evidence of Mary's acquiescence to a plot involving her own murder she had Mary brought to trial. After signing Mary's death warrant, the Queen became hysterical when the sentence was carried out – even trying to push the blame onto her ministers.

On another vital issue, marriage, the Queen remained adamant. As a child she had declared "I shall never marry," and although she continually entertained suitors – even well into middle age – it seems unlikely that she ever considered them seriously. It may be that her fear of marriage stemmed from an early association of marriage and death. This is not entirely surprising, considering the fate of her mother, Anne Boleyn, and of Henry's fifth wife, Catherine Howard. Reluctance to share power was another strong reason for remaining single.

Her ministers and Parliament had their own fears of a nation torn by civil war after her death. They continually begged her to marry so as to produce an heir. Elizabeth fobbed them off with vague promises and kept on toying with her suitors. As suitors they had strategic value. For example, she kept the Duke of Anjou on tenterhooks for three years in order to keep alive the

Above left: the execution of Mary, Queen of Scots, at Fotheringhay Castle, Northamptonshire, on February 8, 1587. Three stages of Mary's death are shown in this sketch: 1, her entry from the left; 2, her preparation; and 3, her execution. Elizabeth was so upset after the sentence was carried out that she tried to blame it on her ministers.

Above: Elizabeth being borne aloft by her courtiers in a ceremonial procession at the height of her reign. She demanded total loyalty from her court. When her favorite, Sir Walter Raleigh, married secretly, Elizabeth considered it an insult to her as a monarch and a woman. This painting is attributed to Robert Peake the Elder.

Above right: "Your loving friend Elizabeth R." The queen's signature on a letter written for her to the Earl of Lennox in 1570.

prospect of a French alliance, and so check the aggressive tendencies of Philip II of Spain.

But Philip could not be fended off for ever. He was angered by English piracy (to which Elizabeth turned a blind eye). Also he believed that he had a right to the English crown, Mary Tudor having bequeathed it to him. In 1588 he sent his formidable Armada north. Elizabeth remained convinced that war could be avoided until the eleventh hour, and she refused to allocate sufficient supplies for her navy. Nevertheless, that navy, largely Elizabeth's creation succeded in driving off the Spanish invaders.

This victory kindled an enormous sense of national pride among the English, along with renewed and intensified affection for their Queen. The last 15 years of Elizabeth's reign saw her idolized, almost as a goddess. She was the subject of extravagant verses extolling her virtues and splendor. More enduringly, the heightened national consciousness found expression in a burst of creative activity, crowned by the plays of William Shakespeare.

The old Queen, painted, bewigged, and fantastically costumed, served as a living symbol of her country's new greatness. Underneath the trappings was a shrewd, indomitable woman who had called that greatness into being. On her deathbed she finally named her successor: James VI of Scotland, the son of Mary Stuart.

William the Silent
1533-1584

stamp out heresy in the Netherlands at whatever cost. This policy, implemented ruthlessly by his appointees, caused many of his subjects to emigrate. Others were provoked into violence. William and other nobles, both Catholic and

Right: this 1832 painting by Cornelis Kruseman depicts William being accused of disloyalty by Philip II of Spain in Vlissingen in 1559, while the latter prepares to leave the Netherlands. William's loyalty to Philip conflicted with his sympathy with the people of the Netherlands. He realized that Philip intended to subjugate the Netherlands by force.

Left: a portrait of William the Silent by the Dutch painter M. van Nierevelt.

The Count of Nassau-Dillenburg, a moderately prosperous German nobleman, was not greatly pleased when his 11-year-old son William inherited from a cousin the principality of Orange in southern France and the extensive Nassau estates in the Netherlands. Now one of the richest nobles in Europe, the boy was required by his position to live at the Imperial Court of Charles V in Brussels, as well as to become a Catholic. But the Count never dreamt that his son would go on to become the founder of a new nation.

A self-confident, likeable boy, William won the affection of the Emperor, and quickly acquired the social graces expected of him. (His nickname "the Silent" derived from his ability to conceal his feelings, not from a taciturn manner.) As a young man he led a worldly, rather self-indulgent life.

His life took a more serious turn after Philip II of Spain became ruler of the Netherlands in 1555. William was Stadtholder (Philip's lieutenant) of the provinces of Holland, Zeeland, and Utrecht, and he regarded loyalty to his sovereign as his overriding duty. This loyalty soon came into conflict with his sense of justice, and his growing sympathy with the people of the Netherlands. He and other members of the governing class began to realize, with increasing alarm, that Philip intended to strip away their traditional powers. Philip was also determined to

Protestant, petitioned Philip to take a more lenient line – in vain. Philip's reply was to send the Duke of Alva at the head of an army. Alva's Council of Troubles, known as the Council of Blood, soon made it clear that heretics were not

Below: the painting "the Milch Cow" of 1585 is a satire on the exploitation of the Netherlands by the Prince of Orange (William the Silent).

NGETIME SINCE I SAWE A COWE .
WNDERS REPRESENTE
HOSE BACKE KINGE PHILLIP RODE
NG MALECONTNT .

THE QVEENE OF ENGLAND GIVING HAY
WHEARE ON THE COW DID FEEDE .
AO ONE THAT WAS HER GREATEST HELPE,
IN HER DISTRESSE AND NEEDE.

THE PRINCE OF ORANGE MILKT
AND MADE HIS PVRSE THE PA
THE COW DID SHYT IN MONSIEW
WHILE HE DID HOLD HER TAY

Left: a detail from a stained glass window in Saint John's Church, Gouda, installed in 1603. It shows William the Silent (bottom center) at the siege of Leyden. The Spanish laid siege to the town in 1574. Relief was brought and the siege raised by flooding the surrounding countryside. Food and other supplies were transported in barges. William founded a university at Leyden.

Below: this contemporary print depicts William being shot dead by Balthasar Gerard.

the only ones to be punished. It confiscated the estates of the troublesome nobles, arrested them, and had some of them executed. William and his family escaped to Germany.

He raised an army during his five-year exile. He also tried, without much success, to enlist foreign support. Although William regarded the struggle against Spain as primarily a political one, with religion a subsidiary issue, he was forced to cast in his lot with the Calvinists. Their militancy, though distasteful to him, provided not only recruits, but also the necessary strength of purpose. Gradually, William was to adopt the Calvinist faith. But he never stopped working for a united Netherlands in which all beliefs would be tolerated.

William re-entered the Netherlands in 1572 with an army of 20,000 men. By the end of the year he held one-third of Holland and parts of Zeeland and Friesland. But the war was just beginning. The Spaniards rallied. By the spring of 1574 they had the important city of Leyden under siege. The heroic raising of the siege by flooding the surrounding countryside and bringing relief to Leyden in barges saved the city, and Holland too. William commemorated the event by founding a university in Leyden.

If fighting the Spanish was the toughest challenge William faced, creating a unified nation from a collection of autonomous provinces was not much easier. A large step forward was the Act of Federation, passed in 1576, which united Holland and Zeeland, and conferred on William extensive military powers. In the south, resistance against Spain was growing, and William was called upon to lead the opposition. But soon the split between the Calvinist-dominated north, and the Catholic-dominated south began to widen. The joining of some southern provinces in the Treaty of Arras (1579) and the subsequent Union of Utrecht, including the main northern provinces, ended prospects for unifying the entire Netherlands.

A year later, William published his *Apology*, a document justifying his rebellion and, for the first time, accusing Philip of being unworthy of his subjects' loyalty. The following May, the Estates General of the United Netherlands (the north) signed the Act of Abjuration, proclaiming their independence of Spain, and chose the Prince of Orange as temporary head of the government.

But Philip had put a price on William's head. One assassination attempt failed. For the next few years, William continued building the new nation under the titular sovereignty of the ineffectual Duke of Anjou. Then one day, on his way from dinner, he was shot dead. The assassin was a young man named Balthasar Gerard, a cabinetmaker's apprentice who had ingratiated himself with William. Gerard had bought the weapon from William's unsuspecting bodyguard with money lent by William himself. It proved a misplaced act of generosity.

Prince Maurice
1567-1625

Maurice of Nassau, the future Prince of Orange, was a student at the University of Leyden when his father, William the Silent, was shot dead. The young man immediately became Stadtholder of Holland, and was soon stadtholder of most of the other seven provinces that made up the United Netherlands.

Maurice was William's second son. He did not take the title of Prince of Orange until the death of his elder half-brother, who was kept hostage most of his life by Philip II of Spain. His mother was William's second wife Anna. She was an emotionally unstable woman, whose erratic behavior may have contributed to her son's rather withdrawn, suspicious nature. Although he lacked the winning charm that had made his father a natural leader, Maurice was a master strategist, in both war and politics.

Right: Maurice moved quickly to suppress the military forces (*waardgelders*) established by each city and town. Accompanied by a large force of his own troops, he made a series of visits to the insubordinate townships. This 1627 painting by Paulus von Hillegaert depicts Maurice disbanding the *waardgelders* on the Neude, Utrecht, on July 31, 1618.

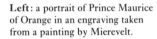

Left: a portrait of Prince Maurice of Orange in an engraving taken from a painting by Mierevelt.

Right: Maurice conferring a degree at the University of Leyden in about 1650 in a painting by Hendrick van der Burgh. Leyden University was founded by William the Silent, and Maurice was studying there when he succeeded.

The constitution of the young republic was complex and cumbersome. Overlapping and conflicting powers were vested in both the provincial States (legislative bodies), and in the States General. But soon an uneasy triumvirate emerged, consisting of Maurice, his brother William Louis (directing the military effort), and Johan van Oldenbarnevelt, advocate of the States of Holland and leader of its delegation to the States General, who handled domestic affairs and foreign policy.

Opposite: Prince Maurice and Prince Frederick Hendrik at the Valkenburg Horse Fair from a painting by Adriaen van der Venne.

Far right: Maurice lying in state in 1625. Van der Venne painted the scene on copper.

Maurice had a good grasp of military engineering, and siege warfare, which in those days was of crucial importance. He reduced the size of his army and reorganized it. It was well-trained and adequately paid, in contrast to most others. Beginning in the 1590s, they won victory after victory. The Dutch and the Spanish signed a truce in 1609, fixing the boundary between the

Republic and the Spanish Netherlands approximately where the Dutch-Belgian border runs today.

Meanwhile, conflict was developing between Maurice and Oldenbarnevelt. This elder statesman was largely responsible for drafting the truce. He therefore antagonized the Calvinist clergy, who seemed to regard the struggle against Spain as a holy war and also Maurice, for whom peace meant, potentially, a reduction of his own authority. Oldenbarnevelt feared Maurice's dynastic ambitions. He was committed to upholding the republican ideas and provincial sovereignty of the various States, and supported the more liberal Calvinists against the strictly orthodox party who stood for a clergy-dominated state. But Maurice had the support of the people, who had monarchist sentiments. His followers issued pamplets accusing the States party of planning a *coup d'etat*, and Oldenbarnevelt of secret dealings with the Spanish. The regents (the group from which the States delegates and and municipal officers were chosen) began to feel nervous. Their militias were largely composed of Orangist men. Towns and cities began to raise their own, loyal, military forces, or *waardgelders*.

Maurice quickly suppressed these moves, making a series of visits – accompanied by his own troops – to the insubordinate towns, and

subtly bullying them into disbanding the *waardgelders*. He also began replacing the municipal officers, and deputies with men he could rely on.

In August of that year, 1618, Oldenbarnevelt was arrested by one of the Prince's bodyguard, acting "by order of the States General." He was tried on charges of treason by a court with no legal authority to do so, and was found guilty. Refusing to ask Maurice for a pardon, which would have been a tacit admission of guilt, he faced his execution with dignity.

Maurice had triumphed over the principle of provincial sovereignty and was now king in all but name. The truce expired in 1621 and this time the Dutch faced a more powerful Spanish army. With help from France, Maurice waged the war until his death in 1625. It was to continue for another 23 years.

Henry IV of France
1553-1610

Few men have brought to their country more valuable personal qualities in its hour of need than Henry of Navarre, later Henry IV of France. A patriot and a statesman in a period when most of his countrymen were more interested in religious differences and family feuds, Henry combined military achievements with a shrewd cynicism in matters of faith. He developed the ability to forgive and forget with an autocratic approach to kingship. Henry, first of France's Bourbon kings, was able to bring his country out of a 30-year succession of religious wars, and to restore France to prosperity, power, and a unique position among Eurpean nations.

Navarre, Henry's kingdom within France, lies in the southwest. It was strongly Calvinist – that is, Huguenot. Henry became their political leader during a period when hatred between Huguenot and Catholic led to almost continuous civil war, which often involved the armies of Spain, and the emerging Netherlands.

Three sons of the Italian queen Catherine de Medici, Francis II, Charles IX, and Henry III, ruled France in succession from 1559 to 1589. They were all weak and ineffectual. Their ambitious mother really ruled France. She strove to balance the rivalries of the Huguenots, and the

leading Catholic family, the Guises. Her juggling reached its hideous climax in the massacre of St Bartholemew's Eve in August 1572. At least 3000 Huguenots were slaughtered in Paris alone. Henry, who had just married Catherine's daughter, only escaped death by renouncing his faith – a faith which he had never taken very seriously anyway. But it was not long before he returned to Protestantism and the leadership of the Huguenots.

Left: Henry IV of France in a charcoal portrait drawn in about 1600.

Above: a force of 10,000 men under Henry IV's command laid siege to Paris in 1590. He showed himself an astute political tactician when he announced himself ready to become a Catholic. This won over the Parisians. He was later to remark "Paris was well worth a Mass." This 17th-century color engraving gives an impression of the siege.

In August 1589 the two Henrys – Navarre and Henry III – were finally reconciled after a long period of confused rivalry and civil war. A Catholic friar stabbed the king to death. There being no rivals to his succession, Henry of Navarre became Henry IV of France. Two factors made his position secure. One was the help of the Protestant queen Elizabeth I of England. She sent money and over 10,000 men to support his cause – a factor that led to his decisive victory over the Catholic forces at Ivry near Paris in March 1590. The second was Henry's "perilous leap" in declaring himself ready to become a Catholic. It gives some idea of his personal power, and of France's desperation after so much fruitless religious conflict that Henry's conversion did not lose him the support of the Huguenots.

Henry achieved a major step toward religious toleration in France in 1598. The Edict of Nantes secured for the French protestants a kind of religious toleration unique in 16th-century Europe. Not only freedom of worship but full civil rights were accorded to them. This "perpetual and irrevocable" measure demonstrated once and for all Henry's preference in religious matters,

Bottom left: Henry turned France's religious divisions to his own political advantage. Here he is depicted renouncing Protestantism in favor of Catholicism. This switch helped win him the most coveted prize of all – Paris.

Bottom right: this print of 1695 shows Henry being stabbed to death in the streets of Paris by a Catholic fanatic in August 1610.

for social and political solutions rather than for abstract truth. This underlying policy of *realpolitik* explains his otherwise cynical remark that "Paris was well worth a Mass." But within the Edict were the seeds of its own death. The guarantee of nearly 100 "places of surety" – armed cities such as Montpellier, Montauban, and La Rochelle to provide security to the Huguenots in times of strife – ran counter to all Henry's other policies. They tended more toward monarchial uniformity and centralization in France.

The past 30 years' experience convinced Henry that the state should be represented by the unquestioned authority of the king alone. He often spoke of his kingship being "under the protection of his people." But to the Estates, the representative bodies of France, he spoke more truly when he said that "your most valuable privilege is the favor of your king." Strong centralized government was Henry's ambition and his bequest to France. After 30 years of chaotic conflict, Frenchmen of every creed and class valued efficiency and order above liberty. Henry's ambition for himself, for France, and for the condition of every Frenchman made him popular as well as respected.

Industry flourished in his reign. Sully, his chief minister remained a Huguenot, but gave him his best counsel. Roads, bridges, and canals were improved. Silk, gold thread work, glass, helped bring a strong economy. Henry was the first of the Bourbon kings of France, and he bequeathed to them a prosperous and tolerant country, which was strong and united. His personal attributes of authority and strength of will, bonhomie, and tact had enabled him to achieve the apparently impossible. When a Catholic fanatic stabbed him to death in August 1610, he was ruler of the most united and powerful country in Europe. The tendency of his Bourbon successors to involve France in expensive, and fruitless wars was perhaps inevitable. But his reign laid the foundation for a century in which France was supreme in Europe. After its 16th-century experience that alone was no mean achievement.

Cardinal Richelieu
1585-1642

If Louis XIV of France could truthfully say, "I am the state," it was largely thanks to Cardinal Richelieu. As Louis' father's first minister, this brilliant, ruthless man devoted himself to the creation of a state where the sovereign's authority would be absolute, and in which the grandeur of his court would symbolize the power of the nation. The irony was that the king whose authority Richelieu was supposedly enhancing – Louis XIII – was a figurehead. Richelieu ruled France.

Born into nobility, Armand Jean du Plessis de Richelieu was educated first for the army. He was sent to a seminary when an elder brother turned down the bishopric which the family controlled. Armand was ordained a priest at 22,

and also consecrated Bishop of Lucon, in Poitou.

But the young bishop had no intention of staying in the provinces. His goal was the royal court, the seat of power. Summoned to Paris in 1614 for a meeting of the Estates General (the last such meeting before the Revolution 175 years later), he managed to catch attention of the Regent, Marie de Medicis. He obtained a minor post at court. A combination of lavish flattery, and obvious ability sent him higher up the ladder. He was acting first minister of the Council two years later.

Richelieu allied himself with the Queen Mother, and her unprincipled favorite Concini.

Left: a color engraving of Cardinal Richelieu made in 1789 by Sergent.

Below: the "emblem on the extirpation of heresy and rebellion, by the care of Cardinal Richelieu." Richelieu is shown as the protector of the monarchy from rebellion and heresy. He is shown removing a caterpillar before it attacks the lilies of France. Tethered, the lion of Spain and the German eagle look on helplessly.

But he suffered a setback when the young Louis XIII at last asserted himself, and had the hated Concini murdered, and his mother and her circle banished. It took seven years for Richelieu to persuade the king of his loyalty. In 1624, now a cardinal, he once more took his seat in the Council. From then until the end of his life he worked to build a unified and powerful nation.

The power of the nobles was one of his major obstacles. Some of the great families maintained fortified castles and private armies. If they had an ax to grind against the king, they would revolt, often with the help of another nation. Richelieu ordered the destruction of all fortified castles not used by the crown. His extensive network of spies discovered plots against the king – which he then foiled with a few timely executions.

Similarly, Richelieu curbed the military and political power of the Huguenots, the French Protestants. In the preceding century, France had been continually torn by religious wars. Though tolerant in matters of faith, Richelieu could not countenance the existence of what was, in effect, a state within a state. In 1627, the port of La Rochelle, a Protestant stronghold, was in revolt, as were other Huguenots in the south. The promise of English help stiffened La Rochelle's resistance. But Richelieu was equally determined to break it. He concentrated the royal forces around the city, and succeeded in driving the English fleet away three times. Finally, after a year-long siege, La Rochelle's remaining inhabitants capitulated. Other Huguenot cities fell more readily.

Hapsburg encirclement was another threat. The Empire to the east, Spain to the south, and the Spanish Netherlands to the north were all controlled by this powerful dynasty. Richelieu tried to undermine Hapsburg power by every means at his disposal. Both secretly and openly, he supported anyone with a grudge against the

Hapsburgs. In 1629, his envoy Charnace helped to negotiate a truce between Swedish King Gustavus Adolphus to lead the Protestant forces against the Hapsburg Emperor. Later, Richelieu gave Gustavus a subsidy of 1,000,000 *livres* a year, intending merely that he should keep the Imperial forces occupied while he himself pushed back France's eastern frontier. He became alarmed when it began to look as though the Swedish warrior would conquer and unify all Germany. Gustavus' death in battle solved that problem, and the war raged on. By 1635 France and Spain were conducting their hostilities on the ravaged fields of Germany. France was openly supporting the Protestant German princes. Although Richelieu did not live to see it, the Peace of Westphalia, ending the war in 1648, would have gratified him. It confirmed the wisdom of his policy. The Empire lay in tatters, and Germany was to remain fragmented for more than 200 years.

Richelieu's callous opportunism was only one side of his character. His belief in the potential greatness of France expressed itself in constructively building up the French navy, developing commerce and industry, and encouraging the arts. Under his patronage, the French school of painting flourished, and architecture and the decorative arts proclaimed the grandeur of the

Above: the siege of La Rochelle. Richelieu was determined to break Huguenot resistance. He finally succeeded after a year-long siege.

Below: Richelieu on his death bed in a painting attributed to Philippe de Champaigne.

state. It was he who founded that august literary society and the guardian of the French language, the French Academy.

Culturally, politically, and militarily France was on the threshold of its golden age when Richelieu died. Long afflicted by various illnesses, he had driven himself relentlessly for 18 years.

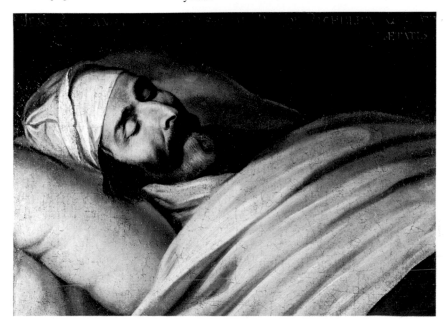

Gustavus Adolphus
1594-1632

Right: the battlefield at Lützen where Gustavus Adolphus was mortally wounded in 1632. The Hapsburg forces can be seen massed in the foreground of the picture. After Gustavus Adolphus was killed leading the Swedish cavalry into battle, his chief lieutenant, Bernard of Weimar took over. Under his command, the Swedish army achieved an unexpected victory.

Left: a portrait of King Gustavus Adolphus. Under his reign, Sweden reached its peak of power and influence.

According to an old prophecy, widely believed among German Protestants in the early 1600s, a "golden Lion" would come down from the north to defeat the "Eagle" of the Holy Roman Empire. He would then conquer Africa and Asia, and finally establish a reign of peace on earth. Christ's second coming was to follow. It is not surprising, therefore, that when the blond-headed Protestant King Gustavus Adolphus of Sweden arrived in Germany at the head of an army, he was met with almost hysterical adoration. And although he did not quite fulfill this messianic dream, he did push back the Emperor's army, rescue the Protestant states, which were on the point of collapse, and contribute to the eventual dissolution of the Empire.

When he became King he was not quite 17. At the outset he faced several crises. His father Charles IX had usurped the throne from the rightful king, Sigismund, also King of Poland. Charles had then gone to war with Poland over some disputed land in the Baltic and the succession to the throne of Russia. At the same time, though financially and militarily weak, he provoked a war with Sweden's traditional rival, Denmark. The country was disunited internally, and the disaffected Swedish nobility only accepted Gustavus as king after he had signed a Charter putting numerous restrictions on his power.

The war with Denmark was brought to a hasty and rather unsatisfactory conclusion in 1613. Four years later the conclusion of the war in Russia brought Sweden two new provinces on the Gulf of Finland, and thus cut off Russian access to the Baltic. But war with Poland was to continue elsewhere for a long time.

On the domestic front, Gustavus showed a conciliatory approach. He appointed the principal author of the Charter, Axel Oxenstierna, as Chancellor. It was a fruitful partnership between King and Chancellor. Oxenstierna put many governmental reforms in train. His reorganization of the treasury made possible Sweden's emergence as a great power. The King established a coherent system of local government, directly responsible to the crown. He made significant reforms in the educational system, designed to increase the number of qualified applicants for the expanding civil service.

His own education had included a thorogh grounding in the arts of war, and he brought to warfare a number of tactical innovations. Lighter, more maneuverable artillery and more flexible formations were among them. He was an audacious commander. And he had a zest for battle and being in the thick of the fight that ultimately caused his death.

Sweden's intervention in the Thirty Years' War was not motivated simply by a desire to save Lutheranism. For 12 years Gustavus avoided becoming directly involved in the conflict, having problems enough with Poland. But the rapid advance of Imperial armies through northern Germany and the avowed Hapsburg aim of gaining control of Baltic trade, followed by the capture of all but four of the German ports, clarified the issue. With French help a

Right: this engraving by the artist Pauli shows Gustavus Adolphus as a military leader in a rather dramatic and fanciful pose. A shrewd politician, as well as a gifted military tactician, Gustavus helped build Sweden into a formidable power.

Below left: the northern empires, with Sweden dominating the Baltic, at the end of the 18th century. Sweden is shown in green, with Russia in pink and Prussia mauve.

Below: the interior of Riddarholms Church with the tomb of Gustavus Adolphus in the center of the picture.

the Imperial army, under the brilliant General Tilly, went from success to success. Then in September 1631, a little over a year after his arrival, Gustavus crushed Tilly's Imperial army at Brietenfeld, near Leipzig. Crippled, it fled to northwest Germany, while Gustavus moved his army triumphantly into the Rhineland. The winter of 1631-32 saw him established at Mainz, and at the center of the labyrinthine politics underlying the conflict. The Swedish army controlled half Germany, and it was the Swedish king who now dealt with the various aims of the French, the English, the Hungarians, and the other interested powers. Gustavus' own aim was to create a strong league of Protestant German states under Swedish control – an idea repugnant to the princes, who feared exchanging one emperor for another.

In the spring Gustavus began moving his army down the Danube, intending to finish off the Hapsburg armies. This plan was thwarted by the reappearance on the scene of the formidable General Wallenstein who attacked Saxony. Gustavus was forced to turn northward. After months of waiting the Swedes attacked Wallenstein near Nuremberg, and were defeated. Morale sank. A third of the army deserted. In November Gustavus had the chance to take Wallenstein – whose army was dispersing for the winter – by surprise. Fog prevented Gustavus from implementing his original strategy. The Swedes were facing another defeat when their king was mortally wounded. His second in command, Bernard of Weimar, turned the near defeat at Lützen into a victory.

With the death of Gustavus, ambitious plans for a Swedish-controlled Protestant bloc crumbled. But Sweden remained in the war until the bitter end, under the leadership of Oxenstierna. At the Peace of Westphalia in 1648, she received more substantial territories on the Baltic, and so became the ruler of that sea until well into the next century.

truce was arranged with Poland, and in 1630 Gustavus landed with his army at Peenemunde.

Paradoxically, he had no German allies at this point. He might be a savior to the masses, but to the Protestant German princes, unable to unite effectively in their own defense, his aims were suspect. Only gradually did he manage to secure their grudging cooperation. Meanwhile,

Charles I
1600-1649

Devout royalists know him as the Martyr King. On January 30 every year memorial services are held in England and Scotland to commemorate the beheading of Charles Stuart. The sensitive, noble features of the Van Dyck portraits reinforce the legend of the tragic victim. It is usual to ignore those aspects of Charles' character, such as obstinacy and political shortsightedness, that contributed to his unhappy fate.

As a child, Charles was weak, prone to illness, and afflicted with a stammer. He idolized his elder brother Henry, a paragon of princely virtues whose death in his teens was regarded as a national disaster. Now heir to the throne, Charles turned for friendship to another hero, George Villiers, Duke of Buckingham. His intense attachment to the charming, headstrong

Above: a print portraying Charles I as a martyr, published after he was beheaded in 1649.

Left: Charles I as portrayed in a well-known official portrait.

Right: a facsimile of an order written by Charles to his Attorney General on January 3, 1642. It demanded that Lord Kimbolton and five members of the House of Commons be arrested for treasonable correspondence with the Scots. The Commons refused to comply with the king's demands. A constitutional crisis ensued, and the English Civil War was precipitated.

Buckingham was one factor in his conflict with Parliament. This began at the outset of his reign in 1625.

The House of Commons had already flexed their muscles in the reign of James I. Keenly aware of the wealth and power they represented, and strongly influenced by Puritan thinking, they viewed the "divine right of kings" (a cherished Stuart dogma) with skepticism and Roman Catholicism represented by Charles' French Queen with horror. Though theoretically willing to prosecute the wars with France and Spain instigated by Buckingham, they objected to paying for his military blunders. In 1626, they threatened to impeach him. To stop this, Charles dissolved Parliament. He then tried to finance the wars by means of forced loans. Those who refused to cooperate were locked up. Finally, desperate for money, he recalled Parliament, which offered the much needed cash provided he guarantee certain civil liberties. The king agreed. The Commons then resumed their attack on Buckingham with renewed vigor. When Buckingham was assassinated, the distraught king blamed the Commons for stirring up hatred of him. His relations with Parliament deteriorated further. In 1629 he dissolved it again.

Thus began an 11-year Personal Rule. It was a reasonably tranquil time for the country and a happy time for Charles, who finally grew to love his wife, Henrietta Maria, and became a father. But in governing the country, Charles made the mistake of giving too much power to his Archbishop of Canterbury, William Laud. Laud's re-catholicizing of the litergy and his strengthening of the church's temporal powers aroused resentment and fear. His attempt to impose Anglicanism on the Scots, warmly supported by the King, stirred up a hornet's nest.

The Scots declared war. Charles was forced to summon a new Parliament in order to obtain funds. When it proved hostile to him, he dissolved it, and called for new elections.

The new Parliament, which met in 1640, proved equally obdurate. They clapped Laud in jail, and brought to trial, for supposed treason, Charles' trusted Minister, the Earl of Strafford. With no real evidence, they found him guilty and forced the king, by means of various threats both political and personal, to sign his death warrant. It was the one action for which Charles never forgave himself.

Forced to agree to a series of measures curbing royal authority, Charles was finally goaded by the queen into retaliating. With several hundred soldiers he burst into the Commons and demanded the arrest of five of his main opponents. But the five had been forewarned, and had gone into hiding. This misguided act roused Londoners to fury. Fleeing the rioters, Charles moved north, while the queen went to Holland, taking the crown jewels with which to buy arms. Both king and Parliament began to raise armies. In August 1642 the Civil War began.

At first, the Parliamentary forces had the advantage of greater numbers, but the Royalists

Left: a contemporary cartoon satirizes the rivalry between the Cavalier followers of the king, and the supporters of parliament, the Roundheads. Charles is caricatured on the left. Austere and puritanical, the Roundheads were so called because their hair was severely cropped short.

ened in 1644 by an alliance with Scotland, which brought 18,000 Scottish troops into the war. The Royalists were now on the defensive and remained so as the Parliamentary army – or Roundheads, as they were called because of their severe haircuts – acquired skill, and discipline. The Roundhead victory at Naseby, in June 1645, effectively ended Royalist hopes, although fighting continued for another year.

After the war ended in 1646, Charles was held prisoner by the Scots, by Parliament, and by the Army – a new political force in the land. Its commander Oliver Cromwell tried to negotiate a new government with the king. But while Charles talked amicably with Cromwell, he was secretly corresponding with the Scots, hoping to regain his throne on better terms. In a letter to his exiled queen in France he assured her that he had no intention of "yielding to the traitor." In the summer of 1648 Charles was again the prisoner of Parliament. They also tried to reach an agreement with him. But the radical element in the Army, led now by the disillusioned Cromwell, succeeded in purging Parliament of its moderate members and had Charles, the "Man of Blood" as they called him, brought to trial. In the face of mounting public support for the king, the illegal tribunal found him

were better trained. They very nearly won the first major battle, at Edghill in Warwickshire, but the outcome was a draw. An attempt to march on London failed, so Charles moved back to Oxford, his headquarters for the rest of the war.

The Parliamentary cause was greatly strength-

Above: this print was issued after Charles' execution. His refusal to reach any kind of compromise with Oliver Cromwell or parliament contributed to his fate.

guilty of "treason" and sentenced him to death. After his beheading, the crowd dipped their handkerchiefs in his blood. It seemed the end of English monarchy. Charles' refusal to compromise made his survival impossible. But the crown was to return 21 years later with greatly curtailed powers.

Oliver Cromwell
1599-1658

28. That Parliament was dissolved a year later in 1629 by Charles I.

During Charles' Personal Rule, Cromwell immersed himself in family matters and local politics. He also experienced a religious conversion. This was to influence his actions for the rest of his life. When, in 1640, he returned to Parliament, he took his place among radicals like his cousin Christopher Hampden, and John Pym.

One of the ironies of history is that the man mainly responsible for the victory of Parliament over King in the English Civil War later became king in all but name, and ruthlessly suppressed parliamentary opposition.

Oliver Cromwell was a contradictory character. As Lord Protector he forbade the death penalty except for murder or treason, and sometimes personally intervened to mitigate sentences. But as Governor-General of Ireland, he cold-bloodedly ordered the slaughter of the civilians of Drogheda and Wexford, while putting down a Royalist-Catholic revolt. This is bitterly remembered by the Irish even today. Although he assumed dictatorial powers, he was always a reluctant dictator. Cromwell was committed, in theory at least, to power sharing between the executive and Parliament. A profoundly religious man, he was keenly aware of his unworthiness before God. At the same time, he was convinced that he was God's instrument, and that his own decisions – arrived at after long periods of prayer – were expressions of divine will.

The Cromwells were a moderately prosperous Huntingdonshire family with a tradition of public service. It was no great surprise when Oliver Cromwell was elected to Parliament at the age of

Above: "The Royall Oake of Brittayne,' a contemporary credited to "Inspiritio Diabolica," or devilish inspiration. The oak tree represents the English monarchy, and the Roundheads are busily cutting it down. Oliver Cromwell is caricatured on the left of the picture, supervising operations.

Left: a portrait of Oliver Cromwell. Under the "Commonwealth" which he ruled a rigidly Puritan regime was imposed – enforced by the *major-generals*.

At the outbreak of the Civil War, Cromwell was commissioned a colonel in the Parliamentary army, and was made responsible for raising a small troop of horse. He soon saw that the Parliamentary cause was not helped by its poorly trained and disorganized army. Cromwell noted the devastating effect of a cavalry charge led by the king's nephew Prince Rupert at Edgehill. He resolved to build his own troop into a similar weapon. By the spring of 1643 he had a regiment of 800 cavalry. They soon earned the nickname "Ironsides" by their intrepid, well-disciplined fighting. At the battle of Marston Moor in July 1644, Cromwell's Ironsides routed the Royalists ("God made them as stubble to our swords," was his characteristic remark). This Roundhead victory destroyed Royalist strength in the North. Cromwell then got Parliament's go-ahead to reconstitute the entire army. The result was the New Model Army, of which Cromwell was General of the Horse. It was imbued with a fervent belief in the justice of its cause. Like Cromwell himself, most of the soldiers belonged to independent Protestant sects, and were as suspicious of the Presbyterians who led Parliament as they were of the Anglican Royalists.

In the tangled sequence of events following the Royalist surrender in 1646, Cromwell tried at first to mediate between the Army, who refused to disband, and the Parliament, of which he was still a member. He also attempted to persuade the king to agree to a proposed constitution.

Cromwell's initial respect for the king vanished when a Scottish royal army invaded England at Charles' request, triggering off the Second Civil War. The New Model Army soon put paid to the royalists. Incensed at the king's

Right: the Great Seal of Oliver Cromwell's Commonwealth. Made in 1651, it depicts a scene in the House of Commons. The Speaker is in his chair while an MP addresses the House. Two clerks sit at a table, which also bears the mace.

Above: Oliver Cromwell at Dunbar in 1650. As Chairman of the Council of State of the new republic, or Commonwealth, Cromwell waged campaigns against Scotland and Ireland. In 1653, he forcibly dissolved Parliament and named himself Lord Protector. This picture was painted by A. C. Gow in 1886.

"prodigious treason," Cromwell determined to bring him to justice.

But Charles' execution further inflamed Royalist feeling. After dealing with the Irish, Cromwell engaged the Scots – now allied with Charles II – and put an end to their new invasion at Worcester in September 1651.

England was now governed, after a fashion, by the self-perpetuating Rump Parliament – the core of radicals who had brought Charles to trial. For more than a year Cromwell observed their actions – and their inaction – with mounting frustration (he particularly objected to the war they had started with the Dutch). Then one day he rose in the House and declared, "You are no parliament. I will put an end to your sitting." So he did, with the help of a body of musketeers.

The remaining years of the Commonwealth, as the republic was called, saw continual struggle for sovereignty. Cromwell's new Parliament, the "Assembly of Saints," passed radically egalitarian measures for several heady months before being dissolved in a *coup* by one of Cromwell's supporters. A written constitution then made Cromwell Lord Protector for life, but also provided for a Council of State and a Parliament with considerable powers. For five years Cromwell struggled with, and dissolved, his Parliaments alternatively. As in the days of King Charles, they quarreled over rights of taxation. Another bone of contention was the rule of the *major-generals*, local government officers to whom Cromwell had given considerable powers. It was they, primarily, who enforced the rigid Puritan restrictions on any form of merriment that characterized Cromwell's rule.

In his foreign policy Cromwell was firmly pro-Protestant and anti-Spain. He made peace with the Dutch, and sent a naval expedition to the West Indies. Here, in due course, the English wrested Jamaica from the Spanish. Pursuing the war into the Spanish Netherlands, England acquired Dunkirk. The successful naval blockade of the Spanish coast increased respect for English sea power.

Throughout its brief existence the Commonwealth was threatened with occasional Royalist uprisings. The government became more and more unpopular. After Cromwell's death its days were numbered. A surge of enthusiasm met King Charles II when he returned in 1660. In a short time, the Puritan republic seemed like a bad dream. But the events of the previous 20 years had shown the Stuarts and their successors that absolute monarchy would not be imposed easily upon their subjects.

Akbar
1542-1605

"A sovereign should be ever intent on conquest." These were the words of Abu-ul-Fath Jalal-ud-Din Muhammad Akbar, and he was true to his words. When he became Mogul Emperor of India at the age of 13 his domain was a mere few hundred square miles around Delhi. At his death, nearly 50 years later, the Empire reached from the Arabian Sea to the Bay of Bengal, and included most of the Indian subcontinent.

Akbar was the third Mogul Emperor of India. Of mixed Iranian, Turkish, and Mongol blood ("Mongul" is a corruption of "Mongol"), he was descended from Ghengis Khan and from Timur. Timur's Indian conquests in the late 14th century had weakened the hold of the Turks and Afghans in that part of Asia. A descendant of Timur named Babar reestablished Mongol rule in India, and conquered large territories from the native rulers. His son Humayun – Akbar's

father – was driven out by an Afghan usurper. He regained his throne shortly before his death.

The teenage Akbar had little interest in governing at first. His chief minister Bairam Khan handled the affairs of state and the conduct of war. Under Bairam Khan's leadership, the shaky Mogul rule in northern India was strengthened and extended.

Akbar dismissed his powerful minister in 1560, and for a while left the government in the hands of a clique. When rivalries within the clique erupted in violence, Akbar dealt swiftly with the chief culprit and assumed control himself. He ruled as absolute monarch from then on.

Even before taking charge of the government, Akbar had displayed statesmanlike qualities by marrying a Hindu princess and allowing her to

Below: this illustration shows Akbar, the third Mogul emperor of India, crossing the Ganges river with his forces.

Below left: an Indian impression of Akbar in procession with his courtiers.

rat. Its ports controlled trade with Western Asia. Three years later, after a difficult campaign, he annexed Bengal. Kashmir was added in 1586. As his reign approached its end, Akbar embarked on the conquest of southern India. By 1601 his Empire reached as far south as Ahmadnagar.

While continually extending his boundaries, Akbar consolidated his rule within the conquered lands. He restructured the system of provincial and local government, bringing chieftains who had formerly enjoyed – or abused – some autonomy into a kind of military hierarchy in which every officer was appointed by and responsible to the Emperor. A keen eye was kept on the revenues produced by each province to make sure that governors were not siphoning off more of the wealth than they were entitled to.

Akbar himself became fabulously rich. His wealth and that of his court financed the manufacture and import of luxury goods, including fine silks and carpets. Official patronage also encouraged arts, which incorporated both Islamic and Hindu traditions. Some European influences found their way into Mogul painting.

Portuguese missionaries were welcomed by Akbar, who, despite being illiterate, had great intellectual curiosity and enjoyed listening to theological debates. He appointed a Jesuit priest tutor to one of his sons. At the age of 36 he is said to have had a mystical experience which left him convinced of his role as interpreter of the divine will. He proclaimed himself the spiritual leader of all his people and disestablished Islam as the state religion. A new religion founded by Akbar combined elements of several faiths. But it remained a cult limited to the Emperor's chosen disciples.

Like many other outstanding leaders Akbar was disappointed in his children. His three sons were drunkards, and the eldest, Salim, had a vicious temper. During the last few years of Akbar's life Salim led a rebellion against his father. A reconciliation was achieved shortly before Akbar's death, and Salim was designated heir to the vast Empire his father had created. It was to last for another 150 years.

continue practicing her religion. This was an extraordinary act for a Moslem ruler. But Akbar was remarkably free of bigotry, and also politically astute. He intended to be acknowledged as sovereign not only by Moslems, but also by the native population. A poll tax formerly levied on all non-Moslems was abolished, and Hindus were recruited into Akbar's government. His marriage to the Hindu princess won him the allegiance of her father – one of the fiercely independent rajas of the province of Rajasthan. Other such alliances followed. Rajput princes became generals and provincial governors of the Mogul Empire.

But most of Akbar's Empire was gained through conquest. In 1573 he conquered Guja-

Above: Akbar's forces attack the fort at Ranthambore in 1563. This action was one of a number of campaigns mounted by the emperor in an attempt to subdue the Rajputs. Bullocks can be seen dragging siege guns into position in preparation for an artillery attack on the fort.

Right: the entrance to Akbar's tomb at Sikandra. No effort was spared in building this magnificent monument, which was completed in 1613.

Louis XIV
1638-1715

Right: Louis XIV's expensive military adventures as well as the extravagant lifestyle of the royal family and the rest of the court at Versailles imposed a heavy burden on the French people. Many were impoverished by the taxes they had to bear. This print shows citizens doing their irksome duty as they queue to pay the tax collector.

Left: this official portrait of Louis XIV shows the "Sun King" at the height of his splendor. The lavishness of the French court provoked envy in other European royal houses. Here, Louis stands in the pose of a keen and accomplished dancer.

Louis XIV the king other kings envied. His court at Versailles set a standard of magnificence imitated, but never achieved elsewhere in Europe. His status as God's representative on earth was not questioned – indeed it was constantly proclaimed, from the elaborate rituals that attended his getting up in the morning and retiring at night to the fact that in the royal chapel his courtiers sat with their backs to the altar, facing him. No presumptuous parliament dared challenge his authority. His formidable army raised fears of French conquest throughout Europe, while a gentler conquest, that of French culture, was welcomed everywhere.

The glory of the "Sun King" in his prime is in marked contrast with the insecurity of his youth. He became king at the age of five, but France continued to be ruled by his father's prime minister Cardinal Mazarin, successor to Richelieu. In 1648 a combination of powerful nobles organized a rebellion – called the Fronde –

against Mazarin and the crown. The civil war that ensued lasted for five years, and was a traumatic experience for the young king. He was left with a lasting distrust of the aristocracy.

After defeating the Frondeurs, Mazarin began teaching his young sovereign the arts of government. Louis proved an apt pupil. He had a remarkable capacity for hard work and attention to detail. These qualities enabled him – after Mazarin's death in 1661 – to oversee every aspect of the government of France and the conduct of his military campaigns. He still found time to lead the numerous court ceremonies, attend Mass every day, go hunting, and consume prodigious meals. Louis also pursued a succession of long and short-term love affairs – without

Above: one of the magnificent rooms in the palace of Versailles, just outside Paris. Still standing, the palace was so extraordinary in its day that its stables were more sumptuous than many a European nobleman's home.

Left: a painting of the *Combat de Vitry*, one of the Battles of the Fronde.

deliberate policy to distract the aristocracy from politics. He exempted them from direct taxation, so preventing them acquiring any material interest in the government, and placed most of the tax burden on those least able to pay – a policy that would later have disastrous results.

Early in his reign Louis reorganized the French army, which had formerly been a motley collection of troops owing primary allegiance to various nobles. With the help of his Minister of War, Louvois, he built a unified and disciplined force under his own control. It was eventually to number 400,000 men.

Louis was continually at war from 1667. He made several unsuccessful attempts to conquer the Dutch Republic. But by 1678 he had gained most of the Spanish Netherlands, and also the province of Franche-Comté, on the Swiss border. French troops occupied Alsace and Lorraine.

Louis made a serious blunder in 1685 by revoking the Edict of Nantes. Harassment of Protestants had not succeeded in forcing them all to convert. So the king – who regarded Protestantism as a threat to the unity of his realm – decided to abrogate their freedom of worship. The resulting exodus not only deprived France of thousands of useful citizens, but also aroused anti-French feeling among the Protestant nations.

The biggest issue at the end of the 17th century was the succession to the throne of Spain, occupied for the moment by the moribund, childless Charles II, Louis' brother-in-law. By various diplomatic maneuvers Louis and his old adversary William III of England reached a compromise solution, only to discover on Charles' death that he had willed his kingdom and its rich empire to one of Louis' young grandsons. If Louis refused the bequest, it would go to the Austrian Hapsburgs. Faced with the old threat of Hapsburg encirclement, Louis gave in.

The War of the Spanish Succession, precipitated by his acceptance, lasted 12 years, and embroiled most of the nations of Western Europe. With only one ally, Bavaria, and with a weakened army, Louis carried on, refusing to accept the crippling surrender terms offered at one point by the Allies. By the Treaty of Utrecht, which ended the war, Louis's grandson, Philip V, retained the Spanish throne, but Spain's European possessions were divided among the Allies.

France itself remained intact, but it was exhausted by the war. Louis was a tired old man, saddened by a series of deaths in his family, including most of his male heirs. He and his second wife, Madame de Maintenon, whom he had married secretly in 1683, lived quietly now, without the glittering festivities of earlier days. In the summer of 1715 Louis' health began to fail. He developed gangrene in his leg. He endured three weeks of agony with dignity. Before dying he admonished his great-grandson, "Do not copy me . . . in my love of warefare; on the contrary, try to live peacefully with your neighbors . . . try to improve the lot of your people . . ."

entirely neglecting his rather pathetic Spanish Queen, Marie-Thérése.

He was lucky to inherit the able minister Jean-Baptiste Colbert from Mazarin's government. After thoroughly reorganizing the nation's finances, Colbert turned his attention to making France self-sufficient, using a variety of measures to encourage industry and commerce. The building and furnishing of Versailles – Louis' lifelong passion – provided a showplace for French craftsmanship, and stimulated foreign demand for French products.

Versailles was more than the king's chief residence. After 1682 it was the seat of government. Hundreds of nobles lived there, seduced by the diverting, indolent life it afforded. It was Louis'

John Sobieski
1629-1696

ority. Any delegate could close the Diet by vetoing any measure. The Diet elected the King of Poland – usually a foreigner – and made sure that he had virtually no power. At that time, most of the Diet delegates were trying to secure the Polish succession for either a French or an Austrian candidate.

When, in 1660, some nobles and most of the army rebelled against the pro-French King John Casimir, Sobieski remained loyal to the crown.

In July 1683 the Turks laid siege to Vienna. Two months later, when it looked as though the beleaguered city would surrender, an international army led by the Polish King John Sobieski came to its rescue. In one day's fighting, Sobieski's army drove the Turks from their encampment and forced them to retreat. From then on Turkish encroachment in Europe began to flounder.

King Sobieski's victory was a remarkable achievement by any standards – his forces were outnumbered by two to one – but given the opposition he faced within his own country and elsewhere in Europe, it becomes truly heroic. Encouraged by the rulers of other nations, Sobieski's country was tearing itself apart. He stood almost alone in recognizing the desperate need to unite against a common foe.

Sobieski had been born into a noble family from the southeastern part of Poland – in those

days a vast country extending almost to the Black Sea. The family had a long tradition of fighting their Islamic and Russian neighbors. John first saw battle at the age of 19, during one of the perennial wars with the Cossacks and Tartars. He was first and foremost a soldier for the rest of his life.

In 1658, Sobieski attended the Polish Diet for the first time. This body was made up of delegates from the smaller regional diets. They were all aristocrats and nearly all committed to holding onto their independence of any central auth-

Above left: a contemporary portrait of John Sobieski.

Above: the battle of Kahlenburg of 1683. Sobieski had formed an alliance with Austria against the Turks. At this battle Polish troops freed Vienna from Turkish occupation.

He was rewarded by being made Grand Marshal, the highest military position in Poland. His marriage to Marie Casimire, a self-centered and devious French aristocrat, drew him further into the French camp at Court.

The long civil war ended in 1666. No sooner was it over than new threats materialized on Poland's eastern frontier. With a force of about 8000, paid for largely from his own funds, Sobieski defeated a much larger force of Tartar invaders at the garrison of Podhajce. On his return to Warsaw, he was acclaimed a hero.

Throughout his career, clever, daring strategy enabled Sobieski to triumph again and again over superior forces. His reputation grew until it was such that the Turkish soldiers credited him with sorcery, and became demoralized as soon as they heard of his approach. But his success on the battlefield was often undermined by his countrymen and allies. He had to deal with recurrent mutinies, particularly among the Lithuanian troops (Lithuania then formed part of Poland),

Above: King Michael Koributh of Poland. He bitterly disliked Sobieski, and attempted to hand over Polish independence to the Turks.

as well as with the political maneuverings of his generals. When the Turks began to menace Poland in 1672, Sobieski's warnings went unheeded. The king, Michael Koributh, hated Sobieski, and made a secret and humiliating treaty with the Sultan, which would have made Poland a Turkish dependency. This piece of treachery at last aroused the Poles to action. They rallied to Sobieski. In the most brilliant of his campaigns, he made a rapid offensive into Turkish-held territory and defeated the enemy at the fortress of Chocim in the Ukraine.

Right: a soldier in the uniform of Sobieski's light cavalrymen. The horse is unencumbered with armor to achieve maximum speed. The feathers made a loud noise when charging to terrify the enemy. The rider is armed with a battle ax, sword, and small round shield.

Following the death of King Michael the next year, Sobieski was elected king after the usual power struggle in the Diet. For a few years after his coronation the country was at peace. But the Turks were mobilizing again. Ostensibly in support of the Hungarians, who were rebelling against their Hapsburg masters, the Sultan's army advanced toward Vienna. King Louis XIV of France, who enjoyed trading advantages with the Turks, put pressure on Sobieski to remain neutral. But Sobieski, although he had no love for the Austrians, saw clearly that a Turkish occupation of Vienna would threaten all of Europe. He formed an alliance with Austria, and succeeded in raising 18,000 Polish troops. In Austria he was joined by allied forces drawn from all over the Holy Roman Empire. Together they moved against the Turks.

Sobieski intended to chase the foe through Hungary and ultimately, in his own words, "to hurl him back into the deserts, to exterminate him, to raise upon his ruins the Empire of Byzantium." But a combination of factors, chiefly mutiny among his troops, finally forced him to turn back to Poland. Still, the Turks were on the defensive, and other nations, including the Venetian Republic and Russia, now responded to Sobieski's call, and continued to push eastward.

Sobieski was continually at war with the Turks and at odds with the Polish nobility for the rest of his life. His own family was torn by rivalry between his sons, and his efforts to establish a hereditary succession, which might have checked Poland's disintegration, were a failure. After his death Poland fell prey to its European neighbors.

William of Orange
1650-1702

Had it not been for Louis XIV of France, William, Prince of Orange, might have spent his life tending his estates, collecting pictures, and hunting. His nation, the United Provinces of the Netherlands, finally achieved peace with Spain in 1648. The burghers who controlled its government were committed to maintaining that peace, and viewed the House of Orange as a potential threat to republicanism. A much greater threat – Louis XIV – was to force the Dutch to turn to William, as they had to his ancestors. Checking the territorial ambitions of the French king became William's driving purpose in life.

His mother was a Stuart, the daughter of

Charles I of England. She died when William was 10. He was made an orphan – his father having died shortly before his birth. A precocious child, he responded readily to the intensive, wide-ranging education given him.

He also received a practical education in the balance of power. He could observe the struggle going on in Holland between those who supported his family, and the anti-Orange party. When Louis XIV appropriated his family's tiny principality of Orange in southern France in 1660, he was enraged but impotent.

He was disillusioned still further when it became clear that his uncle, Charles II of England, was pursuing a pro-French policy, despite the opposition of his pro-Dutch Parliament, and was going to help Louis crush the Republic. In 1672, William was given temporary command of the badly-trained and equipped Dutch army. His 10,000 men were helpless against the powerful French war machine when it invaded the Provinces that same year. Three provinces fell to the invaders. The rest were saved only by means of flooding the countryside. This crisis intensified pro-Orange feeling. William was elected Stadholder of the United Provinces.

The first thing the 22-year-old Stadholder did was to reject the crippling peace terms offered by France and England. He then started enlisting allies and succeeded in winning over the Elector of Brandenburg, the Hapsburg Emperor, and the former enemy, Spain. Building up his army was the next move.

Although he was not much of a military strategist, William loved battle. Normally dour and withdrawn, he came alive on the battlefield. His personal courage won the respect of his foes, as well as his own men.

The war finally ended in 1678. Although France made significant gains elsewhere, it was forced to vacate the Dutch provinces. But Willaim realized that Louis' ambitions would not be so easily suppressed. He worked tirelessly to build a solid alliance against the French, and meanwhile kept an anxious eye on England.

In 1677 he married his young cousin Mary Stuart, daughter of the King's brother James. Life in the Netherlands suited Mary, and she eventually came to love her less than attentive husband. She shared his alarm when her father, a Catholic convert, became King and began to put Catholics in high offices, contrary to the existing laws. James' high-handed treatment of Parliament and the Anglican Establishment rekindled old fears of popery in England at the very moment when Huguenot exiles were telling

horror stories about persecution in France. In 1688, James' second wife gave birth to a son, raising the prospect of a Catholic succession. Soon afterwards, a group of English nobles appealed to William to invade their country, and restore their liberties.

Above: William of Orange becomes William III of England as he and his wife, Mary, are crowned joint monarchs at their coronation in 1688.

now arm himself with English manpower, sea-power, and wealth for his struggle against France. But he would reign as a constitutional monarch. Parliament enacted a Bill of Rights, defining strict limits to a sovereign's power. So the "Glorious" Revolution of 1688 was accomplished.

William was not very popular with the English aristocracy. They resented his coterie of Dutch advisors and intimates. For his part, he found their political struggles tedious. Until the Queen's early death in 1694 he tended to leave the conduct of domestic affairs in her hands, while he pursued his military campaigns. Early in his reign he defeated an Irish force fighting for James at the decisive Battle of the Boyne. A French naval defeat off La Hogue, in the Channel, put an end to Louis' attempts to put James back on the English throne. But war against France continued on the Continent. When peace came in 1697, Louis recognized William as King of England. He had a certain amount of respect for the man who had succeeded in uniting nearly all Europe against him, and whom he had been fighting, off and on, for 25 years. The two kings exchanged ambassadors and temporarily reached agreement on the vexing question of the Spanish succession.

Leading an army of many nationalities, William landed on the coast of Devon five months later. He headed for London. Stunned by defections among his erstwhile supporters and even among his family, James failed to muster any resistance. He was allowed to escape to France.

After lengthy discussion, the specially convened Parliament offered the crown to both William and Mary. They became the only joint sovereigns in English history. William could

Above: William pictured at the Battle of the Boyne in 1689. He defeated an Irish force supporting the claims of the deposed English king, James II. Many Northern Ireland protestants still refer to William affectionately as "King Billy."

Louis' acceptance of the Spanish crown in 1700 revived the possibility of a French-dominated Europe. William quickly formed another coalition against him, the Grand Alliance. Before hostilities got underway he died.

From the childless king the crown passed to Mary's sister Anne. Under her brilliant general, the Duke of Marlborough, the Allies finally achieved William's goal. The balance of power in Europe was restored.

Sir Robert Walpole
1676~1745

Commons, to secure the Hanoverian succession to the throne, and to build the nation's prosperity.

When Walpole was first elected to the House of Commons in 1701 as the Member for Castle Rising, Norfolk, the political scene was dominated by strife between the Whigs and the Tories. These two parties had collaborated in the Revolution of 1688, but the Whigs had since come to regard themselves as the guardians of hard-won liberties against royal absolutism. Meanwhile,

His contemporaries called Sir Robert Walpole a "Prime Minister." They were not referring to his office, for no such office existed in the early 18th century. "Prime Minister" was a term of abuse used by the opposition, who resented Walpole's concentration of power in his own hands. As First Lord of the Treasury, Chancellor of the Exchequer, and effective leader of the House of Commons between 1721 and 1742, he was by far the most important man in the government. He used his power to bring stability to government, and his strengthening of the ties between the ministry and the Commons helped to shape the modern British Parliamentary system.

Walpole was a consummate politician. He was a master at parliamentary debate. He cultivated the manner of the bluff, earthy country squire (which, superficially, he was) to win over the numerous members of that species who inhabited the Commons. At the same time, he enjoyed the life of a wealthy, sophisticated epicurean and confidant of royalty. Apart from his love of power for its own sake, Walpole was motivated by a desire to secure the constitutional gains of 1688. These provided for a balance of power between King, Lords, and

the Tories cherished a certain sympathy for the notion of divine right monarchy and – among some members – for the exiled Stuart Pretender. It was mainly due to Whig pressure that the crown passed, after the death of Queen Anne, to the Protestant Elector of Hanover, George I. Once the Hanoverians were installed on the throne, Tory influence dwindled, and the political battles tended to be fought between one group of Whigs and another.

During Queen Anne's reign, the young Walpole was ousted from his post of Treasurer of the Navy by an incoming Tory government, and was briefly imprisoned in the Tower for supposed corruption. A few years later, he was back in power, and had the satisfaction of helping to bring about the impeachment for treason of his Tory adversaries the Earl of Oxford and Viscount Bolingbroke.

Political infighting among the Whigs during the first years of George I's reign temporarily put Walpole into the opposition. His biggest achievement during this period was the defeat of the Peerage Bill. This government measure would have curbed the royal prerogative to create new peers and thus made the House of

Lords more independent of the king, and, indirectly, of the Commons.

In 1720 Walpole was back in the government in a minor post. He had his great opportunity a year later in the scandal of the South Sea Bubble. The South Sea Company had assumed a large part of the national debt, offering shares of its stock in return. A frenzy of speculative buying forced up the price of the stock to many times its value. Inevitably, people began to sell. In the ensuing panic it was revealed that most of the ministry and the Court were involved in the scheme. Walpole, who had opposed it, was made First Lord of the Treasury and Chancellor, and was entrusted with the difficult task of sorting out the chaos. His political and financial exper-

Above: this satirical print criticises Walpol's role in the "War of Jenkin's Ear." This conflict with Spain was badly mismanaged, and much of the blame was heaped on Walpole.

Above left: the "South Sea Bubble" by Ward from the Tate Gallery, London. It was Walpole who was called upon to sort out the financial mess after the South Sea Company collapsed.

Left: the trade label of the South Sea Company.

tise helped to prevent a general blood-letting, and restored Britain's credit.

The accession of George II to the throne in 1727 strengthened Walpole's position. This was mainly thanks to the friendship and support of the astute Queen Caroline. To the outrage of his opponents, Walpole packed the government with his friends and relatives. His brother-in-law, Lord Townshend, served as Secretary of State for foreign affairs until, in 1730, Walpole took foreign affairs into his own hands.

Although most of the opposition to Walpole centered on his unprecedented power, rather than his policies, there was considerable discontent over his foreign policy. To promote the nation's prosperity he steadfastly kept taxes low and avoided war. "*Quieta non movere*," "Let sleeping dogs lie," was his motto. The opposition claimed that he was careless of Britain's interests, making it the dupe of France and the prey of Spain, whose coast guard in Spanish America was harassing British merchant ships. When a

sea captain named Jenkins produced, in the House of Commons, a shrivelled ear which he claimed to have been cut from his own head by Spaniards, patriotic fervor erupted. Walpole reluctantly agreed to a war with Spain. The War of Jenkins' Ear was the prelude to Britain's involvement in a wider European conflict. It was also the beginning of the end for Walpole. The war was mismanaged, and Walpole bore the brunt of the resulting criticism.

In 1742 a series of defeats on minor issues in the Commons revealed that Walpole had lost the support he needed to carry on governing. He offered his resignation, was given a peerage, and retired to his magnificent country house, Houghton Hall, where he died three years later.

Peter the Great
1672-1725

Russia was still a feudal country in the late 17th century. Tirelessly, relentlessly, Peter the Great bullied the Russian people into building a state that could compete with the advanced nations of the West.

His father, the Czar Alexis, died when Peter was only four years old. The six year reign of his elder half-brother Theodore was followed by a bloody power struggle. At the end of this Peter and another half-brother, Ivan, were proclaimed joint czars. The actual governing of the country was done by Ivan's sister Sophia, while Peter was left to spend his time playing soldier with his servants, learning crafts such as carpentry, metal-work, and masonry, and visiting Moscow's "German" quarters. Here he conversed – and caroused – with foreigners, and began to acquire a knowledge of western ways.

Peter's active rule began in 1695 with the resumption of the war against Turkey. The sickly Ivan died the following year. Peter attacked Azov, a Turkish fortress on the Black Sea, and took it. To secure and exploit his conquest he ordered the colonization of the area, and the building of Russia's first naval station.

Peter took a passionate interest in sailing and seapower. His country had no navy, so he built one. On an incognito visit to Holland in 1697 he worked as an apprentice shipwright. Peter be-

Right: a print depicting the centenary celebrations of St Petersburg. Now rechristened Leningrad, many of the early buildings were inspired by Peter himself. He made St Petersburg the Russian capital, which it remained until the Bolshevik revolution of 1917.

Below left: Peter the Great in the costume of a Dutch sailor.

Below: this ship was rebuilt by order of the young Peter. He later employed his own carpenters, and built a number of ships himself to strengthen Russia's naval power. The ship pictured here was nicknamed "the Grandfather of the Russian Fleet."

lieved in learning things from the ground up. Even before this trip he had begun luring foreign shipbuilders to Russia and scouring his own country for carpenters to work under them. By 1699 14 warships had been built.

But Russia still had no outlet to the Baltic, where its ancient enemy Sweden held sway. The day Peter learned of the signing of a peace treaty with Turkey, he declared war on Sweden. This

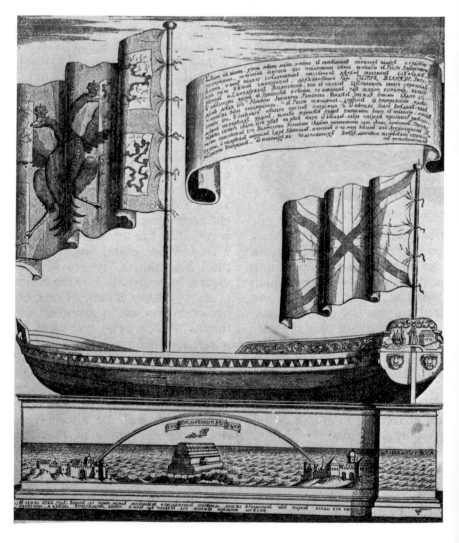

The aristocracy benefitted from new laws increasing their hold on the serfs. But they were also compelled to work for the state. Compulsory service in the army, navy, or government was usually preceded by obligatory education abroad. The character of the aristocracy was changed by Peter's establishment of his "table of ranks." According to this every officer or official had to work his way upward. Status depended not on birth but on rank. By moving up into the top eight ranks, a person of middle or even lower-class origins could become a member of Peter's aristocracy.

All classes resented the highhanded and often brutal methods adopted by the Czar in furthering his vision of the new Russia. Many people pinned their hopes on Peter's son Alexis, who was his exact opposite – lazy, uninterested in

hasty move soon revealed the relative weakness of his army. At the Baltic port of Narva, in November 1700, a Swedish force of 8000 men routed 40,000 Russians. Peter was not put off by this. He began a thoroghgoing reform of his army, borrowing the expertise of foreign officers, and providing it with improved weapons manufactured by his new munitions industry. He was aided, inadvertently, by the decision of the Swedish king, Charles XII, to concentrate on furthering Swedish interests in Poland. The Russians captured Narva and the surrounding territory of Ingria. In 1703 Peter founded, at the mouth of the River Neva, a new city called St. Petersburg (now Leningrad).

War with Sweden continued until 1721. Peter took part in many of its battles himself, including that of Poltava, in the Ukraine (1709), where his army virtually wiped out the Swedish forces. By the end of the war Russia controlled the eastern shores of the Baltic.

While pursuing the war, Peter also set about transforming the Russian economy, church, and government. Dozens of iron works were built, and the manufacture of textiles increased considerably. By the end of his reign foreign trade had grown sevenfold. To encourage trade, Peter made townspeople independent of provincial governors, and let them elect their own municipalities. Eventually, the whole structure of the government, central and regional, was reorganized under Peter's direction. He abolished the office of the Patriarch of the Russian Orthodox Church and replaced it with the Holy Synod, a body subordinate to the Czar. Clergy were required to impress on their flock their duty of obedience to the Czar.

Indeed, the people had little option. Compulsion was a key feature of Peter's rule. Forced labor on a vast scale was recruited for his many projects. Twenty thousand had died building one canal. The new capital of St. Petersburg – a city dear to Peter's heart even when it was still merely a frontier outpost – was the graveyard of thousands of Russian workers.

Above: soldiers of Peter the Great's army. The emperor used brutal methods, and often resorted to military force, in building Russia into a world power. The soldiers shown here are clean-shaven. Peter made soldiers and civilians alike shave off their beards as part of his program to westernize Russian civilization.

warfare, and hostile to his father's reforms. In 1718 Peter issued a manifesto barring Alexis from the succession. Then he ordered an investigation of Alexis' associations, and possible complicity in a plot against himself. On the basis of confessions obtained under torture, Alexis was found guilty of treason and sentenced to death. He died in prison, supposedly of apoplexy.

Peter's own death was precipitated by an act of heroism. Spotting a shipwreck while on a voyage, he plunged into the icy water to help rescue the men, and became ill as a result. He died three months later.

His wife Catherine, who succeeded him, was left with an empire stretching from the Baltic to the Pacific Ocean – the result of continued eastward expansion during his reign. It also included provinces on the Caspian Sea taken from Persia in 1723. The machinery for autocratic rule in the empire had been enormously strengthened. Technologically and militarily it had caught up with western Europe. Culturally, its upper classes now looked west. But the millions of Russian peasants, shackled even more firmly to their masters than before, remained untouched by western ideas. Any changes in their conditions would have to wait for nearly 200 years.

Frederick William, Elector of Brandenburg 1620~1688

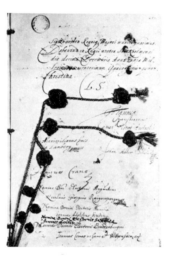

Left: a contemporary portrait of Frederick-William, the Elector of Brandenburg.

Above: the treaty document confirming the Peace of Westphalia of 1648. The military force available to Frederick-William at this time was the embryo of Prussian military might.

Above right: a banquet held on September 22, 1649 in Nuremburg Town Hall to celebrate peace after the end of the Thirty Years' War. Frederick-William is seated at the head of the table.

Frederick William was born to the Elector of Brandenburg and his wife, a grand-daughter of William the Silent in 1620. As the eldest son, Frederick William was heir to Brandenburg, a medium-sized German state whose capital, Berlin, was then an undistinguished provincial town. The duchy of East Prussia, a German territory on the Baltic, which had recently been inherited by the Brandenburg branch of the Hohenzollerns; and a few small states in western Germany would also be his. Of these scattered possessions Frederick William was to form a state that would play an influential role in European politics.

But as a child, he must have wondered whether this inheritance would ever be his. The Thirty Years' War, began two years before his birth, and was raging through Brandenburg. He was sent to a fortress for safety, and spent most of his childhood there. At the age of 14 he went to live in the Dutch Republic, then in its golden age. He studied at the Leyden University, and also spent some time at the court of the stadtholder, Prince Frederick Henry. His four years in Holland had given him a great respect for Dutch commercial and cultural achievements, which he later tried to emulate in his own country.

Frederick William became Elector of Brandenburg in 1640. It was a wasteland. Berlin's population had shrunk from 14,000 to 6,000. Hundreds

of villages had been destroyed. The countryside was plundered by foreign soldiers, and packs of wolves marauded.

The first thing the new Elector did was to extricate his country from a recently-formed alliance with the Emperor and signed an armistice with Sweden, thus achieving a state of neutrality. But for a country with no natural boundaries, a declaration of neutrality was scant protection. Frederick William realized that in order to be secure he must have an army. The few mercenaries that had suffered in the past would not be good enough. A well-trained standing army under his own control was what was needed. By the time the Peace of Westphalia was being formulated he had an army of 8,000 men. This was not large, but it gave him some bargaining power. He acquired eastern Pomerania and several other German territories without actually having made any conquests.

The Brandenburg army was the embryo of the formidable military machine that would later conquer in the name of Prussia, of the German Empire, and finally of Hitler's Third Reich. Small as it was in 1656, when it first saw action in a battle against the Poles, it was the first institution to link the Elector's various possessions. Men of Prussia, Brandenburg, and the other states served in it. The rudiments of a national consciousness were forged. By drawing his officers almost entirely from the landed aristocracy, or *Junkers*, Frederick William established a tradition of militarism among the north German nobility that endured into this century.

During his lifetime, and that of his son and grandson, Frederick William's army seldom fought anybody. He used it mainly as a lever in his convoluted foreign policy. In his efforts to preserve the balance of power and further the interests of Brandenburg-Prussia, he changed sides with dizzying agility. His last alliance was with his nephew, William of Orange, to counter French aggression in the Netherlands.

To stimulate the economy Frederick William actively encouraged immigration by foreigners, such as Polish Jews and French Huguenots, who brought valuable commercial and industrial skills with them. The growth of industry was influenced greatly by the needs of the army. Munitions and textiles took the lead. Many government-sponsored projects were launched to increase income from the crown domains. These made necessary the expansion of the civil service. In the face of opposition from the provincial estates, Frederick William established his right to impose and collect taxes to finance the army. By the time of his death, this institution num-

Right: African natives from the colony of Gross Friedrichburg present gifts to Frederick-William at the port of Stettin in 1682.

Below: Frederick-William and his forces besieging the eastern German port of Stralsund in 1678 during his war against the Swedes.

bered 28,000 well equipped men.

The Great Elector – as he was called after winning a spectacular victory over the Swedes in 1675 – never achieved his goal of annexing western Pomerania, with its coveted port of Stettin (now Szczecin). But he did create an efficiently-run state. His descendants, who bore the title King of Prussia, would wield absolute power in a state that was to include all Germany.

Nadir Shah
1688-1747

Nadir Kuli, "the slave of the Wonderful" – that is, of God. But there was nothing subservient in the character of this formidable soldier who drove Afghan and Turkish invaders out of Persia, and appropriated the legendary jewel-encrusted Peacock Throne of the Mogul Empire.

Nadir was of humble origins. He was born into a family of nomads in Khorasan, in northeastern Persia, and tended sheep as a child. After his father died, Nadir and his mother were captured by Uzbeks and taken north as slaves. He escaped and returned to Persia where he entered the service of a minor provincial governor.

It was not until he was in his 30s that Nadir began his military career. He had married the governor's daughter and become governor himself. Persia was ruled by Afghan invaders at this time, the 1720s. It was in their service that Nadir led an army against Uzbek raiders. When he claimed his promised reward, a high government position, he was beaten and dismissed.

While he was an outlaw, Nadir started to recruit his own army. He then offered his services to Shah Tahmasp, a surviving member of the Safavid dynasty, deposed by the Afghans.

Above: an ambassador from the last Safavid king, Sultan Husain, before Louis XIV at Versailles on February 19, 1715. The sultan surrendered to the Afghans, against whom Nadir Shah fought. His son was supported by Nadir Shah.

Left: an 18th century Persian portrait of Nadir Shah.

Right: this contemporary Persian painting depicts the capture of Delhi in 1739. Nadir Shah is shown at the center of the picture.

Bottom right: the assassination of Nadir Shah in 1747. Surprised in his sleep by a group of his own tribesmen, Nadir Shah killed two of his attackers before he was himself stabbed to death.

Nadir and his army fought the Afghans for three years, finally expelling them in 1730.

Shah Tahmasp rewarded his commander-in-chief by making him governor of Khorasan and several other eastern provinces. There, Nadir's power was virtually total. His next job was to drive the Turks from western Persia, which they had invaded during the Afghan rule. His successes against the Turks were undermined by the Shah himself, whose own military efforts were ineffectual, and who agreed to a disadvantageous treaty with the Turks. Nadir deposed Tahmasp and installed the Shah's young son, making himself regent. In the meantime he sent a message to the Turks: "Restore the provinces of Persia or prepare for war."

The war with Turkey lasted until 1735, and Persia regained considerable territory. Shortly afterwards, Nadir threatened Russia that unless it returned the provinces on the Caspian Sea that Peter the Great had taken, then he would form an alliance with the Turks against Russia. The provinces were returned.

On the death of the young Shah in 1736, Nadir summoned the leading Persian officials and invited them to choose a new ruler. Surrounded by all the evidence of his power, they unanimoulsy voted him the crown. Nadir allowed himself to be persuaded.

The country was impoverished. So it was mainly for plunder that Nadir Shah began marching his army eastward. He made several conquests in neighboring Afghanistan before moving into India, where the once great Mogul Empire was in a state of decadence. Even with considerable military support from one of his princes, the Mogul Emperor could not resist the Persians, and he was forced to surrender. Nadir Shah entered Delhi in triumph and graciously accepted the accumulated wealth of the Moguls, including the celebrated Peacock Throne. When the people of Delhi rebelled, Nadir's army crushed it in an orgy of plunder and killing.

The spoils of the Indian campaign made Persia temporarily solvent. But Nadir Shah had no talent for administration, and he failed to use his newly-won treasure to stimulate the economy. He made several more conquests, and in 1743 began building a navy. With the help of shipwrights and sailors from England, Portugal, and India, he soon had a small fleet in the Caspian Sea and the Persian Gulf.

Nadir Shah became increasingly cruel with age. On one of his campaigns he was ambushed and wounded by two Afghans. Convinced that his son was behind this assassination attempt, Nadir had him blinded. Insurrections against his rule – and there were many – were suppressed

with extreme violence, culminating in the building of a pyramid of heads. While encamped during one of these punitive expeditions Nadir was surprised in his sleep by some of his own tribesmen. Reaching for his sword he killed two of his assailants before another struck him dead.

This humble Khorasan nomad was known to his people as "the Conqueror" when he was king. He made Persia a power to be reckoned with. As Iran it is a powerful industrial nation today. But Nadir Shah had no interest in, and showed no flair for, internal administration. The job of keeping together the nation he had done so much to build had to be left to those around him with a talent for government.

Clive of India
1725-1774

The young Robert Clive sailed for India in 1743 without much enthusiasm – let alone a spirit of adventure. His father, an impoverished country squire and lawyer, had secured him a job as a junior clerk with the flourishing East India Company. In the end, Clive not only achieved spectacular personal success, he also laid the foundations of the British Raj.

After a 14-month voyage Clive disembarked at Fort St. George, Madras, then the most important of the English trading settlements in India. The French and Dutch also had settlements along the Indian eastern coast. By this time, the Mogul Empire, which had ruled India for 200 years, was in decline, and conflicts erupted between rival Indian princes. The European powers exploited these conflicts to further their own interests.

Above: Robert Clive with part of his 800-strong force holding Arcot after relieving Ali, the British candidate for the Carnatic throne, from a besieging French force.

Left: a portrait of Robert Clive in middle age.

France and Britain were at war in Europe. In 1746, the French captured Fort St. George. Clive escaped to another English settlement, Fort St. David, where he volunteered for service in the East India Company's army. He took part in a number of engagements before peace was restored and Madras returned to the British in 1748.

Through their support of rival claimants to the throne of the Carnatic, the state in which

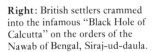

Right: British settlers crammed into the infamous "Black Hole of Calcutta" on the orders of the Nawab of Bengal, Siraj-ud-daula.

Madras was located, the conflict between the French and the British was kept alive. Clive re-entered military service, this time to fight for the British candidate, Mohammed Ali. He was put in command of about 800 men. French-supported troops were besieging Ali in the capital, Arcot. Clive was to lead an expedition to draw them away. He easily captured Arcot, withstood a two-month siege by the returned enemy forces, and finally – out-numbered by about 20 to one – repulsed them. This extraordinary feat made Clive's name. After two more years of fighting, Mohammed Ali was made Nawab, or prince, of the Carnatic. French power in India was broken. From now on the British were in control.

As Commissary for the army, Clive was making substantial profits. By the time of his marriage in 1753 he had amassed £40,000. He and his bride Margaret returned to England, where as the hero of Arcot he was a celebrity, but failed to win a seat in Parliament. He returned to India in 1756 as Deputy Governor of Fort St. David.

Soon after arriving he was given command of an expedition to Calcutta, which had recently been captured by the aggressive new Nawab of Bengal, Siraj-ud-daula. It was during this attack that between 40 and 70 settlers were crammed into the notorious "Black Hole," a tiny cell where about half of them died. Clive recaptured Cal-

cutta, and pursued the Nawab inland. A Bengali conspiracy to dethrone the Nawab made Clive's job easier. His little army defeated those of the Nawab's troops that remained loyal at Plassey. A new Nawab was installed soon afterwards.

Neither Clive nor his associates in the East India Company were then thinking in terms of

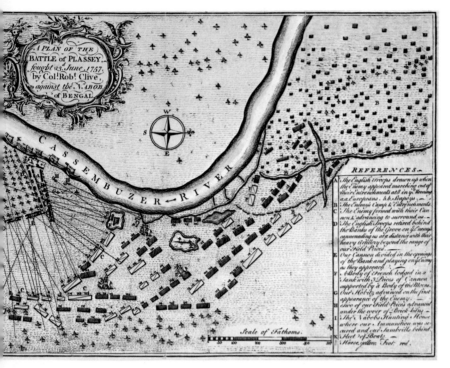

out his combative tendencies. Despite a bitter quarrel with its Chairman, he was once again appointed Governor of Bengal in 1764.

During this last term of office Clive won from the Mogul Emperor, the *diwani*, the right to collect the revenues of Bengal and the adjoining provinces of Oudh and Orissa. Anything left over after all governmental expenses had been met would go to the Company. The figurehead Mogul was content with a generous allowance. This profitable arrangement also had symbolic value. It gave the stamp of legitimacy to the growing British power in India.

For two years Clive ably administered his territory, then in 1767 left India for the last time. He had amassed a great fortune in India, as had other Company men. The British public became increasingly critical of these "Nabobs", as they were called. In 1772 a Parliamentary Committee was set up to investigate irregular financial dealings in India. Clive's enemies made the most of the chance to blacken his name, and as their campaign gained momentum it looked as though he might be required to surrender his fortune. Clive defended himself eloquently. Finally the charge that he had obtained funds illegally was dropped. Then the Commons passed a resolution applauding his "great and meritorious services to this country."

empire building. They simply wanted to continue to make large profits with no interference from the locals. It was almost by accident that, little by little, the British began to extend their control in India. As leader of the only effective

Above: the battle plane of Plassey where a force commanded by Robert Clive defeated the Nawab on June 23 1757.

Above: Robert Clive and Mir Jaffa meet face to face after the battle of Plassey.

Right: An official of the East India Company enjoys a traditional expression of hospitality – a water pipe. It was Robert Clive who was largely responsible for securing the company's interests on the Indian sub-continent. The British Raj was born.

military force in Bengal, Clive had power over the Nawab, though he had his hands full dealing with Indian intrigues, plus occasional challenges from the French and the Dutch.

Returning to England in 1760, after serving two years as Governor of Bengal, Clive won a seat in Parliament, and was made an Irish baron. Politics within the East India Company brought

For more than 20 years Clive had suffered intermittently from acute abdominal pains. His health improved during a trip to Italy in 1773, but the following autumn, he had an exceptionally severe attack, and in his agony slit his throat.

William Pitt the Elder
1708-1788

Left: Pitt the Elder, Earl of Chatham, from a painting in the National Portrait Gallery, London.

Below: Frederick, Prince of Wales. Pitt's friend, he was also his ally against Walpole.

"I know that I can save this country and that no one else can." The supreme self-confidence of these words – spoken by William Pitt soon after the outbreak of the Seven Years' War – turned out to be justified. This mercurial, domineering man gave Britain a badly-needed coherent war policy and led it to victory.

Pitt entered politics in 1735 as Member of Parliament for the sparsely populated borough of Old Sarum, Wiltshire, which his family controlled. He soon took his place among those Whigs opposed to the long rule of Sir Robert Walpole, who, they claimed, was giving Britain's interests second place to those of the king's electorate, Hanover. Taking advantage of the bitter enmity between George II and his son, they grouped themselves around the Prince of Wales, and looked forward to better things in the next reign. This hope was frustrated by the Prince's death in 1751.

Right: King George II. He and his son, Frederick Prince of Wales, detested each other.

Pitt quickly gained a reputation as a firebrand with his attacks on Walpole and the king. After Walpole's resignation in 1742 the Prince's faction – still out in the cold – condemned the new ministry for its handling of the War of the Austrian Succession. Pitt was scathingly critical of the pouring of money into the protection of Hanover to the neglect of the war against France. "It is now apparent," he told the House of Commons, "that this great, this powerful, this formidable Kingdom is considered only as a province of a despicable electorate."

Pitt's ardent patriotism won him great popularity among the British. The merchants of the City of London were particularly keen on him. Their signs, like his own, were fixed on the growing empire overseas. Another reason for Pitt's public esteem was his integrity. In 1746 the king was prevailed upon to give Pitt, whom he naturally loathed, the post of Paymaster to the forces. By tradition this job entitled its holder to various gifts and commissions, all of which Pitt refused, living modestly on the basic salary.

For the next nine years, through occasional shifts in the government, Pitt continued as Paymaster. He married Lady Hester Grenville when he was 46. The marriage was to tie him even more closely to this politically influential family, as well as bring him personal happiness.

War was again brewing in 1775, and Pitt resumed his criticism of the Continent-centered foreign policy that had so dismally failed in the previous war. He was dismissed from his job for his pains. When war broke out between Britain and France, the weakness of the government became apparent. The Mediterranean island of Minorca was lost through ineptitude in Westminster. A public outcry resulted, and a new

ministry was formed, with Pitt as Secretary of State.

Once in office, Pitt surprised everyone by continuing subsidies to Hanover and to Frederick II of Prussia, who was fighting an alliance of France, Austria, and Russia. But he realized that the defeat of France overseas – his primary object – depended partly on keeping it busy in Europe. In recent years the French had become very powerful in India and North America. They now controlled the Great Lakes and were constantly extending their possessions.

Pitt countered the French threat with an intensive, aggressive use of naval power. The British Navy blockaded the French coast, captured several French colonies in West Africa,

the West Indies, and gave support to the East India Company in India. Pitt especially concentrated on the campaign in North America, and showered detailed directives on his newly appointed commanding officers. One of these, General James Wolfe, led a daring night advance up the heights of the city of Quebec, and on the following day defeated the French in a 15 minute battle. By the next year, 1760, Britain had conquered Canada.

In that same year the old king died and his grandson George III came to the throne. Pitt soon found himself at odds with the new monarch and with his chief advisor, the Earl of Bute. Both seemed bent on ending the war as soon as possible. Differences over the conduct of the war and the peace negotiations led Pitt to resign in 1761. By the Peace of Paris, signed in 1763, France regained several of its former possessions and kept its fishing rights in Canada – concessions bitterly opposed by Pitt in the Commons. But Britain's supremacy in India and North America was firmly established.

Pitt had had his finest hour, but he remained in politics. In 1766, George III asked him to form a new government. He was created Earl of Chatham. His brief ministry was not a success. The art of political maneuvering was never his forte. He was frequently ill with the gout and with manic-depressive phases, referred to as "gout in the head." In April 1778 he made his final appearance in the House of Lords, so ill he could hardly stand. Though long sympathetic to the grievances of the American Colonists, he

Above: this print depicts the British capturing Quebec from the French in September 1759.

Below: Pitt the Elder collapses in the House of Lords in 1788.

resolutely opposed their independence. It was with some of his old style that he now attacked a proposal to withdraw British troops from the Colonies. Then he collapsed in his chair. A month later he was dead.

Frederick the Great
1712-1786

Frederick II had an unhappy childhood. His father, King Frederick William I, was a coarse, brutal man. He suffered from porphyria, the same disease that afflicted King George III of England. His sufferings goaded him into uncontrollable rages. Young Frederick was a handy victim. The recipient of innumerable kickings and beatings, he was also treated with psychological cruelty. When he tried to escape to England at the age of 18, the king had his friend and accomplice, a young army officer named Katte, sentenced to death for attempted desertion. Frederick was forced to watch the execution.

After a period of probation Frederick was par-

doned by his father, and given his own residence outside Berlin. There, away from the disapproving parental eye, he could indulge his love of literature, music, and philosophy. Culturally, Frederick was an ardent francophile. He spoke and wrote French fluently, German only brokenly. He was profoundly influenced by the writings of the Enlightenment. This 18th century philosophical movement's main characteristics were a belief in reason and natural law, and a skeptical attitude toward organized religion. Frederick himself was to become the embodiment of the "enlightened despot" – an absolute monarch who governs with wisdom and benevolence.

Within a few weeks of becoming king in 1740 Frederick abolished press censorship, religious

Below left: a contemporary portrait of Frederick the Great.

Below: Frederick the Great enters Berlin at the end of March, 1763. The Peace of Hubertusberg had been signed on February 15 of that year.

discrimination, and torture. He later reformed and codified the laws. The death penalty was only to be inflicted for the most serious crimes by the personal order of the king, who often waived it. Although he ruled absolutely, Frederick did not consider himself the personification of the state, as Louis XIV of France did, but rather its "first servant." Like Louis, he had an enormous capacity for work. He never spared himself, even when in later years he suffered from many ailments. "One does as one wishes with the body," he said, "when the soul says quick march it obeys."

Frederick had inherited a fine army. He soon showed that he meant to use it. Later in life he was to feel keenly the horrors of war, but at 28 he was eager for glory and intent on enlarging and enriching his nation. Scarcely had Maria Theresa come into her inheritance when, with-

out warning Frederick, marched his army into neighboring Silesia, one of the richest of the Hapsburg lands. He took it in seven weeks. The invasion was the first phase of the many-sided conflict that involved most of Europe between 1740 and 1748, and is known as the War of the Austrian Succession. In this war France, Bavaria, and other nations joined Prussia in trying to dismember the Hapsburg Empire. During it Frederick revealed a talent not only for warfare but also for duplicity. Anxious to prevent French domination of Germany, he betrayed the plans of his ally to the Austrians. By the Treaty of Breslau, in 1742, Prussia retained nearly all of Silesia. Later, Prussia reentered the war, and after a few reversals emerged with its earlier gains intact.

After the Treaty of Dresden, in 1745, Frederick enjoyed 11 years of peace. At his magnifi-

Above: Frederick's friend von Katte is executed. Frederick can be seen witnessing the execution from a window.

cent palace of Sans Souci he entertained leading wits, writers, and musicians (including the great Johann Sebastian Bach), practiced his flute, and wrote several books. Voltaire lived at Sans Souci for a while, but he and Frederick brought out the worst in each other. Their friendship ended in a rather squalid row in 1753, and their relationship was never completely repaired. Women were not very welcome at Sans Souci. With a few notable exceptions Frederick disliked their company. His Queen, Elizabeth Christine, had a separate court of her own and rarely saw her husband. They had no children.

In 1756 the pattern of European alliances changed radically when France and Austria signed a pact. One of the provisions was that France would help her new ally recapture Silesia. Russia, with her eye on East Prussia, joined the coalition. So did Sweden and Saxony. Proceeding on the principle that the best defense is offense, Frederick invaded Saxony. It finally capitulated, but Frederick found himself very much on the defensive against the new alliance, with only one strong ally, Great Britain.

Britain, which had its own quarrel with France, provided large subsidies, but the fighting in Europe was done by Frederick's army. He proved himself a brilliant strategist and won several important victories early in the war. But as time went on it looked as though the formidable coalition would be too strong for him. After one disastrous battle he contemplated suicide. The following year, 1760, the Austrians occupied Berlin.

Frederick's luck changed dramatically when, in 1762, the Russian Empress died. Her successor, Peter III, idolized Frederick, and promptly changed sides. France then withdrew from the war, having lost much of her overseas empire to Britain while fighting Prussia at the same time. Soon, only Austria and Saxony remained. Exhausted and impoverished, they agreed to peace terms restoring the *status quo ante bellum*. So, in 1763, the Seven Years' War came to an end.

Frederick devoted himself as energetically to rebuilding his country's economy as he had to expanding its boundaries – though his agricultural reforms and industrial projects were only moderately successful. The fertility and industry of Silesia were a great asset. In 1772, in the first partition of Poland, Frederick acquired West Prussia, thus joining his eastern and western dominions (apart from a few small scattered possessions). Always alert to the possibility of war, he built up his army to its former strength and maintained it in a constant state of readiness. It was while reviewing his troops in the rain that "Old Fritz" – as he was affectionately known by his soldiers – caught the chill that precipitated his final illness.

His nephew, Frederick William II, inherited a nation that was now the strongest in Germany, destined to become ever more powerful in the years to come.

Maria Theresa
1717-1780

Long before the Hapsburg Emperor Charles VI died in 1740, the Holy Roman Empire had virtually ceased to exist as a meaningful political entity. But the Hapsburgs had meanwhile acquired another empire. This embraced not only Austria but the kingdoms of Hungary and Bohemia, large parts of Italy, and the former Spanish Netherlands as well. Charles's heir was his daughter Maria Theresa, then a young woman of 23. Being a woman, she could not wear the crown of the Holy Roman Empire. But Charles had gone to some lengths to obtain the pledges of other European rulers that they would respect her right to inherit all the Hapsburg domains intact.

Maria Theresa was soon to discover how meaningless these promises were. Frederick II of Prussia invaded Silesia within a month of her accession. Six months later, Austria itself was invaded by the French, and shortly after by the Elector of Bavaria, who was later made Holy

Roman Emperor. Spain attacked Hapsburg lands in Italy. Many of the Queen's own nobility were siding with the invaders. Her treasury was empty, and her army at half strength.

Maria Theresa faced disaster. But she showed courage and tenacity. Against the advice of her elderly ministers, who feared an insurrection if the Hungarians were allowed to arm, she appealed for help to the Hungarian Diet. Her speech was eloquent and reasonable, and probably combined with the sight of a beautiful woman in distress had the desired effect. The Hungarian Diet rose to their feet to acclaim their Queen. They also voted her an army.

Far right: this illustration shows the death of Maria Theresa. She is seated third left. It was in her son Joseph's arms that she died of a lung infection. He is kneeling beside her.

Left: Maria Theresa with her husband Francis. Out of her 13 children only Crown Prince Joseph appears in this picture.

Right: Maria Theresa reviews her troops at Heidelberg on 28 September 1745. Her forces were fighting on a number of fronts at this time, and were overstretched.

With this help and with subsidies from Britain and the Dutch Republic, Maria Theresa's forces fought on several fronts for eight years. She made some mistakes, particularly in giving important commands to second-rate generals, such as her husband Francis. But her perseverance was matched with luck. The war against Britain had decisively weakened France. When those two nations agreed to peace in 1748, the War of the Austrian Succession ended too. Maria Theresa was bitterly disappointed at not regaining Silesia, but she held on to the rest of her empire. It could have been worse.

She emerged from the war a confident, capable ruler. Her husband was now Holy Roman Emperor, but it was the Empress who ruled – with

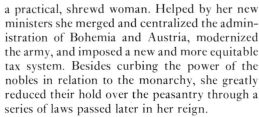

the occasional interruption of childbirth. She had 13 children. Intensely domestic, and more than a little possessive of her wayward husband, she was also skilled in using tears and scenes to get her way. But behind the dramatics, she was

Above: the Schloss Schönbrunn palace, home of Maria Theresa. The Hofburg Palace in Vienna was her other home.

a practical, shrewd woman. Helped by her new ministers she merged and centralized the administration of Bohemia and Austria, modernized the army, and imposed a new and more equitable tax system. Besides curbing the power of the nobles in relation to the monarchy, she greatly reduced their hold over the peasantry through a series of laws passed later in her reign.

Maria Theresa's most able minister, Prince Wenzel Anton von Kaunitz, shared her determination to win back Silesia. He engineered the reversal of alliances that joined Austria to her traditional enemy France. When war came, in 1756, it was, like the previous one, fought on many fronts. Factors beyond Kaunitz' control eventually led to the withdrawal of both France

and Austria's other strong ally, Russia. The retaking of Silesia, which for a while seemed a certainty, had to be abandoned.

After the death of Francis in 1765 Maria Theresa reigned with her son Joseph II. It was a trying experience for both of them. Joseph was thoroughly imbued with the ideas of the Enlightenment. He also craved for the glory of conquest. His mother, though she had humanitarian instincts, was basically conservative. She was firmly opposed to Joseph's proposals for religious toleration, and her foreign policy was, as it had always been, defensive. Over her strenuous objections Joseph, backed up by Kaunitz, joined in the first partition of Poland in 1772, by which Austria appropriated the region called Galicia.

Maria Theresa arranged many diplomatic marriages for her children. The most important was the marriage of her youngest daughter Marie Antoinette to the future Louis XVI of France in 1770. To her anguish, it soon became clear that her daughter was incapable of conducting herself with the prudence and discretion her situation demanded. Trying frantically to make up for her failure to prepare the girl adequately beforehand, Maria Theresa bombarded her with letters warning against her frivolity and intrigues: ". . . by your own fault you may well find yourself plunged into deepest misery . . . I hope I shall not live until misfortune overtakes you . . ."

She did not. The Empress had lain in her grave for 13 years when her prophecy was fulfilled. Maria Theresa was unusual for a woman in her time. She could win over hardened politicians by the force her personality and powers of persuasion.

133

Catherine the Great
1729-1796

Catherine the Great, Empress of All the Russias, began life as Sophia Augusta Fredericka of Anhalt-Zerbst, daughter of one of the more obscure German princes. She was related through her mother to the Grand Duke Peter, heir to the Russian throne. After a period of delicate negotiations with Peter's aunt, the Empress Elizabeth, it was decided that the two children should marry.

Thus, at the age of 14 Princess Sophia arrived in Russia to take up a new life. She soon won the approval of the Russians by her diligent study of their language. Her willing conversion to the Orthodox faith, on which occasion she took the name Catherine, also improved her popularity. As for her betrothed, he was an unpromising young man. Though the grandson of Peter the Great, he had been born a German, and loathed Russia. Sickly and infantile, he at first welcomed Catherine as a playmate. But after their wedding, he was unable to consummate the marriage. Not surprisingly, their relationship deteriorated.

As the years dragged by, Catherine resolved that she, not her incompetent husband, would one day rule Russia. After Elizabeth's death in 1762 Peter ensured his own downfall by his erratic behavior – chiefly his decision to change sides in the current war, and support his hero Frederick the Great of Prussia. The army was overwhelmingly behind Catherine. Six months after Peter's accession some officers staged a *coup d'état*, proclaimed Catherine Empress, and took Peter prisoner. He was forced to abdicate and was later assassinated, probably without Catherine's knowledge.

Aware that she was not only a foreigner but also a usurper, Catherine bent her considerable energies to increasing Russia's power and identifying herself with her new nation. Her ambition was to build a Russian-dominated Orthodox empire extending throughout the lands still controlled by the Ottoman Turks. Russia went to war with Turkey in 1768. A succession of Russian victories made it look as though Catherine's ambition might be realized. To avert a European war – the probable outcome of a Russian conquest of the Balkans – Frederick of Prussia persuaded Catherine to settle instead for a slice of Poland. He and Austria would also take a share. Catherine later participated in two more partitions of Poland, absorbing over half of that unhappy country. Poland now ceased to exist. These gains, along with lands won from the Turks, provided Russia with 200,000 square miles more territory.

Below left: a portrait of Catherine in middle age. A resourceful ruler, her numerous reported affairs were the talk of Europe.

Further strains were imposed by the Empress, who suspected Catherine of spying for Prussia and kept the young couple under constant supervision. After several years Catherine had a love affair and produced a son – officially credited to Peter. Catherine rarely saw the little heir as he was promptly appropriated by the Empress.

Above: Alexander Golizyn and 30,000 men defeated a 100,000 strong Turkish force at Chotin in 1769. Russia's conflict with the Turks was cultivated by France.

Extremely well-read and an admirer of the liberal philosophers of the day, Catherine created an image of herself as an enlightened despot. To be sure, Catherine had some liberal instincts. She instituted several reforms, such as increased religious toleration and the virtual abolition of torture. A commission representing

form St. Petersburg, making it one of the most beautiful cities in Europe, she also had built more than 100 new towns. These were solid achievements with nothing in common with the artificial villages which her lover, Prince Potemkin, had constructed for her triumphal tour of the Crimea in 1787.

Of Catherine's many lovers, Potemkin was special. He was the only one she shared power with. They remained close friends long after their liaison ended. It was Potemkin who achieved the peaceful annexation of the Crimea in 1783, greatly strengthening Russia's presence on the Black Sea.

all classes except the serfs was summoned by her to frame a new constitution. But it was clear that Catherine meant to retain absolute authority herself, and the delegates apathetically discussed the remaining points without coming to any conclusions.

In her policy toward the serfs Catherine showed the limits of her "enlightenment." Before becoming Empress she had declared her intention of freeing them. Now, realizing that she depended on the support of the nobility, she dropped the idea. With typical generosity she gave away to favorite nobles huge tracts of crown lands. The free peasants living on these lands now became serfs bound to the new landlords. The once free peasants of the Ukraine were also condemned to slavery at the stroke of Catherine's pen. By the end of her reign there was hardly a free peasant left in Russia.

It was slave labor that sustained the luxurious, westernized culture of Catherine's Russia and it was slave labor that toiled on her numerous building projects. Not only did Catherine trans-

Above: a page from a 19th century Russian biography of Catherine the Great. The achievements illustrated are mostly military, and the captions are laudatory.

Above right: Catherine the Great visiting the serfs. On this tour, Potemkin had the villages smartened up, as still happens when the mighty visit their subjects. But poverty could not be completely hidden. Ragged serfs watch their sumptuous visitors from behind their log dwelling.

Right: English cartoonist George Cruickshank caricatures Catherine on her deathbed. shrinking from a vision of her evil past. Catherine the Great is still a legend for her stupendous sexual appetite.

Catherine remained a vigorous, healthy woman well into her 60s. Idolized by the Russians, she returned the compliment, claiming that they excelled all other nations in "courage, strength, and wisdom." Her sudden death, of a stroke, was deeply mourned. Russia was much more powerful after her rule than before. Yet she failed to provide it with a capable successor. Fearful that her son Paul might claim his inheritance early, she had excluded him from affairs of state, forbidden him to serve in the army, and kept him ignorant of his prospective duties. Not surprisingly, he proved unequal to them, and after a few years he was removed in yet another *coup*.

Benjamin Franklin
1706-1790

Gazette. Gradually he became a wealthy man. His newspaper flourished – not least because of the pithy wisdom of its best-known feature, "Poor Richard's Almanac" – and so did his printing business. Turning his attention to civic affairs, Franklin organized Philadelphia's first circulating library, its first fire department, and established an academy which later developed into the University of Pennsylvania. He also experimented with electricity, bringing him fame in European scientific circles.

Left: this print shows Benjamin Franklin just after he arrived in Philadelphia poor and hungry. It probably describes the period when Franklin, having fallen out with his brother, decided to strike out on his own in the big city. Although Franklin certainly faced privations in his early life, there is little evidence that he was ever poor and hungry.

Right: apart from being a considerable political thinker and statesman, Benjamin Franklin was a scientist of the first rank. Illustration shows Franklin demonstrating his key on a kite experiment, whereby he proved the conductivity of electricity.

Benjamin Franklin once wanted to open a swimming school in London. Had he pursued the swimming school project, he would almost certainly have made a success of it. He had succeeded brilliantly in his numerous other careers. Whether as printer, journalist, inventor, scientist, civil servant, legislator, or diplomat, Franklin had never failed. He is best remembered for the crucial role he played in the struggle for independence.

Franklin was born a first-generation American in Boston. At the age of 12 he was apprenticed to his older brother James, who ran a printing shop, and published one of the Colonies' few newspapers. Under the pseudonym "Mrs. Silence Doggod," young Ben wrote a number of satirical articles for the paper which greatly irritated the Boston government.

Growing hostility between the two brothers led Franklin to run away from home and try his luck in Philadelphia. He worked there as a printer for several years, and briefly followed this track in London. In 1729, he bought out his employer, the owner of a struggling new publication which Franklin renamed the *Pennsylvania*

He was becoming involved in politics at the same time. In 1750 he was elected to the Pennsylvania Assembly and two years later was appointed Postmaster-General of America. This job brought him into contact with important men throughout the Colonies.

Franklin was one of the first advocates of union among the Colonies. The aim was not to achieve independence, an idea not even contemplated in the 1750s, but to help strengthen the British Empire against France. In 1754 he coauthored a Plan of Union. This was approved by a convention meeting in Albany, New York, but rejected by the colonial assemblies.

Conflict between the Pennsylvania Assembly and the colony's proprietors, the Penn family, brought Franklin to London in 1756. After five years of patient negotiating, he persuaded the British Government to make the Penns pay taxes on their lands, and so contribute to the defense of the colony during the French and Indian War (the American phase of the Seven Years' War).

Franklin again visited London on the colony's business in 1764. He stayed 10 years. During this period relations between Britain and the

American Colonies rapidly deteriorated. The main cause of friction virtually was the question of whether Parliament, in which the colonists were not represented, had the right to impose taxes on them. The Stamp Act, which levied a tax on legal documents and newspapers, met with such fierce opposition that it was quickly repealed. But irritating new laws were passed, and in the Colonies agitators fanned public discontent into sporadic riots. King George III's Government responded by sending over more troops to try to make the colonists behave. In London, Franklin labored in the cause of reconciliation, along with his liberal friends in Parliament. His efforts were to no avail.

When Franklin returned to America in 1775 fighting had already begun. He was immediately elected to the Second Continental Congress. The following year he served on the committee that helped prepare the Declaration of Independence.

Now 70 years old, Franklin embarked on his most important mission: securing the aid of France against Britain. He arrived in Paris to find himself a celebrity. Courted by the fashionable world, honored by fellow scientists and philosophers, Franklin clearly represented to the French the spirit of the Enlightenment in America. France naturally favored a split in the British Empire, but did not want to risk another war with Britain. Covertly, Franklin negotiated with French foreign minister Vergennes for secret loans and arms shipments to the hard-

Right: One of the ways in which Franklin proved his worth to his fellow Americans was his skill as a political negotiator. Here, Franklin is in Paris discussing a peaceful end to the War of Independence with British agent Richard. These discussions contributed to an end to the war, with the American colonists the victors.

Below: the Committee of Five present the Declaration of Independence to Congress. With Thomas Jefferson, Franklin helped draft the declaration. Franklin is on the extreme right of the picture, while Jefferson is in the center.

pressed American forces. In 1778 the first big American victory at Saratoga, New York, induced the French to give open support to the Colonies. Franklin drafted the treaty of alliance.

The war still had nearly four years to run. That the Americans finally did win was largely due to French help which Franklin had done so much to secure.

Franklin's career was not yet over. In 1787, two years after returning home, he took his seat as the oldest delegate to the convention that was to draw up the country's new Constitution. Although Franklin was not entirely happy with the result, he put aside his objections and urged its ratification. His support, and that of George Washington, played a major part in its eventual adoption and the establishment of the world's earliest democracy.

George Washington
1732-1799

George Washington would not make an ideal presidential candidate in the United States today. Aristocratic, aloof, with a distaste for party politics, he would be out of place in the hurly burly of a nominating convention.

But when the young United States elected their first president in 1789, Washington was the inevitable choice. As commander-in-chief

Above right: Washington takes command of the American army in Cambridge Massachusetts in 1775. A cultured and gentle man, Washington proved himself a shrewd political organiser when he helped arrange a boycott of British goods. He went on to become an able military commander.

Left: a contemporary portrait of George Washington. Standing beside him in profile is Lafayette.

of the American forces during the War of Independence he had proved himself a natural leader.

Washington was the son, by a second marriage, of a fairly prosperous Virginia farmer, who died when the boy was 11 years old. His mother was a domineering woman, and it must have been a relief for George when he moved into his elder half-brother Lawrence's household at Mount Vernon in 1745. Lawrence was kind and generous to the boy. He introduced him to the elite of Virginia society. To his sketchy formal education George added some self-taught social graces. He painstakingly copied out 110 "Rules of

Civility and Decent Behavior," and soon felt at home in this cultivated world. Being good at mathematics, Washington took up surveying as a profession and surveyed a large area of northern Virginia. When Lawrence died in 1752 George inherited his Mount Vernon home. The management and improvement of this beautiful estate was to be a source of great satisfaction throughout his life.

But soon the young landowner became involved in political and military matters. He was appointed by the Governor to deliver an ultimatum to the French, who were encroaching on Virginia's territory. When the French and Indian War began in 1754 Washington was commissioned a lieutenant colonel. He later served with distinction under the English General Braddock.

Washington resigned his commission in 1758 after being elected to the House of Burgesses, the Virginia legislature. That winter he married a rich young widow, Martha Custis. For the next 15 years he enjoyed the life of a country gentleman, while fulfilling his legislative duties for a few weeks every year. Virginia was one of the colonies most opposed to the new British taxes and other restrictive laws. In 1764 Washington helped to organize a boycott of British goods.

The Continental Congress met for the first time in Philadelphia in 1774. Washington was one of the Virginia delegates. When fighting broke out between British and Americans in Massachusetts the following year, Congress made him commander of the fledgling American army.

his entire army was remaining in the north. Meanwhile he marched it quickly south, where General Cornwallis had established his British army at Yorktown, Virginia. After a French naval victory off the Virginia coast, Washington led the allied forces in the siege of Yorktown. Cornwallis surrendered two weeks later. Although fighting was to continue for another 18 months the Americans had won their independence.

After the signing of the peace, Washington retired to Mount Vernon. The newly liberated states, joined in a loose confederation, soon began to realize the necessity of a stronger union. A longstanding advocate of such a union, Washington attended and presided over the Constitutional Convention that met in Philadelphia in 1787. When he was unanimously elected president, his sense of duty overcame his reluctance. He was inaugurated in New York City, the first capital, in 1789.

Washington's presidency lasted for two terms, and was marked by a sharp conflict between his Secretary of the Treasury, Hamilton, who advocated a strong central government, and his Secretary of State, Thomas Jefferson, who upheld the rights of individual states. Although Washington tried to reconcile the two parties, he tended to favor Hamilton's policies. He sup-

Few, if any, generals have fought a war with so many disadvantages as Washington. To begin with, he had no experience of leading forces in open-field battles. This handicap was in large part responsible for his first serious defeat on Long Island, New York, in August 1776. His army was a hastily assembled force in which enlistment was only for one year. So by the time men were fully-trained their term of duty was expired. After repeated entreaties to Congress, Washington finally got the enlistment period lengthened. He was less successful in obtaining supplies. For a number of reasons, not least lack of public confidence in the paper currency, Congress failed to provide anything like enough food and clothing for the troops. Indeed, they often went into battle barefoot. While Washington and his ill and ragged army spent a cruel winter encamped at Valley Forge, Pennsylvania, intrigues were afoot to replace him.

In the face of these manifold problems, Washington showed indomitable strength of character. His physical courage and determination won him the respect and confidence of his troops. Washington also achieved some successes. For example, his surprise attack on Hessian mercenaries at Trenton and other victories in New Jersey saved the American cause after the New York disaster. But by 1781 that cause looked all but lost, even with French help. The arrival of 3000 more French troops and a French fleet gave Washington the chance to strike the decisive blow. By an elaborate ruse he fooled the British commanding general, Clinton, into believing

Above: George Washington is inaugurated President of the United States at the Old City Hall, New York in 1789. Another revolution was about to unleash itself in France.

ported his plans for the assumption by the Federal Government of the states' debts, and for the establishment of a national bank. In his foreign policy Washington resolutely kept America neutral, despite strong pressure from Jefferson's party to support the revolutionary French government in its war with Britain. In his Farewell Address on leaving the presidency, Washington warned against the "baneful effects of the spirit of party" and the dangers of entangling alliances. Both of these principles have long since been rejected, but Washington's hand in creating a strong and independent nation is still gratefully remembered by Americans.

Thomas Jefferson
1743~1826

laration of independence. He wrote the first draft. Though tinkered with by other delegates, the final document was mainly Jefferson's work. Its basic proposition – that governments are instituted among men to secure the "inalienable rights" of "life, liberty, and the pursuit of happiness" and that when a government becomes destructive of these ends, men have the right to alter or abolish it – did not originate with Jefferson. It was one of the accepted ideas of the En-

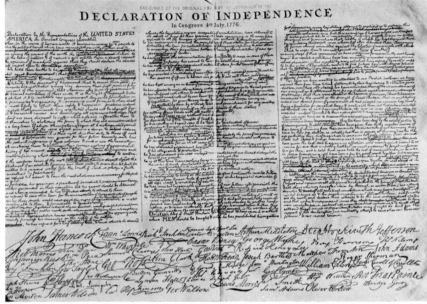

Above: the Declaration of Independence bearing all its signatories. Thomas Jefferson was largely responsible for the wording of the declaration. For its time, the declaration was enlightened, and was almost unique among the pronouncements of governments in declaring the equality of mankind to be self-evident. It still sefves as a model of constitutional democracy.

Below: slaves being unloaded at Jamestown, Virginia, from a Dutch man-of-war. Jefferson failed to get slavery abolished, but managed to stop their importation.

Thomas Jefferson, the third President of the United States, was a man of many talents. A leading statesman of the young republic, he was also an accomplished writer, architect, inventor, violinist, and botanist. His wide-ranging curiosity was born of great intellect.

Jefferson was the son of an enterprising and successful western Virginia farmer. As a youth he was attracted to the study of science. But, as this field then offered few career opportunities, he opted for law. He studied at the College of William and Mary, in Williamsburg, capital of the colòny. While a student he occasionally attended the House of Burgesses. Here he heard the fiery Patrick Henry exhorting the colonists to resist British "tyranny." Later, Jefferson was to serve in the Burgesses for six years, right up to the eve of the Revolution.

Jefferson was one of the Virginia delegates to Second Continental Congress of 1775. A year later, after an attempted reconciliation with Britain had failed, the Congress appointed a committee, including Jefferson, to draft a dec-

lightenment. But Jefferson's eloquent statement of it inspired not only his American contemporaries, but revolutionaries of other countries too.

Jefferson returned to Virginia and again entered the legislature. He tried, against tough opposition, to liberalize its laws. His proposals for free education, an enlightened criminal code, and the gradual emancipation of the slaves were defeated. But his bill ending the importation of slaves became law. After a 10-year battle his Statute for Religious Freedom, which effected a separation of church and state, was passed.

Jefferson was elected Governor of Virginia in 1779. His term of office was disrupted by the invasion of the British army. In 1781, he retired to his beloved estate, Monticello. His wife Martha's death left him very despondent, but pushed him back into public life. In 1784, he sailed for France, entrusted with the task of promoting trade between that nation and the infant republic. He lived there for five happy years, during which Jefferson explored European civilization and exercised his considerable talent for diplomacy.

The French Revolution erupted in 1789. Jefferson returned home and accepted President Washington's invitation to become Secretary of State. He soon clashed with Secretary of the Treasury Hamilton. Hamilton's party were the Federalists and were for a strong central government controlled by the moneyed interests, and closely allied to Britain. Jefferson wanted to diffuse power into smaller units, more responsive to the republic's wealth producers, mainly the farmers. He also profoundly distrusted the British. Jefferson's party, then called the Republicans, became the modern Democratic Party.

Jefferson resigned from the Cabinet in 1793. Later, he served as vice president under John Adams. He was elected president himself in 1800. His first term began with economic cut-

Right: Jefferson was a shrewd politician who inevitably made some enemies. His most influential political adversary was Alexander Hamilton.

Below: probably the turning point of the American War of Independence, the British defeat at Princeton in 1777 at the hands of the American rebel army.

though he was, Jefferson viewed the prospect of a great power controlling the Mississippi and New Orleans with alarm. So he sent James Monroe to France to do some bargaining. The result was the purchase in 1803 of nearly all the land between the Mississippi and the Rocky Mountains. Whether or not this was constitutional, the territory was to be a great source of wealth for the United States. From Jefferson's point of view it had the added advantage of averting an alliance with Britain, which French control of Louisiana would have made inevitable.

During his second term the prospect of war with either Britain or France grew ever more likely. Each power was doing its best to cripple its enemy's trade, and each passed laws preventing a neutral nation from trading with the other. American shipping was caught in the squeeze. Jefferson was determined to avoid war. Instead, he got Congress to pass the Embargo Act, which forbade Americans to trade overseas. Intended to put economic pressure on the European powers, the Act inflicted severe hardship on Americans. Several of the New England states were brought to the brink of secession. Just before Jefferson left office it was repealed.

Back at Monticello, Jefferson cultivated his

backs. Both military spending and taxes were sharply reduced. In view of Jefferson's economy drive and his earlier protests against assumption of extra powers by the central government, it seems strange that the high point of his administration was the purchase of the Louisiana Territory. Napoleon had acquired this vast territory from Spain in 1800, though it remained in Spanish hands for a while. An admirer of the French

Above right: Lewis and Clark guided by Sacajawea. Jefferson sponsored this famous expedition into the American interior. The fertile lands they discovered encouraged the territorial expansionism of the young nation. White America's greed for ever more land proved a disaster for the "first Americans" - the Red Indian

estate and pursued his many intellectual and creative interests. His last public achievement was the establishment of the University of Virginia. Chartered in 1819, it was Jefferson's own creation. He designed both its buildings and curriculum.

Jefferson's active, productive life came to a close on July 4, 1826, the 50th anniversary of the signing of the Declaration of Independence.

Jean-Jacques Rousseau 1712~1778

"Man is born free, but everywhere he is in chains." So wrote Jean-Jacques Rousseau in *The Social Contract*, published in 1762. This proposition has inspired revolutionaries right down to the present day. When Fidel Castro was fighting in Cuba in the 1950s he carried a copy of *The Social Contract* in his pocket.

Rousseau was born of working-class parents in the independent city-state of Geneva. His mother died shortly after his birth, and his father left home 10 years later, having run foul of the law. The young Jean-Jacques received the rudiments of an education and began drifting from job to job. But he read widely, and developed an acute sense of the injustice of the world as he saw it.

Rousseau left Geneva at the age of 16, and was befriended by an aristocrat, Madame de Warens, who became his first mistress. She also persuaded him to become a Roman Catholic (he later reconverted to Calvinism), and helped him with his education.

Rousseau journeyed through France and Italy, making a living mainly by copying, and sometimes teaching, music. He served as secretary to the French ambassador to Venice for a while, and did some writing.

By the 1740s Rousseau was beginning to make a name for himself and to meet established writers, such as Diderot and d'Alembert, for whose *Encyclopedia* he wrote articles on music and political economy. At about the same time

Right: Rousseau's first meeting with the aristocrat Madame de Warens. She became his first mistress when he was 16, and helped him with his education.

Left: this painting pictures Rousseau in the romantic surroundings of a leafy garden.

he took a young washerwoman, Thérèse Levasseur, as his mistress. They remained together for the rest of his life and had five children – all of whom Rousseau deposited in an orphanage.

Civilization both attracted and repelled Rousseau. In his first important work, *A Discourse on the Sciences and Arts*, he attacked both the arts and the sciences as the products of human vanity, and the perpetuators of inequality. The printing press received special condemnation from a man

whose ideas, thanks to the printing press, were to transform western thought.

His most popular work was undoubtedly *La nouvelle Héloise*, a sentimental novel idealizing the virtues of pastoral life. It set a fashion for going "back to nature." Even the dissipated Marie Antoinette and her courtiers played at being peasants in a mock village at Versailles.

In his second discourse, *On the Origins of Inequality Among Men*, Rousseau asserted that humans are naturally good, but are corrupted by society. He supported this assertion with a good deal of misinformation about life among primitive people. But he was one of the first serious thinkers to claim that a person's character is moulded by environment. This belief is the basis of most modern sociological thought.

The Social Contract revealed a change in Rousseau's attitudes toward society. He now held that although society was corrupt, it could be put right and so produce good men. The ideal society, in his view, was one in which all citizens identified with the state and fused their individual wills into what he called the "general will." This concept had little to do with such democratic notions as majority rule, and compromises between conflicting interests. The general will was, rather, the expression of the society's values (at least the values of most adult males). True freedom was found by conforming to the general will. Dissidents should be forced to admit their error, and recalcitrant cases put to death. These principles are at work in the modern world, in societies where what the "general will" is is decided by a handful of leaders – seemingly without the need to consult anybody else. On the other hand, Rousseau emphasised the right of people to participate in their government, and was passionately commited to the idea of equality.

In his lifetime Rousseau's works were condemned by both monarchical, Catholic France and republican, Protestant Geneva. His books were banned and warrants issued for his arrest. Luckily for him, he continually received help from influential friends. For example, the Scottish philosopher David Hume persuaded George III to give him a pension. But Rousseau persisted in believing that his friends were plotting against him, and in the end antagonized many of his benefactors. He died in a beautiful little country house placed at his disposal by a French nobleman.

By the time of the French Revolution 11 years later, Roussea's ideas had become part of the intellectual climate. The "Declaration of the Rights of Man and Citizen," produced by the National Assembly in 1789, owes much to *The Social Contract* in both style and substance. Of

Right: An illustration from Rousseau's work *Discours sur L'inégalité,* showing the *beau sauvage* meeting civilized man.

course, other influences were at work during the revolution – not least the anticlericalism professed by Rousseau's old enemy Voltaire. The revolutionaries drew on several political philosophies in shaping the new regime. But when they were most idealistic and humanitarian, as when they were most dogmatic and repressive, they were following the teachings of Rousseau.

Below: a plate from an early illustrated edition of *Emile.*

Louis XVI
1754-1793

Some of the more romantic French revolutionaries liked to see parallels between the Old Régime and the excesses of Imperial Rome. They would sometimes refer to King Louis XVI as "Caligula." Nothing could be more absurd than this comparison of a mad, bloodthirsty emperor who believed himself a god and a benevolent, mild-mannered gentleman who never wanted to be a king in the first place.

In more tranquil times, Louis XVI might have reigned successfully. He had liberal instincts. While he ruled hospitals were built, forced labor for public works was abolished, and Protestants were granted freedom of worship. He had plans to reform the prisons. But France was already headed for a conflict when Louis took the throne in 1774. Good intentions and modest reforms would count for little.

Late 18th century France was a feudal society, in which the nobility had become increasingly powerful. They controlled the *parlements*, the supreme law courts of the land and the only

Right: the "National Assembly" meeting in a tennis court after Louis had had them locked out of their chamber. This meeting at Versailles in May 1789 swore not to disband until they had drafted a constitution for France.

Below: Louis XVI with his Queen Marie Antoinette, and members of his family. Louis was a moderate, if unimaginative ruler, and his demise was probably largely due to the arrogant and unfeeling behavior of his wife. She is chiefly remembered for her "let them eat cake" remark when told that the French lower classes were starving for bread.

check on the monarchy. At the time, they were busily asserting many of their ancient rights over the peasantry. The peasants (most of them landless laborers) and the growing urban proletariat were severely hit by rising prices, which far outstripped wage increases. The bourgeoisie were doing well financially, but they deeply resented the privileges enjoyed by the aristocracy, par-

ticularly their control of high government offices.

A financial crisis brought the conflict to a head. Louis had inherited a large national debt from his predecessors, and had doubled it with the cost of aiding the American Colonies. Not surprisingly, efforts to reform the tax system so that the nobility and the Church would pay their share had been blocked by the *parlements*. By the

1780s the situation was critical. The government could not continue borrowing. The necessary funds would have to be raised by taxation.

Under pressure from the *parlements* Louis summoned the Estates General to attempt to deal with the crisis. Representatives of the three estates – clergy, nobility, and the rest of the population – met at Versailles in May 1789. The bourgeois representatives of the Third Estate insisted on a combined assembly voting by head, rather than letting each estate vote separately, each having an equal voice. By these means they would obtain a small majority. After winning a few liberal priests and nobles to their side, they declared themselves the "National Assembly." Louis had them locked out of their chamber so they met in a tennis court and swore not to disband until they had given France a constitution. On July 14, 1789 an angry mob stormed the Bastille. This prison had become a symbol of royal tyranny. Its governor was forced to surrender. The French Revolution had begun.

By siding with the aristocrats, Louis had lost the initiative. He also made the great mistake of relying on the advice of his queen, Marie Antoinette. Her extravagance and her interference in affairs of state – particularly by trying to get French support for the foreign aims of her native Austria – had earned her the hatred of the French people. Some of this dislike was now directed against Louis.

While the National Assembly worked to build a constitutional monarchy, the peasants and the urban poor demanded some immediate relief from the sufferings caused by a meager harvest. There were food riots in Paris. In October 1789,

Above: several thousand angry women march on the royal palace at Versailles in October 1789. They had heard rumors that flour was being hoarded there.

a crowd of several thousand women, angered by rumors that flour was being hoarded at Versailles, marched on the palace. Some deputies went with them. They forced the king to give his assent to the acts passed by the Assembly. The next day the royal family were escorted to Paris and installed in the Tuileries Palace, where they could be more closely observed.

Any remaining chance that Louis might cooperate with the Revolution vanished when, in 1790, the Assembly enacted the Civil Constitution of the Clergy. This act stripped the Church of its property and placed it under state control. The pope denounced the act. Louis, fearing for his soul, refused to sign it at first. But early in 1791 he was forced to do so.

Finally, Louis was persuaded by the queen to try to escape to the eastern frontier, where he might gather support to overthrow the new régime. Disguised as servants, he and the queen, their children, and the "Mme de Korff" (the royal governess) slipped out of Paris. Only a few hours later the party was overtaken by the National Guard at Varennes.

Some of the members of the Assembly still tried to save the monarchy. But events were slipping out of their hands. In June 1792, exactly a year after the flight to Varennes, a mob broke into the Tuileries. Louis, displaying admirable calm, defused some of their wrath by graciously inviting them to view the royal apartments.

By August Paris was in a ferment. Terrified by

Above: the head of Louis is held up to the cheering mob after his execution in 1793. He was accused and convicted of active hostility to the aims of the revolution. The detested Marie Antoinette followed her husband to the guillotine in October 1793.

the approach of a foreign army and enraged by the Duke of Brunswick's Manifesto ordering the release of the king, the Paris mob again stormed the Tuileries, and then the Assembly, where the king had gone for protection. The new municipal government, the Commune, forced the Assembly to dissolve.

Meanwhile, the royal family were incarcerated in a small gloomy fortress called the Temple. Then the revolutionaries discovered some of Louis' private papers, which revealed his hostility to the revolution. He was brought to trial, pronounced guilty, and beheaded. The following October the hated Marie Antoinette followed him to the scaffold.

Jean Paul Marat
1743-1793

Jean Paul Marat once described himself as "the wrath of the people." His inflammatory writings helped to launch the violent phase of the French Revolution. He had an unlikely background for such a passionate revolutionary, being born in Switzerland of respectable middle-class parents. Indeed, he was for most of his life a liberal-minded monarchist.

After receiving a degree in medicine from the University of Bordeaux, Marat spent 12 years in England. He established a medical practice there, and also began writing. In 1774 he published *The Chains of Slavery*. In it he condemned despotism, while praising kings who exercised their power with wisdom and restraint.

Right: the front page of Marat's famous radical newspaper *L'ami du Peuple* (the Friend of the People). This 1793 edition demanded the overthrow of the Girondins. Marat was assassinated largely as a result of this appeal.

Below: Jean Paul Marat is hailed as a hero of the revolution. Probably the most radical of the French revolutionary leaders, Marat was also the most popular with the common people. His attacks on the higher clergy and the nobility were vitriolic.

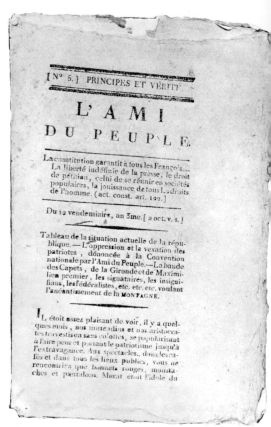

Returning to France in 1777, he became doctor to the bodyguard of the king's brother, the Comte d'Artois. Many other aristocrats soon became his patients. While in this lucrative practice, Marat wrote between 1777 and 1789, eight books on physics, two novels, and miscellaneous other works. His scientific writings were favorably received in France and abroad (Benjamin Franklin attended a demonstration of his experiments). But they failed to win him

the prize he most coveted: membership in the Academy of Sciences. Marat characteristically interpreted the rejection as a malicious personal affront. Some years later, he wrote: "The Academy, finding that it couldn't stifle my findings, tried to make it appear that they were its own discoveries. Three different academic bodies visited me on the same day trying to persuade me to present myself as a candidate. Several crowned heads sought me out on account of the fame of my works!"

At the outbreak of the French Revolution, Marat shared the prevailing mood of optimism. His first pamphlet praised Louis XVI – "the best of kings" – for summoning the Estates General. Louis' attempts to block certain reforms a few months later provoked a more critical response: "It is not . . . the pitiful groans of his subjects reduced to despair that disturb his tranquility; it is the exhaustion of his treasury . . ." Marat's growing indignation at the misery suffered by the masses and his belief in their natural collective sovereignty increasingly conflicted with his conservative tendencies. He never overcame this conflict. On the one hand he described working-class people as "the only ones who have courage and feeling"; on the other hand, they were "so vain, so foolish, so imbecile, that it is almost impossible to save them." At one period he advocated a dictatorship as the only way to bring about a just society.

He launched his newspaper, *L'Ami du peuple* (The Friend of the People), in September 1789. It achieved a wide readership in weeks. One of its editorials provoked the march on Versailles

Left: Marat portrayed at work at his desk. This painting is the work of Marat's close friend Laplace.

Below: Charlotte Corday just after she had stabbed Marat. Marat's body can be seen on the right of the picture.

by a hungry mob, who succeeded in bringing the royal family back to Paris. Marat was declared an outlaw for his part in the insurrection and was forced into hiding. On this and many similar occasions, the "friend of the people" found his friendship reciprocated. He sheltered among working-class Parisians and continued to publish his newspaper.

The intransigence of the king, the plots of the *émigrés*, and the cautious approach of many of the revolutionaries infuriated Marat. *L'Ami du peuple* became more and more insistent on the need for some therapeutic bloodletting in order to rid the country of counter-revolutionary elements. His suspicions often proved well-founded. But his paranoid nature saw treachery in every corner, and his incessant cries for vengeance undoubtedly caused the deaths of some innocent people.

Historians differ over the extent of Marat's complicity, if any, in the September Massacres of 1792. Some claim that the Paris Commune's Committee of Surveillance, of which Marat was a member, ordered the killings. Others maintain that they were the spontaneous action of a group of soldiers angered by the belief that traitors at home were aiding the advance of foreign armies. In any event, some 1200 inmates of Paris prisons, mainly priests, were killed in only about a week. Whether or not Marat bears any responsibility for the massacres, he and the Committee issued a letter to the other French departments expressing approval of the killings and urging them to do likewise.

Shortly afterwards, Marat took his seat as one of the Paris delegates to the National Convention, the legislative body of the newly established French Republic. A power struggle was soon raging between the far left, particularly Marat, and the Girondins, former radicals who now adopted a more conservative line. The Girondins attempted to have Marat expelled from the Convention, but without success. Throughout the spring of 1793 Marat's newspaper called for the overthrow of the Girondins. Rising prices, a food shortage, and the threat of invasion made the Parisians increasingly militant. On May 31 some of them broke into the Convention and forced it to arrest 31 of the Girondin leaders. Some of the Girondins escaped. Most were later executed during the Terror.

Marat's role in the crushing of the Girondin party brought about his death. A young woman named Charlotte Corday became convinced that Marat was the chief perverter of the aims of the Revolution, and that it was her sacred duty to kill him. Pretending to need Citizen Marat's help, she gained admission to the house where he lived with his devoted common-law wife Simonne Evrard and then into the room where he sat in a curious boot-shaped bathtub treating the skin disease that afflicted him. She plunged a knife into his chest.

Robespierre
1758-1794

Maximilien Robespierre was called "the Incorruptible." Ordinary human frailties – for money or the pleasures of the flesh – were foreign to him. He could not be bought. It was power that mattered to Robespierre. Whether he wanted power for its own sake, or to further his vision of a new society, remains in dispute. But whatever his motives Robespierre did achieve great, though brief, power. With this power, he was able to impose the notorious Reign of Terror on France.

Like most of the other French revolutionaries, Robespierre was of the bourgeois class. Born in Arras, in northern France, he was the son of a lawyer, who had deserted the family shortly after the death of his wife. His children were left to be reared by grandparents.

A good student, Robespierre received a scholarship to study law in Paris. There, he discovered the writings of Rousseau. He was particularly attracted to Rousseau's concept of "virtue" as the mainspring of a reformed society.

Throughout his life, Robespierre insisted on the paramount importance of "virtue." He once defined it as "love of the fatherland and its laws, the magnanimous devotion which submerges all private interests in the general interest."

Robespierre practiced law in Arras for eight years. He was chosen to represent the city at the meeting of the Estates General in 1789. He was a frequent speaker in the National Assembly (later called the Constituent Assembly) and

Above: a painting depicting the opening of the Estates General. Robespierre was a lawyer in his native city of Arras in northern France, and was chosen to represent the city in the Estates General.

called for a host of liberal reforms including universal suffrage and, ironically, an end to capital punishment. He was one of the founders of the Friends of the Constitutions, or Jacobin Club.

After the Constituent Assembly was replaced by a newly constituted Legislative Assembly in 1791, Robespierre performed most of his eloquence in the Club. There, he attacked the policy of the dominant Girondin party, who wanted to export the Revolution by force of arms. "Restore order in your own house before you carry liberty elsewhere," he urged. But France went to war with Austria, chief supporter of the old regime, in the spring of 1792.

The overthrow of the king that August and the disbanding of the Legislative Assembly brought Robespierre back into the center of events. As a member of the revolutionary Paris Commune and the chief Paris delegate to the National Convention, he became one of the leaders of the extreme left. He urged Louis XVI's execution, and actively opposed the Girondins. Partly thanks to his efforts, they were expelled from the Convention.

The new republic was threatened as much by uprisings in the provinces as by foreign armies. There was civil war in the south and west. Once Robespierre assumed control of the Committee of Public Safety, in July 1793, he revealed his

Left: a contemporary painting of Robespierre. The main architect of the "Terror", Robespierre turned France into an intolerant dictatorship where the slightest deviation from orthodoxy could result in imprisonment, or death.

Left: a contemporary cartoon attacks Robespierre's policies. Each pile of heads at the foot of the guillotine represents a section of French society. The largest pile are the common people. They, not the aristocrats, suffered most under the "Terror."

intention of ruthlessly suppressing any counter-revolutionary activity. The number of political trials and executions increased, and in September the Convention passed the Law of Suspects. This gave the government extensive powers to imprison people without trial. The Terror began in earnest. Most of the executions took place in the provinces. Contrary to popular belief, only a tiny minority of the victims were aristocrats; 70 percent were peasants and laborers.

Although Robespierre used the Terror to stifle opposition to the state, he was not as blood-thirsty as the Hebertists. This party claimed to represent the working class. It tried to supplant Christianity with a cult of "Reason," and used the Terror as an excuse for orgies of killing. Robespierre sent their principal leaders to the guillotine in March 1794. He did the same to Danton and his Indulgents shortly afterwards.

Having eliminated the opposition, right and left, Robespierre had virtually a free hand. He intensified the Terror. By the Law of 22 Prairial (one of the new months in the revolutionary calendar), accused persons were forbidden to speak in their own defense. This newly stream-lined "justice" enabled the Revolutionary Tri-bunal to convict 50 or 60 suspects a day and kept the guillotine busy.

But in the meantime, the excuse for the Terror was losing its validity and subsiding. Despite his initial objections to the war with Austria Robes-pierre had prosecuted it vigorously, and ordered mass conscription. French forces eventually numbered 800,000 men. In June 1794 the army

invaded the Low Countries. The Allies (which now included Austria, Britain, and the Nether-lands) put up little opposition. Meanwhile, the civil war was petering out.

Robespierre lost the support of the Paris work-ing class. In the Convention, most of whose members were cowed into a state of terrified submission, a conspiracy against him was brew-ing. Ever vigilant, Robespierre appeared before the Convention and informed the members that

Above: Robespierre was over-thrown on July 27 1794. This painting depicts Robespierre being shot in the jaw during the ensuing fighting in the Convention. It is not known whether Robespierre was shot by an assailant, or shot himself.

"there exists within your bosom a league of scoundrels who are at war with public virtue!" He refused at first to name names. The following day, 9 Thermidor (July 27), the plotters struck before he could do so. Amid cries of "Down with the tyrant!" they took over the rostrum and ordered his arrest. The Paris Commune organ-ized a counterattack on the Convention. But after 12 hours of chaotic maneuvering, during which Robespierre was shot – or shot himself – in the jaw, the *coup* was accomplished. Robespierre and his close associates were declared outlaws and quickly dispatched by the guillotine.

After his death the Revolution entered a phase called the "Thermidorian reaction." The Terror subsided, and the Committee of Public Safety had its wings clipped by the Convention. Even the Jacobin Club was closed. The "republic of virtue" was as far away as ever.

Georges Jacques Danton
1759-1794

beau, a moderate revolutionary leader who worked for the king, refers to "the 30,000 (livres) that we have given to Danton." Exactly what service Danton performed for this sum is not known. He may have been an informer.

The contradictions, the shifting currents, the idealism, and the ruthlessness of the French Revolution are exemplified in the life of one of its leading figures – Georges Danton. He is, for many, the most sympathetic of the revolutionaries. A robust, sensual man, he courageously urged moderation when the radical forces that he had done so much to create were in a position to destroy him. But there are shadowy areas in Danton's life, and he remains an enigmatic figure.

He came from the province of Champagne, of peasant stock, though his father practiced law. Danton also studied law. After qualifying at Reims he went to Paris. There, in 1787, he bought the office of advocate to the King's Council, married, and moved into the Cordeliers district on the Left Bank.

This neighborhood was one of the most politically active in Paris. Danton became one of its leaders. Shortly after the Revolution began he was elected its president, and the following year he founded the Club of the Cordeliers. He also became a member of the newly formed Society of the Friends of the Constitution. Commonly known as the Jacobin Club, this organization pushed the Revolution into ever more radical directions.

In the first three years of the Revolution, Danton kept in the background. In fact, some evidence suggests that he may have been in the pay of the Court. For example, a letter from Mira-

Top Danton (left) with Robespierre (center), and Jean Paul Marat – the three most significant leaders of France after the Revolution.

Above: a print showing the storming of the Bastille prison on July 14 1789.

By the summer of 1792, Danton was a member of the Paris Commune, and had acquired a reputation as one of the foremost radicals – largely through his attacks on moderates such as the Marquis de Lafayette. He was one of the instigators of the August 10 march on the Tuileries, which overthrew the monarchy. After this, Danton was appointed Minister of Justice and be-

strike at innocent people. No one wishes to see an individual treated as a guilty person just because he doesn't have sufficient revolutionary vigor."

This rather weak protest was followed up in the following months by articles in *Le Vieux Cordelier*, a newspaper produced by Danton's friend Camille Desmoulins. They criticized the Committee's assumption of greater powers and urged the release of the thousands of suspects then detained in the Paris prisons. The moderate line of Danton and his followers, called the Indulgents, began to gain support in the Convention.

Early in 1794 Danton made the mistake of defending Fabre d'Églantine, a revolutionary accused of involvement in an East India Company swindle. Robespierre quietly added this to the list of charges he was preparing against Danton and his friends. Although warned of the danger he faced, Danton seemed curiously unperturbed. Urged to flee France, he replied "One does not carry one's country on the soles of one's feet." He was convinced that his popularity

came, in effect, the head of the Executive Council. Only two months later he resigned this post in order to take a seat in the new National Convention. The long-smoldering conflict between him and the moderate Girondin party ignited when the Girondins demanded an examination of his ministry's books and discovered embarrassing gaps. The next spring General Dumouriez, commander of the republican army, defected to the Austrians. Danton and the Girondins accused each other of complicity with Dumouriez. But it was the Girondins who were discredited and, under pressure from the Paris Commune, expelled from the Convention.

Meanwhile, Danton had been instrumental in establishing the Revolutionary Tribunal, a body entrusted with trying those accused of treason against the republic, and the Committee of Public Safety, which was to serve as an emergency government until the war with Austria could be ended. Danton was head of the Committee for its first few months. To pacify the increasingly militant working class, the Committee introduced price controls and various egalitarian measures. But Danton's efforts to negotiate a peace with Austria were unsuccessful.

Danton's term on the Committee expired in July 1793, after which the Committee was controlled by Robespierre. The number of political trials increased that autumn. Danton began to oppose the government, urging that the Revolution be stabilized. He spoke out not only against the excesses of the Hébertist party, who were committing atrocities in the provinces, but also against the deliberate policy of Terror with which Robespierre was suppressing the counter-revolution. "Perhaps the Terror once served a certain purpose," he said, "but it ought not to

Above: a *Tribunal de Prison* in session in 1789. These tribunals decided which prisoners should be sent to the guillotine and which spared. They were notoriously corrupt, and Danton campaigned against them, and other excesses of the Revolution.

Right: "the zenith of the French glory. The pinnacle of justice." An English cartoon bitterly lampoons the French Revolution for brutality and injustice.

Above: publisher of the newspaper *Le Vieux Cordelier* Camille Desmoulins accompanies Danton in a tumbril ride to the guillotine. Robespierre had them convicted, with others, of conspiring to overthrow the republic. No evidence was offered.

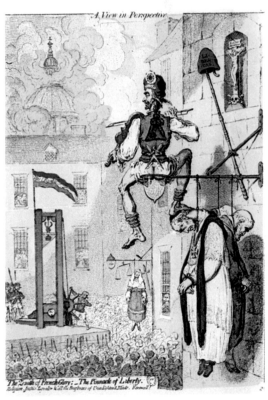

would protect him from the guillotine. When he was arrested he assured his wife, "They will not dare to do it."

Brought before the Revolutionary Tribunal, Danton angrily denied the charges against him – the chief one being that of conspiring with Dumouriez to overthrow the republic. No evidence was brought to support the charges, but he was predictably pronounced guilty. "Vile Robespierre!" he cried. "You too will go to the scaffold!" Danton and his friends went to the guillotine a few hours later.

Napoleon Bonaparte
1769-1821

The rise and fall of Napoleon Bonaparte is one of the most dramatic stories of history. In a mere 20 years this Corsican army officer became Emperor of France and master of most of Europe, only to end up as a prisoner on a remote island in the south Atlantic. His formidable military and political genius ultimately proved unequal to his boundless ambition.

Napoleon's family, minor Italian nobility,

Above right: after his armies had defeated Austria, Napoleon turned his attention to Egypt. During the invasion Napoleon received his first taste of British sea power in the Battle of the Nile. This print depicts the Battle of the Pyramids of 1798.

Opposite page: Europe in 1812, when Napoleon was at the height of his power. Areas directly ruled by France are shown red, and dependent states pink. The allies against Napoleon are marked in orange, and independent states in gray.

Left: a portrait of Napoleon as a young man.

When it looked likely that the expansionist members of the government would be ousted by conciliatory royalists, Bonaparte sent a contingent to Paris to prevent it. He then concluded the Treaty of Campo Formio with the Austrians. This recognized the French conquests.

Bonaparte's next adventure was an invasion of Egypt, intended to cripple British trade with India. The country fell easily, but proved difficult to hold on to. In the Battle of the Nile, Admiral Nelson demonstrated the British sea power that would later help to bring Napoleon down.

Returning to France, he joined a conspiracy to overthrow the Directory. The *coup d'état* of Brumaire (November 10, 1799) established a new republic, the Consulate, with Bonaparte as

had aligned themselves with Corsica's French government. He was educated in military schools in France. Three years before the outbreak of the Revolution, he received his commission. He became an enthusiastic supporter of the upheaval. His revolutionary activities in Corsica forced his family to seek asylum in France.

Napoleon first made a name for himself by capturing the port of Toulon, held by royalists and British. This achievement earned him the rank of brigadier-general when he was only 24. Back in Paris in 1795, he defended the National Convention from a royalist uprising, and later made himself useful to the precarious new government, the Directory.

Bonaparte was given command of the Army of Italy in 1796. He drove the Austrians from northern Italy and established a republic there. He then invaded Austria itself.

Right: Napoleon on a visit to a textile factory in Rouen, 1802. The French bourgeousie provided Napoleon with much of his political support. In return, he encouraged the development of French manufacturing industry.

leon's installation of his brother Joseph as their king. Elsewhere the car rolled along a bit more smoothly. Even so, a good deal of fighting was needed. One coalition after another was formed to stop Napoleon's advance. But with his mastery of strategy and his formidable *Grande Armée*, he seemed virtually unstoppable.

In 1810, having divorced his first wife Josephine, the erstwhile Corsican revolutionary married a princess of the House of Hapsburg. The following year the Empress Marie Louise produced a son, thus securing the Bonaparte dynasty. Napoleon was now at the height of his power. He dominated all of the European continent except the Balkans. The French Empire stretched from the Netherlands and northern Germany down into Italy, including Rome. Satellite states, most of them governed by Napoleon's relatives, surrounded the Empire. Beyond them lay nations such as Austria, Prussia, and Russia that had come to terms with him – temporarily.

There remained one stubborn adversary, Great Britain. Napoleon's original intention had been to invade Britain. But to do this he would have to decoy the mighty British Navy away from its shores. In the event, his strategy failed. Nelson defeated the French fleet at Trafalgar, and so ended the threat of a French invasion. Napoleon tried economic warfare next. His Continental System, imposed in 1806, forbade the import of British goods throughout continental Europe. It was not a success. Britain continued to prosper, and the law was openly and furtively flouted.

When Russia, disillusioned with the Franco-Russian alliance, withdrew from the Continental System, Napoleon once more marched his army eastward. The Russian campaign of 1812 ended in disaster. Napoleon's troops retreated through vicious winter weather, and died of exposure and starvation on the way. Out of 611,000 men who entered Russia, only about 200,000 lived to tell the tale.

Now that the colossus was revealed as vulnerable, other European powers joined forces against him. Napoleon managed to raise another army from the war-weary French, and he kept on fighting. But in March 1814 the Allies reached Paris. He was forced to abdicate and was sent into exile on the Mediterranean island of Elba.

The next year, while the Allies were reconstructing Europe at the Congress of Vienna, Napoleon escaped. Arriving in France, he found the people dissatisfied with the restored Bourbon monarchy and ready to help him revive the Empire. He resumed control of the government and the army, and marched into Belgium. He was defeated by an allied force under the British Duke of Wellington in the epic Battle of Waterloo.

This time the exile was permanent. The British sent Napoleon to the tiny island of St. Helena. He lived for another six years, passing the hours by cultivating a garden and dictating his memoirs.

First Consul. He was effectively dictator. Proving himself as capable in ruling a nation as in leading an army, he restored order in areas torn by civil strife, stabilized the currency, and reformed taxation along more equitable and efficient lines. He reached an agreement with the Catholic Church and reorganized the education system. Law was codified. His Civil Code, the Code Napoleon, endures in France today. It has profoundly influenced the legal systems of those countries that came under Napoleonic rule.

Convinced that it was his destiny to unite all Europe under his rule, Napoleon had himself made Emperor of the French in 1804 and continued his program of conquest. "I don't want to harm anyone," he once remarked, "but when my great car of policy is launched, it must pass. Woe to those who find themselves beneath its wheels!"

Quite a few found themselves exactly there. He meted out especially savage treatment to the Spaniards, who had the temerity to resist Napo-

Above: Napoleon aboard the *Bellerophon* on his way to final exile on St Helena after his defeat at Waterloo in 1815.

William Pitt the Younger
1759~1806

Few politicians have exemplified the concept of politics as "the art of the possible" more fully than William Pitt the Younger. He was British prime minister for nearly 20 turbulent years. His cool head and realistic policies helped the nation recover stability after its defeat in the Americas, and guided it through several crises both foreign and domestic.

The second son of William Pitt the Elder, Earl of Chatham, William showed early signs of intellectual brilliance. As a child he was dubbed "the philosopher." After being educated by tutors he entered Cambridge University at the age of 14. Although he qualified for a law career, he set his heart on entering the House of Commons. In 1780 he was returned to Parliament by one of the pocket boroughs – constituencies con-

trolled by powerful men without reference to the electorate. It was an ironic start to a career of a man who was to champion Parliamentary reform.

Pitt revealed his independent spirit in his first few years in Parliament. Although he joined liberals such as Edmund Burke and Charles James Fox in denouncing the American war ("conceived in injustice...nurtured and brought forth in folly"), he refused to become tied to their party. He differed from them sharply in his respect for the king's traditional rights to veto legislation and appoint ministers.

Right: "The Giant Factotum Amusing Himself" – a cartoon by Gillray satirizes Pitt's taxation policy. The war against France imposed a huge burden on the British exchequer, so Pitt introduced new taxes to pay for it. His imposition of income tax was particularly resented, even though the rate was a mere 2½ pence (six old pence) in the Pound and only the well to do paid it.

Left: a portrait of William Pitt the Younger. He became Britain's youngest ever prime minster before his twenty-fifth birthday in 1784.

Opposite page: the Battle of Trafalgar in 1805. Pitt's fiscal policies had helped strengthen the British fleet, which under Nelson's command, inflicted a crushing defeat on the French. Napoleon's naval power never recovered.

In 1784 Pitt was appointed First Lord of the Treasury and Chancellor of the Exchequer – in effect, prime minister – of a new government. He was only 25. Considering his inability to manage his personal finances, Pitt dealt masterfully with the country's. He established a sinking fund to repay the massive national dept. A believer in free trade, he slashed the exorbitant customs duties that had made smuggling such a lucrative business. At the same time he estab-

lished new taxes and facilitated their collection. Greatly increased revenues resulted. Later, during the war with France, he introduced the highly unpopular income tax. The 1786 economic treaty he concluded with France proved very advantageous to Britain.

The controversial issue of the East India Company's activities was resolved by Pitt's India Bill. This established a Board of Control and other government machinery to supervise the Company's rule in India. Pitt's system remained in operation until the Indian Mutiny, 60 years later.

A modern prime minister can usually rely on strong, regular support in the House of Commons. Pitt was not so lucky and so had to back down on several of his cherished policies. Parliamentary reform was one of them. The overwhelming majority of the Commons would not countenance making the electoral system more truly representative, and thus putting their seats at risk. The first Reform Act was not passed until 1832. The abolition of the slave trade, which Pitt joined his friend William Wilberforce in supporting, was blocked for many years by commercial interests represented in Parliament.

The French Revolution provoked sharply divergent responses in Britain. Many hailed it as the dawn of a new age of freedom. Others thought it a catastrophe. Each side urged that the government take positive action. But Pitt was resolutely committed to non-intervention. So long as the revolution remained a purely French affair, Britain would not interfere. The French advance into the Austrian Netherlands

Right: a Gillray cartoon depicts George III with Napoleon Bonaparte. Napoleon is portrayed as an insignificant little nuisance.

Below: rebels plundering the palace of the Bishop of Ferns in May 1798 during the Irish troubles.

sion of Britain. To counter this menace Pitt organized a coalition with Austria and Russia. This was intended to defeat Napoleon on land while the British Navy defeated him at sea. Only the second half of his strategy was successful. Soon after receiving the news of Nelson's victory at Trafalgar in 1805, Pitt learned that Napoleon had overwhelmed the Austrian forces at Ulm. News of the Russians' shattering defeat at Austerlitz quickly followed.

Pitt's long-failing health broke down under the strain. He had forestalled the invasion but failed to stop Napoleon's advance through Europe. Early in 1806 he died. His last words were, "Oh, my country! How I leave my country!"

(Belgium) in 1792 drew a sharp warning from the British Government. Early in 1793, France announced the annexation of Belgium and declared war on both Holland and Britain. Pitt was now a war leader.

He was not an outstanding war minister, and for some years the conflict went badly for Britain. But he worked tirelessly to build coalitions against the French. In this area he had some success. Meanwhile another crisis loomed. The Irish – increasingly restive under a parliament responsible neither to themselves nor to Westminster – organized a rebellion. Despite some French support, the revolt was crushed.

Pitt hoped to solve the Irish problem by uniting the country with Britain and giving the vote to the Catholic majority. His Union bill passed through Parliament, but then ran up against a royal veto on Catholic emancipation. Though temporarily free of his recurring mental illness, George III was as stubborn as ever. He would not be persuaded. Blocked on this important issue, Pitt resigned in 1801.

He returned to power three years later, just as Napoleon Bonaparte was preparing an inva-

Wellington
1769-1852

The Countess of Mornington took pride in her elder sons Richard and Henry. They had both shone at Eton and Oxford, but her third son was another matter. "I vow to God I don't know what I shall do with my awkward son Arthur," she declared. Not profiting from the benefits of Eton, he was sent to a French military academy, in the hope that he might make a passable soldier. Seldom has such lack of confidence proved so unjustified. The unpromising Arthur Wesley (as his Anglo-Irish family originally spelled their name) went on to become one of Britain's greatest military heroes, the victor of Waterloo. He has the credit for finally stopping Napoleon.

It took some years for his military talent to show itself. Commissioned in 1787, he obtained, through family influence, a position as aide-de-camp to the Viceroy of Ireland. Also, from 1790, he held the Wellesley seat of Trim in the Irish parliament. His first active service came in 1794, when, as a lieutenant-colonel, he led his regiment in some successful minor engagements in Flanders.

India, his next post, was more challenging – particularly after the arrival of his brother Richard as governor-general in 1798. Having proved himself in a successful war against the Sultan of Mysore, Arthur Wellesley was made

Above: the armies of Napoleon Bonaparte go down to final defeat at Waterloo in 1815. British forces under Wellington's command defeated the French, with Prussian help. After an unpromising start to life, Wellington became Britain's greatest military hero.

Left: the famous portrait of Wellington by the Spanish painter Francisco Goya.

Opposite: Wellington's magnificent funeral cortege. He was given a state funeral after his death in 1852.

governor of Mysore, and then commander of the British forces in a war against the Marāthā princes. British rule was greatly expanded by his victories in India. They won some high praise from his brother: "You have infinitely surpassed all that I could have required of you . . ."

Endowed with a knighthood, Wellesley returned home in 1805. He married the sweetheart of his youth, Kitty Pakenham, and entered the House of Commons. Here, he defended his brother's expansionist policies in India against his many critics. He became a close friend of Viscount Castlereagh, then Secretary of State for War, whom he served as military advisor.

So far, Britain's contribution to the war against Napoleon had consisted mainly of large subsidies and successful naval engagements. The War in the Peninsula brought the British army into the struggle on a much greater scale. It was also to make Arthur Wellesley – who became Viscount Wellington in 1809 – a hero.

He first went to Portugal in 1808 to help a Portuguese uprising against Napoleonic rule, sharing command with two mediocre generals. The British won the campaign. But the peace treaty was so lenient toward the French that all three commanding officers were recalled home for a court-martial. Wellesley emerged from the trial with his own reputation intact – even enhanced – thanks to glowing tributes from his subordinates.

It was mainly due to Wellesley's pressure that the British Cabinet agreed to pursue the war in the Peninsula in the first place. He returned to Portugal in 1809 to renew a struggle that would last another five years. In the end, the British, with help from Portuguese and Spanish guer-

revolution and the destruction of British institutions. Accordingly, he firmly opposed parliamentary reform, one of the most pressing issues of the day. His 1830 declaration against reform brought down his government. He became the target for public abuse. On the other great issue, Catholic Emancipation, the Duke took a more progressive line. He saw that civil war in Ireland was the alternative to granting the Catholics political rights and made an all-out effort to overcome the opposition to emancipation of his fellow Tories and George IV. He finally succeeded in passing a bill granting it in 1829.

rillas, expelled the French. For the first few years Wellington fought a defensive war, forcing Napoleon to use up troops needed elsewhere in a vain attempt to drive the British out of the Peninsula. Wellington's offensive coincided with Napoleon's disastrous adventure in Russia in 1812, and gave momentum and encouragement to the Allied cause. After finally liberating Spain from Napoleonic rule in 1814, Wellington pursued the enemy into France. Here, he received news of Napoleon's abdication.

The following year, as commander of an allied army, Wellington inflicted the final defeat on the intrepid Corsican at Waterloo. His victory cost a staggering number of lives. Wellington, who has been somewhat unfairly dubbed "the Iron Duke," wept for the fallen. He hoped he had fought his last battle.

But peacetime was to embroil him in battles of a different kind, and to dim the luster of his military triumphs. After serving capably as commander of the occupation in France, he returned to political life in England. He held a minor post in the Tory Cabinet between 1818 and 1827. He became prime minister in 1828.

Wellington had a well-developed distaste for political infighting, which had hampered the war effort, and a profound fear of liberalism, which he saw as the thin entering wedge of

Right: Wellington in old age. A brilliant military leader he was not such a conspicuous success when he turned his hand to politics.

Below: "Sailor Bill" or William IV was served by Wellington as Prime Minister.

Wellington never really retired. He served as foreign secretary and minister without portfolio in Sir Robert Peel's government. For the last 10 years of his life he was commander-in-chief of the army, motivated by the sense of duty that had sustained him in more active days. Wellington's political career was not as inspired as his military one. He was too rigid to adapt to the changed social conditions of what had become the world's first industrialized nation.

James Monroe
1758-1831

Left: James Monroe was descended from Welsh and Scottish settlers. One of his ancestors had fought for Charles I during the English Civil War.

Below: Louisiana territory being handed over to the United States after it had been purchased from France for $12,000,000 in 1803.

James Monroe was a member of the Virginia aristocracy and a protege of Thomas Jefferson. As such, he was destined to play a part in the development of the young United States of America. He was the fourth Virginian to become its President before 1825. His presidency was a period of relative tranquility called the "Era of Good Feeling." The United States began to pursue a positive, independent course in world affairs.

Monroe was descended from Welsh and Scottish settlers, one of whom had fought for Charles I in the English Civil War. Like Jefferson, he studied law at the College of William and Mary. In 1776 the 18-year-old student enlisted in a Virginia regiment to fight in the War of Independence. He later returned to his studies, this time under Governor Jefferson. This move smoothed the way into the political career he had chosen.

He was an outstandingly successful politician. Between 1782 and 1794 he was elected to the Virginia House of Delegates, to the Continental Congress, to the US House of Representatives, and to the Senate. Like his teacher, Jefferson, Monroe was a Republican and a supporter of

France. It was largely due to his admiration for France that he was appointed minister to that country by George Washington in 1794.

One of his most important tasks was to reconcile the French government, the Directory, to John Jay's treaty with Britain. This agreement amicably settled several points of dispute remaining after the American Revolution. Monroe did not go out of his way to justify the treaty. Instead, he assured the French that a new Republican government would speedily revoke it. Ignorant of Monroe's duplicity, but sensing that he was not the right man for the job, Washington recalled him.

After serving for three years as Governor of Virginia Monroe returned to France in 1803. This time he was President Jefferson's Minister Plenipotentiary, and was entrusted with helping the resident minister, Robert Livingston, negotiate the purchase of New Orleans. When Napoleon's Foreign Minister Talleyrand offered to sell the entire Louisiana Territory, the Americans closed the deal for $12 million.

As Jefferson's minister to Britain, Monroe could not resolve the differences – chiefly to do

with shipping – that led to the War of 1812. Back in America, he returned to Virginia politics. He again served as Governor, before being appointed Secretary of State by President Madison. He succeeded Madison as President in 1817.

Peace both at home and abroad characterized most of Monroe's eight years in office. A brief war with the Seminole Indians of Florida in his first term led to the purchase of that territory from Spain. Conflicts over the spread of slavery into the western lands were satisfactorily settled

the suggestion of the British Foreign Minister Canning that the two nations jointly proclaim the Western Hemisphere out of bounds for European intervention. But Monroe's cautious Secretary of State, John Quincy Adams, urged that the United States make a unilateral statement, which would warn off Britain as well as the other powers. The resulting statement, issued on December 2, 1823, declared that "the American continents . . . are henceforth not to be considered as subjects for future colonization by

by the Missouri Compromise of 1820. This balanced the number of free and slave states in the Union.

The most notable achievement of Monroe's Presidency was the "Monroe Doctrine." A series of wars of independence in Latin America had, by 1822, created a group of new nations occupying nearly all of the territory south of the United States. There was a real possibility that the reactionary governments of Europe, following the policy advocated by *Metternich*, might intervene in Latin America. This threat was viewed with alarm by Great Britain which was now enjoying greatly increased trade with the new republics. The United States was even more worried. Therefore, Monroe welcomed, at first,

Top: Monroe's cautious Secretary of State, John Quincy Adams.

Above: the meeting at which the "Monroe Doctrine" was formulated. It laid down the United States' right to protect its own spheres of influence, and pledged not to become involved in the internal or external affairs of the European powers. It survived intact until the 20th century.

any European powers" and that the United States would regard any attempt by a European nation to impose its political system on a sister American republic as "dangerous to our peace and safety." Monroe also promised not to intervene in European wars.

In those days the United States was in no position to back its declaration with force. For some years, it was the presence of the British Royal Navy in the Atlantic that discouraged any projects for colonizing in the Americas. But Monroe had firmly established a fundamental principle of American foreign policy, acknowledged and adhered to by his successors until Woodrow Wilson took the United States into World War I.

William Wilberforce
1759-1833

In 1784, William Wilberforce, a British MP and a friend of Prime Minister William Pitt the Younger, travelled to Europe with his mother and sisters. A friend, Isaac Miller went along with him. During the journey, the two spent a lot of time reading and talking. When Wilberforce returned to England in 1785, he was a changed man. Along the way, he had been converted to Evangelical Christianity, and had resolved to dedicate his life to religion. His resolve led him into the fight against slavery already underway in England. Largely through his efforts, Parliament ended the West Indian slave trade in 1806. Slavery itself was abolished in Britain and the empire in 1833.

Wilberforce's personal popularity with supporters and opponents alike was of considerable help in his winning the fight for abolition. As a boy in Hull, he was popular with his friends. At Cambridge, he kept a huge Yorkshire pie in his rooms and welcomed one and all to share it. After Cambridge, Wilberforce decided on a career in politics, and was elected to the House of Commons in 1780 along with his Cambridge classmate, William Pitt. The two found they

both agreed with many radical causes such as Parliamentary reform. When Pitt became prime minister in 1784, Wilberforce was one of his strongest supporters.

In 1787, after his religious conversion, Wilberforce was approached by well-known abolitionists Granville Sharp and Thomas Clarkson. They appealed to him to lead the campaign in Parliament to end the slave trade. Wilberforce agreed. He soon became known to his colleagues in the Commons as an eloquent speaker, and a

Above: Tuareg slavers at work. Africans were brutally driven from their homes and transported to labor in the fields and plantations of the New World.
Right: the fearful overcrowding of the slave ships.

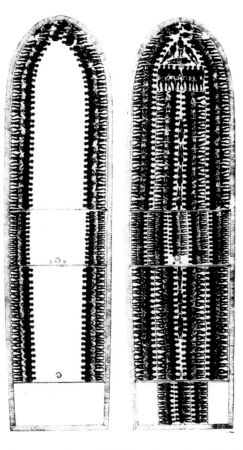

tireless introducer of bills and motions in the cause of abolition. He also became a leading member of the so-called "Clapham Sect," a group of abolitionists who held meetings at his

came to the conclusion that complete emancipation was the only solution. Therefore, from 1821 on, they urged passage of an anti-slavery law. Progress was again painfully slow, and Wilberforce retired in 1825 before success had been achieved. But he continued to speak, and served as vice president of the Abolition Society, an organisation formed by young supporters in 1823. The struggle in Parliament was carried on by a former collaborator of Wilberforce, Sir Thomas Foxwell Barton. In 1833, the Act of Abolition, ending slavery throughout the British Empire, was finally passed. Wilberforce lived to hear of the second reading, but died a month before it became law.

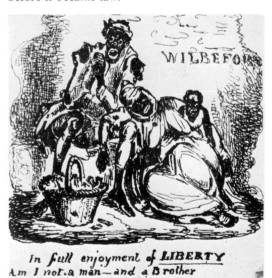

In full enjoyment of LIBERTY Am I not a man—and a Brother

house on Clapham Common, South London.

Wilberforce and the abolitionists won many converts to their cause, but failed to gain legislative victories for many years. The Tories in control of Parliament depended on West Indian planters and slave traders for support. Many other members believed abolition would damage the British economy. Not until Pitt died and was temporarily replaced by a liberal coalition was a law finally passed in 1806 outlawing the slave trade.

This achievement after almost 20 years of hard fighting, won Wilberforce respect and admiration and allowed him to turn to other issues such as Roman Catholic emancipation, and the introduction of Christianity into India. But the slavery issue would not go away. The 1806 act had ended British participation in the slave trade, but it did nothing to improve the lot of those already enslaved. Wilberforce and his supporters

Above: whip brandishing slave drivers supervise slaves on a West Indian sugar plantation. Slave owners varied in their attitudes. But many were brutal, and slaves often died from overwork and ill treatment. Wilberforce fought to put an end to such abuses in British possessions, and the only way to do that was to abolish slavery.
Above right: slavery in action in the United States. This cartoon shows two slaves being forced to run the gauntlet at West Point Military Academy in the early 19th century. Slaves were often subjected to acts of cruelty.
Right: a pro-Wilberforce leaflet reading "in full enjoyment of liberty am I not a man and a brother." Even sympathetic publications like this grotesquely caricatured black people.

William Wilberforce did not begin the movement for abolition, nor did he shepherd the final emancipation bill through Parliament. But he, more than anyone else, through 40 years of determined struggle aroused the conscience of the British people, and gathered the necessary support to end slavery in Great Britain and its empire. Parliament expressed its appreciation of his long struggle by insisting that he be buried in Westminster Abbey. A grateful nation subscribed money to pay for the statue to be placed nearby.

Metternich
1773-1859

Left: Prince Clemens von Metternich portrayed in strikingly romantic and militaristic pose.

After the French Revolution and the Napoleonic wars a mood of conservative reaction settled over Europe. The ideals of social justice kindled by the Revolution were still very much alive, but those in power were determined to restore, as far as possible, the old order. The personification of this reaction was Prince Clemens von Metternich, Austria's Foreign Minister.

Metternich was born of a noble family in the Rhineland town of Coblenz. He entered the University of Strasbourg to study diplomacy at the age of 15. Unlike many of his fellow students, the revolutionary spirit of 1789 left him cold. When life became dangerous for aristocrats he returned to Germany, completing his studies at the University of Mainz.

His first diplomatic assignments were in Brussels, where his father was Austria's minister plenipotentiary, and in The Hague. Later, forced to flee to the Netherlands by the advancing troops of the French Revolution, the Metternich family went to Vienna. Here, a marriage was arranged between Clemens and Princess Eleonore Kaunitz, granddaughter of Maria Theresa's foreign minister. After serving in Dresden and Berlin, Metternich was appointed Austria's ambassador to France in 1806.

Metternich opposed Austria's policy of ap-

peasement toward Napoleon from the outset. Over the years his methods of dealing with Bonapartist aggression were refined. In 1809, encouraged by French reverses in Spain, he persuaded his government that the time was ripe for renewing the war. Austria was roundly defeated and Metternich – now foreign minister – was forced to sign a humiliating peace treaty. He behaved more cautiously from then on. Metternich negotiated the marriage between Napoleon and the Hapsburg princess Maria Louise. This gained some breathing space for Austria. As Napoleon was preparing to invade Russia in 1812, Metternich signed a treaty with Napoleon promising military assistance, with the prospect of handsome rewards for Austria if France won. At the same time, he secretly reassured Russia, Prussia, and Great Britain of Austria's friendship and his intention of reviving the Coalition. After Napoleon's humiliating defeat in Russia, Metternich extricated Austria from its treaty. In 1813, having secretly rearmed, Austria joined the Fourth Coalition to defeat Napoleon.

Metternich's guiding principle was, as ever, the maintenance of the balance of power. He had no wish to cripple France. The Treaty of Paris (1814) reflected his views, and dealt fairly with the former enemy.

Soon after the signing of the treaty, representatives of all the European nations met at the Congress of Vienna, called to try to restore equilibrium to Europe. Metternich played a key role in the formulation of the numerous solutions produced by the Congress. Two of the

Right: the Congress of Vienna. Metternich played a key role in formulating the numerous decisions that were eventually reached. Called to try to restore stability in Europe, the Congress was more successful in this considerable task than anybody expected. The settlements dealing with Germany and Italy were of key importance.

Left: Europe as it appeared after the Congress of Vienna. Metternich strove hard to try to negotiate settlements that would stick, and preserve European security.

Right: Metternich was a repressive ruler who had a distrust of freedom of speech and expression. This 1835 cartoon comments on the Germany of censorship, police spies and informers. Entitled "The Thinkers' Club", the captaion above the table reads "How long are they going to let us think for?"

Above: Metternich's signature, ending with a flourish. An unbending autocrat, Metternich was the main target of the French revolutionaries' wrath in 1848.

most important settlements were those dealing with Germany and Italy. In place of the defunct Holy Roman Empire, Metternich created a German Confederation, a loosely-knit league of 38 states, of which Austria was the dominant partner. He wanted to form a similar Austrian-dominated confederation in Italy, but this did not materialize. But Austrian hegemony in Italy was assured through re-appropriation of Tuscany and the creation of the kingdom of Lombardo-Venetia within the Austrian Empire. For the time being, Metternich agreed to the retention of the throne of Naples by Napoleon's brother-in-law Joachim Murat. But when Joachim tried to launch a movement for Italian unity

and independence a few years later, Metternich, with allied help, crushed the movement and installed a Bourbon monarch in Joachim's place.

Metternich had little sympathy for the new nationalistic trends, and he was alarmed by the rather mild activities of a German student movement dedicated to promoting German unity. At a conference held in Carlsbad in 1819 he prevailed on the other German states to take steps against such groups. The Carlsbad Decrees dissolved the student political clubs and imposed press censorship.

In order to preserve the peace after the Congress of Vienna, the powers agreed to meet frequently and deal with any incipient problems. Several such congresses met, the last at Verona in 1822. They did reach some satisfactory agreements. Metternich's suggestion that they should join in collective intervention whenever any government was threatened by revolution was rejected by both France and Britain. Only the more autocratic powers, Russia and Prussia, joined Austria in this agreement.

Within the Austrian Empire – the "land of silence" – unrest manifested itself among all segments of society: Slavs, Hungarians, peasants, Italian republicans, Polish aristocrats, German intellectuals. Metternich's cautious moves to reform the governmental structure were vetoed by the ultra-reactionary Emperor Francis II. After Francis' death in 1835, power struggles between Metternich, the Regent, and other ministers made any positive approach to the coming crisis impossible.

The crisis was precipitated by the French Revolution of 1848. Emboldened by the news from Paris, the Hungarian radicals demanded an end to Austrian absolutism. Within days, Viennese working men and students had staged an insurrection. Metternich was their main target as the personification of autocracy. His equally autocratic opponents in the government used him as a scape-goat, forcing him to resign.

Metternich spent several years in exile in England and Belgium. After the revolution had subsided and the reactionary forces were once more in control, the aging statesman was invited to return to Vienna. There, he lived for another eight years, a revered figure frequently consulted by the young Emperor Francis Joseph on affairs of state. But Metternich's style of rule was a thing of the past.

Simón Bolívar
1783-1830

The 21-year-old Simón Bolívar stood on an Italian hill with his tutor and made a vow: "I swear before you, by the God of my fathers and the honor of my country; I will not rest, not in body or soul, till I have broken the chains of Spain."

Bolívar kept his promise. He drove the Spaniards from his own country, Venezuela, and from the countries now known as Colombia, Ecuador, Peru, and Bolivia – the last named in his honor.

Bolívar was a creole, that is of Spanish descent but not born in Spain. So, despite his family's wealth, he was a second-class citizen. Spanish colonial rule was firmly in the hands of native-

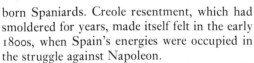

Left: a portrait of Simon Bolivar. He was an untiring fighter for South American independence. Bolivia, named in his honor, was one country he helped to free from the Spanish yolk.

Right: Bolivar, as a creole had suffered Spanish racialism at first hand. Many of the men who fought alongside him were descended from slaves imported by the Spanish. This picture shows Bolivar at the death of one of the many black fighters among his followers.

born Spaniards. Creole resentment, which had smoldered for years, made itself felt in the early 1800s, when Spain's energies were occupied in the struggle against Napoleon.

The first Venezuelan *coup*, in 1810, was directed ostensibly against the rule of Bonapartist Spain. Its leaders professed loyalty to the legitimate king Ferdinand VII, but soon the republicans, including Bolívar, had their way and Venezuela declared its independence. At Bolívar's suggestion, the exiled General Francisco Miranda returned to Venezuela, and took command of a republican army. Only part of Venezuela, including the capital, Caracas, rallied to the republican cause. Most cities remained royalist, and would remain so for years. A republican government was set up, with Miranda as its chief executive. But royalist troops, commanded by Domingo de Monteverde, soon

crushed the fledgling republic. Miranda, who had outraged the patriots by surrendering, tried to flee. He was captured with the help of the indignant Bolívar, who very nearly lost his passport when he told Monteverde, "I helped arrest General Miranda in order to punish a traitor to my country, not to serve Spain!" But Monteverde allowed him to leave Venezuela. He could hardly have suspected that the young hot-head, who had shown little military skill up to then, would become Spain's most formidable adversary.

Bolívar went to the neighboring colony of New Granada (Colombia), whose revolutionary leaders reluctantly gave him a command. Disobeying orders, Bolívar attacked the royalist stronghold of Tenerife and captured it. He went on to score more victories, re-entered Venezuela,

Bolívar was at one point president not only of Colombia (New Granada) but also of Peru and Bolivia. He disliked administrative duties, and tended to leave the job of governing to his vice-president. But he did have political goals beyond independence. His Bolivian Constitution provided for a president-for-life, gave the vote to all citizens (except domestic servants) who could read, and outlawed slavery. Bolívar's great dream was a commonwealth of all the South American states.

His dream was not shared by most of the revo-

and unleashed his *guerra a muerte*, war without quarter. No one who had helped the royalist cause would be spared. Bolívar's lightning attacks proved fruitful, and his power to inspire loyalty won new recruits to the cause. A new republic was established at Caracas in 1813. Bolívar was virtually dictator.

He experienced an impressive series of triumphs and defeats over the next 17 years. At one point, in 1815-16, Bolívar was a penniless exile in Jamaica and Haiti, whose President Pétion helped the patriots organize an invasion of Venezuela – once again under Spanish rule. Three years later he led an army over some of the most dangerous passes of the Andes, and descended on the Spaniards of New Granada. Once liberated, New Granada chose Bolívar as its president.

lutionaries. Their sights extended no further than their own countries, or even their own provinces. Venezuela, which Bolívar liberated permanently in 1821, became part of the new state of Gran Colombia, which also included Colombia and Ecuador. But many Venezuelans began agitating for independence from Gran Colombia. Some even regarded Bolívar as a traitor.

Bolívar's own vice-president, Santander, opposed his centralist policies. More and more people took Santander's side. Implicated in an attempt on Bolívar's life, Santander was sent into exile. But the forces at work in the new states were too strong for Bolívar. Wracked by tuberculosis, he resigned from the presidency in 1830, and prepared to leave for Europe with his mistress Manuela. He got no further than Cartagena, where he died.

José de San Martín
1778-1850

Born in Argentina, then the United Provinces of La Plata, José de San Martín spent his boyhood in Spain, and as a young man fought for the mother country in its war against Napoleon. But he was acutely conscious of being a creole, and his own country was making its first tentative

Right: the declaration of Argentinian independence in July 1916. Independence was declared at Tucuman. San Martin was encouraged by the new governments bold stance, and in January 1817 crossed the Andes to invade Chile.

steps towards independence. San Martín played a decisive role in the achievement of that independence.

San Martín retired from active duty in the Spanish Army in 1811, and was granted a transfer to Lima, Peru. He did not go to Peru, but to London. There he met other South Americans, who were making plans for the liberation of their own countries.

San Martín returned to Buenos Aires with some other revolutionaries, and was given authority to form a corps of mounted grenadiers by the triumvirate ruling the United Provinces. Although nominally loyal to the deposed Ferdinand VII, the government was determined to win absolute independence.

San Martín shaped his grenadiers into a force that won several battles against the royalists. He was then given command of the ragged Army of the North, stationed near the Peruvian border. He realized at once that a defensive action was not enough. It was vital to destroy the royalist stronghold in Peru. He conceived an audacious plan to achieve this. The geography of Peru made an overland invasion impossible. So he decided to lead his army westwards over the Andes into Chile, which had a strong revolu-

tionary movement. He would launch a sea invasion of Peru from a liberated Chile.

Concealing his plans from the Buenos Aires government, San Martín applied for, and received, a post as governor of a western province. He capably governed the province of Cuyo between 1814 and 1817. Meanwhile, he built up an army of 5200 men, and a network of agents in Chile entrusted with keeping revolutionary sentiments alive.

Argentina's formal declaration of independence in 1816, and the inauguration of a new government favorable to bold policies gave San Martín his chance. With official blessing he completed his painstaking preparations. In January

Right: San Martin with his friend, the Chilean revolutionary, Bernardo o'Higgins lead their force over the Andes mountains into Chile. Chilean royalist forces were taken by surprise.

1817 – mid-summer in those latitudes – he crossed the Andes. He tricked the Chilean royalists into thinking he would invade farther south. With the bulk of the royalists elsewhere, San Martín quickly conquered the capital, Santiago. The Chilean revolutionary Bernardo O'Higgins, who had gone with San Martín on the perilous march, was installed as supreme director of the new government. Chilean independence was established a year later.

San Martín then built a navy. Under the daring Scottish officer Lord Cochrane, the Chilean navy broke the royalist blockage of Valparaiso and went on to raid the coast of Peru, at the same time propagandizing among the natives.

Above: the Scottish naval officer Admiral Lord Cochrane. He commanded the Chilean navy which San Martin had built up.

By 1820 Cochrane's raids had sufficiently intimidated the Peruvian navy, and San Martín was able to land his forces along the coast. His plan was to proceed cautiously, gathering support among the people before engaging the viceroy's forces. Meanwhile, the Spanish government was adopting a more conciliatory policy to its colonies. The Peruvian viceroy met with San Martín to negotiate terms. But San Martín was not interested in compromise, and the negotiations failed. He blocked Peru's main port, and continued to propaganda war. The viceroy withdrew to the mountains, taking his troops with him, and the people of Lima declared their wish for independence and invited San Martín to enter the city. He declared himself Protector of the country until the royalists could be expelled.

At this point San Martín's fortunes took a turn for the worse. The royalist forces were difficult to budge. San Martín was an inept ruler. His rapacious officials added to his own unpopularity. His meeting with Simón Bolívar in 1822 was not a success. San Martín obviously hoped for Bolívar's cooperation in driving the Spanish from Peru. He returned to Lima convinced that this was impossible. There, he found that the citizens had thrown out his corrupt chief lieutenant, Monteagudo. Thoroughly dispirited and in bad health, San Martín resigned. The independence of Peru was finally achieved in 1824 by Bolívar.

In that same year, after living for a while in Chile and in Argentina – where he had many enemies – San Martín sailed for Europe. Now a widower, he lived for another 27 years. During that time he had the satisfaction of seeing his reputation among South Americans improve. He died when he was 72 and was to become Argentina's most venerated hero.

Queen Victoria
1819~1901

"I shall ever remember this day as the *proudest* of my life!" wrote the 19-year-old Queen Victoria in her journal on the day of her coronation, June 28, 1838. To the spectators in the Abbey with memories of her aged uncles, the eccentric William IV and the dissolute George IV, the radiant young Queen must have made a nice change. They were witnessing the beginning of a new era. During her reign, Britain reached the peak of its power, and came to rule a quarter of the world's people.

The image of Queen Victoria evokes that of a dour, stout old lady who was "not amused." But she really often enjoyed a joke. Early in her reign the Prime Minister, Lord Melbourne, gave her fatherly guidance and reassurance. Having lost her own father in infancy, Victoria appreciated his advice. Under Melbourne's tutelage the Queen became an ardent Whig. Later, under the influence of Benjamin Disraeli, she would be a no less ardent Tory.

Non-political monarchy was still a long way off, but the political power of the monarch declined considerably during Victoria's reign. By the end of her reign three-quarters of the adult male population had the vote. But the queen wielded considerable influence.

It was with some reluctance at first that Victoria allowed her beloved husband Prince Albert to share some of her responsibilities. He effici-

Right: the Great Exhibition opens at the Crystal Palace London in 1851. It displayed wares from all over the world, and served as a showplace for Britain's industrial supremacy. Victoria is at the center of the stage and her husband, Prince Albert, is on the right. After Albert's death from typhoid in 1861, Victoria was inconsolable.

Above: Whig Prime Minister Lord Melbourne. It was Melbourne who guided the Queen through her constitutional duties early in her reign.

ently reorganized the royal household, and was soon attending her audiences with ministers and reading dispatches to her. The Great Exhibition of 1851 was Albert's project. He also occasionally interested himself in the conduct of foreign policy – still, to some extent, within the royal prerogative. His tactful rewording of Prime Minister Palmerston's angry note to the American government over the seizure of two Confederate agents on a British ship averted war with the United States.

Albert's death from typhoid in 1861 left Victoria in a profound and prolonged state of grief. She withdrew from public life and stubbornly resisted all efforts to bring her out of seclusion. Her popularity suffered as a result. Her sense of duty was finally reawakened by the Conservative leader Benjamin Disraeli, prime minister between 1874 and 1878. After the Indian Mutiny of 1857, an uprising of Indian troops against the British, the government abolished both the East India Company and the puppet Mogul Empire, and assumed direct control of the subcontinent. Disraeli now arranged for the queen to become in title what she was in fact: Empress of India. In 1876 he purchased from the Khedive of Egypt 44 per cent of the shares of the Suez Canal Company, making Britain the principal share holder of this vital new waterway.

Of Disraeli's main antagonist, William Ewart Gladstone, the queen did not approve. Gladstone served as prime minister four times between 1868 and 1894. He was one of the liberal Tories who had joined with the Whigs to form the Liberal Party. He sponsored many of the progressive measures of the day, including the secret ballot, state-supported education, the legalizing of labor unions, and the end of religious discrimination at Oxford and Cambridge. On one issue – women's rights – he was a reaction-

Above: Benjamin Disraeli
presenting Victoria with the crown
of India from a cartoon based on
the tale of Aladdin "New Crowns
for Old."
Right: a poster celebrating Britain's
industrial progress.
Below: a family group at
Darmstadt in 1894. Victoria is in
the center of the picture.

ary. In this Queen Victoria agreed with him;
"this *mad, wicked folly*" she called it. Otherwise,
she found Gladstone and his principles odious.

A main bone of contention was the Irish Question. The queen had little understanding of the sufferings endured by the Irish peasants under their callous landlords. All that she felt was needed were severe measures against Irish "terrorists." She thoroughly objected to Gladstone's bill to disestablish the Anglican Church in Ireland, so that Catholics would no longer have to support it financially. But later, when the bill reached the House of Lords, she personally used her influence there to obtain its passage, and so avert a parliamentary conflict. Similarly, in 1881 she smoothed the way for Gladstone's Land Bill, which corrected some of the injustices borne by the peasants. By now the Irish were pressing for Home Rule. Gladstone eventually supported them. His advocacy of Home Rule for Ireland further alienated the queen and split the Liberal Party.

Victoria also disliked Gladstone for what she considered his inadequate defense of British interests abroad. His delay in sending relief to General Gordon, besieged at Khartoum in the Sudan, and Gordon's subsequent death at the hands of Sudanese terrorists, provoked an angry telegram from his sovereign. Gordon exemplified the spirit of empire-building; sent to evacuate British and Egyptian troops from the Sudan, he had tried a counter-offensive. Victoria much admired this heroic but misguided effort. Victoria's Diamond Jubilee of 1897 featured the glory of the Empire. It also produced a great outpouring of patriotism and affection for the queen. She symbolized the nation's manifold achievements, its power and influence throughout the world. Indeed, Britain became the world's leading power under Victoria's reign.

Leopold I of the Belgians
1790-1865

Charlotte's death in childbirth left Leopold grief-stricken and at loose ends. For 10 indolent years he travelled around Europe, keeping an eye open for any opportunities that might come his way. In 1830 such a chance presented itself. Greece, newly independent of Turkey, offered him the throne. Though tempted by the offer, Leopold turned it down – partly because it looked as though a Regent might be needed when his young niece Victoria became Queen.

Right: Princess Charlotte, the only daughter of England's Prince Regent, became Leopold's first wife in 1817. He married her for the usual diplomatic motives of the time. But he fell in love. Her death two years later shattered Leopold.

Left: a portrait of Leopold I by Winterhalter. Early in her reign, Queen Victoria thought highly of Leopold's advice. Other European rulers were not so impressed.

Below: "a Rough Passage to Belgium." The Dutch made a surprise attack on Belgium only two weeks after Leopold became king.

To Queen Victoria "Uncle" Leopold was the trusted mentor of her childhood. Many other crowned heads thought he was something of an upstart, the elected king of an inconsequential little country. In fact, Leopold was an able ruler and dedicated peacemaker, who helped bring prosperity and security to the newly-created state of Belgium.

Born a German, he was a member of the ruling house of Saxe-Coburg. This family also produced Queen Victoria's mother, her husband Albert, and any number of other royal consorts. As a youth Leopold served as an officer in the Russian army (his commission having been obtained through family influence). In 1814, as a lieutenant-general, he escorted the victorious Russian Czar and Prussian King into Paris.

Shortly after this triumph, Leopold asked for the hand of Princess Charlotte, the only child of England's Prince Regent. Originally attracted only by the prospect of one day sharing power with the Queen of England, Leopold gradually fell in love with the Princess, and she with him. Their wedding, in 1817, was followed by two years of idyllic happiness.

The Revolution of 1830, which overthrew the restored Bourbon dynasty and installed the "Citizen King" Louis Philippe d'Orléans, caused tremors north of the border in Belgium. Ruled for 300 years by foreigners – first the Spanish, then the Austrians, and then the French – Belgium had been joined to the Dutch Netherlands to form the Kingdom of the Netherlands in 1815. The centralizing tendencies of the Dutch King, William I, were strongly resisted

two parties, the Catholics and the Liberals. Although a constitutional monarch, he found plenty of scope for governing, particularly in the directing of foreign affairs. He also actively promoted the growth of Belgian industry. Under his reign Belgium prospered.

So content were the Belgians under their king that one old republican politician complained that there was "too much happiness and prosperity in Belgium to hope for another revolu-

by the Belgians. The Belgian National Congress declared Belgium's independence from Holland in 1830. Many Belgians wanted to unite with France, but the other great powers would not allow this. At a conference in London, the British and the French negotiated terms for an independent, neutral Belgium. They agreed on Leopold as a suitable king for the new nation, and obtained his assent. The powers then persuaded the Belgian Congress to accept him. On July 21, 1831 the new King of the Belgians entered Brussels and took an oath to uphold his country's constitution.

But King William would not give up half his kingdom without a struggle. His army marched into Belgium. Even after massive French forces came to the aid of the Belgians the Dutch still held Antwerp. They did not give it up until 1839, when King William signed the Twenty Four Articles, the treaty affirming Belgium's independence.

With characteristic thoroughness, King Leopold learned all he could about Belgium. He encouraged the development of a sense of national pride, and he moderated disputes between the

Above: French troops in Belgium in 1831. When the Dutch attacked, French forces were sent to Belgium's assistance.
Below: a funeral parade in Berlin during the 1848 revolution. Revolt swept Europe in that year, but Belgium largely escaped. Leopold was an unassuming ruler and deserves some of the credit for avoiding the upheaval typical everywhere else.

BLACK

tion." Revolution spread like a brush-fire through most of Europe in 1848, the Belgian government remained secure. Leopold offered asylum to political exiles, including such diverse characters as Karl Marx and Leopold's old friend and frequent critic Prince Metternich.

Keenly aware that his nation existed only with the consent of the great powers, Leopold worked tirelessly to prevent war, negotiating patiently whenever conflict threatened. His diplomatic maneuvers included a considerable amount of matchmaking, culminating in the marriage of his daughter Charlotte (by his French Queen Louise d'Orléans) to the Archduke Maximilian of Austria. Leopold had always distrusted Napoleon III, whom he suspected of having designs on Belgium. But when the French Emperor broached the idea of establishing Maximilian as ruler of Mexico, Leopold's frustrated dream of empire overcame his better judgment. He persuaded his son-in-law to accept. Fortunately, he would not live to see the tragic outcome of that adventure. Leopold's achievement was to preserve Belgium's territorial integrity against her more powerful neighbors.

Benito Juárez
1806-1872

Benito Juárez was a president of humble origins. Also like Lincoln, he brought his country through its most serious crisis. But Juárez' country, Mexico, was politically much more fragile than the United States. It was divided against itself, and was invaded by a foreign power. For three years of his presidency Juárez hid in one provincial town after another. A puppet installed by Napoleon III of France attempted to govern.

Juárez was born in the state of Oaxaca, 15 years before Mexico won its independence from Spain. Orphaned as a child, he was brought up

by an uncle. This uncle taught him to read. Impatient to continue his education, Benito ran away from home at the age of 12.

In the city of Oaxaca the young Indian became a servant to a kindly bookbinder, who encouraged him in his studies. Juárez once planned to become a priest, but when an Institute of Sciences and Arts was established in Oaxaca, he enrolled to study law.

Above: General Santa Anna, the autocratic ruler of Mexico. He became president, and later dictator in 1853.

Left: Benito Juárez, the inspiration of Mexican independence. He fought, politically and by force, against Mexico's corrupt dictator General Santa Anna. Santa Anna is better known for his attack on Texan independence fighters at the Alamo.

While Juárez was establishing himself as a lawyer and bringing up a family in the 1880s and 1840s, the young Republic of Mexico was tottering under a series of military *coups* and rebellions. In 1846, the country was embroiled in a disastrous war with the United States. Half its territory was lost in the conflict. Each new government kept going with massive foreign loans. Meanwhile the Church and other landowners became richer and richer at the expense of the vast Indian majority, who remained illiterate and desperately poor.

Pressure for reform increased in the late 1840s. In 1847 Juárez, a passionate reformist, was elected governor of Oaxaca. While governor he built several hundred schools, reorganized the military forces, and put the state's finances in order.

General Santa Anna became president in 1853, then dictator. Reformers, including Juárez, were forced into exile in the United States. The ebb and flow of Mexican politics soon brought them back. In 1857, with a new liberal constitution and a new government in Mexico City, Juárez was made minister of the interior. Scarcely had he assumed his duties when yet another *coup* forced the liberals out. As the legal successor to the exiled president, Juárez took command of the constitutional government and waged a three-year war against the Usurpers. He entered Mexico City as president.

The enormous foreign debt left by his predecessors was his first headache. To put the shattered country together, Juárez and his cabinet suspended payments on the foreign debt.

Left: the execution of Maximilian, puppet of Napoleon III of France, on June 19 1867. Juárez returned to Mexico City less than a month later, on July 15.

States torn asunder by civil war, he saw his chance. He sent to Mexico 28,000 French troops. They drove Juárez and his supporters out of the capital, clearing the way for the new sovereign, the Hapsburg Archduke Maximilian, and his wife Carlotta.

Maximilian was an idealist and shared some of Juárez's liberal beliefs. For example, he wanted to nationalize Church property and grant freedom of religion – ideas that soon landed him in trouble with the Vatican. But Maximilian's good intentions were unaccompanied by any talent for administration or political determination. His government achieved little, apart from lining their own pockets.

By 1867 events were turning in the Juáristas' favor. The American Civil War was over, and Americans were raising funds to help Juárez. Meanwhile, the United States Government put pressure on Napoleon. More dangerous pressure was being applied to France by the Germans. Napoleon began to bring home the troops that had been keeping the Juárez forces (now about 40,000 strong) at bay. Maximilian's response to this betrayal was not to abdicate, as Napoleon suggested, but to make a last-ditch stand. He and his few remaining loyal troops were captured at Querétaro. In May 1867 Juárez ordered his execution by firing squad.

Once again Juárez returned to Mexico City in triumph. Now, at last, he was able to implement some of his reforms. But his government was an uneasy alliance of conflicting interests, and some of his measures made enemies of former friends. One of these was General Porfirio Díaz, who led an unsuccessful rebellion against Juárez. Five years after Juárez's death, of a heart attack, in 1872, Díaz became dictator of Mexico. He abdicated in 1911 and died four years later.

His stated intention of paying the money back as soon as the country was on its feet did not satisfy the French, British, and Spanish. They all sent ships and troops to Mexico to force payment. But France's allies withdrew when they discovered that Napoleon III had more ambitious goals than mere debt-collecting.

Encouraged by exiled Mexican monarchists, Napoleon planned to create a French-dominated empire in the New World. With the United

Below: Juárez returns to Mexico City. He was reelected president of the Republic of Mexico in August 1867.

Louis Kossuth
1802-1894

Hungary in 1848 was considerably larger than it is today, but it was not a true nation. The several ethnic groups in its population were dominated by a Magyar (Hungarian) nobility. Until the beginning of the 18th century most of it had been ruled by the Hapsburgs. A nationalistic spirit had been kept alive among the proud Magyar nobles. Most significant of the leaders of the Hungarian struggle for independence was the fiery patriot Louis Kossuth.

Kossuth was not really Hungarian. His father was a Slovak of the minor aristocracy, and his mother was German. Still, he supported the Magyars' cause, not only against Austria but also against the claims of Croats, Transylvanians, and other minorities. After qualifying as a lawyer Kossuth obtained a position as agent for a wealthy landowner, a countess. She launched his political career by sending him as a substitute delegate to the Hungarian Diet in 1832. Kossuth's political views developed during the Diet's four-year sitting. Unlike other radicals, notably Count István Széchenyi, who emphasized the need for economic and social reforms, Kossuth believed that the overriding need was for political independence from Austria. Substitute delegates were not empowered to speak in the Diet, so Kossuth began writing reports of the sessions. These reports naturally reflected his own views, and were copied by his friends and circulated throughout the country. They won him many adherents, but antagonized the government. In 1837 he was arrested and convicted of subversion.

He was released from prison in 1840 and became the editor of a political journal – continuing his agitation for Hungarian liberty. In 1847 he was elected to represent the county of Pest in the new Diet and quickly assumed leadership of the radical party.

Right: Louis Kossuth addressing the Hungarian Diet (parliament). A fierce patriot and advocate of independence, Kossuth struggled to free Hungary from the autocratic yolk of the Hapsburg empire.

Opposite page: Hungarian forces capture the fortress at Buda on 21 May 1849. This was one of the most significant acts in Hungary's revolt against Hapsburg rule.

Left: Louis Kossuth making a speech to an independence rally. He combined total belief in his cause with passionate oratory.

Although divided, the radicals managed to push through some minimal reforms when they received the news of the 1848 Revolution in Paris. Kossuth seized the chance to demand an end to Austrian oppression. The speech, printed in German and circulated in Vienna, helped spark off an insurrection that rocked the Austrian government and stimulated other revolts throughout the Empire. The Hungarian Diet, alarmed by popular uprisings in their own country, enacted the March Laws. These established a new, more democratic legislature and granted new liberties, including freedom of the press and of religion.

Kossuth was appointed minister of finance in the new government. His headstrong behavior aggravated the differences between the Hungarians and the Vienna government, which still exercised some control over Hungary. The various Hungarian minorities rose in revolt when Kossuth declared that he would impose the Magyar language on all non-Magyars – over half the population.

An Austrian-supported Croat army invaded
Hungary in September 1848, and set off a civil
war. The prime minister, Batthyány, resigned.
Kossuth now head of the committee of national
defense, effectively became a dictator.

Early in 1849 the restored and strengthened
Hapsburg regime repudiated the Magyar constitution and appealed to the Russian Czar for
help in crushing the revolution. That August
100,000 Russian troops invaded Hungary. Despite valiant fighting, the Hungarians were
finally defeated. Kossuth fled to Turkey.

He made a tour of the United States and England in 1851, in an attempt to win support for the
Hungarian cause. Although he was welcomed as
a hero in both countries, official support was not
forthcoming. Kossuth spent the rest of his life
in exile in London and Turin, watching with
anguish the cruel repression imposed on his
country by the victorious Austrian government.
In 1859 he collaborated with Napoleon III by
planning a Hungarian revolt to coincide with the
French-Piedmontese war against Austria. But

Above: Louis Kossuth addresses
the crowd at the foot of Nelson's
Column, London, in 1851. His
political message was greeted with
extraordinary enthusiasm in
England.

the early armistice made by Napoleon put an end
to these plans. A few years later, in 1867, the
establishment of the Dual Monarchy gave Hungary almost complete autonomy under the Hapsburg crown. Kossuth bitterly opposed this compromise, but it endured until World War I.

Camillo Benso di Cavour
1810~1861

Italy was a patchwork of separate states in the 1850s. Only one of these, the kingdom of Piedmont-Sardinia, was in a position to lead the others toward unity. Unlike Lombardy-Venetia it was free of foreign rule, and unlike Naples – whose despotic Bourbon regime was called "the negation of God erected into a system of government" – it enjoyed certain political liberties. The House of Savoy was a constitutional monarchy. It was fortunate in having as its prime minister an able and patriotic man, Count Cavour.

Although he had a well-earned reputation for cool-headed maneuvering, Cavour could be temperamental as well. As a youth, his insubordination at the military academy he attended greatly distressed his aristocratic family. Later, his outspoken republicanism resulted in his being subjected to police surveillance.

Having alienated the king, Charles Albert, Cavour was unable at first to pursue his chosen career of politics. He resigned his army commission in 1831, and spent the next few years traveling. He particularly liked England and France, and greatly admired their industrial development and constitutional governments.

Back in Piedmont, Cavour successfully managed a large family estate and accumulated a substantial fortune. The emergence of liberal trends in the Piedmontese government in 1847 enabled him to found a progressive newspaper called *Il*

Risorgimento ("The Resurgence") – the name given to Italy's struggle for independence and unity.

Cavour finally entered politics in the eventful year of 1848, during which Piedmont attempted, without success, to liberate Lombardy from Austrian rule. After two years in parliament, Cavour joined the Cabinet as minister of agriculture, all the time working to create an alliance of moderates to counter the influence of the right and the left. King Victor Emmanual II asked him to form a government in 1852. As prime minister Cavour encouraged the development of Piedmontese industry, the building of railroads, and free trade. He also introduced liberal reforms including curbs on the power of the Church.

Cavour realized that the expulsion of Austria and the unification of Italy could only be accomplished with the help of one of the great powers. In 1854, he sent Piedmontese troops to fight on the side of the British and French in the Crimean War. At the ensuing peace conference he was able to present the case for Italian independence. But despite considerable anti-Austria feeling, the western European powers were reluctant to take action against her.

Cavour then tried subtle persuasion on Napoleon III. He held out the prospect of a French-dominated Italy once Austria was expelled, while keeping his plans to create a strong unified Italy independent of France well hidden. Napoleon swallowed the bait. At a secret meeting with Cavour in 1859 he agreed to give Piedmont military aid – on condition that Austria be provoked into being the aggressor.

By building up the Piedmontese regular army and commissioning Garibaldi to recruit and train a volunteer force drawn from all over Italy, including Austria's domains, Cavour provided the necessary provocation. Austria declared war on Piedmont. French troops crossed the Alps.

Below: Garibaldi meets King Victor Emmanual II. With Garibaldi, Cavour was a passionate believer in Italian unity. His close study of the British and the French democratic systems had helped him to become a shrewd politician. Victor Emmanual asked him to form a government in 1852.

The war lasted only two months. The allies won significant victories in the north. Elsewhere in Italy revolutionary groups, encouraged by Cavour, staged uprisings in support of union with Piedmont. Then Napoleon, under pressure from Prussia, signed a separate peace with the Austrians. Lombardy was to be joined to Pied-

mont but Venetia retained by Austria. Cavour, furious at the king's ready acceptance of the truce, resigned.

The following year, having made his peace with the king, Cavour returned to office and resumed his cautious maneuvering for unity. By ceding Nice and Savoy to France he was able to

Below: the 6000 strong demonstration against the Quirinale in 1848. The crowd gathered on November 16, and when Pio Nono refused to grant their demands, opened fire—killing a bishop in the process. Swiss Guards returned the fire.

Left: map shows the progress towards Italian unity. Lombardy (light green) was joined to Sardinia (gray) in 1859. In 1860, Garibaldi added further states (mid-green). Venetia (dark green) joined in 1866, and Rome (white) in 1870.

annex several Italian duchies. But without French help he could not go much further. Meanwhile, Garibaldi, on his own initiative, sailed off to Sicily and proceeded to conquer all of southern Italy.

With Garibaldi installed as dictator of Naples, Cavour now executed a strategic masterstroke. On the pretext of checking the advance of Garibaldi's revolutionaries, Cavour sent the Piedmontese army south. They bypassed Rome, where Napoleon's troops guarded the pope, but acquired most of the papal states and other territories *en route*. Garibaldi's magnanimous withdrawal in favor of the king made it possible to unite north and south and so create an Italy nearly as large as it is today. Only Rome and Venetia remained outside the fold. Cavour would not live to see them acquired.

In February 1861 delegates to the first Italian parliament met in Turin to begin the difficult task of bringing political unity to their diverse land.

Garibaldi
1807~1882

When the Italian soldier-patriot Giuseppe Garibaldi made his fourth visit to England in 1864, enterprising servants from the house where he was staying sold bottles of soapsuds from his washbasin. High-born ladies begged for locks of his hair. In Sicily, colored posters pictured him as Christ blessing the faithful. A more realistic appreciation of his qualities was offered by President Abraham Lincoln in 1861. He offered him a command in the Union Army, Garibaldi declined.

Garibaldi was born in the Mediterranean port of Nice. His father and grandfather were both sailors. Early attempts to steer Giuseppe toward the church or the law were defeated by the lure of the sea. He spent his youth sailing the Mediterranean and the Black Sea, occasionally fighting pirates. He met the exiled republican revolutionary Mazzini in Marseilles in 1833, and pledged himself to fight for Italian unification. As one of the leaders of an abortive insurrection in Genoa the following year, Garibaldi became *persona non grata* with the Piedmontese government and was forced into exile.

Garibaldi went to South America. There, he became involved in the struggle of Rio Grande

Right: Garibaldi's republic in Rome was short-lived. On the orders of Napoleon III of France, French forces under the command of Oudinot occupied the city in 1849 and reinstated the pope. Counter-revolution was taking a grip on the rest of Italy, and Garibaldi went into exile.

for independence from Brazil. He later fought for Uraguay against Argentina. In those struggles, he developed a characteristic style of fighting which relied heavily on guerrilla tactics and improvization.

Garibaldi returned to Italy in 1848 and offered his services to King Charles Albert of Piedmont, who had declared war on Austria. His offer was turned down. The king and his government were suspicious of his republican leanings. Garibaldi

looked elsewhere for the chance to serve the cause of liberation. Eventually, he and his little army arrived in Rome, which had been taken over by revolutionaries and declared a republic. Garibaldi was elected to the new Roman assembly. Soon he found himself back in the more congenial role of a soldier, fighting the troops of Napoleon III. It was a lost cause. The French occupied Rome and restored the pope. All over Italy the forces of counter-revolution gained control. Once more, Garibaldi went into exile.

For the next five years. Garibaldi roamed the Old World and the New, and lived for a time in New York City. After returning to Italy in 1855, he bought half of the tiny island of Caprera. This was to be his home – sometimes his prison – for the rest of his life. He practiced farming there, without much success, and enjoyed a simple life with his family.

Enjoying a reputation as a patriot and man of the people, Garibaldi was approached by the Piedmontese prime minister Cavour, who realized that he would be useful when the projected war with Austria materialized. Garibaldi had long-held republican views. But his political opinions were somewhat incoherent. He had little respect for parliaments, and favored the idea of a benign dictatorship. His one fixed goal was Italian unification. If this could be achieved

Left: Guiseppe Garibaldi. In 1861, United States president Abraham Lincoln offered him a command in the Union Army. Garibaldi refused.

Below: an earlier fighter for Italian unity, Guiseppe Mazzini. A staunch republican, Mazzini was in exile in Marseilles when Garibaldi met him in 1833. After the meeting, Garibaldi pledged to fight for Italian unity.

most readily under the royal house of Piedmont, he was willing to support the king.

When war came in 1859 Garibaldi led his volunteers in several engagements in Lombardy, helping to capture this region from Austria. Later, frustrated by the armistice imposed by France and embittered by the ceding of Nice and Savoy, Garibaldi resolved to continue the struggle alone. He recruited about 1000 volunteers – called the Redshirts because of their

about 2000 Sicilian recruits, miraculously forced the 25,000-strong Bourbon army to surrender Palermo.

Now established as dictator of Sicily, Garibaldi introduced a few social and economic reforms before continuing his march of conquest. In August 1860 his now much larger army crossed the Straits of Messina, and advanced on Naples. Poor morale among the Bourbon troops made his job easier. Within three weeks Naples

Below: Garibaldi (center) at the defense of Rome in 1849. His forces failed to save the city from an army sent by Napoleon III of France. Napoleon feared that a united Italy would challenge French dominance in Italy.

had fallen to him.

Although he now distrusted Cavour, Garibaldi still supported the king. When the Piedmontese army moved south two months later, Garibaldi gave up his conquests to Victor Emanuel in favor of Italian unity.

Garibaldi's career was by no means at an end. He sat for a while in the new Italian parliament – an experience that made him more skeptical of representative democracy than ever. He also led several unsuccessful expeditions to free Venetia and Rome. The Italian government, following a tortuous and confused foreign policy, sometimes helped and sometimes frustrated these efforts. Twice, Garibaldi was arrested and forced to retire to Caprera. Rome and Venetia were acquired peacefully as a result of conflicts between Prussia, France, and Austria.

By the time of his death, Garibaldi had become disillusioned with the Italy he had helped to create. Its government was riddled with corruption, and its social and economic ills were as glaring as ever. In his will he had stipulated that his body be cremated, but the government prevented this and gave him a magnificent burial.

uniforms. With them he sailed to Sicily, then part of the kingdom of Naples. He quickly won popular support in Marsala. After a few weeks of intermittent fighting his Redshirts, along with

Above: Garibaldi received a tumultuous welcome when he entered Naples in 1859. He went on to take Sicily into Italy.

179

Abraham Lincoln
1809-1865

Abraham Lincoln personified a favourite American concept – that of poor boy makes good. He was born on a farm in Indiana into a poverty striken, illiterate family. Only 12 months of his life was spent at school. But he early developed a keen appetite for reading. He was marked for success. In Indiana, that meant politics.

After doing a variety of jobs, as railsplitter, soldier, shopkeeper, and postmaster, he ran for the Illinois legislature in 1834, and was elected. While serving in the legislature Lincoln studied law. He was admitted to the Bar in 1837. Clearly a young man on his way up, he attracted the ambitious, wellborn Mary Todd. After some hesitation on Lincoln's part, they were married. The marriage was not happy. Lincoln's prolonged bouts of melancholy and his wife's violent temper – a sign of her mental instability – put a severe strain on their relationship.

In the first 10 years after his marriage, Lincoln's early promise seemed unlikely to be fulfilled. In his two years in Congress he antagonized his party, the Whigs, by his opposition to the Mexican War, and was later passed over for public office. He pursued his law practice without enthusiasm.

Meanwhile, the nation was moving toward its great crisis. The issue was the extension of slavery into the territories. The government had tried to keep a balance between the number of slave and free states for years. But the North was becoming more and more insistent on stopping the spread of slavery, while the South was urging its extension with missionary fervor.

Right: a slave auction in progress in the United States in 1852. Lincoln's attitude to those states that still allowed slavery was cautious – slavery was wrong and must be eradicated "in time." More radical voices were demanding immediate abolition.

Below right: Lincoln visits one of his generals, probably Grant, at the height of the American Civil War.

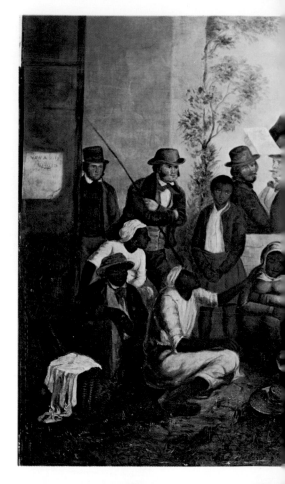

CHARLESTON
MERCURY
EXTRA:

Passed unanimously at 1.15 o'clock, P. M., December 20th, 1860.

AN ORDINANCE

To dissolve the Union between the State of South Carolina and other States united with her under the compact entitled "The Constitution of the United States of America."

We, the People of the State of South Carolina, in Convention assembled, do declare and ordain, and it is hereby declared and ordained,

That the Ordinance adopted by us in Convention, on the twenty-third day of May, in the year of our Lord one thousand seven hundred and eighty-eight, whereby the Constitution of the United States of America was ratified, and also, all Acts and parts of Acts of the General Assembly of this State, ratifying amendments of the said Constitution, are hereby repealed; and that the union now subsisting between South Carolina and other States, under the name of "The United States of America," is hereby dissolved.

THE
UNION
IS
DISSOLVED!

Above: Lincoln's presidential victory provoked what had long been threatened – secession of the southern states over the slavery issue. The Charleston Mercury reports the break up of the Union. Civil war was soon to follow.

Left: Lincoln, a symbol of the American "dream" – the poor boy who "made it."

A new anti-slavery party, the Republican Party, was formed in 1854. Four years later, the Illinois Republicans nominated Lincoln to oppose the incumbent Democratic Senator Stephen Douglas. During the race the two candidates met in a series of debates. At these historic meetings Lincoln proved that as an orator he was a match for the formidable Douglas. He reiterated his conviction that the nation could not endure "half slave and half free." Slavery was wrong and it must, in time, be extinguished.

Lincoln lost the election, but the campaign won him a national reputation. He was nominated for the presidency two years later. His

election was ensured by a split among the Democrats, whose extreme pro-slavery members nominated a rival candidate.

Lincoln's election provoked an act the South had long contemplated: secession. Even before he was inaugurated, seven states had declared themselves independent and formed the Confederate States of America. Later, four more states joined. A civil war between the Union and the Confederacy broke out in April 1861.

The North fared badly during the first two years of war. Southern strategy triumphed again and again. The North's greater resources and its blockade of the southern coast would only grad-

ually influence the course of the conflict. But as the war continued, Lincoln showed his own gift for strategy. At the most critical moment – General Robert E. Lee's invasion of Maryland in September 1862 – Lincoln overruled his advisors and recalled the brilliant but troublesome General McClellan, and gave him command of the Army of the Potomac. McClellan's hard-won victory at Antietam checked the Confederate advance and averted European recognition of the Confederacy. Shortly after Antietam, Lincoln issued the Emancipation Proclamation, freeing the slaves. For the moment, the freedom was theoretical, but the Proclamation gave the Union cause a moral force – particularly in foreign eyes – that it lacked before.

The struggle raged another two and a half years. The South fought valiantly, but its second invasion of the North was checked at Gettysburg. In the Mississippi region the intrepid General Ullyses S. Grant won several important Union victories. Lincoln gave Grant command of the entire Union Army. Lee finally surrendered to Grant in April 1865.

Less than a week later, while attending the theater, Lincoln was shot in the head by a southern extremist, an actor named John Wilkes Booth. He died the following morning.

His death was a loss for the South as well as the North. In the bitter years of Reconstruction that followed, few seemed to remember these words from Lincoln's Second Inaugural Address:

"With malice toward none; with charity for all; with firmness in the right . . . Let us strive on to finish the work we are in: to bind up the nation's wounds; to care for him who shall have borne the battle, and for his widow and his orphan – to do all which may achieve and cherish a just, and a lasting peace . . ."

Napoleon III
1808-1873

Left: Napoleon III. He shamelessly exploited the reputation of his uncle Napoleon Bonaparte in order to climb to power.

The French radicals revolt of 1830 paved the way for the "Citizen-King." But they had not given up hope of a Republican France. Even the constitutional monarchists were advocating extending the franchise. The people, bored by the drab mediocrity of the government, yearned for the glorious days of Napoleon. With the 1848 revolution, a man bearing this magical name turned events to his own advantage.

The legend of Napoleon had burned brightly in the household of the exiled Hortense Bonaparte, the wife of Napoleon's brother Louis. Their son, Prince Louis Napoleon, was very much aware of his heritage. After the Emperor's son died in 1832, Louis was considered the Bonaparte claimant to the French throne.

He completed his military training – though he was never much of a soldier – and in 1836, helped by officers of the Strasbourg garrison, he attempted a *coup*. It was a complete failure, and Louis Napoleon was forced into exile. After a brief period in the United States, he lived in England for a while. Here, he wrote pamphlets. One presented the "Napoleonic idea" as one of humanitarian and social progress reconciling order and freedom under the benign leadership of a "providential man."

Louis Napoleon made a second attempt at a *coup* in 1840. This was as much a fiasco as his first try, and the French government sentenced him to life imprisonment. He spent six years

Right: a decree of Napoleon III issued after he staged a coup on December 2 1851. He could not get National Assembly support for a second term as president, so he peremtorily dissolved the Assembly, reduced the suffrage and imposed press censorship. He had earlier cooperated in expelling 33 socialist deputies from the Assembly.

Below: Napoleon's wife, the Empress Eugenie with his son Prince Louis, 1858.

confined in a fortress, where he continued his studies and writing. Then he managed to escape and flee to England.

The Revolution of 1848 brought him back to France. Although the republicans regarded him with suspicion, he had enough supporters to be elected to the new Constituent Assembly. The new constitution provided for a president, to be elected by universal suffrage. Louis Napoleon stood and received 5,400,000 votes. His nearest

AU NOM DU PEUPLE FRANÇAIS.

LE PRÉSIDENT DE LA RÉPUBLIQUE
DÉCRÈTE:

Art. 1.
L'Assemblée nationale est dissoute.
Art. 2.
Le Suffrage universel est rétabli. La loi du 31 mai est abrogée.
Art. 3.
Le Peuple français est convoqué dans ses comices à partir du 14 décembre jusqu'au 21 décembre suivant.
Art. 4.
L'état de siége est décrété dans l'étendue de la 1ᵉ division militaire.
Art. 5.
Le Conseil d'État est dissous.
Art. 6.
Le Ministre de l'intérieur est chargé de l'exécution du présent décret.
Fait au Palais de l'Élysée, le 2 décembre 1851.

LOUIS-NAPOLÉON BONAPARTE.
Le Ministre de l'Intérieur.
DE MORNY.

rival only managed 1,500,000.

As President of the Second Republic, Louis Napoleon showed little sympathy for republicanism. In an uneasy alliance with the dominant monarchists in the Assembly he supported the ousting of 33 socialist deputies, imposed press censorship, and reduced the suffrage. One of his first acts on the international scene was to send an army to Rome to restore the pope, forced out by the city's new republican government.

Unable, under the existing constitution, to serve a second term and lacking enough support in the Assembly to get the constitution changed, Napoleon staged a *coup* in December 1851. He dissolved the Assembly and restored universal suffrage. The nation dutifully elected him President for 10 years. He proclaimed the Empire.

The Emperor, who called himself Napoleon III in deference to his late cousin who would have been the Second, ruled France with a firm hand. The Legislative Body had little power. Its members were elected through a process carefully controlled by the government. Censorship and police surveillance kept unwelcome ideas under wraps.

On the positive side, Napoleon III kept his promise to improve the nation's material prosperity. He encouraged the building of railroads and other engineering projects, and established investment banking to finance growth in industry and agriculture. Many fortunes were made. Even the working classes benefitted. Some progressive measures, such as those creating new hospitals and public housing and legalizing labor unions, gave Napoleon a reputation as a "socialist" in ultra-conservative circles.

"The Empire means peace," Napoleon had declared in 1852. But the heir of Napoleon I was hardly likely to adhere to a peace policy. When

French trade in the Near East was threatened by Russian advances into Turkey, Napoleon sent his army to join the Turks. Britain did too. The Crimean War (1854-1856) temporarily checked Russian expansion into the Mediterranean.

Italy had a special place in Napoleon's affections (as a youth he had fought in an Italian rebellion), and he was sincere in his wish to free it from Austrian rule. But he did not want to see it a unified nation. His aid to Piedmont in the brief war of 1859 freed Lombardy. But by making a separate peace with Austria he tem-

Above: Napoleon III meets Bismarck on September 3 1870. The day before, the French had capitulated in the Franco-Prussian war. Bismarck (right) is obviously aware that Napoleon is now an impotent ruler.

Above right: the Prussians besiege Paris in 1870. Parisians suffered dreadfully during the siege. Napoleon remained indifferent.

porarily checked Italian unification. The ambiguity of his Italian policy was glaringly obvious in the French occupation of Rome, which continued until the outbreak of the Franco-Prussian War. In bolstering the temporal power of the pope he was strongly influenced by the ultra-Catholic party, including his wife, the Empress Eugénie.

The Empress also played an influential role in the disastrous Mexican venture, in which Napoleon's army ousted President Benito Juárez and installed the Hapsburg Archduke Maximillian as Emperor of Mexico. The Mexican "Empire" – in effect, a French satellite state – collapsed in 1867.

Napoleon also failed in his attempts to win additional territory for France in return for his policy of benevolent neutrality toward Prussian aggrandizement in Germany. With the Empire steadily losing popularity at home, Napoleon's advisors advocated war against Prussia as a way of restoring public confidence. Such an action might also secure the desired territorial gains. In 1870 a suitable provocation appeared. A member of the Prussian House of Hohenzollern was offered – and temporarily accepted – the

Spanish crown. This triggered an aggressive response from France. The Prussian Chancellor Bismarck cleverly exploited this.

When war came in July 1870 the French army's inferiority to the Prussian was shown up. Two months later the French suffered a decisive defeat in the battle of Sedan. The Emperor was taken prisoner by the Prussians, while in Paris revolutionaries proclaimed a new republic. The following spring, after being released, he and the Empress retired to England, where he died two years later. His wife lived until 1920.

Bismarck
1815-1898

In 1815 the Congress of Vienna busied itself tidying up Europe's boundaries and enshrined the status quo as the key to future peace. That same year the wife of a Prussian landowner gave birth to a son who was to sweep away many of those boundaries to create a new German Empire.

Otto von Bismarck showed no early signs of having any remarkable talents. He spent most of his time at the University of Göttingen carousing and fighting duels (25 within nine months), but he did manage to pass his law exam at Berlin. As manager of some family estates Bismarck behaved like a typically uncouth country squire. His neighbors called him "the wild man."

Friendship with a group of devout and intel-

Right: Prussian forces defeat the Austrians at Koniggratz, July 3 1866. The Austro-Prussian war was a disaster for Austria.

Left: Otto von Bismarck, the "Iron Chancellor." A passionate believer in military strength as a method of ruling, Bismarck inspired the militaristic approach to German foreign policy that wreaked havoc in the first half of the 20th century.

lectual people, including his future wife Johanna, had a civilizing effect on the young Bismarck. Their right-wing idealism strongly influenced his thoughts.

The new liberal trends that followed the 1848 revolution kept Bismarck out of politics for a while, but a more conservative constitution was established in 1850, and he was elected to the new parliament. Soon afterward he was chosen by the king to represent Prussia at the Frankfurt

Diet, the deliberative body of Metternich's German Confederation. Eight years at Frankfurt convinced Bismarck that Austria would never accept Prussia as its equal. He resolved to build a Prussian-dominated Germany from which Austria would be excluded.

Hoping to obtain high office in the government, Bismarck was disappointed in 1859 to be put "in cold storage" as Ambassador to Russia. This was followed by a brief term as Ambassador to Napoleon III's France. He was recalled to Prussia by a government crisis: a row between King William I and the parliament over the budget. William appointed Bismarck prime minister, whereupon Bismarck successfully asserted the government's right to collect and spend tax revenues as it pleased. In his first speech to the parliament he made his famous remark: "The great questions of our day cannot be solved by speeches and majority votes. . . . but by blood and iron."

Now in a position to formulate foreign policy, Bismarck began to undermine Austria's ascendancy in Germany. His maneuvering in this cause occasionally brought him into conflict with the king.

Disputes over the two German duchies of Schleswig and Holstein, which had earlier been ceded to Denmark and which Bismarck intended to annex, brought war with Austria. Bismarck first joined forces with Austria against Denmark. Having regained and occupied the duchies after a brief war, the Prussians and Austrians began to fall out over their governing.

184

Bismarck secretly encouraged these disputes. At the same time, he secured guarantees of neutrality from the other powers.

The Austro-Prussian War of 1866 was over almost as soon as it started and ended with Prussia victorious. By the terms of the peace treaty Prussia annexed several north German states outright and grouped the others north of the Main river into a new North German Confederation. Bismarck imposed an authoritarian

Above: an 1870 French cartoon about the "Ems Dispatch." Entitled le Roi s'amuse, the drawing shows Bismarck standing behind William I manipulating the toy soldiers.

months the Prussians had established headquarters at Versailles. It was there that Bismarck experienced his greatest moment of triumph, the proclamation of the German Empire. The rulers of the south German states were persuaded to join the Empire, which was further enlarged by the acquisition of Alsace and Lorraine.

Prince von Bismarck – as he now was – governed the Empire for another 19 years. Always concerned primarily with foreign policy, the "Iron Chancellor" worked tirelessly to build alliances to ensure stability in Europe. Styling himself an "honest broker," he labored for three years to avert war between Russia and Britain in the Near East. He finally succeeded.

In domestic affairs he was less successful. A bitter struggle with the Roman Catholic Church

constitution on the Confederation. Power was concentrated in the hands of the Prussian king and prime minister.

The Franco-Prussian War of 1870 was less a product of Bismarck's ambition than of French war fever, inflamed by the traditional French fear of a unified Germany. But once Bismarck realized the likelihood of war, and the possibility that the south German states might be drawn into union with Prussia as a result, he set about provoking war with characteristic cunning. He encouraged the Spanish to offer their throne to a Hohenzollern prince, a move guaranteed to antagonize the French. When that project failed, he made clever use of a telegram from William I reporting a cool but civil exchange with the French ambassador. By ingenious editing he altered the telegram to suggest an exchange of insults. This abridged "Ems Dispatch," published in German and French newspapers, triggered the war.

Once again, the Prussian army was victorious. Bismarck's careful diplomatic groundwork had succeeded in isolating France. Within a few

Above: William I is declared Kaiser of Germany at Versailles, where the Prussian army had established headquarters after the Franco-Prussian war. Bismarck is standing to the right of the picture.

was followed by an equally implacable fight with socialism.

Bismarck's combative personality was partly responsible for his differences with William II, who became emperor in 1888. The new emperor's tendency toward saber-rattling, combined with relatively liberal domestic policies, naturally infuriated the chancellor. In 1890 Bismarck's attempts to sabotage the emperor's plans for an international labor conference precipitated the final break.

Marx
1818-1883

Karl Marx was "a type of man all compact of energy, . . . with a thick black mane of hair, . . . a man who had the right and power to command respect . . . a man convinced of his mission to dominate men and make them to follow him." His philosophy remains one of the major structures in the history of human thought. A philosophy of human history leads to a doctrine of social revolution, followed by a practical strategy of social revolution. Behind all is a vision. "Communism is the true appropriation of human nature through and for man. It is the return of man to himself as a social, that is a truly human, being."

Marx's father was a lawyer who had converted from Judaism to Christianity. The young man studied law and graduated in philosophy. He became editor of a Rhineland newspaper in 1842, but his radical editorials led to its closure by censorship the following year. Marx emigrated to Paris where he met his lifelong friend Friedrich Engels, and became a socialist. They both joined the Communist League in 1847. Founded as the League of the Just with the slogan "All men are brothers," it was one of a number of socialist groups founded in Paris, Brussels, and

Far right: the Paris Commune of 1870. Marx saw the Commune as a forerunner of working-class revolution. But it collapsed, and its ringleaders summarily shot. The French army was arbitrary in its choice of "ringleaders." Some men were shot because they "looked intelligent."

Right: Friedrich Engels membership card for the International Working Men's Association. Karl Marx helped form the Association, and is one of the signatories on Engels' card.

Below: Marx' political ally, and friend and benefactor, Friedrich Engels. Engels was a constant source of financial support for Marx, whose only other form of income was a pittance from occasional pieces of journalism. Engels and Marx wrote the *Communist Manifesto* together.

London by German exiles. Marx and Engels wrote the famous Communist Manifesto for it. The fraternal idealism was augmented with a program for "the forcible overthrow of the whole existing social order." Coincidentally, it appeared at the same time as the Paris Revolution – February 1848. Twenty years later, the Manifesto's influence was to permeate Europe.

The failure of the 1848 revolutions convinced Marx of the need for political parties dedicated to revolution. Banned from most European countries, he lived mostly in London from 1849. Marx devoted himself to his studies in the British Museum Library. As a result, he and his family lived in such grinding poverty that one of his children died. He was paid a pittance to act as a correspondent for the New York *Tribune* newspaper. But Engels, who managed the Manchester branch of his family's prosperous textile business was his chief source of financial support.

In 1866 Marx helped found the First International of Working Men's Associations in Geneva. He hailed the Paris Commune of 1870 as a forerunner of working-class revolution. But the *Communards* had little contact with com-

munism. And the First International was soon torn asunder by dissentions between Marx and anarchists led by the Russian Bakunin. It disbanded in 1876.

The first volume of Marx's historic and monumental work *Capital* had appeared in 1867. Volumes two and three, edited by Engels, followed in 1885 and 1894. Marx's first philosophical influence had been Hegel, but it was modified by the materialism of Lugwig Feuerbach. In the 1840s he had devoured the works of the classic economists from Adam Smith to Riccardo, and the French School of Saint Simon, Louis Blanc, and Proudhon. Marx rejected the traditional appeal of "natural law" and the rights of man. Instead, he appealed to the inevitability of the historical process as presented by his theory of dialectical materialism.

The dialect proceeded by the conflict of opposites. A historical phenomenon, such as the social system (the thesis) produced its own opposite

PYRAMIDE A RENVERSER

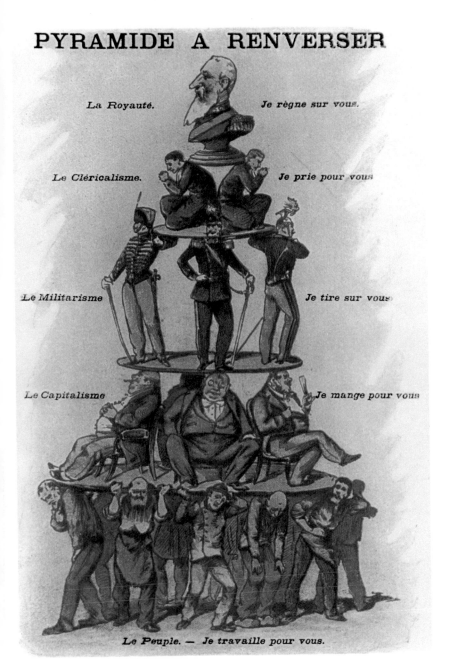

La Royauté.   Je règne sur vous.

Le Cléricalisme.   Je prie pour vous

Le Militarisme   Je tire sur vous

Le Capitalisme   Je mange pour vous

Le Peuple. — Je travaille pour vous.

The idea that private property is the root of social injustice was already old when Proudhon trenchantly wrote "Property is theft." "But," said Marx, "philosophers have only interpreted the world; the point is to change it." This could only occur through revolution: "because the ruling class cannot be overthrown in any other way, and also because only revolution can rid the revolutionary class of the accumulated rubbish of the past and fit it to reconstruct society."

Marx's mighty achievement has affected almost all subsequent historical and economic theory, even though it has been heavily criticized outside the communist world. It has been re-shaped to meet changing conditions by communist scholars and has numerous derivative forms. Communism is claimed as the official creed by the rulers of half the world's population. But many western Marxists insist that the state of society existing in the "communist" nations can better be described as "state capitalism."

(the antithesis) to yield a higher synthesis. Marx identified the "two great hostile camps" of his own age as the bourgeoisie (the thesis) and the proletariat (the antithesis). The former controlled the means of production of the industrial state, and exploited both the world's resources and the labor of the proletariat. Since the liberal democratic state served the interests of the bourgeoisie it must be a sham, and parliamentary government a mask for capitalist class rule. The rivalries of national states are likewise a distraction from the proletarian's true objective. Patriotism was fostered to hamper international working–class solidarity. A world proletarian revolution would be necessary to establish the "dictatorship of the proletariat" (the historical synthesis). With power held by the class which by definition has neither property nor the possibility of exploitation, exploitation itself will come to an end and a truly classless society emerge.

Above: a Belgian socialist cartoon entitled "a Pyramid to Overturn." At the top of the pyramid sits the royal family and nobility, supported by the Church. The armed forces props up both, and they are in turn supported by the capitalist class. Bearing the weight of the whole lot is the working class.

Right: Karl Marx' grave at Highgate cemetery, North London. His rallying call in the Communist Manifesto, "Workers of the world unite. You have nothing to lose but your chains", has inspired generations of socialists.

Paul Kruger
1825~1904

The Great Trek is the most significant event in The Afrikaners' history, and has entered their mythology. The young Paul Kruger took part in it. His people were farmers of mainly Dutch descent, and were dissatisfied with the British rule in the Cape Colony. They decided to seek new lands where they could govern themselves and preserve their own way of life. Thousands of families joined the exodus. Taking their horses, cattle, and sheep with them, they headed north. The Kruger family finally settled in the Transvaal. Intensely religious, Paul Kruger believed, as did the other pioneers, that God had intended this land for the Afrikaners. Later, as President of the Republic of South Africa (the Transvaal), Kruger was a stubborn opponent of British imperialist aims in that part of Africa.

In the Republic's early years Kruger held both military and civil positions under its first president, Andries Pretorius. He was there when Pretorius concluded the Sand River Convention in 1852. Britain acknowledged the new country's independence. Another Afrikaner nation, the Orange Free State, received recognition later.

In the 1870s the British Government began pressing for a confederation of the south African

Right: a meeting held in support of the Boers' cause is disrupted by anti-nationalists.

colonies and states. It was argued that this would give them a united policy *vis à vis* the native tribes and promote their mutual safety. The Afrikaners were reluctant to join such a confederation. This could be dealt with simply by annexing the Republic, and then the Orange Free State. In 1877 the British, claiming that the Republic's government had virtually broken down, forced the president to resign. A British government was installed.

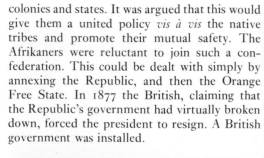

Left: a Daguerrotype print of Paul Kruger as a young man. The thumb of his right hand is missing. He cut it off himself after being injured by a bullet.

Above: a British cartoon comments on the conduct of the Boer War. It is captioned "How the British public gets its news."

Kruger now emerged as a resistance leader. He went to London twice to plead his country's case, but to no avail. Back home, he organized protest meetings and passive resistance. At one mass meeting, 2000 Boers declared their willingness to give their lives to regain their country's independence.

War was precipitated in 1880 over a farmer's refusal to pay some taxes. It lasted less than three months, and the Boers fought with remarkable tenacity. The peace treaty, called the Pretoria Convention, effectively restored the Republic's independence, though Britain retained a vague "suzerainty" over it. Kruger, a skilled negotiator despite his uncouth manners, won most of the concessions. But there still remained some points on which the Boers were dissatisfied. In 1883, Kruger again went to London, where he secured a revised treaty.

He served as President of the Republic from 1883 to 1902. Besides controlling the administration, he dominated the legislature, or *Volksraad*. He usually got his way by sheer force of will, along with a good deal of shouting. Though his rule was quasi-despotic, President Kruger made himself available to listen to any citizen and would spend part of each day chatting with people on his front veranda, while his wife dispensed endless cups of coffee.

The devout, homogeneous, agrarian society over which Kruger presided was soon challenged by an influx of foreigners. Mainly British, these invaders were lured by the rich gold deposits in the southern part of the country. Kruger regarded these "outlanders" with profound suspicion and treated them accordingly. Although they contributed most of the tax revenues, only the most primitive public amenities were made available to them. A 14-year residence requirement for naturalization kept them from wielding political influence, and Kruger's economic policies caused widespread dissatisfaction among them.

In 1895 the outlanders, encouraged by Cecil Rhodes, prime minister of the Cape Colony, planned an uprising, which was to be supported by British troops led by the Administrator of Rhodesia, Dr Jameson. Kruger, heard of the plot, and offered some concessions. The uprising was abandoned, but the raiders, not having received the message, went ahead according to plan, and were defeated. Kruger handled the affair with great skill. He showed clemency to the conspirators and released Jameson, whose action the British government was forced to disown.

But the raid stirred new fears among the Boers of a British takeover. The government passed new laws restricting freedom of the press and assembly and began to make massive arms purchases. In May 1899 a conference was held at Bloemfontein, in the Orange Free State, to try to reach a settlement. It was a failure. Kruger made

Right: a French anti-British cartoon at the time of the Boer War. The translation of the captions reads "a proposed monument to be erected to commemorate England, eternal champion of justice and protector of the weak."

some concessions on the key issue of the franchise, but not enough to satisfy the British.

Both sides now made ready for war. Kruger demanded in October 1899 that British troops massed along the Republic's borders be withdrawn. His ultimatum was turned down flat. Two days later the Boer War began.

Kruger had the bitter experience of seeing his country vanquished. When the British occupied the capital, Pretoria, he went into exile, while Boer guerrillas carried on the struggle. He went to Europe, where he was acclaimed as a hero in many countries. But he failed to elicit any support from their governments. In 1902, both the Republic and the Orange Free State were brought into the British Empire.

Two years later, Kruger died in Switzerland. His body was taken to Pretoria for burial.

Below: a band of South African police raised in support of Kruger during the Boer War in 1899.

Cecil Rhodes
1853~1902

Right: Boers attacked by Zulus during the Matabele war in 1896. Rhodes opened up Southern Africa to speculative pioneers in search of diamonds and gold. Not surprisingly, the natives resisted this invasion of their lands.

Left: a *Punch* cartoon of 1895 depicts Rhodes standing astride Africa – a comment on his stated ambition to rule the whole of the African continent. The title of the cartoon, "Rhodes Colussus", is taken from the Collusus of Rhodes, a statue which once straddled the harbor of the Greek island of Rhodes.

Right: Rhodes at the Great Indaba in the Matoppo Hills, negotiating the peace at the end of the Matabele war, September 1896. He was negotiating from strength, and the concessions wrung from the Zulus were immensely profitable to Rhodes. The natives were less happy.

The extension of the British Empire was Cecil Rhodes' single-minded mission. Unsubtle, arrogantly confident and a man of towering energy, he believed that power was inseparable from money. By the time he was 35 Rhodes controlled South Africa's diamond industry through his De Beers Company. He extended Britain's African territories by nearly 1,100,000 square miles and left a huge fortune for educational endowments. But his conflict with President Paul Kruger of the Transvaal deepened hostility between English and Afrikaaner.

The son of a country parson, he was a sickly boy and was sent out to Natal to work on his brother's farm when he was only 16. When diamonds were discovered at Kimberley the brothers staked their claims. Cecil Rhodes was financially independent at 19, and returned to England to study at Oxford. His undergraduate years were continuously interrupted by visits to southern Africa to control his mushrooming financial interests.

After Oxford, Rhodes was elected to the legislature of Cape Colony in 1881. A fellow member commented: "This is the future man of South Africa, perhaps of the world."

Cape Colony was founded as a supply base by the Dutch East India Company in the 1650s. It had been British since the early 1800s. The Orange Free State and the Republic of the Transvaal lay to the northeast. They had both been founded by migrant Dutch farmers – the Boers. Tension between British and Dutch was considerable. Meanwhile, the African peoples, Bantu and Zulu, struggled to resist both sets of invaders. Rhodes planned a British expansion northward through Bechuanaland (now Botswana). He dreamed of eventually linking with the British protectorate in Egypt to cut a British swathe through Africa "from Cairo to the Cape" a distance of over 4,500 miles.

Rhodes financed settlements in southern

Rhodes had been prime minister of Cape Colony since 1890, and ruled it as an autocrat. He limited the franchise by education and income qualifications, and angered white opinion by guaranteeing certain rights to Africans.

He was impatient to realize his great dream of a federation of self-governing Boer and British states within the Empire. Colony and Company lands, ruled by Rhodes, almost encircled the Boer republics.

The once poor Transvaal had become rich with the discovery of gold on the Witwatersrand in 1884. Foreign prospectors, many of them British, were controlled by stringent legislation and a restricted franchise. They began plotting against the Kruger government of the Transvaal and approached Rhodes, who had substantial mining interests on the Rand. At the end of 1895 armed British volunteers, led by a friend and colleague of Rhodes, Dr Leander Starr Jameson, mounted a raid into the Transvaal. This was the famous Jameson Raid.

In the words of a contemporary Englishman it was "an adventure childishly conceived, clumsily executed and. resulting in immediate

Right: a French cartoon comments on the failure of the Jameson Raid. It shows the British "Dans le Petrine". Dr Leander Starr Jameson, a friend of Rhodes, had led a band of British volunteers in an attack on the Transvaal. The raid was a total failure, and is one of Britain's greatest military fiascos against the Boers.

and ignominious failure." The raiders were captured and handed over by President Kruger to the Imperial authorities. Jameson was sent to London for trial, and jailed for 18 months. Rhodes resigned and was spared worse humiliation only by the famous "Kruger telegram". In this, Kaiser William II of Germany congratulated the Boer President. Infuriated by this "interference," British public opinion would not tolerate proceedings against the Empire's hero.

Rhodes devoted the remainder of his life to developing Rhodesia. Ruthless and aggressive, he nevertheless believed that "enlargement of the British Empire" served "the cause of peace, industry and freedom." And to Rhodes, the end justified the means.

Bechuanaland and in 1889 negotiated trading and mining rights up to the Zambesi River with the Chief of the Matabele, Lobengula, for his British South Africa Company. A British Royal Charter gave the company the right to rule the region. Rhodes sent pioneers to occupy further territories, and had the charter extended for regions north of the Zambesi (Northern Rhodesia, now Zambia). Trading had become annexation. Rhodes once remarked, "I would annex the planets and the stars if I could" and he confessed that "sometimes I have adopted means in removing opposition which were rough and ready." The defeated Matabele were forced to accept the new white settlements in 1896.

Theodore Roosevelt
1858-1919

Theodore Roosevelt was probably the most energetic man ever to occupy the White House. He approached his job with almost superhuman enthusiasm, and transformed the nature of the United States presidency. Under his reign, it ceased to be merely an executive post and acquired the more positive role it still possesses.

Roosevelt was born into a prosperous family. His severe asthma and other ailments might have condemned him to an idle life. But politics had a natural appeal for a young man with his competitive nature, and soon after graduation from Harvard in 1880 he was elected to the New York State Assembly as a Republican. A recurrence of asthma led him to go west, where he spent two years as a cattle rancher. This experience intensified his love of the outdoors and made him an ardent conservationist.

Returning east, Roosevelt held several civil service appointments, including that of assistant secretary of the navy. With the Spanish Ameri-

Right: Roosevelt with his Rough Riders at San Juan Hill during the Spanish-American war in 1898. His time with the Rough Riders made Roosevelt into a national hero.

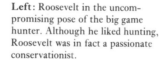

Left: Roosevelt in the uncompromising pose of the big game hunter. Although he liked hunting, Roosevelt was in fact a passionate conservationist.

Above: a 1904 cartoon portrays Roosevelt in negotiation with Kaiser William II of Germany. In dealing with foreign powers, Roosevelt was careful not to involve the United States in military risk or expense. He was influential with the German Kaiser.

can War of 1898 he left his desk to resume the "strenuous life," this time as commander of a company of volunteer cavalry in Cuba. Roosevelt and his Rough Riders' exploits made him an American hero.

Political battles next claimed Roosevelt's interest. After being elected governor of New York, he launched a campaign against political cor-

ruption. The alarmed Republican bosses then engineered his nomination as President McKinley's running mate. They hoped that the oblivion of the vice-presidency would render him harmless. An assassin's bullet felled McKinley six months after his inauguration in 1901. "Teddy" became president.

To the consternation of his own party leaders, the traditional supporters of big business, the new president soon showed that he meant to

clamp down on those who were making vast fortunes at the public's expense. Chief among his targets were the trusts – super-corporations that controlled particular industries and, in many cases, kept prices artificially high. He established a department of commerce and labor, empowered to collect facts that would facilitate prosecutions under the existing, neglected, anti-trust laws. Armed with this data, Roosevelt successfully took out law suits against a number of trusts for illegal operations.

In 1904, having been re-elected by a huge majority, he introduced legislation to regulate railroad fares. Another important piece of Roosevelt legislation was the Pure Food and Drug Act, the first step toward consumer protection by the government. Roosevelt also established the right of government to arbitrate on disputes between labor and management. His intervention in a coal miner's strike in 1902 won a modest increase in pay for the miners and public acclaim for the president. Though he had misgivings about organized labor and supported the open shop, Roosevelt supported the unions' demands for better pay and shorter hours as part of the

"Square Deal" he promised the country as a whole.

Combining traits that are seldom found together these days, the domestically progressive Roosevelt was also an unabashed imperialist. He firmly believed it was the duty of the United States to maintain order in the Western Hemisphere. While upholding the Monroe Doctrine (non interference in the affairs of other nations), he added to it the assertion that "Chronic wrong-

can commissioners sorted out the Republic's finances, providing for repayment of foreign debts. When a series of revolutions occurred, the US Army moved in to restore order, remaining until 1924.

Roosevelt's treatment of Colombia was just as highhanded. Negotiations with Columbia for the right to build a canal across the Isthmus of Panama ground to a halt in 1903. The possibility had arisen of securing this right from the pro-

Above: this rather fanciful print depicts Roosevelt mediating between the two sides in the Russo-Japanese war in 1905.

vince of Panama by supporting its secession from Columbia. Roosevelt approved, and the Panamanians, bolstered by the presence of three American warships, won their independence in a bloodless revolution. The United States leased from Panama a 10-mile-wide strip of land cutting across the Isthmus. They then built the Canal, which opened for traffic in 1914.

Under Roosevelt's leadership the United States began to play a part in settling differences between other powers. He personally guided the negotiations, held in Portsmouth, New Hampshire, that ended the Russo-Japanese War of 1905. The following year he sent an American representative to a conference dealing with a crisis between France and Germany over Morocco. America's help in formulating the resulting agreement was a significant departure from its traditional neutrality in European affairs and set a precedent for later involvement overseas.

Roosevelt's last two years in the White House were marked by a growing split between conservative and progressive Republicans. After leaving office, he returned to politics in 1912 as the presidential candidate of his newly-formed Progressive Party. This move worked to the Democrat's advantage. Ironically, it was to be the Democrats who would follow the trail marked out by Teddy Roosevelt, adding a "New Deal," a "Fair Deal," a "New Frontier," and a "Great Society" to the "Square Deal" which expressed the government's responsibility to the people.

doing" on the part of another American nation "may force the United States . . . to the exercise of an international police power." This "Roosevelt corollary" to the Monroe Doctrine (later repudiated) was a response to financial corruption in the Dominican Republic, which had raised the bogey of intervention by European creditors. Roosevelt intervened instead. Ameri-

Above: in domestic policy Roosevelt took action against some of the excesses of the unbridled capitalism of the United States. This US cartoon portrays Roosevelt the "trust buster" taking on, and defeating the combined opposition of the American railroad bosses.

David Lloyd-George
1863~1945

Chancellor of the exchequer from 1908 and British prime minister from 1916 to 1922, Lloyd George was the architect of Britain's first welfare legislation, the leader who steered the country's economy and morale through the horrors of World War I, and one of Britain's greatest orators. He was also one of the wiliest politicians of the 20th century.

Left: David Lloyd-George at the hustings. Lloyd-George is probably one of the most accomplished British politicians of the 20th century. An effective orator, he had a considerable following among the common people.

Party challenged their credentials as the party of social reform. Lloyd George's 1909 "People's Budget" tried to steal Labour's thunder. It was directed against the privileged classes, with higher death duties and super tax among its proposals. It passed through the House of Commons, but was thrown out by the Lords despite two general elections in 1910 and 1911. Lloyd George campaigned virulently against the aristocracy. "A fully equipped duke costs as much to keep as two Dreadnought battleships and dukes are just as great a terror." Finally, the Lords were forced to pass the budget when the new king, George V, agreed to Asquith's request to create as many new lords as would be needed to pass the measure. The Parliament Bill of 1911 removed the Lords' right to veto a bill and con-

His father died when David was only one, and the family went to live with an uncle, Richard Lloyd, in Caernarvon, Wales. Lloyd, a local preacher of great power, financed his training as a solicitor. Lloyd George qualified in 1884 and married Margaret Owen four years later. In 1890, he entered parliament as Liberal MP for Caernarvon Borough. He held the seat until 1945 when he was created Earl Lloyd George of Dwyfor.

He burst into political controversy as an ardent leader of Welsh nationalist aspirations, wedded to non-conformity in religion, and earned national and local unpopularity by impassioned speeches against the Boer War. His extra-marital adventures became common knowledge. But his energy, his personal charm, and talent helped him to the top.

When the Liberal Party came to power in 1905, Lloyd George entered the government as president of the Board of Trade. In this post, he displayed remarkable flair as an arbitrator in industrial disputes. Three years later, the new liberal prime minister, Herbert Asquith, made him chancellor.

It was a time of personal tragedy. Lloyd George's beloved daughter Mair had died in 1907, aged only 17. At the same time the Liberals were in political trouble. The rising Labour

Above: Liberal Prime Minister Herbert Henry Asquith appointed Lloyd-George Chancellor of the Exchequer in 1908. His "People's Budget" a year later tried to outflank the rising Labour Party by going a small way along the road to a welfare state.

Left: troops blinded by chlorine gas on the Somme during World War I painted by the war artist John Singer Sargent. Lloyd-George was scornful of the incompetence of many of the military leaders, and detested their callousness.

fined them merely to the power to delay.

In the same year Lloyd George presented his National Insurance Act. This laid the foundations of the British welfare state. After the outbreak of World War I he was appointed minister of munitions. His energy and unorthodox methods irritated civil servants but, by bringing businessmen into the organization of munitions planning and winning the cooperation of the trade unions, he radically improved output.

War Minister from June 1916, he was often at odds with the army top brass. He distrusted their military assessments and despised their profligate expenditure of other men's lives.

He succeeded Asquith as prime minister of a coalition government with the Conservatives in December 1916. Many Liberals believed he had

Above: the recurring struggle of the Irish people for their freedom from Britain dogged Lloyd-George's premiership. Picture shows the bombed interior of the Dublin General Post Office after the Easter Rising of 1916. He earned the distrust of the Irish population when he sent the Black and Tan terror gangs into the conflict.

Left: Georges Clemenceau, Woodrow Wilson and David Lloyd-George after the signing of the Versailles Peace Treaty in 1919. Lloyd-George tried unsuccessfully to dissuade Clemenceau from some of the harsher penalties to be imposed upon the defeated Germany. The terms of the treaty crippled the German economy, and gave Nazism a stepping stone to power.

maneuvered Asquith's resignation, and the split in the party hastened its rapid decline in the 1920s and 1930s. Lloyd George tightened up the administration of war. He raised public morale and forced the Admiralty to institute a convoy system which dramatically reduced German U-boat successes in the Atlantic.

Following the Armistice of 1918 he won a resounding electoral victory. With Prime Minister Clemenceau of France and President Woodrow Wilson of the United States, Lloyd George was a principal arbiter of the post-war settlement reached with the Treaty of Versailles in 1919.

He then turned his attention to Ireland. Aiming to crush opposition he at first authorized the formation of the notorious "Black and Tan" British terror gangs. But then, in a marathon of complicated negotiations, won Irish agreement to the establishment of the Irish Free State in 1921.

The following year he was accused of selling honors to raise party funds. He then split the coalition with his belligerent policy toward Turkey in her war with Greece and resigned the premiership. The Conservatives won the ensuing election. Lloyd George was reduced to the uncongenial task of leading the failing Liberal Party (1926–31) and to writing his *War Memoirs* and the vitriolic, highly personal *Truth About the Peace Treaties*.

A maverick of genius, though untrustworthy in his enemies' eyes, David Lloyd George was perhaps the one man who could have given purpose and stature to the sorry mediocrity of interwar British politics. But his own free-lancing and independence of party meant that once he lost power he lacked the party machine to recover it.

195

Georges Clemenceau
1841~1929

Called "the Tiger," Georges Clemenceau was often much disliked by the electorate as well as political rivals during his turbulent career. But at the age of 76 he became the hero of France. In November 1917, Clemenceau was appointed prime minister to lead France to Victory in World War I. This he did and then went on to fight ruthlessly for France's crippling demands on Germany at the Peace Conference of Versailles in 1919. In the words of Sir Winston Churchill, Clemenceau, "with his quaint stylish cap, his white moustace and burning eye . . . he embodied and expressed France."

Clemenceau was born in a traditionally Catho-

Left: Clemenceau speaking in the Chamber of Deputies. His uncompromising radicalism made him many enemies.

lic and royalist region of France of a family which, by contrast, had a long tradition of radicalism and anti-clericalism. In his 20s he left France and worked for a time as a teacher and journalist in the United States. After his return to France he became prominent in left-wing Parisian politics. During the Siege of Paris by the German army in 1870, Clemenceau tried to mediate between the radical Commune and the new National Assembly. He resigned from the Assembly when it decided to attack the Commune. After entering the Chamber of Deputies he soon won numerous enemies for his guerrilla political tactics, violent speeches, and vitriolic journalism. His readiness and skill as a duellist did not endear him to anyone either. A prominent leftwinger, Clemenceau was hounded from public life in 1893 for sup-

posed corrupt activities.

But this did not shut him up, and he continued his journalistic barrage from the political wilderness. He wrote for *L'Aurora*. In 1898, the novelist Emile Zola published his open letter *J'accuse* in this same paper. This lambasted the government for its handling of the case against the Jewish army officer Alfred Dreyfus. Clemenceau joined the pro-Dreyfus forces against the reactionary establishment.

A member of the Senate from 1902, Clemenceau formed his first administration four years

Right: a contemporary French cartoon attacks Alfred Dreyfus. Dreyfus was a Jewish army officer convicted for spying for the Germans on the flimsiest of evidence. The anti-semitism endemic in French society and in the army ensured Dreyfus' downfall. Clemenceau, along with Emile Zola, championed Dreyfus against the establishment.

later. It presented a bold reforming program. But, despite a three-year tenure, few of its measures became law. Ironically, this left-wing administration fell because of its ruthless suppression of a series of strikes.

In an interview in 1908 he had vented his suspicion and dislike of Germany. "For France the danger of invasion is very real. We know that on the outbreak of war . . . German armies will invade France by way of Belgium." Out of office, he attacked Germany in his journal "The Free Man" and, from 1914, the French government's handling of the war. The official censor moved against the paper. Clemenceau rechristened it "The Chained Man."

By 1917 there were mutinies in the French army. The politicians were considering a negotiated peace. Poincaré, president of France, called Clemenceau to office to restore the patriotic "sacred union" of the French people. The old Tiger, now 75, turned in fury on the defeatists. Foch, the most widely respected general in France, was made allied supreme commander. Staunchly supported by Clemenceau he withstood a series of violent German offensives. On 18 July 1918, Foch unleashed the counteroffensive that led to victory in November.

Above: Allied troops occupy the left bank of the Rhine river after the Armistice in 1918. France wanted to occupy large western territories of the defeated Germany, but had to be content with demilitarization of the Rhineland.

Left: the Versailles Peace Conference in progress. Woodrow Wilson is standing at the center of the picture, while Clemenceau sits at his left.

Clemenceau presided over the Versailles Conference called to extract peace terms from Germany. Urged by Foch and French nationalists he demanded French military occupation of large areas of western Germany. But he had to be content with demilitarization of the Rhineland and US and British military guarantees, which soon proved worthless. But the provinces of Alsace and Lorraine, taken by Germany in the 1870 Franco-Prussian war, were returned to France. Clemenceau also secured a considerable reduction in Germany's armed forces and huge reparations.

In his prime the Tiger spoke "with the force and velocity of an express train." At Versailles the express train had slowed. But Clemenceau dominated the final, humiliating ceremony at which the German representatives signed the terms of surrender. "Clemenceau made a sign to the ushers. There was an absolute hush. The Republican Guards flashed their swords into their scabbards with a loud click. 'Let the Germans enter,' said Clemenceau, his voice distant but harshly penetrating. At the end of the ceremony he rasped. 'The sitting is ended.' No more no less." A delegate leant over to congratulate. "Yes," said Clemenceau, "it is a beautiful day."

Woodrow Wilson
1856-1924

Thomas Woodrow Wilson was considered an autocrat by his enemies. The 28th President of the United States, he believed he should be a national leader, not merely an executive, and launched the 20th-century tradition of presidential government.

At home, he initiated a radical restructuring in American society and administration. Wilson was the first American president to play a decisive role in world affairs. He saw World War I as the war "to make the world safe for democracy," and to bring about "the liberation of its people." As founder of the League of Nations, he failed to persuade his own country to join.

He was born in Staunton, Virginia, of Scottish Presbyterian descent. After a brilliant academic career at Princeton University, he became Democratic governor of New Jersey in 1910. His important reforming legislation, and his noble and fiery oratory, won him national respect. He won the 1912 presidential election with a populist campaign against the Republican administration's close links with big business.

In his first year as president, he pushed through major legislation which established the Federal Reserve System, so curbing the power of private banks and trusts, and favoring labor interests. Later in his presidency Congress amended the Constitution to give women the vote, and later to enact prohibition of alcohol.

When war engulfed Europe in 1914, Wilson, aware of America's diverse national origins, kept the country neutral. This policy made him very unpopular when a German U-boat sank the liner *Lusitania* in 1915 with the loss of over 100 American passengers. Germany agreed to re-

Above: beer casks being emptied after the introduction of prohibition. This was not a great success of Wilson's presidency. The sale of alcohol passed into the hands of gangsters.

strict its submarine campaign and Wilson was returned for a second term in 1916. He wished to act as a peacemaker in Europe, and in January 1917 outlined the bases for a League of Nations. But Germany returned to all-out submarine

Above: a French cartoon comments on the United States' entry into World War I. A German soldier stands in a pool of blood as the Stars and Stripes looms up before him.

warfare. In April Wilson asked Congress to declare war. Once committed the president conducted the war effort singlemindedly. Centralizing measures at home were introduced. These had long-term effects on American industry. Abroad, he gave General Pershing sole charge of military operations in France.

Wilson announced his famous Fourteen Points for the Peace in January 1918. These demanded: open covenants openly arrived at, freedom of

Below: American suffragists at a rally in 1907. Votes for women was another achievement of Wilson's presidency.

the seas, reduction of armaments, reduction of international tarrif barriers, adjustment of European colonial claims, the redrawing of central European boundaries on the basis of nationality, and a guarantee of Belgian sovereignty.

The Central Powers accepted them though the Allies at first hesitated. They preferred to see Germany totally humiliated. Many Americans felt the same way, and disliked the idea of American involvement in the internationalist League even more. In 1918 Wilson's political opponents won control of the vital Congressional Foreign Relations Committee. Even so, against all American precedent, the president personally led the delegation to the Versailles Conference. He

feared that, without him, it would end in vengeance upon Germany rather than reconciliation.

Wilson won Conference acceptance of the principle of the League of Nations, and of his own draft of its founding Covenant. But he had to compromise with the allies' demands for territory and reparations from Germany. The treaty signed at Versailles was humiliatingly harsh on Germany and sowed the seeds of a still bloodier holocaust.

Wilson's failure to achieve his own objective of a peace of reconciliation discredited him with the American electorate. It also exhausted him. The Foreign Relations Committee refused to recommend the ratification of the League treaty without crippling recommendations. Wilson embarked on a nation-wide tour in support of the League but suffered a complete nervous and physical collapse in October 1919. Congress was prepared to adopt the Treaty, but with such limiting reservations that Wilson now urged the

Territory ceded by Germany

Ceded by Austria-Hungary

Ceded by Bulgaria

Ceded by Russia

Above: United States troops at the Battle of the Marne, July 1918. Once committed, Wilson gave the US war effort his complete attention. He was awarded the Nobel Peace Prize in 1920.

Left: these two maps show the change in the boundaries, and balance of power, in Europe before and after World War I.

Democrats to refuse their support. He hoped that the 1920 presidential elections would prove a plebiscite in favor of the full Treaty. But the Democratic candidate was defeated by a landslide by Warren Gamaliel Harding.

Wilson received the 1920 Nobel Peace Prize, but retired from politics. He had led America through its largest war to victory, and had won international acclaim. But he was finally rejected at home. Privately, a man of warm personal magnetism, in public he remained aloof and was considered autocratic. This made him increasingly unpopular with the electorate while his attempt to force America into demanding international responsibilities was out of tune with the relaxed mood of the post-war world. The people welcomed Harding's call for a return to "normalcy" – isolationism in foreign affairs and the deceptive delights of the 1920s at home.

Henri Petain
1856-1951

Marshall Henri Petain was one of the great French heroes of the 1914-18 War. His reputation was shattered after he headed the French Vichy government of collaboration with the Nazis after June 1940. A career officer in the French army he won European renown with the defense of Verdun in 1916. At this time the fashionable military theory was that of "attrition." The aim was to kill as many of the enemy as pos-

Le Petit Journal

COMMANDANT L'ARMÉE DE VERDUN

Left: a portrait of Petain on the cover of a 1916 issue of the magazine *Le Petit Journal*. He is captioned the commander of the army at Verdun. After Verdun Petain became a hero in France.

Below: Germans taken prisoner at Verdun are marched into captivity in 1917. Petain salutes them as they trudge past.

sible, not to advance. Victory would go to the nation with the largest population because it had more men to send to the slaughter.

The German commander, von Falkenhayn, chose to attack Verdun because he knew France would defend it almost regardless of the cost. Verdun has been France's principal fortress against Germany since the Franco-Russian War of 1870-71. It had to be defended. Standing in a salient of the front, it was easy to attack. France lost about 300,000 men between February and July. But they inflicted almost equally severe losses on the Germans. With their slogan "They shall not pass," Petain and his men became the heroes of France.

Despite the slaughter the front line remained

where it was. The same was true throughout the war zone. Later in 1916 the French commander-in-chief, Joffre, was replaced by General Robert Nivelle. Although junior to Petain, he knew better how to handle politicians. He also had a plan to "finish the war." But German spies uncovered its details while Nivelle's colleagues, notably the war minister Painleve and Petain, were convinced it would fail. It did, and the senseless, butchery caused mutiny in the French army. 21,000 soldiers deserted. Entire regiments left the front for Paris. Officers who tried to stop them were beaten or killed. On May 15 1917 Petain was appointed commander-in-chief to halt the collapse.

He was a cold man, contemptuous of democratic devices, but his sympathy for the sufferings of the troops was genuine. The ringleaders of the mutiny were shot or exiled, but the chief factor in restoring the army's morale was Petain's visits to more than 100 divisions along the front. He convinced officers and men that the meaningless slaughter of the past would not be repeated. But Petain had little offensive spirit and was replaced as commander-in-chief by Foch.

He became minister of war in 1934. In tune with his defensive approach to war, he pushed forward the building of the huge eastward defensive system known as the Maginot Line. Con-

sidered impregnable, the line had three flaws. It reinforced the French army's defensive mentality, it drained resources from the building of tanks and aircraft, and it was too short. The Germans bypassed it in 1940 and attacked France through the Ardennes forests.

Above: people accused of collaborating with the Germans after the liberation of France. All over France alleged collaborators were rounded up. These, at Vaucelles, are imprisoned in a barbed wire compound.

By May 15, what was left of the French army of the Meuse was everywhere in retreat. Prime Minister Paul Reynaud appointed Petain, at the time ambassador to Franco's Spain, his chief military adviser. But, with General Weygand who had been given charge of the defense of France, Petain urged that an armistice be reached with the Germans. On June 14 the Germans entered Paris. Reynaud resigned on the 16th, and Petain formed a new government. On June 22 it signed a humiliating armistice with Hitler in the same railway carriage in which Foch had dictated Germany's surrender in 1918. German troops occupied north and west France. Petain's government with its capital at Vichy, ruled the central and southern zone. Britain was left to face Germany entirely alone.

The shame of France's position seems to have affected Petain little. A right-wing clerical, anti-republican, he, and thousands like him, saw in defeat the chance to overthrow liberalism. Petain believed he had saved the nation from revolution and social chaos. The archbishop of Lyon hailed him as "the incarnation of suffering France." Frenchmen accepted Petain's authority. Charles De Gaulle's broadcasts from London evoked little response. The Resistance became a significant factor only after the Germans became excessively oppressive irrespective of

Above: Petain on trial for collaborating with the Nazis by heading the Vichy government. Petain is reading his declaration at the trial, which took place in July and August 1945. He was sentenced to death, but Charles de Gaulle commuted the sentence to life imprisonment.

Petain and his prime minister Pierre Laval. Taken to Germany by the retreating Germans, Petain returned voluntarily to face trial for treason. He was sentenced to death and national indignity. Some scapegoat was needed for the enthusiasm with which France had embraced defeat in 1940. De Gaulle commuted the sentence to life imprisonment.

Petain's tragic personal career epitomised the decline in French morale and political self-confidence between the two world wars.

William II
1859~1941

The third and last monarch of a united Germany, William II was cast by his enemies as the villain of the piece in World War I. Today that war is considered the result of a clash of rival imperialisms. Britain feared Germany's growing industrial and naval strength. Personal dynastic illusions of the emperors of Germany, Austria-Hungary and Russia also played their part. In this sense only was William's ebullient and conceited personality a factor in the events leading up to the holocaust.

When William was born, Prussia was the most powerful in a united free trade area of lesser German states. From 1862, under his grand-

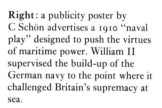

Right: a publicity poster by C Schön advertises a 1910 "naval play" designed to push the virtues of maritime power. William II supervised the build-up of the German navy to the point where it challenged Britain's supremacy at sea.

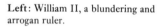

Left: William II, a blundering and arrogan ruler.

father King William I and the "Iron Chancellor" Bismarck, it became the most powerful state in continental Europe. Her king became the emperor of the former German federation. William himself took the throne in 1888 after a three-month reign by his dying father Frederick III. Influenced by his wife Victoria, daughter of the great English queen, Frederick had held liberal views. His son, fascinated by the triumphs of his grandfather's reign, had extravagant ideas of the divinity of kingship and the imperial destiny of Germany.

With considerable constitutional powers as head of the German state, William resented the patronizing authority of Bismarck and sacked him in 1890. European diplomats regarded the talented but unstable young ruler with apprehension. His mother had said "my son has no motive save vanity." Most people recognized beneath the proud posturings an egotistical but insecure nature. Perhaps his withered left arm, about which he was undoubtedly sensitive, was a factor in his insecurities. He pursued generous if paternalistic policies of social reform at home. Abroad he planned a world role for Germany based on his personal insights and royal friendships, notably with "Nicky," Czar Nicholas II of Russia.

But William was blundering as well as arrogant. He supported Russian policies against Japan but supported, equally, Austria's ambitions against Russia in the Balkans. France was angered by his interventions in Morocco which it considered its sphere of interest. William protested friendship to Britain, yet sent a message of congratulation to President Kruger of the Transvaal, Britain's bitter enemy in southern

men, you will live to rue the day you made me do this."

By 1916 the military high command under Hindenburg and Ludendorff had political control of Germany. But by October 1918 the allies were demanding William's abdication as a precondition of peace, and revolution loomed in Germany. Ludendorff saw that defeat was inevitable. He democratized the regime and retired.

Above: William II had fled into exile and Germany was now a republic. Berliners wait in front of the Chancery for Ebert and Scheidemann on November 9 1918. The first job of these leaders of the new Weimar Republic was to reach a peace with the Allied powers. No less urgent was to stem the tide of revolution in Germany.

Left: William II (center) with his military advisors, Generals Von Hindenburg (left) and Ludendorff during World War I.

Below: William II out walking on his 75th birthday (January 27 1934) in exile at Doorn, Holland. His wife walks at his right.

Africa. He sponsored a huge expansion of the German navy. Britain, then the world's greatest naval power, could only see this as aimed against itself. In 1908 he even contrived to affront both English and German public opinion. In a press interview he announced that while he personally was a friend of England, German public opinion was hostile. Even reactionary circles asked him "to act with greater reserve."

In 1914, Austria declared war on Serbia. William assured Austria of German support, believing his personal intervention with "Nicky" would halt Russian mobilization in support of Serbia.

His uncle, Edward VII of England (died 1911), had once written: "My nephew will release the forces of war not as a result of his own initiative, but out of weakness." As William signed the orders for German mobilization on August 1 1914, he said to his generals: "Gentle-

At noon on November 9 Prince Max of Baden, the recently appointed parliamentarian chancellor, announced the emperor's abdication without consulting him. He then resigned the chancellorship. Two hours later the Berlin crowds were cheering the German republic. Germany signed an armistice on November 11 1918.

William fled to neutral Holland. The Dutch gave him Castle Doorn as a home. He died in June 1941, and was given a military funeral on the orders of Adolf Hitler.

He died as he had ruled . . . a symbol of aggressive German militarism. But William believed that he had not sought war. His chancellor, von Bulow, once said: "We seek to put no one in the shade; merely to give ourselves a place in the sun." A colonial empire, a powerful navy, extended European influence – any one was a feasible objective. Pursued together in the unsubtle and provocative style of William and his ministers, they inevitably forced Germany's opponents together.

Eamon De Valera
1882-1975

Eamon De Valera is a dominant figure in modern Irish history. He was born in New York of an Irish mother and Spanish father, but was raised by his mother's family in County Limerick. Educated at the National University of Dublin, De Valera became a fervent nationalist. He joined the Irish Volunteers, and won national prominence in the 1916 Easter Rising against the British.

It was to have been a nationwide rebellion with German help. But the Germans held back and the Irish leadership abandoned the plans. However, a number of Dublin groups, one led by De Valera, seized the central post office and held out for four days. The volunteers lost 250 men and 100 British troops were also killed. At first, Irish public opinion was hostile to the revolutionaries, but when the British military commander executed the leading commandants they were hailed as martyrs. De Valera was spared because of his US nationality and imprisoned. The British were at war with Germany, and regarded the revolutionaries as deep-dyed traitors.

Freed by amnesty in 1917, De Valera formed the Finna Fail "Soldiers of Destiny" party. He was named "President of the Irish Republic"

Top: Irish members of parliament disrupt the proceedings of the House of Commons in 1901 as part of the campaign for Irish independence from Britain.

Above: Irish freedom fighters at a Dublin barricade during the 1916 Easter Rising. During this rising, 250 rebels lost their lives, as did 100 British troops.

by the illegal Sinn Fein (We Ourselves) party. He was locked up again, but escaped in 1918 – fleeing to the United States. There he raised funds for the republican cause. Returning from America at the end of World War I he entered the Dail (Irish Parliament) which was negotiating independence terms with the British. Six northern counties of Ireland, most having a Protestant majority, were to remain an integral part of the United Kingdom with their own provincial government. This was to become the modern state of Ulster. The remaining 26 southern counties were to form the new Irish Free

State, independent within the British Empire but owing allegiance to the crown.

A majority in the Dail accepted these terms, but De Valera led the opposition. They refused the oath to the British crown, and authorized a campaign of violence by the IRA (Irish Republican Army). Ireland was plunged into civil war. De Valera was again imprisoned. This time by the Irish government now led by Liam Cosgrave. He called off the IRA campaign and was released in 1924.

Street violence continued. In 1927, the justice minister, Kevin O'Higgins, was assassinated. In response, Cosgrave introduced a tough Public Safety Act. Among other things, this obliged all Dail members to swear allegiance to the crown or be expelled. De Valera complied and became leader of the opposition in the Dail.

The opposition opposed the payment of land annuities. These serviced the funds raised on the London money market to buy out former British landlords.

De Valera became a prime minister of a coalition government in 1932. In elections the following year, he won a majority of one over all other parties. He abolished the Senate, the Irish upper house, in the late 1930s. The IRA was suppressed for its continuing acts of violence. Ireland broke its remaining links with England under De Valera's rule. He stopped payment of land annuities, and promoted a new constitution. Approved by plebiscite in 1937, this abolished the oath of allegiance, and made Irish the official language of the state, now renamed Eire. The national territory was declared to comprise the whole island of Ireland and the office of president was established. But he never officially declared the country a republic.

De Valera held Ireland neutral in World War II. Nevertheless many Irishmen volunteered for service in Britain's armed forces. The·regime's inability to stimulate industrial growth, halt the flood of emigration to Britain or to improve agriculture, led to defeat in the 1948 elections by a coalition under J. Costello. This government declared Ireland a full republic. De Valera was returned as prime minister in 1951 to 1954, and again in 1957. But he resigned two years later in favor of Sean Lemass in 1959, and became president. He held that office until 1973.

Above left: Madame MacBride addresses a street meeting in support of the demand for Irish independence. Her husband, John MacBride, was executed by the British during the Easter Rising. She is seen attacking De Valera's treatment of militant Republicans. ". . . these are the laws which brought about the fall of Mr Cosgrave and yet are being maintained by Mr De Valera to crush Irish Republicans."

Above: the opening of the Irish Parliament in September. 1922.

Right: Eamon De Valera attending a parade to commemorate the 50th anniversary of the Easter Rising on April 10 1966.

Lawrence of Arabia
1888~1935

would get most of Syria, while Britain controlled Mesopotamia.

Welcomed by Feisal, Lawrence evolved tactics with him "to contain the Turks by the silent threat of a vast unknown desert." The garrison at Medina was immobilized. Its supply line, the Hejaz railway, was sabotaged, and in July 1917 the port of Akaba fell to a daring attack from the landward side masterminded by Lawrence. His energy, self-discipline, and astonishing endurance during a fearful 200-mile desert march helped make 'al-Urenz' a legend. He had adopted

Left: a portrait of T E Lawrence in Arab costume by the Welsh painter Augustus John.

Right: a street in Yenbo. Lawrence's house is the nearest right in the picture.

Below: the Emir Feisal. Lawrence was assigned as the Emir's British Liaison officer.

Arab dress and in Councils of War sat, "bare feet tucked under him, swathed as the others, with gold dagger, girdle round his waist."

In November 1917 Lawrence was arrested,

The Englishman T. E. Lawrence was already a hero of the Arab liberation struggle against the Ottoman empire by the time he was 30. Lawrence's tactics were a model of desert guerrilla campaigning, and his account of the struggle, *Seven Pillars of Wisdom*, is an epic of the effects of war on men. His diplomacy helped establish the modern states of Iraq and Jordan. But Lawrence was an emotionally complex character, and his career ended in controversy.

He was the second of five illegitimate sons of a wealthy landowner. His mother's shame at her love match was to affect his later life. Having studied history at Oxford, Lawrence spent five years in Syria and Mesopotamia studying crusader castles and working as an archaeologist. Increasingly fluent in Arabic, he grew to accept their culture more and more.

In World War I, the British offered help to Arab insurgents against Turkey. Sherif Hussein of Mecca drove the Turks from Mecca and the southern Red Sea ports in June 1916. That December Lawrence was assigned British liaison officer to his son Feisal. He shared the Arabs' dreams of independence. But the secret Sykes-Picot agreement between Britain and France envisaged a post-war settlement in which France

Left: General Allenby (center) enters Jerusalem in late 1917. By the end of that year Allenby's troops had driven the Turks from Jerusalem. Allenby chose to walk into the city, saying he could not ride where Christ had ridden a donkey.

Lawrence went to the Versailles Peace Conference to help fight the Arabs' case.

Winston Churchill thought of him: "one of nature's greatest princes . . . from amid the flowing draperies his noble features and flashing eyes, loaded with fire and comprehension shone forth." But Lawrence's efforts at the Conference failed, and in July 1920 the French drove Feisal from Damascus. Urged by Churchill, now Colonial Secretary, Lawrence played a prominent role in negotiations. In July 1921 these established Feisal as King of Iraq and his brother

while reconnoitring the Turkish-held town of Deraa. There was a £20,000 price on his head but he was not recognized. That night he was sexually assaulted. He escaped and in January 1918 led a crushing Arab victory over the Turks in open battle at Tafileh. Lawrence refused decorations from France and Britain.

His anguish at "exploiting the blood and hope of another people" brought him to the verge of resignation. But, perhaps hoping that rapid Arab victories would forestall the Sykes-Picot plan, he fought on. Early in October 1918 he and Feisal entered Damascus in triumph – just days ahead of the British army under General Allenby. Feisal now learnt of the Franco-British agreement. In comparison, the British "Balfour Declaration" of November 1917, "in favor of a Jewish national home in Palestine," seemed secondary. In January 1919, at Lawrence's prompting, Feisal reached an understanding with the Zionist Leader, Chaim Weizmann.

Above: the Cairo Conference of 1921. Winston Churchill is seated front row center. It was his job as Colonial Secretary to deal with those ex-Turkish Arab provinces not considered ready for independence

Abdulla as ruler of Trans-Jordan under British mandate.

But Lawrence became deeply depressed. He despised himself for his "fraudulent" role in the Arab campaigns, his illegitimate birth and the bestial humiliation of Deraa. In search of "mind suicide" through drudgery, he enlisted as a mechanic in the Royal Air Force under the name of Ross. The press had the story within weeks. Lawrence next sought obscurity as "T. E. Shaw" in the Tank Corps. In 1925, on the verge of mental breakdown, he was transferred back to the RAF. In 1928 he completed *The Mint*, a harsh account of life in the forces. His Dorsetshire cottage of Clouds Hill provided a haven where he could keep contact with such friends as the dramatist George Bernard Shaw and his wife Charlotte; a passion for powerful motorcycles provided his chief relaxation. He was killed in a crash in 1935. Lawrence remains an enigmatic figure to this day.

Lenin
1870-1924

Lenin is the founder of Bolshevism and the father of Soviet Russia. He is also one of history's most successful revolutionary leaders. A dominant figure of 20th century history, his writings, with those of Karl Marx, established Marxist-Leninism as the doctrine of world communism.

Born Vladimir Ilyich Ulyanov, he early adopted the revolutionary pseudonym Lenin.

Below: Lenin portrayed in a modern propaganda poster in Moscow. Such a display reveals a "cult of personality", of which Lenin himself strongly disapproved.

Lenin's parents were school teachers. His eldest brother, Alexander, was executed in 1887 for plotting the assassination of Czar Alexander III. Lenin was deeply influenced by this event, and he inherited Alexander's copy of Marx's *Capital*.

After an education punctuated with revolutionary activities he qualified brilliantly in law from the University of St Petersburg. Lenin was soon absorbed in Marxist studies and propagandizing among workers' groups with Krupskaya who was to become his wife. He spent some months in Geneva in 1895 with Russian Marxist exiles, notably Plekhanov. Returning to Russia with banned political literature, he was exiled to Siberia. There he continued the studies which led to the major work *The Development of Capitalism in Russia*, and brilliant polemics against rival revolutionaries.

Released in 1900 Lenin returned to Geneva. Here with Plekhanov and others, he launched the revolutionary journal *Iskra* ("The Spark"). In his 1902 pamphlet *What is To Be Done?* he advocated the need for an elite party of dedicated revolutionaries. A meeting of the Russian Social Democratic Party held in Brussels and London in 1903 split on this issue. Lenin's supporters won a majority on the Central Committee, and dubbed themselves Bolsheviks – Russian for "majority." The Mensheviks ("minority") argued for a popular mass party. They won control of the central committee the following year. Lenin resigned and the movement split.

Lenin lived abroad from 1907. He was in Zurich when risings in Petrograd forced Czar Nicholas II to abdicate in March 1917. Popularly elected soviets were formed in Petrograd, Moscow and other cities. Lenin said in January of that year: "we of the older generation may not live to see the decisive battles of the coming revolution." He now found himself with other revolutionaries being transported through Germany in a sealed train provided by the imperial German authorities keen to see the Russian war effort disintegrate completely.

Left: Russian troops kneel before Czar Nicholas II as he blesses them with an Icon during World War I. By the end of 1917, Nicholas had been deposed and Lenin ruled the country as president of the Council of People's Commissars.

Left: picture from a Russian book portrays the "Storming of the Kremlin" in 1917. In fact, the first phase of the revolution was accomplished without bloodshed.

Above: the national seal of the Bolsheviks, bearing the hammer and sickle and the words "Russian Socialist Federative Soviet Republic. Workers of all countries, Unite!"

Below: Lenin's corpse lies in state. His Last Testament denouncing the behaviour of Stalin was suppressed.

He was rapturously received at the Finland Station, Petrograd. But the Bolshevik revolution still had to be won. The Petrograd coup, directed from the Smolny Convent by Leon Trotsky, came at last on November 6–7 (October 24–25 in the old calendar). Food supplies and key services were taken over bloodlessly, and the provisional government disbanded.

Lenin, as president of the newly formed Council of People's Commissars, declared the new regime's determination to withdraw from the war with Germany, and to nationalize all land without compensation. Elections were called. But the Bolsheviks won only 175 of 700 seats. The Assembly was disbanded in January 1918 by Red Guards. Lenin was now virtually a dictator of central Russia, with Trotsky and Joseph Stalin among his chief lieutenants. Opposition wilted in the Red Terror mounted by the Cheka security organization. But the country at large was prey to ambitious regional party officials and adventurers. Civil war broke out

between white (Counter-revolutionary) and Red sections of the army. Western countries sent in troops to overthrow the Revolution. By August 1918 about 30 rival regimes were operating on Russian territory.

Peace with Germany was bought at the Treaty of Brest Litovsk. It was bought dearly. Russia lost one third of its agricultural land and its population, four fifths of its coal, and half its industry. Anti-Bolshevik rebellions broke out and the civil war continued. The communists, under Trotsky, fought their way to eventual victory in 1921. Lenin had meanwhile set up the Comintern in 1919 to further world revolution which he believed inevitable.

Industry was nationalized and grain requisitioned. This policy of War Communism produced bitter opposition from the peasantry who had not dispossessed their feudal landlords merely to hand over their gains to the communists. Trotsky put down a menacing mutiny among the Kronstadt naval garrison near Petrograd.

In March 1921 Lenin introduced the New Economic Policy which relaxed state centralism, allowed features of private enterprise and somewhat mollified the peasantry. Nevertheless, the party machine strengthened its grip and Stalin, general secretary of the party, increased his influence. Lenin foresaw danger but after several illnesses brought on by his titanic labours, died virtually paralysed by a stroke

Before Lenin, classical Marxist theory presented Russian revolutionaries with a dilemma. The theory stated that the revolution should come when a country had passed through a "bourgeois," industrialized stage. But Russia was largely a backward peasant society. Lenin's writings showed that a socialist revolution could occur in such a society. The Mensheviks by contrast, argued that Russia should move to revolution gradually through the bourgeois phase posited by pure Marxist theory.

Lenin sought to show that war is the natural condition of capitalism and that imperialism is its last stage. He preached the duty of Bolsheviks to actively encourage revolution in other countries. He firmly believed in the necessity of revolution. "A Social-Democrat must never forget that the proletariat will inevitably have to wage a class struggle for socialism even against the most democratic and republican bourgeoisie."

Trotsky
1879-1940

Lenin himself did not fulfil as many revolutionary roles so brilliantly as Leon Trotsky. His writings on Marxism covered and shaped its development over the first 40 years of this century. He directed the revolutionary tactics which brought the Bolsheviks to power in October 1917. As father of the Red Army he protected the Revolution in its early years.

Born Lev Davidovich Bronstein, Trotsky was the son of a prosperous farmer. Brilliant at

Right: *Trotsky and the First International* by the Mexican painter Diego Rivera. This painting is now in Mexico where Trotsky died.

Left: Trotsky's 1915 passport photograph. He had been to Switzerland in 1915 to attend the Zimmervuald Conference. Thirty-eight socialist delegates from 11 countries had met to discuss ways of ending World War I.

school, he joined a Marxist group at the age of 17. He was arrested for the first time two years later. Using falsified papers in the name of Trotsky, one of his jailers, he escaped from a term of Siberian exile in 1902. He fled to London where he helped Lenin on the revolutionary journal *Iskra*.

Trotsky returned to Russia in 1905. As chairman of the St Petersburg Soviet, he was involved in the Revolution of that year which forced concessions from the Czarist regime. Trotsky was one of the Social Democrats who tried to continue the revolutionary strike action, and was arrested when the Soviet was suppressed. He escaped a second exile to Siberia and 1907-14 worked as a journalist in Vienna. At the outbreak of World War I he lived as an active revolutionary in Paris and then New York. He returned to Petrograd after the overthrow of the Czarist regime by the February Revolution of 1917. Trotsky was the principal director of

the Bolshevik coup that October.

Trotsky became commissar for foreign affairs after the Revolution. He had charge of the negotiations at the Treaty of Brest Litovsk with Germany in 1918 which confirmed Soviet Russia's withdrawal from World War I. Massive territorial concessions were made to Germany as the price of peace.

Trotsky then took over the conduct of the civil war against the Whites, and the western intervention forces which followed. From the remnants of the Czarist army and other scattered elements Trotsky welded the Red Army into the fighting force which saved the Revolution.

But the Revolution faced a dire threat from within. In March 1921, newly recruited peasant sailors at the Kronstadt naval base near Leningrad, mutinied in protest at the Bolshevik monopoly of power. Trotsky immediately ordered an attack across the ice. Ten days of fighting in driving snow followed.

During the civil war, Trotsky was the party's greatest figure after Lenin. But his growing mutual distrust with Stalin, a secondary but important figure, began to erode his position. He next clashed with Lenin. Stalin was named general secretary of the party. When Lenin died in 1924 he was able to keep Trotsky from the succession. The rivalry found ideological expression in the fierce debate over whether socialism should be confined to Russia (Stalin's view) or be propagated by world revolution (Trotsky). And Stalin controlled the party machine. Trotsky was sacked as commissar, expelled from the Politburo, and from the Party in 1925. In 1929 he was exiled from the USSR. He lived first in Turkey, then in France, from 1935 in Norway and from 1937, when Stalin pressured the Norwegian government to expel him, in Mexico.

In exile Trotsky mounted a brilliant and scathing critique of Stalin. In response, Stalin

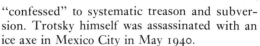

Below: Lenin and Trotsky surrounded by a delegation of the Red Army, March 1921. The Army had just put down the Kronstadt Rebellion.

"confessed" to systematic treason and subversion. Trotsky himself was assassinated with an ice axe in Mexico City in May 1940.

Trotsky's writings, with those of Lenin, were a brilliant adaptation of the philosophy of revotionary strategy of Marx – shaped for an industrial society – to the backward peasant based society of Czarist Russia. In the great debate between the Mensheviks and Bolsheviks, Trotsky never fully committed himself, but saw clearly that

raised the bogey of a supposed Trotskyite plot as the excuse to murder thousands of supposed collaborators. A series of grotesque show trials were mounted in 1936, 1937 and 1938. Virtually all the leaders of the Bolshevik 1917 Revolution, friends of Lenin and venerated by the Party,

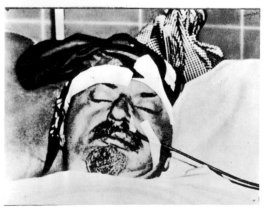

Above: under Stalin, Trotsky's role in the Revolution was denied. The picture on the left shows Lenin speaking to troops in Moscow before they leave for the front during the Civil War, May 1920. Trotsky stands to the left of the platform. The picture on the right is of the same scene. Trotsky has vanished and the platform has grown – both the work of Stalin's censors.

Left: Trotsky pictured soon after he had been assassinated with an ice-pick by an agent of Stalin in May 1940.

Lenin's theory of an authoritarian party would lead to a dictatorship.

His writings include *The History of the Russian Revolution*, one of this century's great works of literature, a brilliant biography of *Stalin* and *The Permanent Revolution*. The Marxian "permanent revolution" is one which "makes no compromise with any form of class rule . . . and can only end in the complete liquidation of all class society." Such passages and Trotsky's notes on "The Art of Insurrection" make him one of the most influential of revolutionary theorists. Trotsky's beliefs still inspire socialists around the world.

Ataturk
1881-1938

Above: Ataturk (right) with Rafet, who had been given the command of the Third Army in Turkey's war against the Greeks. The Greeks landed at Smyrna in 1921. Turkish sovereignty was virtually extinguished.

Right: this print shows Ataturk and his forces attacking Greek troops at Sakarya – August 1922.

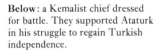

Below: a Kemalist chief dressed for battle. They supported Ataturk in his struggle to regain Turkish independence.

The founder of modern Turkey, Mustafa Kemal Ataturk grew up under the last decadent regime of the Ottoman empire which still ruled much of the Balkans, Syria, Iraq and North Africa. He ran away from school to enter a military academy. Then, like many young officers, he joined the Young Turks opposition movement.

For a time, Kemal was chief of staff to the movement's leader Enver Pasha who forced the installation of a more liberal sultan in 1909. Turkey's enemies took advantage of the upheaval to grab territory from the empire. Most of the Balkan territories were lost, and Italy conquered Lybia in 1912. Enver Pasha welcomed Germain aid. With the outbreak of World War I in 1914 Turkey joined the Central Powers against the Allies. Kemal had won distinctions in Turkey's various wars but he was becoming increasingly disillusioned with Enver Pasha's growing concern with imperial affairs. Kemal formed the Turkish Nationalist party in 1919. Later that same year Greek forces occupied the city of Smyrna (Izmir) on Turkey's west coast. Seizing the mood of national outrage, Kemal convened a nationalist congress at Erzerum. He was outlawed by Sultan Mohammed VI.

Constantinople was occupied by Allied troops after Turkey's defeat in World War I, and Mohammed VI was next obliged to sign the humiliating Peace of Sevres. This confirmed Smyrna as a Greek possession, established

Armenia as a separate republic, and confined European Turkey to Constantinople and its environs. The Ottoman empire was liquidated and Turkish sovereignty was virtually abolished – even in the lands left to the Turks. A large Greek force landed at Smyrna to enforce the terms of the treaty in 1921.

The Ankara Assembly withdrew from their allegiance to the sultan and organized national resistance. In a series of brilliant campaigns, Kemal reoccupied Armenia and routed the Greeks. At the Congress of Lausanne in 1923,

Left: the Gallipoli Campaign was a fiasco for the Allies in World War I. Here, troops land at ANZAC cove in the Dardanelles.

The sultans had been the spiritual heads of Islam, the "caliphs," successors of the prophet. Could the revolutionary Turkish regime legitimately end this function as well as the political role? Religious lawyers in the Ankara Assembly argued that conditions for the investiture of a true caliph had been fulfilled only during the reigns of the first four caliphs. Their successors had claimed the title falsely, and the modern Islamic community had the authority to chose its own form of government. Such political

Right: Ataturk looks on as one of his subjects demonstrates writing in Latin script, 1930. Ataturk introduced a Latin alphabet into Turkey.

theorizing was no doubt necessary but, as Kemal admitted, the caliphate had had to go because it had forced the Turkish people to serve an international ambition against their national interests.

Kemal secured the frontiers by treaties with Yugoslavia, Rumania, and even Greece. Friendly relations were established with Soviet Russia. Foreign influence was excluded even at the cost of turning away much needed foreign capital. Kemal was virtually a dictator of this one-party state. He pushed through reforms with an energy rarely equalled in the history of government.

All former titles, religious as well as secular, were abolished. Elections to the national assembly were by universal male suffrage. Religious orders were suppressed. Polygamy, allowed by Islamic law, was forbidden under Turkish law. Full emancipation of women was proclaimed in 1934, and they were given the vote. In 1928 Islam ceased to be the state religion. The entire traditional legal system was dismantled and European codes adopted. Even the wearing of the fez was prohibited. Islamic script was replaced by the Latin alphabet and all Turks under the age of 40 were forced to go to school to learn it. Ankara displaced Constantinople as capital.

From grand principles to seemingly petty but symbolic details, the westernization of Turkey achieved by Kemal Pasha was rapid and fundamental. Opposition and risings were ruthlessly suppressed but when, in 1934, Kemal received the title of Ataturk, "Father of the Turks," few doubted that the honor was deserved.

the Allies agreed to improve Turkey's treaty terms. Eastern Thrace, Smyrna and other territories were handed back and Turkey's internal sovereignty recognized. It was a symbolic as well as a real achievement. The powers which had defeated Turkey under the sultan had now been brought to terms by the Turkish nationalist republicans.

Kemal was elected president of the republic. The sultanate had been abolished in 1922. Two years later the caliphate went too. Controversy raged throughout the orthodox Islamic world.

Franco
1892-1975

Francisco Franco y Bahamonde was dictator of Spain for 36 years. He came to power when the rebel army finally defeated the forces of the republican government in the Spanish Civil War. Franco enjoyed undisputed authority from 1939 until incapacitated by illness in the last year of his life.

A Galician by birth, he came from a family of four generations of naval officers. Franco broke the tradition by entering the army's Infantry Academy at Toledo. He graduated at 17 and volunteered for active service in Spain's colonial campaigns in Morocco.

Efficient and aloof, he became full commander of the recently formed Spanish Foreign Legion in 1923. The war against the forces of the Moroccan guerilla leader Abd-el-Krim was faltering and becoming increasingly unpopular in Spain. Indeed internal affairs were sliding towards anarchy, largely because of autocratic interference in government by King Alfonso XIII. Since his accession in 1902 there had been no fewer than 33 governments. Then, in 1923, with the king's permission, Miguel Primo de Rivera took over as virtual dictator.

Franco won national standing when the Spanish Foreign Legion played a major role in

Left: General Francisco Franco. Throughout his reign Franco held Spain in a repressive and dictatorial grip. Since his death, there has been a political upsurge, and Spain has established a constitutional democracy in tune with the rest of western Europe.

Right: King Alfonso XIII. His autocratic interference in political affairs bedeviled government in Spain.

Opposite above: a recruiting poster for the airforce issued by the Socialist Workers Party during the Spanish Civil War. The slogan reads "to vanquish fascism join the airforce."

Opposite: Pablo Picasso's pictorial protest at the bombing of Guernica. Franco had authorized the bombing of urban civilian populations. The bombing was carried out by the German *Luftwaffe*. It was practice for what they were to inflict on civilians during World War II.

defeating the Moroccan rebels in 1926. He was promoted brigadier-general, and in 1928 became director of the Zaragossa military academy.

But Rivera's regime and the monarchy itself were overthrown in 1931, and replaced by a republic. Franco, a prominent rightist and monarchist, was retired to the reserve list and the Zaragossa academy closed. Two years later he was once more in the public eye when a new right-wing republican regime gave him command of troops sent to quell a rising of miners in the Asturia region. Next he was appointed chief of the army's general staff.

In the few months he held this powerful position Franco tightened discipline and so made himself familiar as commander to the army's senior officers. But in 1936 the left-wing Popular Front parties won the elections. Strikes and street violence mounted. Franco appealed to the government to declare a state of emergency. They ignored him, and he found himself effectively exiled as military commander of the Canary Islands.

Right-wing officers proclaimed a rising against the republican government in July 1936. Franco flew to Morocco to take charge of the revolt there. In September he was nominated head of the Spanish state and supreme commander. General Emilio Mola became commander of the army in the north. Franco's forces advanced rapidly northwards and began to besiege Madrid. The Civil War seemed to be at an end. But government forces fought on until March 1939.

International Brigades of volunteers came to help the republican government. Arms and materiel came from the Soviet Union. Franco received troops, equipment and aircraft from Hitler and Mussolini. International opinion was outraged when he authorized bombing of open cities, notably Guernica. Franco insisted on un-

conditional surrender. He reorganized the Falange (Spain's Fascist Party) as his official political organ, and began a purge in which tens of thousands of his opponents were killed.

Once in power, he banned all criticism and opposition. Despite his sympathy with Europe's other fascist dictators, he held Spain aloof and officially neutral throughout World War II. A meeting with Hitler at Hendaye in 1940 yielded the German leader little, but ensured Spain immunity from invasion by the German forces occupying France. After the war Spain was at first ostracised by the international community. But in 1953 the United States signed an agreement in which Spain received economic and military aid in return for providing military bases. The same year Franco signed a concordat with the Vatican which reaffirmed the close interdependence of church and state in Spain. By 1960 Spain had relinquished its colonial power in Morocco, been admitted to the United Nations and the Organization of European Economic Cooperation. America's President Dwight D. Eisenhower made a state visit to Spain that same year. In the 1960s the country's economy expanded through tourism and increasing industrialization.

Franco had proclaimed Spain a monarchy in 1947, with himself as regent for life. In 1954 he designated as his successor Don Juan Carlos (born 1932), the son of Don Juan and grandson of Alfonso XIII. Twelve years later a new law, approved by referendum, appointed Spain's first prime minister since 1939 and made marginal relaxations in the regime's oppressive authoritarianism. Tensions later developed between liberal forces and right-wing Falangists. But when Franco died, Don Juan Carlos ascended the throne with remarkably little opposition.

Mussolini
1883 - 1945

Benito Mussolini embodied the politics of elitist, anti-socialist nationalism. Communism was the arch enemy, and liberal democracy was the arch victim of the 1920s and 1930s. He joined with the German Führer Adolf Hitler in the Rome–Berlin Axis of 1939 and entered his war in June 1940. Mussolini's ambitions helped precipitate the European crisis, but the war destroyed his regime.

Although one of the victorious Allies of World War I, Italy felt aggrieved by the terms of the Versailles Peace Treaty of 1919. It was given no share of Germany's former colonial possessions

Above: Mussolini's famous march on Rome on October 28 1922. Picture shows fascists with Mussolini at their head passing through the arch into the Piazza Del Popolo. King Victor Emmanuel III invited Mussolini to form a government.

Left: Benito Mussolini pictured in characteristically belligerent pose.

and the Adriatic port of Fiume, which she claimed, was internationalized. Fiume was seized by a romantic band of nationalists in September 1919. They flew into the territory led by the aviator-poet Gabriele D'Annunzio. But, to popular resentment, Italian troops restored the city to international control.

At the same time, social discontent wracked the nation. Communist workers' soviets clashed with armed anti-communist veterans. Chief among these were the street fighters mobilized by the ex-corporal and one-time socialist journalist, Benito Mussolini. They were uniformed in

black shirts, like D'Annunzio's sky raiders. For their badge they wore the ancient Roman emblem of authority, the *fasces* – an ax bound in rods. These "fascists" gained a modest 35 seats in the 1921 elections. But, following a government resignation in 1922, Mussolini, reassured by influential supporters, staged a coup. Some 30,000 Blackshirts marched from Milan to Rome. King Victor Emanuele III invited Mussolini to form a government, and the 400 non-fascist deputies voted him dictatorial powers for one year. His indefinite dictatorship was heralded, in 1924, when the murderers of the socialist leader Matteotti received only token sentences.

Tight party organization, modelled on the communist cell system and led by veterans of the "March on Rome," plus intensified police repression, ensured the triumph of fascism. The individual was held to be subject to the state under the supreme leader or "Duce." He embodied the aims of the state and inspired its destiny. War was the way to strengthen the state and toughen its citizens. Victory was assured against nations that did not want to fight. They were "decadent."

The regime tried to turn Italy into a corporate state. Strikes were banned and free trade unions were replaced by state controlled labor organizations. These were matched by national confederations of employers. Party members were imposed on company boards. For many years Mussolini was his own minister of corporations. Party control was extended to social and leisure activities. Police intimidation stifled any opposition. Political murder completed the picture of a

RECONDITIONED CAESAR —

—ALMOST AS GOOD AS NEW

by ILLINGWORTH

system where the individual was always subservient to the interests of the state, or, more correctly, the party.

The Italian economy did improve and the draining of the Pontine Marshes, a vast malarial zone near Rome which had defeated the best efforts of engineers of ancient emperors and medieval popes, was a major achievement. But the endemic poverty of southern Italy was barely touched. The government also failed to curb the Mafia.

Late in 1934, Mussolini decided to attack Abyssinia (Ethiopia). It lay between Italy's east African colonies of Eritrea and Italian Somaliland. The League of Nations declared Italy an aggressor in October 1936, and imposed sanctions – except on the vital commodities of coal and oil. The English and French foreign ministers, Hoare and Laval, worked out compromise concessions at Abyssinia's expense. They were leaked to the press and public outrage in Britain killed the plan. The League's sanctions were ineffectual. Mussolini added Ethiopia

Left: the British cartoonist Roy Illingworth lampoons Mussolini being pumped up by Hitler. Allied propaganda claimed that Mussolini was a puppet of the German Fuhrer, with no freedom of action. By about 1942, this assessment was probably correct.

to the Italian empire. What was left of the League's prestige vanished.

Mussolini next committed Italian troops in support of Franco's rebellion in Spain. Perhaps he hoped that a grateful Franco would help fulfill his ambition to dominate the Mediterranean. Certainly Italian money and armed intervention helped the future Spanish dictator's cause. In Easter 1939 Italy annexed Albania, a supposedly friendly protected state. Even such easy triumphs had been unpopular in Italy. The disastrous intervention in World War II robbed the regime of all popular support.

The Rome–Berlin "Axis" of 1939 was strengthened by Hitler's long standing admiration for Mussolini who had overthrown a democratic regime and yet forced the liberal democracies to accept him as an equal. At the Locarno Pact in 1925 Mussolini had joined France and England in guaranteeing a major settlement of Europe's post-Versailles frontiers. They had accepted him as a mediator at the Munich pact of 1938 which dismembered Czechoslovakia in Germany's favor, even though, shortly before, Mussolini had stood by when Hitler annexed Austria. For this the Führer had sworn eternal friendship to the Duce.

But Mussolini only went to war when, in June 1940, France was all but beaten by Germany. Three years later the Duce was dismissed by his own fascist Grand council and imprisoned. Hitler mounted a daring rescue and reinstalled him as head of a puppet regime. Following the German collapse Mussolini was captured by partisans and shot.

Mussolini had ruled for 21 years. He had brought Italy an appearance of power which deceived many European statesmen. The Lateran Treaty of 1929 still governs relations between the Italian state and its problematic partner, the Roman Catholic Church. But many Italians resent the role of the Church in their lives.

Right: Mussolini and his mistress Clara Petaci hanging by the feet from the rafters of a Rome garage. From a height of power and adulation, Mussolini's reputation sank until he was hated and reviled by the Italian people.

Hitler
1889 - 1945

Below: the militarism of Nazi Germany on display. Hitler reviews a military parade in Berlin, held in honor of his 50th birthday on April 21 1939.

In 1921 Hitler, responsible for the German Worker's Party's propaganda, became its president having renamed it the National Socialist German Workers' Party ("Nazi" Party). At this stage the party's support was still negligible but the worsening economic situation worked to its advantage.

Thousands were later to attend its rallies, and Captain Ernst Rohm, a party member and a staff officer of the Bavarian district army command,

Adolf Hitler established the most brutal tyranny in Western European history and was the prime instigator of World War II. The dictator of Germany and founder of the Nazi party was the son of a minor Austrian official. From 1908, both his parents having died, Hitler lived in Vienna as an "art student", though he was twice rejected for entry into art school. Imperial Vienna's cosmopolitan population and the strong currents of European anti-Semitism shaped the obsessive racialism which dominated Hitler's life.

He went to Munich in 1913, and served as a volunteer in the German army during World War I. Though only a corporal, he won the Iron Cross First Class, Germany's highest award for valor. In Munich after the war, he acted as an undercover army agent in the tiny German Workers' Party to vet it for communist and socialist elements. Army officers throughout Bavaria were working to subvert the new social democratic Weimar republican regime led by Freidrich Ebert. They and other right-wingers charged that the republic by signing the 1918 Armistice had "stabbed the army in the back." In fact, it was the army top brass which urged the conclusion of an armistice in the first place.

Above left: the dust jacket of Hitler's book *Mein Kampf* (My Struggle). His belief in the need for extra living space for Germany (*lebensraum*) is clearly set out. And for those who wished to take notice, the book gives a terrifying outline of Hitler's views on the future of the Jews.

Below: Hitler (left) with three old Nazi henchmen, Gregor Strasser, Ernst Röhm, and Hermann Göring pictured on July 16 1932.

organized storm troopers (*Sturmabteilung* or SA) from workless exservicemen, to promote street violence. Other early party members included Rudolf Hess, Hermann Göring and the "Jew Baiter of Nuremberg" Julius Streicher. In November 1923, General Ludendorff, who with Field Marshall von Hindenburg had led Germany's war effort, joined ex-corporal Hitler in an attempted coup against the Bavarian provincial government. This "beer hall putsch" was a fiasco.

Hitler was sentenced to five years imprisonment but was released after barely nine months. He wrote *Mein Kampf*, "My Struggle" while in jail. The book outlined his racialist obsession with the Aryan master race. The *Volk* was the natural unit of mankind and the Germans were the greatest such *Volk*. The Führer or Leader embodied the *Volk*. Hitler's brilliant propaganda techniques were also described in *Mein Kampf*.

The 1929 Slump threw millions out of work and ruined many a small business. Hitler found a ready audience among these unfortunate people. He made influential contacts with prominent German industrialists.

In the 1930 elections the Nazis won six million votes. At vast party rallies, brilliantly stage-managed by Joseph Goebbels, Hitler used his compelling demagogic oratory to proclaim racial hatred and the glorious future awaiting the German people once they were reunited and rearmed and the Versailles treaty overthrown.

The aging President von Hindenburg appointed Hitler chancellor in January 1933. He immediately called new Reichstag (parliamentary) elections. The Reichstag fire, blamed on Communists, helped win the Nazis votes. The new assembly voted Hitler dictatorial powers under the Enabling Act.

In June 1934, at the urging of Heinrich Himmler, Hitler ordered the assassination of Rohm and many of his SA colleagues in the "night of the long knives." Rohm had been demanding more radical revolution, and the army top brass bitterly resented him for his ambition to turn the SA into an alternative armed force at the service of the party. Hitler became undisputed Führer and the armed forces swore allegiance to him personally.

Versailles had created newly independent states from the former Austro-Hungarian empire, and reestablished Poland. As a result, various German populations were ruled by Slavs while Austria was debarred from uniting with Germany. Hitler saw this as fragmentation of the German *Volk*. In 1936, Hitler ordered the reoccupation of the Rhineland, demilitarized by Versailles, and allied Germany with Benito Mussolini's Italy in the "Axis". Next he incorporated Austria into Germany (Anschluss). The 1938 Munich agreement with Britain and France, dismembered Czechoslovakia. This country, under Eduard Benes, had become a

Below: the first American tanks enter the shattered center of Cologne, March 1945. The Allies demanded the unconditional surrender of Nazi Germany as a pre-condition to the end of the war in Europe. Hitler refused to consider capitulation. As a result Germany was industrially and politically destroyed.

model democracy in Central Europe after World War I. It was now enslaved by Nazism. Despite his virulent anti-Communism he signed a pact with Stalin's Russia. Germany could thus attack Poland without any interference from the Soviet Union. Hitler invaded Poland on August 31, 1939. Britain and France at last declared war on September 3. Russia took the eastern half of Poland while Germany took the rest.

A brilliant German *Blitzkreig*, masterminded

by Hitler, forced France's capitulation in June 1940 but Britain held firm. Throughout the war Hitler maintained tight control of military strategy. The invasion of Russia in June 1941 (operation "Barbarossa") was followed in December with a declaration of war on the United States after the Japanese had attacked Pearl Harbor.

Meanwhile Himmler was charged with supervising the "final solution of the Jewish question," Nazi jargon for the systematic extermination of Europe's Jewish populations. In July 1944 an attempt on Hitler's life headed by the army officer Klaus von Stauffenberg came within an ace of success. From January 1945, as the Third Reich crashed toward defeat Hitler and a small group of henchmen, chief among them Joseph Goebells the brilliant head of Nazi propaganda, retreated to a bunker headquarters in Berlin. On April 29, after a ceremony of marriage with Eva Braun, his mistress of 12 years, Hitler committed suicide followed by Eva and the Goebells family.

In the 1930s Germany was undeniably the most powerful industrial nation in Europe. To many Germans it seemed Hitler would win it its "rightful place" in world affairs. In fact he ensured her division between liberal democracy and Communist imperialism, arch-enemies of the Nazis' "supreme German *Volk*."

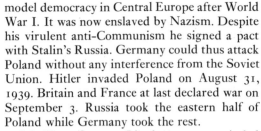

Left: "the Third Reich? No!" – an anti-Nazis poster of the early 1930s. Having gained power, Hitler ruthlessly crushed all forms of opposition and set about building the most fearsome police state of modern history. The traditional scapegoat, the Jews, were not the only victims. Thousands of trade unionists, socialists, and Christians were thrown into concentration camps. Those who remained obstinate in their opposition to Nazism were treated with the utmost brutality, and eventually killed.

Himmler
1900 - 1945

At the height of his power, Heinrich Himmler was, second only to Hitler, the most powerful man in Nazi Germany. He was certainly the most feared. Himmler came to control the Gestapo, the Security Police (SD) and the Criminal Police. He was head of the political and armed SS. This last was to number 500,000 men by 1944. He controlled a vast slave labor force in the concentration camps which was put to work in SS controlled factories. He ruled a state within a state.

Himmler was earning a living as a poultry farmer in 1928; the following year Hitler gave him command of the 200-man strong SS. Formed four years before, this was the *Schutz-staffel*, "Security Echelon", the black shirted elite of the Nazi street gangs. Himmler transformed it into the main weapon of terror in the Nazi state.

Above: this SA rally poster depicts the perfect Aryan type beloved of Himmler's racial fantasies.

Left: this captured German war painting depicts Himmler in the pose of a dashing military leader.

Below: the Gestapo identity disk, carried by all members of that justly notorious organization.

But it remained under the orders of Ernst Rohm, Hitler's friend, and founder of the brown shirted SA, or *Sturmabteilung*.

When Hitler became German chancellor in January 1933 Rohm, who with Gregor Strasser ranked almost with Hitler in the Nazi movement, urged that the German army be subordinated to his SA. The army high command vehemently objected, and Hitler needed their support to stay in power. Rohm was assassinated by Himmler's SS execution squads in the "night of the long knives" of June 29–30 1934. Strasser went into exile. Estimates of the numbers killed vary from Hitler's own figure of 77 to one historian's estimate of 922. Two years later Himmler replaced Hermann Göring as head of the Gestapo (*Geheimstaatspolizei*, "Secret Police"). Later he merged all the security services into the *Reichs-versicherheitshauptamt* the "Reich Security Main Office."

In 1938 Himmler provided the bogus evidence (a homosexual liaison by General Fromm), which enabled Hitler to discredit the leadership of the

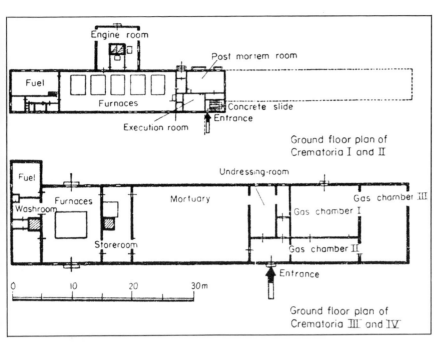

Engine room

Post mortem room

Fuel

Furnaces

Execution room   Entrance

Concrete slide

Ground floor plan of
Crematoria I and II

Undressing-room

Fuel

Washroom

Furnaces

Mortuary

Gas chamber III

Gas chamber I

Storeroom

Gas chamber II

0   10   20   30m

Entrance

Ground floor plan of
Crematoria III and IV

armed forces and himself assume command in chief. During World War II his jobs included responsibility for the conquered lands in eastern Europe.

Nazi theory, for Himmler a revealed "truth", supposed that humanity was subject to a Nordic Aryan "master race." There were also various sub-human *untermensch* species. Most sub-human of all were the Jews, the fiendish enemies of the blond haired Aryan. This psychotic, science fiction scenario, led to the "final solution of the Jewish question." From 1941 this meant systematic mass murder.

Possibly, some dim sense of human shame flickered even in Himmler since he warned that "this page of glory in our history is never to be written." But the bureaucratic machine he controlled with such able lieutenants as Reynhard Heydrich and Adolf Eichmann, built the extermination camps and traveling firing squads which, it · has been estimated, killed about 5,000,000 Jews. Jews were not the only victims. Slavs, Gypsies, and at least 2,000,000 Russian

Top: the ground floor plan of Crematoria 3 and 4 at Auschwitz extermination camp Poland. The victims were told that they were merely about to take a shower. It was intended that they should not guess their true fate until they were actually locked in the gas chamber. The crematoria themselves were surrounded by lawns and flower beds to create an innocent impression. About 2,000,000 people were murdered at Auschwitz.
Top right: an International Red Cross worker reveals the charred remains of one of Himmler's victims in an oven at Buchenwald concentration camp.
Above: three starving concentration camp survivors. Few lived to tell of the horror of the camps, so ably supervised by Himmler. Millions were either executed, or died from starvation and SS brutality. Disgusting medical experiments of no scientific value were regularly performed on unwilling inmates.

prisoners of war died in the killing factories. At least 12,000,000 civilians, innocent of any crime, were murdered by the Nazis. Millions more were conscripted as slave labor and deported from their home. "Whether nations live in prosperity or starve to death", said Himmler, "interests me only in so far as we need them as slaves for our *Kultur*." They gave their labor and, when dead, their persons. German industry cooperated with the SS in running the camps. Large chemical companies like I. G. Farben provided Zyklon B for the gas chambers, and engineering concerns built the crematoria. The clothing of the dead was salvaged, their jewellery and gold fillings deposited in bank vaults, and their bones used as fertilizer. The catalogue of Heinrich Himmler's efficiency spares us no horrors.

Himmler's talent for administration, essential for a successful public servant, was compounded by a literalistic and obsessive belief in the tenets of Nazism. Among the truths he held to be self evident was, that "the race of Slavs is built upon a sub-human race invigorated by a few drops of Aryan blood." He took an active interest in the work of the SS Institute for the Research and the Study of Heredity. He found time to investigate folklore, archaeology and runic inscriptions for evidence of Aryan superiority and expected confirmation in astrological prediction. Himmler should have been merely a dangerous crank. As it was he became absolute master of half the German administrative and military machine.

In mid-April 1945, urged by his staff to rescue something from the ruins of defeat, Himmler attempted negotiations through a neutral intermediary, Count Ffolk-Bernadot of Sweden, with the advancing Allied forces in the north of Germany. He was captured by British soldiers in May, but killed himself before he could be tried as a war criminal at Nuremberg.

Churchill

1874 - 1965

Winston Churchill was one of the most controversial figures in British politics for 40 years. He won his title to greatness as the leader of Britain and the figurehead of European resistance to Nazi Germany in World War II.

The son of Lord Randolph Churchill and Jenny Jerome, daughter of an American tycoon, Churchill was descended from the English general, the Duke of Marlborough. He joined the army and saw service in India, the Sudan and

Below: Winston Churchill depicted on probably the most famous British propaganda poster of World War II.

Below right: Churchill seated at the left of his mother Lady Randolph Churchill – the former Miss Jennie Jerome. Churchill's brother, John Strange Churchill sits on her right.

the Boer War. His account of that war, of his capture and escape, made him nationally known, and he was elected to parliament as a Conservative in 1900. But in 1906 he "crossed the floor" of the House of Commons and joined the Liberal government. He was home secretary from 1910 to 1911 and then first lord of the admiralty.

In 1915 he promoted the disastrous World War I expedition against Turkey at Galipolli in the Dardanelles. Temporarily discredited, he went on active service with the army in France. He took up office again in 1917 in the Liberal government led by David Lloyd George. First, he served as minister of munitions, then as minister for war and from 1921 as minister of the colonies. At the war office, in 1919, he keenly supported military intervention against the Bolshevik regime in Russia.

Churchill again joined the Conservative Party and was chancellor of the exchequer from 1924 to 1929. His most controversial decision was to revalue the pound, which critics believed helped worsen Britain's huge unemployment figures. During the 1926 General Strike, Churchill edited the official *British Gazette* propaganda sheet. In this he described the workers as "the enemy" to be forced into "unconditional surrender."

Churchill opposed the reduction of the voting age for women to 21 in 1928. He was also critical of the transformation of the British Empire into the Commonwealth, and opposed conciliating Indian nationalism. On this last issue he left the Conservative party's leadership and stayed in the political desert for nearly 10 years.

The rise of Hitler filled Churchill with foreboding. He was almost alone in denouncing the British government's appeasement of the German Führer's demands in Europe. Of Prime Minister Neville Chamberlain's Munich agreement with Hitler he said: "We have sustained a defeat without a war." After Chamberlain declared war on Germany on September 3 1939, Chamberlain appointed Churchill first lord of the admiralty.

Germany attacked Holland and Belgium in May 1940 and Chamberlain resigned. Churchill became prime minister. Three days later he told the Commons: "I have nothing to offer but blood, toil, tears and sweat." After World War II

he was to write: "I felt as if I were walking with destiny, and that all my past life had been but a preparation for this hour and this trial. . . . My warnings over the last six years had been so numerous, so detailed, and were now so terribly vindicated, that no one could gainsay me."

As war leader, Churchill had only one objective – total defeat and unconditional surrender for Nazi Germany. That Britain did not, like France, surrender and so give fascism undisputed ascendancy in Europe was largely due to Churchill's inspiring radio oratory, to his masterly handling of Parliament, and his dogged leadership of the war effort. He was ably backed by a coalition war cabinet, while Britain was loyally supported by Commonwealth governments.

When Hitler invaded Russia in June 1941 Churchill welcomed Joseph Stalin as a partner. In December of the same year Hitler declared war on the United States. Despite his close understanding with President Franklin D. Roosevelt, Churchill, who intervened frequently and often unfortunately in Britain's military policies, was unable to persuade the Americans to mount a major offensive against Germany from the south. He was later equally unsuccessful in talking them into making a rapid eastward push in Europe to forestall Communist takeover there.

The British recognized Churchill's heroic contribution as a war leader but did not trust him to carry out a socially just reconstruction of peacetime Britain. While he was at the Yalta Conference, with Stalin and Roosevelt, his party was crushingly defeated at the polls. He

Above: this photograph from the famous pictorial weekly *Picture Post* shows workers listening to one of Churchill's speeches on the radio in a public house in London's East End. Among the audience are demolition workers taking a break from clearing debris from bombed building after the *blitz* of 1941. The pub is the Black Dog in Shoe Lane London EC4. Churchill's radio speeches played their part in sustaining the morale of the British people.

Below: Churchill on the balcony of Buckingham Palace with the royal family during the celebrations of Victory in Europe – May 8 1945. Left to right are Princess Elizabeth, Queen Elizabeth, Churchill, King George VI, and Princess Margaret. Despite his reputation as a war leader, Churchill and the Conservative Party were routed by Labour in the 1945 general election.

was succeeded as prime minister by the Labour leader Clement Attlee. When Churchill returned as prime minister in the 1951 elections, the welfare state was entrenched in Britain. He spoke eloquently for a united Europe, but made no practical moves to join the budding European institutions. In 1953 he was honored with the Order of the Knight of the Garter by the new Queen, Elizabeth II and received the Nobel Prize for Literature. He retired as prime minister in 1955, though remaining in Parliament. He died in 1965. After a state funeral attended by representatives from all over the world he was buried at his own wish in the village churchyard of Bladon in Oxfordshire, near the Marlborough ancestral home.

Churchill's books, among them his life of *Marlborough, A History of the English Speaking Peoples*, and his six volume *The Second World War*, reveal the deep sense of history which inspired his love of his country and a towering mastery of English prose.

F. D. Roosevelt
1884 - 1945

The 32nd president of the United States was the first American politician to seriously tackle the misery of unemployment. His "New Deal" policies during the depression years of the 1930s brought relief to millions. In the 1940s Franklin Delano Roosevelt became a dominating figure among the Allies in World War II.

Son of a prosperous family, Roosevelt entered politics as a member of the New York senate in

1910. He was a reform Democrat and campaigned vigorously for Woodrow Wilson in the 1912 presidential election, and was assistant secretary to the navy from 1913 to 1920. As the Democrats' vice-presidential candidate, he shared in his party's crushing defeat by the Republicans in the 1920 election.

He was struck down by poliomyelitis in 1921. It paralysed him from the waist downwards. In 1927 he formed the Warm Springs Foundation at a health resort in Georgia to help other victims of the disease. By this time, Roosevelt was back in politics. He was elected governor of New York in 1928 and at once launched a vigorous social reform program. In 1932 he presided over the investigation into the corrupt "Tammany Hall" Democrat administration in New York city which forced the resignation of Mayor James Walker.

More important in the national perspective was the "Brain Trust" of advisers recruited by Roosevelt to help New York's recovery from the dire effects of the Slump which followed the Wall Street crash of 1929. He stood for president, and won handsomely in November 1932.

Above left: a portrait of Franklin Delano Roosevelt by Douglas Chander.

Above: the Tennessee Valley Authority's Norris Dam in east Tennessee. This irrigation scheme was one of the major achievements of Roosevelt's "New Deal" – a program of policies designed to relieve some of the worst consequences of the economic depression of the 1930s.

Far right: the Yalta Conference of February 1945 fixed the borders of post-war Europe. Roosevelt, a sick man, sits between Winston Churchill (left) and Joseph Stalin (right).

His inaugural speech earned him a charismatic reputation. He proclaimed his "firm belief that the only thing we have to fear is fear itself". Roosevelt now embarked on the "New Deal" measures. These extended government control over industry and agriculture, and aimed to revive the economy by massive injections of public funds.

New government agencies administered public employment schemes, regulated banks and stock exchanges, challenged private control of the companies in the area of electricity and, with the vast Tennessee Valley Authority, irrigation. The federal government was intervening to an unprecedented degree in private enterprise. Critics pointed to the often conflicting and wasteful schemes devised by the Brain Trust and other advisers which had accompanied Roosevelt into office. Conservatives frankly viewed "that man in the White House" as a "traitor to his class." The Supreme Court declared a number of the New Deal measures legally invalid, and the president's attempt to reorganize the court failed. But his "one-man" attack on the economic depression of the 1930s made him an internationally respected figure. In 1936, Roosevelt won his second presidential term with a crushing victory. It was clear that the beneficiaries of the New Deal appreciated his efforts, even if his big business critics did not.

Abroad, Roosevelt opened a "good neighbor" policy with Latin America, appealed for peace to Mussolini and Hitler, and maintained good relations with Japan. When war broke out in Europe in 1939 both Republicans and Democrats

opposed military involvement, but favored friendly neutrality to Britain. In domestic politics many, including leaders in his own party, were outraged by Roosevelt's unprecedented decision to go for a third term. But 1940 saw another decisive victory. In the campaign he pledged the electors "your boys will not be sent into any foreign wars."

Even so Roosevelt's administration actively helped the anti-German war effort. In March 1941 Congress passed the Lend-Lease Act. This was to provide aid "as the President deems satisfactory" to nations whose defense was vital to the security of the United States. Britain was the only recipient until November when aid was given to Russia.

In August Roosevelt met Winston Churchill on a warship off the Newfoundland coast where they signed the Atlantic Charter, a statement of common aims. It became a foundation document of the declaration of the United Nations signed by 26 combatant nations on January 1 1942. By this time the United States itself had been in the war almost one month following the Japanese attack on Pearl Harbor on December 7, 1941.

While leaving the conduct of operations to the military, Roosevelt was heavily involved in diplomatic exchanges and a series of conferences with the Allied leaders. In 1944, with Harry S. Truman as his vice-presidential running-mate, he won a fourth astonishing term as president. At the Yalta Conference in February 1945 Roosevelt, already a sick man, Churchill, and Stalin made vital decisions on post-war Europe.

Above: Pearl Harbor in flames after the Japanese attack on December 7, 1941. This attack catapulted the United States into World War II. The vociferous isolationists were silenced.

The four occupation zones of conquered Germany were agreed and territorial settlements in Asia made with Russia. Roosevelt died two months later.

Roosevelt achieved a revolution in American government and as the leader of the world's most powerful nation during World War II played a decisive role in shaping the post-war settlement.

Eisenhower
1890 - 1969

After the war in Europe, Eisenhower commanded the United States occupying forces in Germany, and was also chief of staff in the US army. In 1948 he resigned his military positions to become president of Colombia University, New York. This move to civilian life did not lead Eisenhower into politics immediately. He refused offers of the Republican presidential nomination and then, in December 1950, took leave of absence from Columbia to become the first Supreme Allied Commander of NATO. In 1952 he again retired from military life. This time he entered politics triumphantly, decisively beating the Democratic candidate Adlai Stevenson in the 1952 presidential elections.

Although Eisenhower cut taxation and hoped to limit the role of the federal government, world tensions during the "Cold War" period led him to demand vast military appropriations from Congress in the country's largest ever peace time federal budgets. Other important federal initiatives included a "partnership" policy in developing hydro-electric resources and the Canadian-American treaty for the construction of the St Lawrence Seaway, opened for navigation in 1959.

Left: General Eisenhower's major role as Supreme Commander of the Allied forces in the Invasion of Europe was taking responsibility for overall strategy, as well as attempting to reconcile the often conflicting interests of national military leaders under his command.

Known universally as "Ike", Dwight D. Eisenhower was a formidable general and became one of the most popular United States presidents. As first supreme commander of the North Atlantic Treaty Organization NATO he played a prominent role in shaping the present Euro-American defense structure.

A career soldier, Eisenhower served in World War I as commander of a training camp for tank warfare. Between the two world wars his postings included four years in the office of the assistant secretary for war. He was appointed chief of operations and then commander of United States forces in Europe in 1942. In November he commanded the American landing forces in the joint British-American campaign in north Africa, the first major western offensive of the war. The following year he directed the successful invasions of Sicily, and southern Italy came the next year. Eisenhower was appointed commander-in-chief of the Allied invasion of northern Europe which he led to victory with the help of the British Field Marshal Bernard Montgomery and the flamboyant American general George Patton.

Right: on the road to the Presidency of United States. Eisenhower celebrates winning the nomination at the 1952 Republican National Convention. With him is his vice-presidential running mate Richard M Nixon. Also present are Mrs Patricia Nixon (left) and Mrs Mamie Eisenhower (right).

Eisenhower won his second term in 1956 with an even more decisive victory over Stevenson. Liberals suspected Republican credentials in areas of social policy. But in 1957 Eisenhower made a notable landmark in United States social policy. He enforced a Supreme Court ruling banning segregated education for blacks and whites. Governor Orval Faubus of Arkansas had

Above: troops of the 101st Airborne Division escort Negro students into the Central High School, Little Rock. Eisenhower had ordered in federal troops to enforce a Supreme Court order banning racial segregation in education.

Above: Soviet leader Nikita Khruschev meets dancing girls on the set of the film Can Can in Holywood during a state visit to the United States in 1959. His meetings with Eisenhower were intended to help reduce tension between the two countries.

called in the Arkansas National Guard to prevent school integration in the town of Little Rock. Eisenhower ordered in federal troops.

Following the death of the Russian leader Joseph Stalin in 1953 Eisenhower looked to relaxation in the Cold War with "Iron Curtain" countries. But he had taken power in the middle of the witch-hunt against supposed communists in the administration, engineered by Senator Joe McCarthy. Moreover, Eisenhower's secretary of state, John Foster Dulles, was dedicated to the containment of what he considered the world threat of revolutionary communism. The United States buttressed the nationalist Chinese regime of Chiang K'ai-shek in Taiwan against Mao Tse-tung's China, increased its support for the corrupt regime in southern Vietnam, intervened with military and economic aid to authoritarian regimes in the Middle East, and opposed Nasser in Egypt. But in 1956, when Britain, France, and Israel attacked Egypt after Nasser's nationalization of the Suez Canal, the United States sided with general world opinion to force its allies to withdraw. The Anglo-French initiative coincided with an anti-communist revolution in Hungary which America may have been secretly fostering. It was crushed by armed force by Soviet Russia.

International tension eased in 1959 when Eisenhower received the Russian leader Nikita Khruschev on a state visit to the United States. The Russians angrily cancelled a planned return visit when, early in 1960, the American U2 spy plane was shot down over Soviety territory and its pilot Gary Powers was captured.

But for all the many tensions, Eisenhower's presidency can be seen, in retrospect, as a period of comparative peace abroad and prosperity at home. The Korean War had been brought to an end in June 1953, as many Americans believed, thanks in large measure to Eisenhower himself. Thereafter the United States was involved in no major international conflict. Eisenhower was president during a period of unprecedented growth in the United States economy. But the benefits were very unevenly spread.

Stalin
1879 - 1953

Party machine bureaucrat, monstrous tyrant, charismatic war leader, father of his people, bloody and ruthless megalomaniac – few figures of modern history have been so variously assessed as Joseph Vissarionovich Stalin has been assessed as all of these. He ruled Soviet Russia with an iron hand for 25 years, during which time he extinguished all opposition.

The son of a shoemaker called Djngashvili, Stalin studied for the priesthood at the theological seminary in Tiflis in his native Georgia. Expelled for insubordination he joined the Caucasus Social Democrat party and in 1903 followed Lenin's Bolsheviks in the split with the Mensheviks. He changed his name to "Stalin," "man of steel." Repeatedly arrested for revolutionary action, Stalin first met Lenin at a conference in Finland in 1905. Seven years later he moved to St Petersburg and became editor of *Pravda* then the party's journal of doctrinal debate. Exiled for life to Siberia in 1913 he was amnestied after the fall of the Czarist regime in 1917.

After the October Bolshevik Revolution of that year, Stalin became commissar of nationalities, a member of the Politburo (the party's policy-making body). In 1919 he was appointed commissar of the inspectorate established to supervise the workings of the new civil service.

Right: the fate of those sent into corrective labor by Stalin's secret police chief, Beria, is shown on this map. They labored in woods, mines and factories – some for many years. Many never lived to tell the tale.

Left: Joseph Stalin (left) on the battlements of the Kremlin. By the 1930s Stalin had liquidated nearly all the old Bolsheviks of the 1917 revolution, and established a brutal dictatorship. A "cult of personality" was erected which glorified Stalin's every word, and falsified his role in Russian Communist history.

He also acted as liaison officer between the Politburo and the organizational bureau, and in 1922 became general secretary of the central committee of the Communist Party. Now he had power in the country at large and increasingly controlled the apparatus of the party.

Just before his death Lenin in his "last testament" drew attention to Stalin's undemocratic tendencies and recommended that he be dismissed. But this testament was suppressed. Power passed to a triumvirate of Stalin, Zinoviev and Kamenev, all old Bolsheviks, who determined to exclude their brilliant rival Leon Trotsky. But by December 1927 Stalin had engineered the expulsion of all three from the party, now under his control. Mass recruitment of new members had diluted the influence of the Old Bolsheviks. It was now a party of administrators and bureaucrats, not of revolutionaries. Many people joined merely to obtain, or keep, the sought after and better paid soft jobs. Trotsky

observed it was "the supreme expression of the mediocrity of the apparatus that Stalin rose to his position."

But Stalin had also brought to the party a new idea. Leninist theory states that the only way to secure true socialism is for the revolution to spread throughout the capitalist world. But it did not, and this produced a great ideological debate. Trotsky urged Russian intervention in revolutions abroad to promote world revolution. But Stalin turned Leninist theory on its head by propounding "socialism in one country."

At the 1925 party congress, Stalin said "the main task of our Party is to fight for the victory of socialist construction in the USSR." Above all, this meant industrialization. The 1927 Con-

228

gress instructed the State Planning Commission to produce a Five Year economic plan. The pace was punishing. "It is sometimes asked whether it is not possible to slow down the tempo a bit" Stalin admitted in a famous speech. He went on, "No Comrades, it is not possible.... We are 50 or 100 years behind the advanced countries. We must make good this lag in 10 years. Either we do it or they crush us."

The 1927 Congress also determined to "pursue the offensive against the kulaks" (wealthier peasant farmers). They had made good profits during Lenin's New Economic Policy, but the industrial program demanded cheap food for the factory workers. Furthermore if Russia was "to be transformed from an agrarian country into an industrial country" which the capitalist world could not "crush", the kulaks had to be eliminated as a class and hundreds of thousands of inefficient small holdings "collectivized" into large, more efficient units.

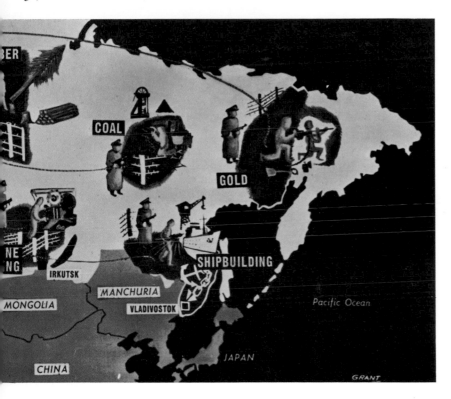

Enforcing this policy produced a fearful upheaval. State mobilized terror gangs stalked the countryside. The kulaks, rather than yield, destroyed machinery and slaughtered livestock. Millions of them were deported to forced labor camps, millions died. They were either murdered or starved by the unimaginable disruption of agriculture. Between 1928 and 1933 the national herd of horned cattle sank from 70 to 34 million.

But during these years, when the western world was suffering its worst ever economic depression, Soviet heavy industry was revolutionized – without foreign capital and without foreign technicians. Living standards undoubtedly declined, thousands of people died building factories in sub-zero temperatures. But

heavy industrial production rose dramatically. The totalitarian regime tightened its grip and the personality cult of Stalin was fostered. The murder of his associate Kirov in 1934 heralded a wave of judicial murders, organized by the dreaded secret police OGPU. All surviving members of Lenin's Politburo, senior service chiefs and thousands of lesser "traitors" and "saboteurs" were killed. The old Bolsheviks were wiped out.

Nazi Germany posed an external threat now. Stalin agreed a pact with Hitler in August 1939 but Germany invaded in June 1941. Russian patriotism was kindled by specially reinstating old church leaders and the cult of Stalin. When peace came, a quarter of all Soviet property had been destroyed and 20,000,000 Soviet citizens killed. In his dealings with the Allied leaders, Roosevelt and Churchill after the war, Stalin proved an astute diplomat. But at home cultural repression was complete and a new purge was being planned when Stalin died of a cerebral hemorrhage.

The horrors of the Stalinist era are notorious. The achievements are remarkable. The Revolution was fighting for its life in 1920. In 1945, having born the brunt of the German war machine Soviet Russia emerged as one of the two world superpowers. "There can be few parallels in history of latent strength being brought into play so effectively." But Stalin's brutal repression, his elimination of any dissent, and his building of a fearsome police state destroyed Russia's claim to be regarded as socialist.

Right: a portrait of Stalin is burned in Budapest during the Hungarian uprising of 1956. Despite his condemnation of Stalin's dictatorial methods, his successor Nikita Khruschev crushed the Hungarian revolt by Russian force of arms.

Charles De Gaulle
1890 - 1970

Charles de Gaulle was the figurehead of French resistance to the Nazis in World War II. After the war he restored France's fortunes and increased its influence in the world.

A career officer, de Gaulle was three times wounded at Verdun in 1916. His career between the wars was chiefly notable for a book on the strategy of mobile tank offensives. This was dismissed by the cavalry obsessed French high command but eagerly studied by the German army. Briefly a minister in the last French government before Petain's Vichy regime, de Gaulle fled to London in June 1940. He broadcast an appeal for support. But France, and

virtually the whole French empire, accepted Petain's collaborationist policies.

De Gaulle founded the Free French movement and continued his broadcasts. His name slowly became the symbol of French resistance.

With the allied conquest of North Africa in 1943, de Gaulle joined the French commander in Algiers, General Henri Giraud. He later displaced him as president of the French National Committee of Liberation.

Britain and the United States doubted de Gaulle's influence in France. The Americans

suspected him of dictatorial ambitions, while the British, especially Churchill, found him arrogant and obstructive. Neither intended him to have a hand in the military government of post-war France.

The Nazis were driven out and Paris was liberated in August 1944. But wherever de Gaulle went in liberated France the Free French quietly took over from the Vichy local officials. The chaos and blood letting which many feared

Right: this painting by Anthony Gross portrays seven members of *La Compagnie Tito* (Côte du Nord, Brittany) – anti-Nazi resistance. People like these risked their lives for France, while De Gaulle exhorted them via the BBC from England.

would follow the fall of Vichy did not materialize – apart from a few unpleasant incidents.

De Gaulle directed French affairs for the next 14 months. He thought Communism was the biggest threat. The election of October 1945, the first in which French women had the right to vote, returned the Communists, Socialists and pro-Gaullist Catholics as the largest parties. The Assembly's first job was to enact a new constitution. De Gaulle as head of government excluded Communists from key ministries, but was unable to impose his plans for a presidential rather than parliamentary constitution. He resigned in January 1946.

Party politics soon fragmented the Fourth Republic. De Gaulle held aloof. In 1953, believing that only further upheaval could cure "the disease of French political anarchy" he retired completely from public life to the village of Colombey-les-deux-Eglises, to write his memoirs and await the "inevitable" call to save the nation. It came in May 1958.

A massive French army had been fighting liberation forces in Algeria for years. French settlers feared a sell-out and by May 1958 a group of Algerian-French colonels seemed poised to oust the Paris government. On June 1 the Assembly accepted de Gaulle as prime minister. The colonels thought he would yield to their demands. In fact he introduced a presidential constitution in France and prepared the ground for Algerian independence. It came in 1963.

Presidential tours to every French *departement*, magisterial television appearances and

Right: the cartoonist Papas lampoons De Gaulle's arrogance. The caption says "Britain will make a high level approach to join the EEC."

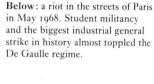

BRITAIN WILL MAKE A HIGH LEVEL APPROACH TO JOIN THE EEC

Below: a riot in the streets of Paris in May 1968. Student militancy and the biggest industrial general strike in history almost toppled the De Gaulle regime.

national referendums to endorse the president's policies were carried out with a style bordering on the monarchical. Cartoonists caricatured him as Louis XIV. De Gaulle once observed "authority requires prestige and prestige requires remoteness." He practised the principle among his own people, for whom he had an only thinly veiled contempt. Abroad, his truculent chauvinism won the respectful dislike of both friends and enemies. He withdrew French forces from the NATO alliance in 1966. By his personal veto he excluded Britain from membership of the European Economic Community in 1963, fearing it would threaten France's dominance in the Community.

France seemed the dominant power in Europe. By a policy of detente with the Eastern block and close ties with Russia, balanced by criticism of American policy during the Vietnam War years, de Gaulle aimed to build world influence and developed France's independent nuclear deterent. He established contacts with Red China and toured in South America and Canada. There, in 1967, he electrified the Anglo-Saxon world by calling for a "Free Quebec".

But in France, his social policies were kindling student discontent and industrial anger at pay and conditions. In May 1968 disturbances broke out which came close to revolution. The students were supported by the largest industrial general strike in history. While Prime Minister Pompidou acted promptly de Gaulle seemed uncertain. But television oratory brought a landslide Gaullist victory in government elections. The following year, de Gaulle lost a referendum to endorse his presidency. The aging autocrat retired to Colombey.

Tito
born 1892

Tito is the father of modern Yugoslavia. He maintained Yugoslav independence against Soviet Russia in the 1950s, and led his country to a dominant position in the Third World.

Born Josip Brodz of a Croat father and Slovene mother, Tito was a subject of the Austro-Hungarian empire. He became a metal worker, joined a trades union, and then the Social Democratic Party of Croatia. While with the Austro-Hungarian army on the Russian front in World War I, he was captured by the Russians. After the Russian Revolution of 1917 he fought with the Red Army in the ensuing civil war. He returned to Croatia in 1920. His homeland was now part of the newly proclaimed kingdom of the Serbs, Croat and Slovenes under King Peter I of Serbia. After increasing tension, World War I was finally sparked off when a Serbian nationalist

by the name of Prinsip, assassinated the Austrian Archduke Ferdinand in protest at Austria's annexation of Bosnia and Herzegovina at Sarajevo. Serbia was then overrun and its government fled to the Greek island of Corfu. There, with representatives from Croatia, Slovenia and Montenegro, it proclaimed the new kingdom, with its capital at Serbian Belgrade.

It was an unstable state. The Southern Slav peoples were divided by religion – Orthodox and Catholic Christians and Moslems – and by language and traditions. Croatia set up a separate parliament in Zagreb in 1928. The Serbian monarchist government suppressed it and changed the name of the state to Yugoslavia ("Southern Slavia"). In 1934, Croatian and Macedonian nationalists murdered the king and his son Peter II took the throne.

That year, Brodz was released from a five-

Right: Tito (right) with his Partisan staff in their hideout in Ngar Drvar during World War II. The hideout (below) was reached by steep paths cut out of the mountainside. Before reaching the cabin where Tito lived, visitors were subjected to a critical examination by Partisan guards.

Left: Marshal Tito is an independently minded communist leader who has refused to allow Yugoslavia to be dominated by Moscow. He has adopted a policy of non-alignment in foreign affairs.

year prison term. Now dominant in the Croat-Slovene Communist Party he had been a revolutionary agitator under various pseudonyms, among them "Tito." In Moscow in 1935 he joined the Balkan section of the Comintern, survived Stalin's purge of Yugoslav Party members in Russia, and became secretary general of the Executive Council of the Comintern. He returned to Yugoslavia and reorganized the Communist Party. It sent a volunteer force to fight on the Republican side of the Spanish Civil War in 1937.

In World War II, Yugoslav resistance was at first dominated by the right-wing Serbian monarchist Chetnik forces led by Draza Mihailovic. But Tito's Partisans, fighting in the mountains, soon proved more important. They withstood seven major German offensives, and were soon in conflict with Mihailovic who was also representative of the exiled King Peter. Despite Moscow's opposition Tito established revolutionary administrations in areas under his control. He then convened the Partisan Assembly which set up a provisional government of Yugoslavia. Maneuvering between the Soviet Union and the western Allies, he successfully

Right: an Allied propaganda poster condemns Nazi brutality in Yugoslavia. Tito and the Partisans were effective, and the Germans meted out punishment on innocent civilians.

Herzegovina, Macedonia, Slovenia, and Montenegro.

Tito had a national reputation and, despite his communism, support from the West. Resolutely independent he supported the communist rising in Greece, fought to incorporate Trieste into Yugoslavia, and attacked the Catholic Church. Western anger increased. In 1948, Stalin expelled Yugoslavia from the Comintern, hoping to force the isolated country into the Soviet bloc. Instead, the nation rallied behind its leader and elected him president in 1953. Renewed moves to understanding between Russia and Yugoslavia were shattered by the Soviet invasion of Hungary in 1956. In the 1960s, President Tito assumed a world role, visiting Asia, Africa, and Latin America. With presidents Nehru of India and Nasser of Egypt, he convened an important conference of "non-aligned" nations.

The Soviet invasion of Czechoslovakia in 1968 outraged the Yugoslavs. Tito denounced it as "violating the sovereignty of a socialist country and a blow to socialist and progressive forces throughout the world." He also tightened Yugoslav military readiness. His country's form of "decentralized socialism", combined workers' participation in decision making with some capitalist features. It was a break with Soviet orthodoxy, and Tito's independent foreign policy was an affront to Moscow's authority in European communism.

But Yugoslavia's nationalities remained in uneasy federation. In 1970, when the aging Tito was still among Europe's most elegant and talented statesmen, plans were drawn up for a collective leadership to follow him. But he continued as leader, perhaps the only man who could command allegiance from the country's diverse populations.

evaded their pressures to share government with the royalists.

He was elected Yugoslav premier in 1945, and in November his party won elections to the constituent assembly which proclaimed Yugoslavia a federal republic consisting of the Soviet Socialist republics of Serbia, Croatia, Bosnia and

Wilhelmina
of the Netherlands

1880 - 1962

Queen of Holland for nearly 60 years, Wilhelmina was dearly loved. In Holland's darkest hours of Nazi occupation she was trusted by her people. She embodied the spirit of the nation's resistance to tyranny.

Wilhelmina's father, King William III, died in 1890, when she was only 10 years old. Emma, her mother, acted as regent. The young queen was inaugurated in the Nieuwe Kerk, Amsterdam in 1898. She married the German duke, Henry of Mecklenburg Schwerin three years later. Their daughter Juliana was born in 1909.

Wilhelmina soon revealed a dominating personality, a serious attention to business, and strong views on policy matters. These qualities were combined with an almost mystical devotion to the tradition of her noble and royal ancestors. But the queen scrupulously observed the constitutional restrictions of her authority.

Below left: a wartime poster shows Wilhelmina sternly discouraging Dutch workers from reporting to the Germans for enforced labor.

Below: Princess Juliana and Prince Bernhard take their children Beatrix and Irene for a walk in London in 1940.

partly due to Wilhelmina. She was also party to the decision to allow the Kaiser William II political asylum and the Dutch government's refusal to extradite him for trial as a war criminal. The queen also opposed her ministry's proposal to open diplomatic relations with the USSR but she could do nothing to prevent economies in Dutch defense expenditure, nor divert the administration of Hendrik Colijn from its "adaptation" policy during the depression years of the 1930s.

Devaluation of the currency was delayed, and economies enforced which reduced the standard of living and worsened unemployment. Appalled by the external weakness and internal hardship of her country the queen more than once considered abdication. She decided to do this during the Jubilee year 1938, the 40th anniversary of her accession. Princess Juliana and her husband

ZIJT GIJ 'S VIJANDS SLAAF? MELDT U DAN!
ZOO NIET, DAN NIET!

Resistance leaflet: a stern Queen Wilhelmina exhorts Dutch workers not to report for enforced labour

During World War I the Netherlands kept neutrality while Germany overran neighboring Belgium. In the chaos which followed the war in Europe, revolution swept Germany and looked likely to spread to Holland. That it did not was

Prince Bernhard had great difficulty in dissuading her. The year was a happy one for the royal family. Juliana and Bernhard had a baby daughter, Princess Beatrix, in January. The first week of September was given over to national celebrations; the prime minister observed somewhat complacently that throughout Europe

parliamentary democracy seemed secure only in those states which had retained their constitutional monarchs.

Wilhelmina was irritated by her ministers' apparent indifference to the threat posed by Hitler's Germany. Bypassing her ministers, she ordered Dutch military attachés abroad to report direct to herself on German armaments. She obtained up-to-date briefings on the state of Dutch defenses in conferences with senior military officers. This private information did little to boost her faith either in her ministers, or the military leader van Reynders.

The Netherlands hoped to protect its neutrality just as in World War I. Some border territories were flooded but defensive measures were low-key to avoid provoking the Germans into a pre-emptive attack. When the invasion came on May 10 1940, vital bridges were still standing. On the advice of her ministers Wilhelmina fled to London three days later. The Dutch army was still in the field, but on May 15 the German air force systematically bombed the undefended city of Rotterdam. The historic center of the town was flattened and thirty thousand people were killed. The Dutch had no choice but to surrender or watch their country destroyed. Nevertheless, the Dutch home fleet and air force joined the British and the East Indian navy continued at war in the Pacific. Both were under the direction of the Netherlands government in exile in London. Money to maintain these forces was raised in part from Dutch assets in the United States. Wilhelmina's broadcasts from London, the one hopeful Dutch voice confidently predicting victory, rallied public morale and made the queen herself dearly loved.

In June 1942 she visited her daughter Juliana in Ottawa in Canada. Then she flew on to

Above: Queen Wilhelmina inspecting Dutch troops in 1939.

Below: the coronation of Queen Juliana after Wilhelmina's abdication in 1948.

Washington DC and addressed Congress in August on the occasion of the signing of the American agreements on Lend-Lease with the Netherlands. In exile, free of answerability to parliament, Wilhelmina enjoyed greater influence in ministerial discussions. She returned to the Netherlands on March 13 1945, after its liberation, to a loyal and enthusiastic welcome. But the queen was soon disappointed. She had expected increased power for the crown in the post-war settlement. In 1948 she abdicated in favor of her daughter, giving health reasons. Her immense popularity was clear at the celebrations for the 50th anniversary of her accession.

Carl Gustav Mannerheim
1867 - 1951

Carl Gustav Mannerheim led Finland into the ranks of free nations. He was already past 50 when he first appeared on the public scene. Born of Swedish parentage like many Finns, Mannerheim seemed poorly qualified to inspire his countrymen. He spoke little or no Finnish until late middle age, and then only badly. But it was largely through Mannerheim's leadership that Finland took its place among the world's independent nations. Today it is the only close neighbor of the Soviet Union with western

against the Soviet Union. They were supported by a German force of a mere 12,000 men. The next year, he retired into private life when his country established a republic rather than the monarchy he had wanted.

Finland was faced by threatened Soviet aggression in 1931. Mannerheim was recalled to be chairman of national defense. In the next eight difficult years, he managed to build the Mannerheim Line, a 90-mile defense spanning the Karelian Isthmus between Finland and

democratic institutions.

Finland was almost the last European country to achieve nationhood. For centuries this land of lakes and forests was a mere province, first of Sweden and then, after 1808, of Russia. During the Bolshevik Revolution of 1917 the Finns seized their opportunity to declare independence. It was Mannerheim who carried the attempt through to success.

As a young man of 22, Mannerheim joined the Russian army, Finland then being part of Russia. He became a corps commander in World War I. In 1917 he returned to Finland, which had declared its independence on December 6, and was occupied by a Soviet force of 40,000. Mannerheim led virtually untrained Finnish fighters to victory in a bloody four-month war

Above: the famous Mannerheim line. Diagram shows a series of lines of electrified barbed wire, concrete tank obstacles and massive granite boulders. Minefields and tank traps were also prepared for extra defense. A series of forts were built, mostly underground, and connected by trenches. The white arrows show the range of the forts' guns.

Above left: Carl Gustav Mannerheim was over 70 when he was called upon to lead the defense of Finland from the Russians.

Right: Soviet troops breach the Mannerheim line.

Russia. It consisted only of field fortifications, trenches, and 66 concrete machine-gun posts, a flimsy structure against the might of the Red Army. During the 1930s, while the rest of Europe was trying to restrain Hitler's expansionism by diplomatic means, Finland faced massive territorial demands from Stalin. Mannerheim, aware of his country's weakness, argued for a compromise. Stalin warned a Finnish delegation in 1939: "I well understand that you wish to remain neutral, but I can assure you it is not possible. The greater powers will simply not allow it." He underlined this warning when he and Hitler made their famous Nazi-Soviet non-aggression pact in August 1939. In December Soviet forces attacked, threatening the whole 800-mile Finnish frontier.

Again Finland called upon its national hero, and at the age of 72 Mannerheim became commander-in-chief. This was his finest hour. In the bitter struggle of the "Winter War," nine poorly equipped Finnish divisions faced 27 larger

Soviet divisions equipped with heavy artillery and tanks. The Mannerheim Line held. White-clad ski troopers harassed Soviet columns in the north. Finnish defenders destroyed almost 1000 Soviet planes during bombing raids on Finnish cities. It was a heroic defense. Mannerheim was amazed. "I did not believe that my own men could be so good, or that the Russians could be so bad."

But superior numbers told, and the Mannerheim Line began to crumble. The Finns had hoped that Britain and France – by February 1940 both at war with Stalin's ally Germany – would lend support. But on March 6 Sweden and Norway, desperate to maintain neutrality, refused to allow Allied troops to cross their countries to reach Finland. The Mannerheim

Below left: the Finnish capital Helsinki recovers from a Russian air raid on December 12 1939. Superior firepower eventually brought Russia an expensive victory.

Above: a Finnish wire cutter clears a path for his comrades through the barbed wire in the depths of the "winter war". The war against tiny Finland cost Soviet Russia 1,000,000 men.

Line broke. On March 13 Finland accepted terms that gave the Soviet Union all the territory Stalin had demanded. Though beaten, the Finns had reason for pride. Khruschev later admitted that 1,000,000 Soviet troops had died in the fighting. Churchill spoke with his usual eloquence: "Finland alone – in danger of death, superb, sublime Finland – shows what free men can do. The service Finland has rendered to humanity is magnificent."

The effects of Finland's valiant resistance were far-reaching. The country was saved from Soviet occupation. Fear of Russian power spreading into Scandinavia encouraged Hitler's attack on Denmark and Norway in April 1940. Most important of all, the Winter War led Hitler to underestimate the Soviet Union's military strength. He attacked his former ally in June 1941. This was to prove his most disastrous mistake.

In 1941 Finland, then allied with Germany, attacked the Soviet Union in the hope of getting back its lost territories. Mannerheim, still commander-in-chief, gained some early victories. But the tide of the war in the east had turned, and Soviet armies advanced steadily as the Germans retreated. Mannerheim, who had become president of Finland in 1944, was compelled to sign an armistice with Stalin in September of that year. The peace treaty gave still more Finnish territory to the Soviet Union and imposed a severe war debt on the young nation. Mannerheim led his country for two more years until ill health forced him to retire.

Chaim Weizmann
1874 - 1952

Born in Russia, Dr Chaim Weizmann was a British citizen for much of his life. He was a distinguished scientist and a dominant figure in the world Zionist movement for 50 years. Dedicated from youth to the conviction that the Jews were a people entitled to their own state in Palestine, he, with David Ben Gurion, established the modern state of Israel, becoming its first president in 1948.

Zionism, rooted deep in the Jewish consciousness, found revived vigor in 19th-century Russia. In 1896, the Viennese Jew, Theodor Herzl, published *The Jewish State*. About 200 Jews of all nationalities and social classes answered Herzl's call for a conference at Basel, Switzerland, in 1897. It formulated a program "to create for the Jewish people a home in Palestine secured by public law." When the Turkish empire, which then ruled Palestine, refused to allow full-scale colonization, Herzl accepted a British offer of territory in Uganda. "Let the sovereignty be granted us over a portion of the globe large enough to satisfy the rightful requirements of a nation; the rest we shall manage for ourselves." But at the 1903 Zionist conference many delegates, notably the Russians, opposed any idea of homeland outside Palestine.

Above: anti-semitism was endemic in central and eastern Europe for centuries. This print shows a Jew being assaulted in the presence of the military in Kiev in 1881.

Two years before, Weizmann had secured the foundation of a Jewish National Fund to buy land in Palestine. It continued a work of settlement, heavily financed by Baron Edmond de Rothschild. By 1914, the enterprise had the seeds of a "national" undertaking.

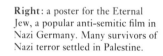

Right: a poster for the Eternal Jew, a popular anti-semitic film in Nazi Germany. Many survivors of Nazi terror settled in Palestine.

Opposite above: A J Balfour speaking in Dartford, Kent, in 1910.

Opposite right: Moshave Beit Yosef, a "stockade and tower" settlement in the Jordan valley.

Opposite: early settlers in Palestine pictured in 1884.

Left: a bronze bust of Chaim Weizmann by Benno Elkan.

During World War I Weizmann, a lecturer in chemistry at Manchester University, became a director of the British Admiralty laboratories. They were working on a synthetic process for the manufacture of explosives. He was also president of the British Zionist Federation and the friend of Lloyd George, Arthur Balfour, Winston Churchill, and the Rothschild family. His international contacts included the American Justice

Louis Brandeis, friend of President Woodrow Wilson. In 1917 Weizmann's lobbying produced a letter from British foreign secretary Balfour to Lord Rothschild, the leading figure of British Jewry. "His Majesty's Government," it read, "view with favor the establishment in Palestine of a national home for the Jewish people and will use their best endeavors to facilitate the achievement of this object, it being clearly understood that nothing shall be done which may prejudice the civil and religious rights of the existing non-Jewish communities in Palestine, or the rights

and political status enjoyed by Jews in any other country."

The contradictions of the famous "Balfour Declaration" were compounded by an assurance given two years earlier to the Arab leader, Sherif Hussein, that Britain was "prepared to recognize and support the independence of the Arabs in all regions" of the Turkish empire excluding north west coastal Syria – a limitation aimed at satisfy-

ing Britain's imperial ally France. In this web of budding national aspirations and international power politics, Weizmann labored to build an understanding with the Arabs through Hussein's son the Amyr Faysal. Not surprisingly, he did not meet with complete success.

Weizmann assumed leadership of the world Zionist Organization in the 1920s. Palestine was administered by the British under a League of Nations mandate. The Jewish population, quadrupled through immigration between 1924 and 1940, was administered through the Jewish Agency headed by David Ben Gurion. Arab resentment at Jewish immigration was reflected in increasing violence against the settlements. They mounted their own defense organization, the Haganah, in response. As war clouds gathered over Europe, Britain sought to placate Arab hostility and so free its troops policing the mandate. The 1939 White Paper drastically curbed Jewish immigration and land purchase. It was rejected by the League, by the Arabs who held out for full independence, and as "a classic step-by-step sell-out of a small nation," by Weizmann. He nevertheless served as a British scientific adviser during World War II.

When it ended he became active in the diplomatic preparations for the foundation of the new state of Israel. It was proclaimed on May 14 1948. His name is commemorated in Israel's Weizmann Institute of Science.

239

David Ben-Gurion
1886 - 1973

David Ben Gurion was the first prime minister of the new state of Israel. Along with Chaim Weizmann the leader who made it possible. Ben Gurion was the charismatic figure of modern Zionism.

Christened David Gruen, he was born in Poland at a time when Zionist dreams of a Jewish state in the homeland of the Biblical Hebrews were stirring in Eastern Europe. David's father was a local leader of the "Lovers of Zion." Wealthy European Jews were buying land in Palestine, then part of the Turkish Ottoman empire. David went to work in the Jewish agricultural settlements there when he was 20. He adopted the Hebrew name of Ben Gurion and formed the Zionist socialist party dedicated to "the political independence of the Jewish people in this land."

Expelled by the Turkish authorities at the beginning of World War I Ben Gurion lived in New York for a while. He returned to Palestine after it had been liberated by the British army helped by Arab forces under T E Lawrence (Lawrence of Arabia).

After the war Palestine was administered under a mandate for the League of Nations. The Zionist Organization, claiming to speak for "the Jews of the world" urged that "Great Britain should act as the Mandatory power." The Mandate required Britain "To place the country under such political, administrative and economic conditions as will secure the establishment of the Jewish National Home." Britain was already committed to such a policy by the 1917

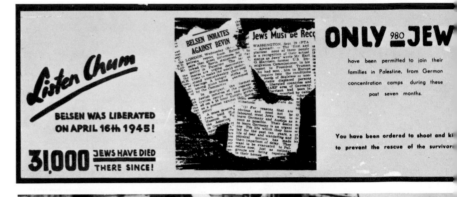

Top: a protest leaflet issued by the Hagana. This is one of many produced to be passed clandestinely to British soldiers sent to police Palestine in 1945.

Above: a Jewish immigration ship. Thousands of Jews tried to enter Palestine after World War II.

Opposite: David Ben Gurion in retirement. After his resignation from the government in 1953, Ben Gurion went to live in the isolated Kibbutz of Sde Boker in the Negev desert.

"Balfour Declaration." But it had also promised to support Arab independence. The promises were irreconcilable. In 1939, to the fury of Ben Gurion, a British government White Paper abandoned the Balfour Declaration.

Now chairman of the world Zionist Executive, he was also the dominant figure in Jewish Palestine. He had founded the Histadrut, confederation of Jewish workers. This was the principal Jewish organization which, with the Haganah armed forces, defended the settlers against terrorism by the Arab inhabitants. Ben Gurion also became leader of the Mapai Israel workers' party, and was head of the Jewish agency which helped the British administer Jewish affairs in Palestine.

Winston Churchill was sympathetic to Zionist

aims but could do little as Britain's war effort in the Middle East relied heavily on Arab goodwill. Ben Gurion determined to recruit the American Zionist Organization. At a meeting in New York in May 1942 it passed the Biltmore Resolution "That the gates of Palestine be opened to immigration and that Palestine be established as a Jewish Commonwealth." After World War II, shiploads of Jewish refugees from the horrors of Hitler's Europe were turned back by the British

Below: a Jewish settlement in the Negev with a boundary in the shape of the Star of David. The full scale Israeli offensive to break the Egyptian cordon and relieve the 27 Negev settlements began on October 15 1948, after the Egyptians had violated the truce by attacking an Israeli food convoy.

Right: Israelis celebrate on Independence Day.

The new state faced hostile neighbors and floods of immigrants. Ben Gurion extended the system of settlements in the desert areas, encouraged the *kibbutz* collective farms, inaugurated a unified system of public education to foster national unity, and met Arab incursions with violent reprisals. In 1956, in collusion with the Anglo-French action against Egypt at the time of the Suez crises, Israel occupied Gaza. Ben Gurion, who had only been briefly out of

office since 1948, resigned the premiership in 1963. His attempt to recover power at the head of his own splinter party failed. He retired to a *kibbutz* in the Negev desert in 1970.

His life's work was summed up in the title of his book *The Rebirth of Israel*. If Chaim Weizmann had inspired the philosophy of Zionism, it was David Ben Gurion who made its realization possible.

Royal Navy attempting to enforce its government's restriction on immigration. Terrorist action in Palestine by the Jewish Irgun organization and the Stern Gang put further pressure on the British army and authorities in Palestine.

Despite Arab objections, the United Nations announced the partition of Palestine into an Arab and a Jewish State in 1947. Violence intensified. On May 14 1948 Ben Gurion formally read his country's declaration of independence. Arabs and Jews clashed in set battles and calculated terrorism.

Arab irregular troops and the Arab Legion faced the combined forces of the Irgun, the Stern Gang and the Haganah. They were outnumbered and defeated in a series of campaigns. By the time armistice terms were signed early in 1949 Israel had expanded her territory by roughly one third over the UN Partition Plan. It appropriated more land to itself in following years.

Eduard Benes
1884 - 1948

A founder of modern Czechoslovakia, Eduard Benes was Czech foreign minister and then president throughout the inter-war years. The Munich settlement between, France, Britain and Hitler's Germany in 1938 opened the way to German occupation of Czechoslovakia. Benes saw no alternative but to give in to Hitler's demands. He ratified the settlement then resigned the presidency. France and Britain's betrayal of the Czechs at Munich did not satisfy Hitler's territorial appetite. Europe moved inexorably towards World War II.

At the beginning of the 20th century, the Czech people yearned for independence from the Austro-Hungarian empire ruled by the autocratic Hapsburgs. Thomas Masaryk, a university professor, led the independence party in the Austrian diet from 1907. During World

War I he and Benes, also an academic, founded the Czech National Council in Paris. It proclaimed Czech independence in October 1918. In November Masaryk was acclaimed president in Prague. Benes, as foreign minister, represented Czech interests at the Versailles Peace Conference.

The new state was an uneasy federation of nationalities. The industrialized Czech lands of Bohemia and Moravia were united with agricultural Slovakia which had its own language and independence movement. There were religious differences. National minorities, notably Poles, Hungarians, and three million Germans living in the western Sudeten region further threatened national cohesion. Slovaks were angered by the fact that Czech officials of the former Austro-Hungarian provincial administration dominated

Above: map shows how Czechoslovakia was formed. The shaded part shows the boundaries of the old Austro-Hungarian (Hapsburg) Empire. Apart from Czechoslovakia, parts of the empire were given to Poland, Roumania, Italy and Yugoslavia. The map was taken from the magazine *Weekly Illustrated* of June 4 1938, as was the picture of Eduard Benes (left).

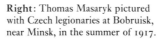

Right: Thomas Masaryk pictured with Czech legionaries at Bobruisk, near Minsk, in the summer of 1917.

the government. The Sudeten Germans, privileged classes until 1918, were even more discontented. Nevertheless, when Benes succeeded Masaryk as president in 1935, with a Slovak as prime minister, the country appeared able to cope with its many problems.

Benes secured his country against any attempt by Germany to alter the terms of the Versailles treaty with a series of alliances in the early 1920s. He reached agreements with Romania, Yugoslavia, and France.

From 1937, Hitler was anxious to neutralize Czechoslovakia. Thrusting between Germany and Austria, its frontiers were ringed with the Sudeten and other mountain ranges. These were honeycombed with a formidable defense system

of gun emplacements and concrete bunkers. The Czech army of 34 divisions was well trained and formidably equipped by the great Skoda armaments factory. The German Führer's generals were under no illusions about the strength of Czech defenses. But thanks to Hitler's opportunistic diplomacy, the unwillingness of France to stand by Czechoslovakia, Britain's eagerness to appease Germany's demands, and Benes's determination not to plunge his country into war, the massive works fell without a fight.

The seeds of the 1938 crisis were sown in 1919. Versailles has invoked the principle of national self-determination to dismember the Austro-Hungarian empire. But within the new Czech frontiers, Slovaks continued to agitate for full independence and the Germans, closely bound to Austria by blood and tradition, could plausibly plead injustice. Benes, disturbed by French reluctance to guarantee him against Germany, hoped to negotiate the extremist Sudeten German party of Konrad Henlein into demands for the dissolution of the country. This he believed would force the French and British to declare war against Germany. Henlein continued to demand only "equal" treatment but, in conference with Hitler, observed, "we must always demand so much that we can never be satisfied."

The British prime minister, Neville Chamberlain, feared the crisis would lead to war. He saw the abstract justice of the Sudetens' claim and foolishly supposed that if it were granted Hitler would be satisfied. But, despite concessions from Benes, Hitler and Henlein continued to step of their demands. On September 29 1938 at Munich, Chamberlain and the French prime minister Daladier agreed a settlement of the Czechoslovakian crisis with Hitler. This opened the Sudeten territories and, incidentally, their mountain fortifications, to Germany. Because he had no other choice, Benes agreed, and then resigned the presidency. By April 1939 Hungary and Poland had absorbed Czechoslovak border territories and the Slovaks had won their independence as a client state of the Third Reich.

Above: British prime minister Chamberlain and French Premier Daladier prepare to betray Czechoslovakia at the Munich Conference of 1938. Benes was not allowed to attend the conference, but had to wait in another room to be informed of what was to become of his country. The British and French anxiety to appease Hitler merely succeeded in delaying war until Nazi Germany was militarily stronger. Left to right are Ribbentrop, Chamberlain, Hitler, Daladier, and the British ambassador to Berlin Neville Henderson.

Right: the Czech capital of Prague, a beautiful city with a terrible history.

Benes spent World War II as president of the Czech government in exile in London. His foreign minister was Jan Masaryk (born 1886), son of Thomas.

Surveying Prague once again from the president's palace in 1945 Benes commented: "Is it not beautiful? The only central European city not destroyed. And all my doing." He and Masaryk remained in office after the Communist coup of February 1948. A few days following Masaryk was reported to have killed himself. In June, Benes resigned the presidency, having refused to sign the new constitution. He died shortly after.

Sun Yat-sen
1866 - 1925

school there and then studied medicine at Canton. Back in Hawaii in 1894 he organized the secret Revive China Society. There followed the Sino-Japanese War. Japan had been modernized on western lines for 30 years. The demise of the antiquated Ch'ing regime seemed imminent. Sun returned to encourage a rising in Canton. It failed and he fled to Europe with a price on his head. He was forcibly held in the Chinese Legation in London pending deportation. But the resulting press outcry compelled his release, and at the same time made him an international name.

In 1897 Sun sailed for Tokyo. During his stay in Europe he read widely in western political and economic theory – notably the works of Karl Marx and the American Henry George.

Tokyo was the home of many Chinese revolutionaries. While there, Sun kept contact with mainland secret societies and, in 1905, formed a new party, the Revolutionary Alliance. It proclaimed The Three Principles: Nationality – the expulsion of the Manchus and western interests; People's Authority – Republican government; and People's Livelihood, an equitable system of land ownership, later to be equated with socialism. The young Chiang K'ai-shek was an early recruit. Within a year the Revolutionary Alliance boasted 10,000 members in South East Asia. Expelled from Japan in 1907, Sun toured Chinese communities in Asia, Europe and the United States.

The Chinese people were regarding revolution increasingly favorably, and the imperial regime,

Sun Yat-sen was a Christian and China's first republican president. Elected after the overthrow of the Manchu Ch'ing dynasty in 1911, he was deeply imbued with Western culture, and was an ineffectual revolutionary. But he has been venerated as the pioneer and father of Revolutionary China by Communists and Nationalists alike.

Sun's ascendancy rested on his eloquence, great personal magnetism, and his unquestioned integrity. His Kuomintang Nationalist party was China's first modern political movement. He mobilized support for the revolution in the large Chinese communities overseas and was a figure of international standing. Sun's life's work ensured that the new China should be a republic at a time when many reformers favored a reconstituted empire on the Japanese model. When he was born, on a poor farm near Canton, Imperial China, for 3000 years the Orient's greatest power, was nearing collapse. European powers had forced the dynasty to yield crippling trade concessions and grant "extraterritorial" jurisdictions whereby European nationals in China were governed by their own laws. Thousands of Chinese artisans and merchants had gone abroad to work.

At 13, Sun went to live in Hawaii with his brother. He was educated at an English mission

incompetent as well as corrupt, alienated the army under Yuan Shih-kai. A rising in Wuhan broke out in October 1911, and spread rapidly. Instead of suppressing the rebels, Yuan negotiated with the republicans. Sun Yat-sen returned to China in triumph. On 1 January 1912 he was proclaimed president of the provisional republic at Nanking. Six weeks later he trustingly resigned his office to Yuan, and prepared his new Kuomintang party for National Assembly elections. In 1913 Yuan, maneuvering to become emperor, suppressed the party. Sun retired to

itself. Sun fled again, this time to Shanghai. Here Adolf Joffe, a Russian Communist agent, found him. To many Chinese, the Russians appeared models of revolutionary technique. Moreover, the Bolshevik government in Moscow had renounced Czarist claims on Chinese border territories. For their part, the Bolsheviks saw China as the natural second front in the world revolution. Sun, who had telegraphed congratulations to Lenin in 1917 and was China's most famous republican, was regarded as the best leader to rally the cause. Sun needed allies. He

Japan once more. Yuan died in 1916. Members of the 1912 Assembly could be bought, and bought cheaply, by special interest groups. This corrupt behavior discredited the experiment with western democracy in the eyes of the Chinese people. In Sun's words "China had not only failed to learn from western democracy but had been corrupted by it." For 10 years Sun struggled to establish a government at Canton as a rival to Peking.

Meanwhile, China was becoming a mere geographical expression. The western powers still enforced their concessions. The 1919 Versailles treaty handed over the German concessions to Japan – the Japanese infiltrated Manchuria. In the rest of China, generals carved out independent "warlord" fiefs in collaboration with absentee landlords.

In 1921 the warlord of Kwantung province helped Sun secure his base at Canton but refused to campaign against the northern warlord regimes. Indeed he began to plunder Kwantung

had no army and the Kuomintang, although widespread, was poorly organized. Chiang K'ai-shek, now his military aide, was sent to Moscow for technical training.

The Whampoa Military Academy was established near Canton. Russian advisers organized the Kuomintang into a well disciplined system of cells, and strengthened its propaganda machine. Members of the recently founded Chinese Communist Party could become individual members but Sun Yat-sen was made life chairman. In 1923 Sun was again installed at Canton, to be joined by Chou En-lai and other communists. He was invited for joint discussions by the warlord regime in Peking in 1925. Despite criticism by his colleagues he went. Sun died in Peking before the discussions began.

When he died his own position was still uncertain and China was in anarchy. But by his charisma and dedication Sun Yat-sen had fired a generation of revolutionaries. Sun inspired the leaders of modern China.

Chiang Kai-shek
1887 - 1975

Generalissimo Chiang K'ai-shek became familiar in the west as leader of free China against the Japanese in World War II. Brother-in-law of China's great revolutionary leader Sun Yat-sen, Chiang had succeeded as head of Sun's Kuomintang ("Nationalist") party after his death in 1925. Chiang fought the Communists for leadership of China for 20 years. From 1950, while countries like the Netherlands and Britain recognized Communist Peking, Chiang's exile regime in Taiwan (formerly Formosa) held China's seat at the United Nations.

In 1923, Sun Yat-sen sent Chiang on a mission to Moscow. He was later appointed commandant of the Whampoa Military Academy, founded at Canton with Russian help. Chou En-lai was a political commisar there. But Chiang sided with traditional landlord and business interests and detested cooperating with Communism.

In 1926 Chiang led the Kuomintang army out of Canton on Sun's long-planned campaign against the warlords of North China. He captured Hunan province, already weakened by Mao Tse-tung's communists. Nanking and Shanghai were also taken – again with communist help. But in April 1927, Chiang ordered mass murders of Shanghai's communists before proclaiming a new Kuomintang government at Nanking. Finally, his troops took Peking and its province from

Above: a public execution in a Nanking street on May 27 1927. The right wing Chinese Nationalists led by Chiang Kai-shek finally broke with the Communists in 1927 and proceeded to kill as many of them as they could lay their hands on.

Opposite above: Chiang Kai-shek reviews the Nanking garrison on January 1949. This was one of his last acts as Chinese leader. He relinquished his 22-year rule to the Communists under Mao Tse-tung on January 21 1949. Chiang established a Kuomintang government on the island of Formosa (Taiwan).

Opposite: a parade in support of Chiang on Taiwan.

the warlord of Manchuria, a collaborator with the Japanese. Yet when Japan annexed Manchuria in 1931 Chiang did nothing.

For him Japan was China's "disease of the skin," the communists its "disease of the heart." Chiang turned south against Mao's Communist Republic in Kiangsi province. Following the advice of his Nazi German military experts, Chiang encircled the republic with a tight blockade in 1934. But Mao's forces broke out, and in summer 1935 reached Yenan in the northern province of Shensi. There they called for a national front against the Japanese. Chiang ordered his army at Sian in Shensi to overrun Yenan.

But the Sian army were Manchus and they refused the order. When Chiang flew to Sian he was held under duress. Chiang refused all compromise, though his life was clearly in danger. Chiang's death would have weakened China even more and Mao sent Chou En-lai to Sian with assurances of full Communist loyalty if he would command the joint forces against the Japanese. Chiang reluctantly agreed. Six months later Japan unleashed a war of unparalleled savagery. By late 1937 they held most of eastern China. The Kuomintang capital was moved to Chungking on the rugged upper reaches of the Yangtse. Chiang, elected leader of the Kuomintang in 1938, began a stubborn defense.

In World War II the western allies recognized Chiang K'ai-shek as President of the Chinese Republic and China's commander in chief. Chiang considered that America's entry into the war in 1941 sealed the ultimate defeat of Japan, and was content to consolidate his position at Chungking. He was determined to exclude communists from government after the war and even confiscated ammunition due for them from the

western allies. But the communists won control of the countryside round the great northern and eastern cities. With Japan's surrender after the atom bomb attacks on Hiroshima and Nagasaki in 1945 they were poised to take the surrender of the Japanese garrisons. Using his authority as Commander China War Zone, Chiang ordered a United States airlift to fly his troops in to take the surrenders and so exclude the communists. America, anxious to reconcile her wartime allies, dispatched a mission under General George Marshall but Chiang broke off the discussions.

His Kuomintang regime at Nanking still claimed to be the only legitimate government of China. But the communists won a series of brilliant battles culminating in the crushing victory of Huai-Hai in December 1948. Their entry into Peking in January 1949 was merely an epilogue. In 1950 Chiang established a Kuomintang government at Taipei, on Taiwan (Formosa). The Korean War of that year led President Harry S Truman to guarantee its territorial integrity.

Chiang held to his proclaimed intention of reconquering the mainland and consolidated a near dictatorial regime, despite bitterness among the native Taiwanese. By the early 1970s Taiwan was economically flourishing but America's detente with Communist China made its political future unsure. In 1971, Peking took China's seat at the United Nations. Taiwan remains an island of unfettered capitalism.

Mao Tse-tung
1893-1976

Lin Piao, founders of the Red Army. A Soviet Republic was soon flourishing in rural Kiangsi. In 1934 Chiang mounted a massive siege. The Communists, 100,000 men, women and children, broke out on the Long March. After a year of military harassment and terrible hardships over a 7000-mile journey, the survivors reached Yenan in northern Shensi. The march was to become a legend of the new China. Yenan became capital of a new republic, and Mao

Father of the Chinese communist revolution, chairman of the Chinese Communist Party from 1935, and leader of the country from 1949, Mao Tse-tung remains the dominant figure of 20th century Chinese history. His writings are revered by world revolutionaries for their theories of permanent revolution and of guerrilla war. Maoism is the doctrine of a major section of western Marxists.

After a village school education in the Chinese classics and a teachers' training course which introduced him to western political literature, Mao took a job at Peking University as assistant to the librarian Li Ta-chao. He soon joined Li's Marxist study group.

China's republicans were already disillusioned with western democratic liberalism when the 1919 Versailles Peace Treaty awarded former German concessions in China to the Japanese. On May 4 1919, Peking university staff and students, Mao and Chou En-lai among them, took to the streets. Two years later Mao was one of the 13 co-founders of the Chinese Communist Party in Shanghai. In 1923 he worked for Sun Yat-sen's Kuomintang to promote revolutionary action in Hunan.

In *Report on . . . the Peasant Movement in Hunan* (1927) Mao argued that a Chinese communist revolution must be based on the peasant masses and not an industrial proletariat. This theory broke with Marxist orthodoxy. When, in 1927, Chiang Kai-shek purged the Shanghai communists Mao fled to the mountains of Kiangsi province to be joined by Chuh Teh and

Opposite: in Red China, judgement by one's peers is highly developed. Here, a Chinese farmer is accused of dishonesty by his fellow farmers. The person selected to defend the accused farmer is known as the People's Tribune.

chairman of the Communist Party in 1935.

Whereas Kuomintang China was governed by corrupt and tyrannical soldiers and officials, the communists maintained tight internal discipline and dealt fairly with the local peasantry. They also demanded a national front against the Japanese. In December 1936 Chiang Kai-shek was forced to agree. Communist guerrillas occupied the countryside around the Japanese-held cities of north-east China. They introduced honest government and redistributed land to the peasants. By 1945, Mao was effectively ruler of 90,000,000 Chinese.

An American mediation mission to Mao and Chiang under George C Marshall failed and the civil war was renewed. The People's Republic of China was proclaimed in October 1949. Despite massive inflation, threat of famine and a collapsed trade, the currency was stabilized by 1951. Mao turned to land reform. Millions of peasants received small freeholdings (later amalgamated into cooperatives). Some landlords were given plots, but thousands more stood trial for previous oppressions, and many were killed. In the 1950–51 Korean war, the People's Liberation Army drove back the United Nations/United States forces. It was China's first victory over a Western army. At the 1954–55 Geneva and Bandung conferences on Vietnam, the diplomacy of the foreign minister Chou En-lai increased China's international standing still further. But during the 1950s China was involved in bitter dispute with Russia.

Mao was incensed by Khruschev's denunciations of Stalin, a major redirection of the communist line on which he had not been consulted. He also feared that Khruschev's policy of peaceful co-existence with the west could develop into a common front against China. The two countries came close to war.

Mao's book *On New Democracy* expressed a profound belief in the creative power of mass opinion and mass participation. He proclaimed the Great Leap Forward in 1958. Thousands of

became president of the Republic.

Though still chairman of the party Mao seemed in decline. But a program of Socialist Education in the schools was preparing the young shock troops of his Great Proletarian Cultural Revolution. In August 1966 1,000,000 young Red Guards assembled in Peking from all over China to be encouraged to denounce Mao's high-ranking party opponents, notably the "capitalist roader" Liu Shao-chi. Mao was supported by

Below: the Communist Chinese People's Liberation Army storm the city of Chinchow under cover of gunfire to force the Nationalist forces to capitulate, late 1948. It was one of the Communist's most decisive victories in the Chinese Civil War.

Lin Piao who had already abolished ranks in the army, and had issued the famous *Little Red Book* of the *Sayings of Chairman Mao* as a compulsory training manual. Liu Shao-chi was eventually forced out of the party. But China fell into

turmoil and the army was called in as the Red Guards got out of hand. Soon Lin Piao himself emerged as the new threat. He died in an air crash in the Republic of Outer Mongolia in September 1971. The following year it was announced that he had been fleeing China after a failed attempt on Mao's life.

Thereafter Mao remained the unquestioned figurehead of China. During his last years effective power may have been in the hands of a counter-revolutionary "gang of four" led by Chiang Ching, his wife. But the work of the great revolutionary himself was done. The foundations of Chinese society had been relaid and the country prepared for its natural role as a major world power.

Russian advisers, vital to China's industrial program had been withdrawn. Now homebuilt furnaces sprang up along the railways throughout China's coalfields. Peasant cooperatives were amalgamated into vast communes to rationalize agriculture and strengthen social solidarity. Both initiatives faltered. Critics objected that Mao's emphasis on ideology weakened efficient economic management. The chief critic, Liu Shao-chi,

Above right: Chinese communists enthusiastically waving *The Thoughts of Chairman Mao* ("the Little Red Book") during the "cultural revolution" of the 1960s. Mao's teachings and writings inspired a generation of Chinese. Since his death the first veiled criticisms of Mao have emerged in China.

Hirohito
born 1901

Emperor Hirohito holds an equivocal place in 20th century history. The grandson of Mutsuihito, founder of the restored empire of 1808, he presided over an era of aggressive Japanese militarism. In 1945 he surrendered his country to the allies – the greatest humiliation in Japanese history. But Hirohito's personal responsibility for the excesses of his country is open to question.

Since the 1890s, Japan's army, directly answerable to the emperor, had made the country a world power. Czarist Russia had been crushingly defeated, Korea annexed and Manchuria infiltrated. World War I in Europe gave Japan the chance to overrun German territories and concessions in China and the Far East, gains confirmed by the 1919 Treaty of Versailles, and move into Europe's Asian export markets.

Hirohito came to office as regent for his father, the mentally unstable Yoshihito in 1921. In that year he visited Europe. At the time, Japanese opinion was turning against democratic constitutionalism. Post World War I slump and the apparently corrupt arrangements between Japan's politicians and big business soured the

domestic scene. Abroad, an Australian veto on the Japanese request for the recognition of racial equality in the League of Nations, and an American ban on oriental immigration further discredited the proclaimed ideals of western liberalism.

In this atmosphere the theories of the revolutionary nationalist Kita Ikki were eagerly received. They outlined the concept of "Showa Restoration", in which capitalists should sur-

Above: the Emperor Hirohito outside the Neijishi Temple in Tokyo blesses troops before their departure for the front during the Sino-Japanese war. To the Japanese, Hirohito was a god. It was a terrible shock to the population when, after World War II, Hirohito renounced any claims to deity.

render their riches and corrupt politicians their power to the emperor. His program, confused but emotive, amounted to state socialism at home and imperialist expansion abroad. It was to be implemented by a military regime holding supreme power under the emperor. These explosive ideas gained wide acceptance among young army officers. Meanwhile, the chiefs of staff increasingly ignored the civilian government.

The army in Manchuria arranged the murder

Right: Japanese farming family returning home exhausted from the fields. While Japan was waging a war of aggressive conquest, many of the ordinary people lived lives of grinding poverty.

of the local governor-warlord. When, despite the emperor's disapproval, the crime went unpunished, it overran the region and set up a puppet state there in 1931. Government approval was neither sought nor given. An imperial order might have halted the army's aggressive policies. But following advice to act scrupulously like a western constitutional monarch, Hirohito gave no direct order for withdrawal. His instructions through the war minister were deliberately held up until the occupation of Manchuria was consolidated.

In October a military coup was discovered but the culprits received only light sentences. In May 1932 the prime minister was assassinated by a group of young officers. At their trial they claimed to have been acting patriotically. Peasant poverty was widespread and many Japanese agreed with the officers' contention that the government's inadequate relief measures were due to corruption. Again the sentences were light. The militarists were in control of affairs.

When, in October 1932, the League of Nations condemned Japan's aggression in Manchuria, Japan's delegates walked out, despite Hirohito's wishes. But the army itself was divided. In 1936 officer insurgents inspired by the ideas of Kita Ikki, attempted a coup supposedly in the name of the emperor. Many government functionaries were murdered. Hirohito bluntly dubbed this action as mutiny. The rebels were executed. But it was a triumph not for constitutional liberalism

Above: the dreadful scene after the bombing of Nanking railway station in November 1937. Japan treated the Chinese people with appalling brutality during the Sino-Japanese war.

Below: Hirohito and his wife on a state visit to Britain. Many people resented his presence, even many years after World War II.

but for one army faction over another. Abroad the regime signed the 1936 Anti-Comintern Pact with Adolf Hitler against the Soviet Union. Japanese armies surged out of Manchuria into China proper. Chiang K'ai-shek retreated deep into the west. By November 1938 China's richest and most populous provinces were under Japanese occupation.

The regime promoted the cult of imperial divinity. Political parties were suppressed in 1940, and General Hideki Tojo became prime minister the following year. War in China continued but, with the attack on Pearl Harbor on December 7 1941, Japan opened hostilities against the United States. Japan at first won prodigious gains in the Pacific and overthrew the British and French colonial administrations in Asia. She proclaimed a Greater East Asia Co-Prosperity Sphere. But the allies slowly fought back and in August 1945 atomic bombs fell on Hiroshima and Nagasaki. Even then, the emperor's broadcast announcing the capitulation was barely credible to many Japanese. Equally shocking was his renunciation of divine attributes the following year. The 1947 constitution made him "representative of the people" with strictly ceremonial powers.

Since the war Emperor Hirohito has been a target for left-wing political protests and occasionally focus of right-wing political nostalgia. In his private capacity he enjoys a reputation as an authority on marine biology.

Harry S. Truman
1884 - 1972

The 33rd president of the United States, Harry S. Truman passed some of America's most important post-World War II social legislation. In foreign affairs he presided over the Marhsall Plan for post-war European recovery and the foundation of the North Atlantic Treaty Organization. He ordered United States intervention with United Nations forces in the Korean war.

A farmer's son, Truman served with the army in World War I in France. Entering local politics in 1922, he went to the Senate in 1934 as a firm supporter of Franklin D Roosevelt's New Deal. He later opposed Roosevelt's third term as president, and won national prominence as chairman of the Senate committee on war

expenditure. This body revealed spectacular bungling on war contracts. Wide support in his own party and from powerful labor groups led to Truman's election as vice-president for Roosevelt's fourth presidential term in 1944.

Roosevelt died in April 1945. Truman became president in the critical last weeks of World War II. He feared that an invasion of Japan would cost thousands of American lives. So to end the war, Truman authorized the use of atom bombs on Hiroshima and Nagasaki.

Right: the birth of the North Atlantic Treaty Organization (NATO), April 4 1949. Secretary of State Dean Acheson signs the North Atlantic Treaty. Truman is standing behind him.

Below: the atomic explosion that virtually wiped out Hiroshima, August 1945. Truman authorized the use of atomic bombs on Hiroshima and Nagasaki to bring a speedy conclusion to the war with Japan. In this they were successful, as well as in claiming about 200,000 civilian lives.

After World War II Truman amalgamated the separate armed services secretariats under a single secretary of defense, appointed by himself. He also won civilian and ultimately presidential control over nuclear fission. It was already clear that the alliance with the Soviet Union would not survive the peace, so United States military capability had to be maintained. The Russians rejected America's Baruch Plan for an international agency controlling nuclear fissile material. The two great powers also disagreed over the unification of the occupation zones of defeated Germany, over general disarmament, and over the formation of an armed force for the newly founded United Nations.

Truman was determined to resist communist expansion in Europe and the Middle East. His method was to extend economic and military aid to countries threatened with subversion or attack. In 1947 secretary of state George C Marshall was sent to Turkey and Greece. A massive aid program to Europe known as the Marshall Plan was developed as a result of this visit. These foreign initiatives were fully supported by Congress but Truman's domestic "Fair Deal" policies were not.

Welfare and civil rights legislation was opposed by the Republican dominated Congress, and by southern Democrats who broke with their party and nominated their own candidate for the 1948 presidential elections. Another Democratic splinter group also ran against Truman in protest against his anti-Soviet policy. All observers expected that he would be roundly defeated by the Republican, Thomas E Dewey. But a hectic whistle-stop campaign, lambasting the "Do Nothing" Republican Congress for blocking his

Above: the Korean war dogged Truman's presidency. This picture was taken at the front by Navy combat photographer Edward A McDade on April 11 1952 – as peace negotiations are taking place.

Above: Hollywood stars fly to Washington to protest at the manner in which un-American Activities Investigations were being conducted. Front row left to right: Geraldine Brooks, June Havoc, Marsha Hunt, Lauren Bacall (Mrs Humphrey Bogart), Richard Conte, and Evelyn Keyes. Back row left to right: Paul Henreid, the group's spokesman Humphrey Bogart, Gene Kelly, and Danny Kaye. The "Cold War" was at its most severe.

social legislation, won Truman the election while Democratic majorities swept into Congress.

Public housing, social security, minimum wage legislation, and racial equality in the government-controlled armed forces were just some of the areas in which he pushed through reforming measures. But even this Congress would not repeal the restrictive Taft-Hartley Labor Act passed over Truman's veto in 1947, or put through his full civil rights program.

On the international stage, Truman's second administration initiated the formation of the Euro-American defense alliance, the North Atlantic Treaty Organization (NATO). In 1948, the Soviet Union blockaded Berlin to land access by the western powers. It was to force them to surrender their position. Instead they mounted a massive airlift. The blockade was lifted in May 1949. The founding document of NATO was signed in Washington in April 1949. It inaugurated the pattern of western defense.

Communist aggression broke out in the Far East. At the end of World War II, Korea had been divided into northern (Soviet) and southern (United States) zones of occupation. Rival governments were established. North Korean forces invaded the south in June 1948. With the Soviet representative inexplicably absent the United Nations authorized member states to intervene on behalf of the south. Truman sent a large United States force commanded by General Douglas MacArthur. Serious initial reverses decided MacArthur to invade Communist China and mount an offensive in the north. Despite wide popular support for MacArthur, the hero of the war against Japan, Truman relieved him of his command in April 1951. Truman's political courage was the greater as the United States was in the throes of the sinister, nation-wide witch-hunt mounted by Senator Joe McCarthy against what he charged was communist infiltration of government.

Truman declined nomination for a third term as president. In retirement he was a prominant commentator on national and international politics. The Harry S Truman Library was opened at his home town of Independence Missouri in 1959.

253

George C. Marshall
1880 - 1959

Left: General George C Marshall. He devised the means for European reconstruction after World War II.

Below: "Attention Reconstruction." This poster was distributed in Germany after World War II to extol the virtues of the Marshall Plan.

great deal of diplomatic activity. When he resigned as chief of staff President Truman gave him the delicate task of mediating between

General George C. Marshall was one of those rare men who followed a successful military career with a distinguished political achievement. He was the architect of the European Recovery Program called the Marshall Plan after him. Its importance in Europe's economic recovery after World War II can hardly be overstressed.

An outstanding staff officer in World War I, Marshall served in China between 1924 and 1927. He headed the United States army as chief of staff from 1939 to 1945, being created general of the army in December 1944. Marshall had urged a direct attack on German-held France from 1942 and opposed Winston Churchill's policy of a front in North Africa. He was over-ruled by Franklin D. Roosevelt. When the European second front was at last established after the D-Day landings of June 1944 the Americans wanted a single supreme commander for northern Europe and the Mediterranean. Marshall was the obvious choice for the post. But separate commands were decided upon and Dwight D. Eisenhower was made commander-in-chief Europe.

Marshall's wartime responsibilities involved a

bourg, the Netherlands, Norway, Portugal, Sweden, Switzerland, Turkey, and Britain. They were joined in October 1949 by the German Federal Republic. The United States and Canada became associate members in 1950. Including, as it did, former enemies and even neutrals, it proved a major agency of European integration. Its immediate function was the administering of the funds now advanced by the US Congress.

In the years 1948–1950 Congress appropriated $10.9 billion for the Marshall Plan. The Economic Cooperation Administration, which administered the program on behalf of the United States government under Paul G Hoffman, ensured self-help by stipulating that each recipient should put into a "counterpart fund" a sum equivalent to the grants received. These

America's wartime allies in China – Mao Tse-tung's communists and the nationalists under Chiang K'ai-shek.

During World War II the United States supported both parties as common allies against Japan. But there were clear signs that the civil war, suspended in the 1930s, was about to break out again. The Americans decided to try to conciliate. Marshall's mission went well at first. A conference was arranged between the two sides. But it got nowhere. What he saw of the corrupt regime of Chiang K'ai-shek led Marshall to recommend his government to consider supporting the communists. But the United States felt bound by wartime agreements with Chiang. Marshall returned home where, in January 1947, President Truman appointed him secretary of state. He busied himself at once with the shattered economies of Europe. Within a month he had engineered immediate American aid to Greece and Turkey. Then he began to prepare for his revolutionary scheme for general European recovery.

Marshall presented the principle of his plan at a speech at Harvard in June 1947. Commenting that post-war Europe would for years be unable to afford reconstruction from its own resources, he went on: "It is logical that the United States should assist in the return of normal economic health in the world, without which there can be no political stability and no assured peace." The British and French governments took up the offer, and invited the Soviet Union to join in a meeting of foreign ministers in Paris that month to draw up a statement of Europe's needs. The Russians held back and when the British and French invited 22 other European states to discuss the plan, forbade the countries under her control to attend.

From these preliminary meetings emerged a series of agencies of European cooperation. The most important was the OEEC, the Organization for European Economic Cooperation. It was formed in 1948 by Austria, Belgium, Denmark, France, Greece, Iceland, Ireland, Italy, Luxem-

Above: two soldiers of the Communist Chinese Fourth Army read a sign written in English and Chinese. It urges strengthening of Sino-US friendship, and the settling of differences in North China – May 21 1946.

counterpart funds could be spent only with American approval. Some critics have pointed out that this stipulation forced the recipients to support United States foreign policy.

Poor health caused Marshall to resign as secretary of state on January 1 1949. In 1950–51 he held office briefly as secretary of defense and was awarded the Nobel Peace Prize in 1953 for the great aid program that bears his name.

Paul Henri Spaak
1899 - 1972

Born near Brussels, Paul Henri Spaak was a dominant figure in Belgian politics for 30 years. He achieved world stature as a principal architect of the European Economic Community.

From a distinguished political family on his mother's side, Spaak trained as a lawyer and entered politics as a Socialist party member in 1932. Four years later he became foreign secretary and, in 1938, Belgium's first Socialist prime minister. Tension was growing in Europe. Hitler had occupied the Rhineland in 1936. Belgium, under King Leopold III hoped to avoid involvement in any coming war. It developed a policy of wary semi-neutrality, im-

Netherlands and Luxembourg which, in 1948, took effect as the Benelux economic union. As foreign minister in Belgium's first post-World War II government, Spaak was a principal draughtsman of the United Nations Charter and was elected first president of the UN General Assembly in 1946. He became prime minister of a coalition government with the Social Christian party in 1947. Important measures included the

Right: Trygve Lie is elected secretary general of the United Nation Organization on February 2 1946. Paul Henri Spaak, the president of UNO, stands behind Trygve Lie, on the left.

Below: Winston Churchill (seated right) visits the Belgian premier and foreign minister Paul Henri Spaak.

plemented by Spaak. At the same time, the country's defenses were strengthened. On May 10 1940, Germany invaded. Only 18 days later Leopold recognized that the military situation forced him to surrender. But he refused to follow his government into exile in London, and was confined for the next four years in the fortress of Laeken.

In exile, Spaak was again foreign minister in the government of Huber Pierlot. He participated in negotiations with the exile regimes of the introduction of women's suffrage and the signing of the Brussels defense treaty with the other Benelux countries, Britain and France in 1948. This was integrated into the North Atlantic Treaty Organization (NATO) the following year.

In domestic affairs the *"question royale"* dominated these years. King Leopold, unfairly criticized by many of his countrymen as a collaborationist, had been taken to Germany in

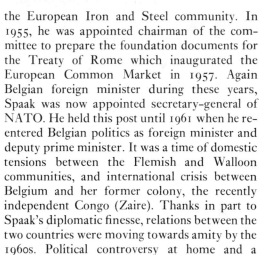

Right: posters urging a "no" vote in the referendum on whether King Leopold should return to the Belgian throne. Many thought Leopold had betrayed Belgium to the Nazis in 1940. Spaak thought there should be a 66 per cent vote in favor of the king. The vote was in fact 57.8 per cent in favor.

June 1944. When Belgium was liberated in September the country was without a head of state. Leopold's brother, Prince Charles, was made regent. The communists vehemently opposed King Leopold's restoration. They were supported by the Socialists and even some Liberals. Despite this opposition, Gaston Eyghens, the Liberal prime minister who succeeded Spaak in 1949, pushed through a bill for a referendum which required a 55 percent vote in favor for the king to return. Spaak argued that the vote should be 66 percent. The referendum in fact produced a 57.8 percent "Yes" vote for the king. He returned to Belgium on July 22 1950. Protesters, among them Spaak, demonstrated in Brussels. The division in the country fell along lines of religion and nationality as well as politics. In the prevailing uproar King Leopold abdicated in August in favor of his son, Baudouin, and left the country.

In the next 10 years Spaak was perhaps the dominant figure in European politics. He earned the nickname "Mr Europe". Spaak was Chairman of the Organization of European Economic Cooperation and president of the Assembly of

the European Iron and Steel community. In 1955, he was appointed chairman of the committee to prepare the foundation documents for the Treaty of Rome which inaugurated the European Common Market in 1957. Again Belgian foreign minister during these years, Spaak was now appointed secretary-general of NATO. He held this post until 1961 when he re-entered Belgian politics as foreign minister and deputy prime minister. It was a time of domestic tensions between the Flemish and Walloon communities, and international crisis between Belgium and her former colony, the recently independent Congo (Zaire). Thanks in part to Spaak's diplomatic finesse, relations between the two countries were moving towards amity by the 1960s. Political controversy at home and a weakening in his commitment to European federalism contributed to his decision to retire from politics in 1966 and enter business.

Below: Spaak is given a traditional welcome in the former Belgian Congo (Zaire).

Gandhi
1869 - 1948

Mohandas K Gandhi's ideas and methods changed the course of history for at least two nations. This small, frail, and gentle man inspired the Indian people to fight for independence using a weapon he had perfected – non-violent civil disobedience. He forced Britain to give up the jewel of its empire.

Gandhi's ideas were rooted in his religion, Hinduism. He grew up believing in non-violence, tolerance, and respect for all living things. Like most Hindus, he sought truth. But unlike others, he sought truth through social and political action.

Gandhi believed that the Indian people could live in justice only if they ruled themselves. But the British had been in India for more than 300 years, and they were not keen to give up their rich colony. To persuade them to think again,

Right: Indian Independence Day on August 15 1947 being celebrated in Paris with the raising of the Indian flag.

Left: Gandhi pictured at a spinning machine. He believed that the revival and expansion of home industry was essential if an independent India was to succeed.

Gandhi introduced *satyagraha* (the force of truth) in 1919. At his suggestion, thousands of Indians refused to buy British goods, attend British schools, or use British courts. They marched in protest against British laws, and even lay down in the streets in front of British vehicles. The British were baffled. They could find no way to fight Gandhi and his followers but to put them in jail. But the Indians regarded going to jail as inseparable from civil disobedience. They lined up proudly to be arrested. It took Gandhi and his followers 28 years before Britain finally withdrew and India gained her independence in 1947.

Gandhi first used *satyagraha* for a different purpose. He had gone to South Africa in 1893 on a one-year legal assignment after earning a law degree in London. There, he found that Indians were subjected to humiliating discrimination. He discovered it the hard way on a journey from Durban to Pretoria soon after his arrival. During the trip he was beaten up by a stage coach driver, expelled from a first-class railway carriage, and denied access to a hotel – all because he was an

Indian. Gandhi's sense of justice was outraged. He made up his mind to fight. He stayed on in South Africa for more than 20 years to lead the Indian community in a struggle for equal treatment.

In the beginning, Gandhi drafted, circulated, and submitted petitions to the local Natal legislature and to the British colonial government. He edited a weekly newspaper, *Indian Opinion*, and formed the Natal Indian Congress, a political organization to represent Indian interests. In 1909, the Transvaal government ordered all Indians to register and be fingerprinted. Gandhi advised his followers to defy the order and they did. This was the beginning of Gandhi's first campaign of non-violent civil disobedience. The South African leader Jan Christian Smuts was eventually forced to agree to better treatment for Indians in South Africa.

Gandhi returned to India as a hero during World War I. Indian troops were fighting and dying along with the British in many parts of the world. They expected to be rewarded with some measure of self-rule when the war ended. Instead, Britain passed the Rowlatt Acts of 1919. These stated that Indians could be jailed without trial for political agitation. Later that year, in Amritsar, a local British commander ordered his troops to fire on a large crowd of unarmed civilians gathered for a meeting. The soldiers killed nearly 400 Indians and injured 1200 more in what came to be known as the Amritsar massacre. Gandhi responded to the Rowlatt Acts and the

village in India. It later became the Congress Party.

Gandhi wanted more than an independent India. He also wanted a unified one in which all of India's religious, cultural, and language groups lived together in peace and tolerance. Even the untouchables, India's lowest caste group, were to be given equal treatment. He had social goals for the new state too. Gandhi was opposed to the complexities of modern societies.

massacre by launching the first of many campaigns of non-violent Civil disobedience. He led protest marches and fasted. Thousands of Indians, including Gandhi himself, were arrested and jailed.

In the early 1920s, Gandhi became the leader of the Indian National Congress, an organization which had been founded in 1885 as a forum for airing Indian opinion, but had since become the center for Indian demands for self-rule. Gandhi changed the National Congress into an effective political instrument with support in almost every

Above: Sikh-Hindu refugees fleeing from Lahore in Pakistan into India. Many refugees were killed in fighting with Moslems as they headed for the relative safety of India.

Instead he favored a simple and austere life for the Indian people based in part on cottage industries which would provide meaningful work and produce essential goods such as cloth. Other Indian nationalists opposed Gandhi on some of these goals.

In 1945, the Labour Party under Clement Attlee took power in Britain, and pushed for immediate independence for India. But a struggle between the Indian National Congress and the Moslem League blocked the way. The League wanted a separate state for India's Moslems. Finally the Moslems prevailed, and India gained independence in August, 1947 as two separate countries. India and Pakistan.

Gandhi was bitterly disappointed at the partition of India and at the violence which followed as millions of Moslems moved from India to Pakistan, and millions of Hindus traveled the other way. He toured the riot areas, fasted, and finally quelled the violence in Calcutta and Delhi. A few days later, on his way to prayers, he was shot and killed by a Hindu fanatic opposed to his tolerance towards Moslems. Jawaharlal Nehru, his successor, said in sorrow: "The light has gone out of our lives and there is darkness everywhere."

Nehru
1889 - 1964

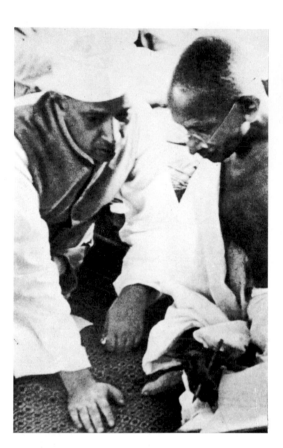

tural production, higher school enrollments, and improved health care. Remarkable progress was made in all these areas, but much of the country's economic growth came in the private sector. India remains one of the poorest nations in the world.

In foreign affairs, Nehru favored a policy of friendly relations with all countries, regardless of ideology. He annoyed western nations by refusing to sign defense pacts with them or to

WIE SICH INDIENS WIRTSCHAFT VERTEILT		
LANDWIRTSCHAFTL. ERTRÄGE (IN HEKTAR)	H	P
JUTE	398,000 ha.	570,000 ha.
BAUMWOLLE	5,572,600 ha.	660,000 ha.
TEE	259,400 ha.	39,300 ha.
REIS	6,993,000 ha.	2,176,000 ha.
WEIZEN	1,700,000 ha.	1,127,000 ha.
ZUCKER	1,065,000 ha.	209,000 ha.
GESAMTSTRECKE DER EISENBAHNEN	25,970 MEIL.	15,542 MEIL.

INDUSTRIE WERKE	BAUMWOLLFABR.	JUTEFABR.	ZUCKER-RAFFINERIEN	EISEN u. STAHL WERKE	PAPIERFABR.	GLASWERKE
H	380	108	156	18	16	77
P	9	0	10	0	0	2

Left: Nehru (left) with the father of Indian independence Gandhi. The two men failed to reconcile moslems and Hindus. In the disturbances which took place after the British withdrawal hundreds of thousands were killed.

Above: this German map depicts a rough profile of the Indian economy.

Gandhi, the man who led India to independence, was a philosopher and an activist. Dressed in a loin cloth and squatting on the ground. He was most at home among poor villagers. His appeal to struggle against British rule was to the masses. By contrast, Jawaharlal Nehru, the man who led India after independence as its first prime minister, was an aristocrat, educated at Harrow School and Cambridge University in England. He was a sophisticated political thinker and a statesman.

Nehru spent almost 10 years in jail during the struggle for independence. Much of his time there was spent reading, thinking, and planning for the future. When independence finally came in 1947, his ideas on what the new state should be like were well formed. They included secularism, parliamentary democracy, and a socialist economy.

The first two became part of the constitution of the new nation in the early days of independence. Nehru tried to bring the third about through a series of five-year plans. These plans called for industrialization, increased agricul-

support them consistently in the United Nations. Many of the other Asian and African nations that followed India to independence in the 1950s also chose non-alignment. Nehru became the unofficial leader of an Afro-Asian block.

His policy of non-alignment suffered a serious blow in 1962 when Red Chinese troops invaded northern India. Indian forces had moved into a disputed border area. The Chinese not only drove them back to their previous position but well beyond. Nehru called for Western arms and got them. But China had made its point, and pulled back.

India's defeat along the northern border worried the Indian people. But Nehru's personal popularity survived.

Nehru joined the nationalist movement soon after he finished his education in England, and returned to India to practice law. But he was bored by the long-winded speeches of his colleagues, and he did not take an active role until 1919 when Gandhi called for action to oppose British repression. Along with thousands of other Indians, Nehru joined Gandhi in acts of defiance against British authority, in protest marches, and in jail sentences.

By the mid-1920s, Nehru was Secretary of the Indian National Congress. In this post he traveled widely to investigate conditions in India. His travels opened his eyes to the abysmal poverty and degradation in which many Indians lived. He became convinced that India needed social and economic reform as well as political independence.

With Gandhi's support, Nehru was elected president of the Congress in 1929. He chaired the meeting in Lahore in which India demanded full independence from Britain for the first time. The Lahore meeting made Nehru a nationalist leader second only to Gandhi. Later, he took

The provincial governments resigned in protest in 1939 when the British government took India into World War II without securing their permission. The National Congress demanded full independence immediately. When Britain refused, Gandhi launched the Quit India movement. Both Gandhi and Nehru were arrested and spent most of the war years in jail.

After World War II, Britain's new Labour government offered independence to India as

part in meetings with the British that culminated in the Government of India Act of 1936. This was one of a series of steps by which Britain gradually gave Indians self-rule.

The 1936 act provided for popularly-elected autonomous government for India's provinces. The elections in 1937 to fill the seats in the provincial legislatures opened a rift between India's Hindus and Moslems that was never mended. Candidates of the Hindu-dominated National Congress won a majority in seven of the 11 provincial assemblies. The Moslem League representing India's Moslems took only three. Fearing Hindu domination, the League asked the Congress to form coalition governments including some Moslems. But Nehru wanted unity and secularism, not separate representation for different religious groups, and he refused. Three years later, the Moslem League formally demanded a separate Moslem state.

Above: the inauguration of the Rihand Dam in January 1963. It can generation 250,000 kilowatts. Nehru attended the inauguration. He believed that the wholesale industrialization of India was the only way to cure the grinding poverty of so many of its people.

soon as Congress and the Moslem League could decide on partition. Nehru reluctantly agreed. Bloody riots between Moslems and Hindus in 1946 had convinced him that there was no alternative. India and Pakistan became independent dominions within the British Commonwealth in August, 1947.

Nehru served as president of the constituent assembly which drafted India's constitution and acted as its government until the first general election was held. In that election, the Congress Party won overwhelmingly and Nehru, as its leader, became prime minister. He held the post until his death in 1964.

Nehru's death left a vacuum in India that no other Indian could fill. But he also left a stable government, a developing economy, and a people who had come to believe as strongly as he had in secularism, socialism, and above all in democracy.

Ali Jinnah
1876 - 1948

Mohammed Ali Jinnah was known as the man with a problem for every solution in the final days of British rule in India. A Moslem, Jinnah stubbornly insisted that India's Moslem minority have a state of its own. No compromise was possible, he said. Only partition of the subcontinent would protect the Moslems from Hindu domination. Both Hindus and British gave in in the end. The Moslem state of Pakistan was created and Ali Jinnah, its founder, became its first head of government.

Moslems made up about 25 percent of India's population just prior to independence. They were the descendants of Arab, Turkish, and other invaders and of converts to Islam during Mogul rule there. Most had been educated in religious schools while Hindus attended state schools established by the British. As a result, Hindus, already more powerful because of their numbers, also held most of the good jobs available in business and the government. Moslems were mostly farmers or workers.

But Jinnah came from a wealthy Moslem family. He was educated as a lawyer in Britain and established a successful law practice in Bombay before joining the nationalist movement in 1905.

Above: dead and dying littering Main Street, New Delhi, after rioting between Moslems and Hindus in 1947.

Left: Mohammed Ali Jinnah, President of the All India Moslem League speaking at the League's legislators' convention. Ali Jinnah concluded his speech by saying "We are prepared to sacrifice anything and everything. We shall not submit to any scheme of government without our consent."

Ironically, Jinnah began his nationalist career as an ardent supporter of Indian unity. He joined the Indian National Congress and worked within it to develop a sense of nationhood among the Indian people. But he soon grew frustrated by the Hindu's seeming indifference to Moslem problems and interests and by his failure to move up in the National Congress.

Jinnah joined the Moslem League in 1913, though he was still a member of the Congress. The League had been formed seven years earlier to protect Moslem rights. It assured Jinnah that it supported Indian unity as enthusiastically as the Congress did. The two organizations were then working closely together. By 1916, Jinnah was president of the League. He played a major role in negotiating the Lucknow Pact between the League and the Congress. The Pact called for a separate Moslem electorate to assure Moslem representation in a future Indian legislature. But cooperation between the two organizations soon broke down, and the Congress withdrew support for the Pact. Jinnah resigned from the Congress in 1930, but he continued to work for Moslem-Hindu unity until 1937. That year Congress refused to include Moslems in coalition

Below: Moslem women wearing burkahs to keep strict purdah wait to vote on the question of whether the Northwest Frontier should join Pakistan or remain part of India.

joined one or the other of them. These states had been ruled by Indian princes before independence in cooperation with the British government. After independence, the states with a predominantly Hindu population joined India,

governments in the provinces.

Disillusioned with the Congress, Jinnah threw all his efforts into the League. Under his leadership, it grew and its influence spread. In 1940, it demanded the creation of a Moslem nation, Pakistan, made up of those parts of India in which Moslems predominated. At first, both the British government and Hindu leaders refused to consider it. But the League showed it had the support of almost all India's Moslems by winning all the Moslem seats in elections for the constituent assembly in 1946. Violent Moslem-Hindu riots added pressure. Jinnah stood firm.

Pakistan was declared an independent dominion within the British Commonwealth in August, 1947. Jinnah became the Govenor-General and was later elected president of its constituent assembly.

The new nation consisted of two regions, West Pakistan in the northwestern part of the subcontinent and East Pakistan in the northeast. These two regions were separated by more than 1000 miles of Indian territory. They had little in common besides the Moslem religion, and friction gradually developed between them. In 1971, East Pakistanis rebelled against the government and set themselves up as a separate nation called Bangladesh.

After India and Pakistan gained independence, a number of princely states on the subcontinent

Below: Ali Jinnah's tomb. His countrymen called him Quaid-e-Azam – Great Leader.

while those made up mostly of Moslems became part of Pakistan. One of the largest princely states, Kashmir, had a predominantly Moslem population, but its prince, a Hindu, joined India. War broke out between Pakistan and India and lasted until the United Nations arranged a ceasefire in 1949. The ceasefire left most of Kashmir under Indian control. Neither nation was satisfied, and the problem of Kashmir remained unsolved.

Jinnah died in 1948 leaving behind a nation with far more problems than solutions. But Pakistan existed and his countrymen gave him full credit. They called him Quaid-e-Azam, Great Leader.

Khruschev
1894 - 1971

When retired Soviet premier Nikita Khruschev died in 1971, Soviet authorities were reluctant to let their people mourn. They delayed announcing his death for several days, decided against a state funeral, and denied permission for his body to be buried in the Kremlin wall where Stalin is buried.

Khruschev, the crude, effervescent, bald-headed man with the infectious grin had loosened the grip of Stalin's 30-year terror. A. pent-up demand for freedom and material goods was unleashed which his successors found hard to control. They must have feared his death would set off new demands for change reminiscent of those to which he responded in the heady days of his rule.

Khruschev first denounced Stalin in a secret report at the 20th Party Congress in 1956. He accused his predecessor of intolerance and brutality and of glorifying himself in a "cult of personality." Important changes in Soviet life followed his speech. The secret police were curbed, political prisoners released, and intellectuals and artists given a limited amount of freedom. Similar changes were wrought in other communist countries. Stalinist leaders were toppled to make way for more moderate replace-

ments. In Poland, where Wladyslaw Gumulka took power, freedom was increased, relations with the Roman Catholic Church renewed, and cultural and economic channels to the West widened. Other Eastern European countries followed suit. But when the post-Stalinist leader of Hungary, Imre Nagy, attempted to withdraw from the Warsaw Pact, the military alliance linking the Soviet Union with its allies, Khruschev sent in Soviet tanks.

Right: a wrecked Russian tank in the university quarter of Budapest. Despite Khruschev's denunciation of Stalin's dictatorial methods, he was quick to crush the 1956 Hungarian uprising by armed force.

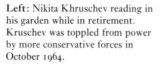

Left: Nikita Khruschev reading in his garden while in retirement. Kruschev was toppled from power by more conservative forces in October 1964.

In 1959, Khruschev met United States President Dwight D Eisenhower on a trip to the United States, and planned to have "Ike" return the call. But the visit was cancelled after an American U2 spy plane was shot down over the Soviet Union in 1960 and its pilot, Gary Powers, captured.

The spy plane incident was the first of a number of disasters that combined to bring Khruschev down. Another occurred after he installed offensive missiles on Cuba, 90 miles from Florida, in 1962. President John F Kennedy took a strong stand. After 13 days on the brink of nuclear war, Khruschev backed down and ordered the missiles removed. Later, as a happy ending to the confrontation, Khruschev, Kennedy, and prime minister Harold Macmillan of Great Britain signed a nuclear test-ban treaty. But the Red Chinese could never forgive Khruschev for giving in on the missiles and a split between the two countries that began with de-Stalinization widened.

Soviet opposition to Khruschev grew when his ambitious plans to increase agricultural production failed and administrative changes took responsibility from some party supporters. His cuts in military spending and his increasingly undignified behavior proved too much. In October, 1964, his many opponents, notably Brezhnev and Kosygin, forced him to retire. The boisterous Khruschev disappeared into quiet seclusion – the first he had had in almost 50 years

first Secretary of the Moscow party with responsibility for completing the Moscow subway. He later received the Order of Lenin for this job. A strong Stalin supporter, Khruschev continued to move up through the ranks of both party and government as many of his associates died in Stalin's purges of the 1930s. He spent World War II in the Ukraine where he restored the purge-shattered party, suppressed separatist movements, and after the German invasion,

Below: West German Chancellor Helmut Schmidt (right) meets Aleksei Kosygin (left) and Leonid Brezhnev – the two men at the head of the overthrow of Khruschev.

Left: a Russian rocket on display in Moscow. Soviet arms spending, as well as space research, greatly increased under Khruschev's rule.

of service to the communist cause.

A poor boy from a peasant background, Khruschev was born in Kalinov, a village in southern Russia. As a child he worked as a herder on his father's tenant farm. Later, after his family moved to Yuzovka in the Ukraine, he took jobs in the mines and factories there. He joined the Communist Party in 1918 and served as a junior political commissar with the Red Army during the civil war. After the war, he completed his secondary education at one of the new Soviet Workers Schools. There, he became a student leader and secretary of the school's Communist Party Committee. When he finished school, he became a full-time party worker. He soon attracted the attention of Lazar Kaganovich, the Secretary-General of the Ukrainian Communist Party and friend of Stalin. In 1929, Khruschev moved to Moscow to attend the Stalin Industrial Academy and soon became involved in that school's and later Moscow's Communist Party organization. By 1935, he was

encouraged resistance. When the Ukraine was liberated in 1944, he worked to restore agricultural production there.

Called back to Moscow by Stalin in 1949, Khruschev again became First Secretary of the Moscow Communist Party as well as Secretary of the Soviet Party's Central Committee. After Stalin's death in 1953, Khruschev was one of a group that inherited power. Through his control of the party machinery in Moscow and the central government, he was able to defeat his chief rival, Malenkov and take power as the First Secretary of the Soviet Communist Party. In 1955, he ousted Malenkov from the premiership and replaced him with a hand-picked candidate, Nicholai Bulganin. The two ruled as a team until a pro-Stalin group made up of Malenkov, Molotov, and Kagin tried and failed to oust Khruschev in 1957. The next year, to signify his complete control, Khruschev named himself the premier giving him the top government as well as the top party post.

Khruschev was 64 years old by the time he reached the top and he ruled for only six years before he was overthrown by more conservative opponents. But in that time he brought about dramatic changes – not so much in communist theory as in its application in the Soviet Union.

John F. Kennedy
1917 - 1963

"The torch has been passed to a new generation of Americans . . ." said John F Kennedy in his inaugural address as 35th president of the United States in January 1961. "A trumpet summons us – not . . . to arms but to a struggle against the common enemies of man: tyranny, poverty, disease, and war itself." With these ringing, almost poetic words, Kennedy set the tone and the goals for his administration. He was to serve just over 1000 days before he was slain by an assassin's bullet in Dallas in 1963. But in that time he inspired the young with his idealism and attracted them into government service. He

Below: Jacqueline Kennedy at her husband's funeral after his assassination in Dallas, Texas, on November 23 1963. She is flanked by Edward Kennedy (left) and Robert Kennedy (right). Robert was himself assassinated in July 1968.

Right: during his presidency, Kennedy pledged that the United States would put a man on the Moon by the end of the 1960s. His pledge was fulfilled in July 1969 when astronaut Edward Aldrin stepped onto the surface of the Moon from the Apollo 11 lunar module.

welcomed new nations into the world community and sent American volunteers to help them. A manned space program was launched during his administration that eventually put a man on the moon. Perhaps Kennedy's greatest act in office was his signing of a nuclear test-ban treaty offering hope for a future without nuclear pollution or destruction.

Kennedy had eight brothers and sisters. Their father, millionaire financier Joseph P Kennedy

encouraged them to think, to try, and to win. One of his sons was expected to become president. When Joe, the eldest son, was killed in World War II, the responsibility passed to John. By that time, John had already graduated from Harvard University and turned his senior thesis into a best-selling book, *Why England Slept*. He had become a war hero in World War II by rescuing his men after their torpedo boat was sliced in half by a Japanese destroyer.

After starting a career in journalism Kennedy ran for the United States Congress from a district in Boston, Massachusetts. Bypassing the regular Democratic party machinery, he relied instead on his friends and family to help him. Day after day he canvassed, ringing doorbells, and shaking hands. His mother and sisters held Kennedy teas to tell voters about him. Kennedy won by a landslide.

Kennedy spent three terms in the House of Representatives, during which he gained a reputation for accessibility to his constituents, and a moderately liberal voting record. He took on the popular Republican party incumbent Henry Cabot Lodge for a seat in the Senate in 1952. "It was those damn Kennedy teas," Lodge

is reported to have said when the election was over with Kennedy the victor.

Kennedy gradually became more radical in the Senate. He showed increasing support for labor, civil rights, and aid for the new nations emerging in Africa and Asia. But he was criticised by liberals for not taking a strong enough stand against Wisconsin Senator Joseph McCarthy and his anti-communist witch hunt. Kennedy had intended to vote against McCarthy in the Senate's censure, but he was in the hospital recovering from a serious back operation when the vote was taken. He remained strapped to a board for six months afterwards and wrote *Profiles in Courage*, another best-seller for which he won a Pulitzer prize.

Kennedy's shift to the left attracted the attention of liberal Democrats who had supported Adlai Stevenson in his unsuccessful bid for the presidency in 1952. When Stevenson was again nominated in 1956, he left the choice of the vice-presidential candidate to the convention. Kennedy almost won. His impressive withdrawal speech reached millions of United States homes tuned in to the convention. He became a national figure overnight.

Kennedy announced his candidacy for the presidency in January 1960. With his younger brother, Robert, as campaign manager, he won primary after primary. He was nominated on the first ballot at the Democratic convention. In the campaign itself, Kennedy answered a widespread fear that his Roman Catholicism would influence his actions as president with an impassioned statement of his belief in the separation of church and state. He also gained credibility by his poise and expertise in a series of debates with the Republican candidate, Richard Nixon. The final vote was close, but Kennedy won by a hair.

With such a narrow margin of victory, Kennedy could not rely on strong public or Congressional support for his legislative program. He did secure approval of the Peace Corps and the Alliance for Progress, an aid program for Latin America. But he failed in his attempts to reform taxes, aid education, provide medical care for the aged, and protect civil rights. In any case, circumstances forced him to spend much of his time on foreign affairs. He had inherited from President Eisenhower a CIA-trained force of Cuban exiles and a plan to invade Communist-dominated Cuba. Trusting military advice, he allowed the invasion to go ahead. But he refused American military support, and the action failed. Instead of toppling Cuban leader Fidel Castro, the Bay of Pigs invasion strengthened his

Above: the Cuban Crisis took the world to the brink of nuclear war. Russia had stationed missiles on Cuba, only 90 miles from the United States mainland. Picture shows the USS *Barry* (foreground) shadowing the Soviet freighter *Anosov. Anosov* is carrying military equipment, including eight Soviet missiles.

Below: Jacqueline Kennedy stands to one side as Lyndon B Johnson is sworn in as President of the United States following John Kennedy's assassination. Johnson was to push through most of the social legislation initiated by Kennedy. His career was to be destroyed by the Vietnam war – also initiated by Kennedy.

prestige and power as a revolutionary leader.

A year later, in 1962, Kennedy announced to a shocked American public that the Soviet Union had installed offensive missiles in Cuba, and that the United States had imposed a blockade to prevent Soviet ships carrying additional weapons from reaching the island. For 13 days, the world teetered on the brink of nuclear war before the ships turned back, and Soviet premier Khruschev announced that the missiles would be removed.

In 1963, in preparation for the 1964 election, Kennedy went to Dallas, Texas to try and heal a split in the local Democratic party there. As he and Mrs Kennedy rode slowly through the city in an open car, shots rang out. Kennedy was dead by the time he reached the hospital and Lyndon B Johnson was sworn in as his successor.

Kennedy's assassination ended a brilliant career and deprived the United States of what might have been a great president. His work was carried on by Johnson, who secured passage of much of the legislation Kennedy had introduced.

Gamal Nasser
1918 - 1970

Five million people attended Gamal Abdel Nasser's funeral. They poured into Cairo from all over Egypt in jammed trains and buses, and lined up 200 deep to catch a last glimpse of his casket. Nasser was a national hero, the first Egyptian to rule an independent Egypt since the pharaohs. More important, Nasser had given the desperately poor Egyptians a sense of national pride and hope for the future for the first time in centuries. Said one government official, "Nasser was everything to Egypt – friend, father, president, king, and even God. And now we are alone."

Millions more mourned for Nasser throughout the Arab world. They too regarded him as their hero. One Lebanese newspaper summed it up: "One hundred million human beings – the Arabs – are orphans."

Nasser aroused strong emotions in life as well as in death. To the Israelis, he was crafty, theatrical, and dangerous. Some Western leaders thought him a maddeningly unreliable Third World leader who took arms and money wherever he could find them. But the fellaheen, Egypt's peasants, understood and were proud of him. He was one of them.

Right: the Aswan High Dam under construction. Completed in 1970, the dam had doubled the supply of water controlling the flow of the Nile river. Its hydro-electricity plant generates much needed power. The dam raised the water level by 200 feet, provided distant oases with extra water. Clouds have been spotted where none had been seen before. Aswan is the greatest industrial achievement of Nasser's reign.

Far right: mourning Egyptians jam the streets of Cairo during Nasser's funeral in 1970.

Like many poor boys in the Third World, Nasser sought to better himself through a military career. He graduated from Egypt's military academy and eventually achieved the rank of colonel before seizing political power in a military coup in 1952. The coup overthrew the corrupt king, Farouk. Egypt became a republic.

At first, Muhammed Naguib, a popular general, served as front man for the revolutionary government, while Nasser pulled the strings from behind the scenes. But the two leaders quarreled. Nasser finally ousted Naguib and took full power. He was elected president unopposed in 1956.

One vestige of foreign control remained in Egypt when Nasser took over. Britain kept troops there, mostly to protect the privately owned Suez Canal. Nasser stunned the world in 1956 by nationalizing the canal. Britain, France, and Israel invaded Egypt and defeated its troops. But the invaders were forced to withdraw by the United States and the Soviet Union, which both backed Egypt in the United Nations. The seizure of the canal was seen as a victory throughout the Arab world. When Nasser began talking to them of Arab pride and strength, he had a sympathetic audience.

The Egyptian president saw how much power and influence the Arabs might have if they stood together. Their numbers, their strategic location, and their oil made them a force to be reckoned with. He dreamed of an Arab union stretching from Morocco to Iraq. But his efforts to forge political links among the argumentative Arabs failed. Egypt and Syria joined briefly in a United Arab Republic in 1958, but Syria withdrew three years later.

Nasser was a little more successful in his efforts to encourage social revolution in Arab countries to replace "feudalist and reactionary" monarchies with modern republics. A republican

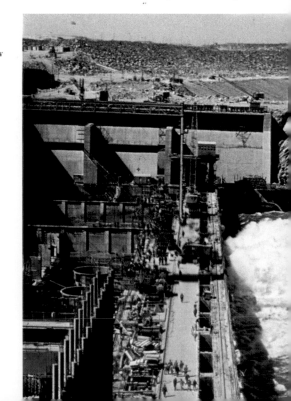

Nations partitioned Palestine and gave a large chunk of it to Zionists for the creation of the state of Israel. Nasser also believed that Israel was an expansionist nation supported and used by outside forces – the world Zionist movement and western imperialist nations. As such, he saw it as a threat to Arab nations. Also, Israel's control of the Negev Desert split the Arab world in two.

As a young officer, Nasser had fought Israel when it was created in 1947. In 1967, believing that Israel was poised to invade Syria, he massed Egyptian troops along the border with Israel and closed the Gulf of Aqaba to Israeli shipping. Israel attacked Egypt, Jordan, and Syria, routed them all, and occupied large chunks of their territory. Egypt lost the Gaza Strip and the Sinai Desert, including the east bank of the Suez Canal. Nasser took full responsibility for the crushing defeat and offered to resign. But Egyptians and other Arabs persuaded him to withdraw his resignation.

The cost of war and defense undermined Nasser's efforts to industrialize Egypt, and to introduce social and economic reforms. But he made a start. By limiting land ownership and distributing the resulting surplus, Nasser provided land for 1,500,000 peasants. The Aswan High Dam, completed in 1970, supplied more land for the landless as well as power for industry. He built schools, clinics, hospitals, and housing. Through industrialization, he increased jobs. Per capita income rose slightly despite huge population increases. But millions remained landless, jobless, and poor.

A great deal was left to be done to fulfill Nasser's dream for Egypt and for the Arab world when he died unexpectedly in 1970. But the massive turnout for his funeral and the grief expressed by Arabs everywhere seemed to indicate that his people shared his dream, and would continue to pursue it.

government took power in Yemen in 1962, but its position was not secured until Egypt had poured men and arms into a costly five-year civil war against Saudi Arabia backed royalists there.

Nasser was more successful in rallying the Arabs against Israel. Like most Arabs, he believed that the Palestinian people had been robbed of their homeland when the United

Above: the entrance to the Suez Canal at Port Said. Nasser's nationalization of the canal provoked the invasion of Egypt by British, French, and Israeli forces. Pressure from the United States and Russia forced them to withdraw.

Golda Meir
1898 - 1978

Born in Kiev in Russia during one of the periodic persecutions of Jews there, Golda Meir emigrated as a child to the United States, and then as a young woman to Palestine. There she tended chickens and took in laundry. Slowly, she worked her way up to a position of leadership in the Jewish community in the critical years before Israeli independence in 1948. After independence, she helped form and lead the new nation as labor, foreign, and finally prime minister. Golda Meir was sustained by her belief that Jews deserved a nation of their own.

When she arrived in Palestine in 1921, it was ruled by Britain on a mandate from the League of Nations. Jewish immigrants, most of them from Russia and Eastern Europe, were settling

Right: crops growing where nothing grew before – "the Blooming Desert." Thanks to irrigation projects, Israel's agricultural acreage has been dramatically increased since 1948. But the Palestinians remain dispossessed, living in refugee camps.

Far right: the six day war of 1967. An Egyptian MIG lies wrecked on the ground. Much of the Egyptian air force was destroyed by Israeli strikes before it could take off. The Israeli intelligence organization, Mossad, provided the strategic information necessary.

in the area, hoping to create a Jewish state there. Meanwhile, Arab Palestinians grew increasingly concerned for their own homes and futures.

Meir and her husband lived first on a kibbutz and then in Tel Aviv. They finally settled in Jerusalem where she went to work for the Histadrut, the General Federation of Jewish Labor. She held the post of secretary of its Woman's Labor Council until 1948. She represented the Council on Histadrut's executive council as well as at international conferences, and spent two years in the United States in the 1930s serving as national secretary for its American counterpart, the Pioneer Women's Organization.

At the same time, Meir pursued a second career in the World Zionist Organization. She began in 1929 as a delegate to the World

Opposite: a view from the Shalom Tower of the Israeli capital of Tel Aviv. This modern city has been built in 30 years.

Zionist Congress and later traveled widely in Europe and the United States on behalf of the organization. In a third career, she sat on the executive council of the National Council through which Jews in Palestine governed themselves under the British mandate.

During World War II, Meir headed Histadrut's political department. When the British arrested many other Jewish leaders in Palestine, she served as head of the Jewish Agency's political department, the top position in the Jewish community in Palestine. In this post, she fought for the release from detention of would-be Jewish immigrants who had tried to enter Palestine illegally. She became a leading spokesman for Zionism with the British authorities.

After Israel's troubled birth in May 1948, Meir spent six months representing the new nation in Moscow. She returned to become a member of the Knesset after the first elections were held early in 1949. Appointed Minister of Labor and Social Insurance by prime minister David Ben Gurion, she built housing for the new immigrants pouring into the country and created Israel's national insurance plan. In 1956, Ben Gurion moved her from the labor to the foreign ministry. Here, she took a strong stand against Israel's Arab opponents and backed the prime minister's policy of swift retaliation. She also courted African support through technical aid and established diplomatic relations with West Germany.

Meir handled Israel's relations with the outside world for 10 difficult years before resigning in 1966 to slow down slightly as secretary general of her party, Mapai. After arranging a

merger of three pro-labor groups, Mapai, Raki, and Ahdut Hasvoda, to create Israel's Labor party in February 1968, she resigned her post and tried to retire. But when prime minister Levi Eshkol died suddenly in February 1969, Labor party leaders divided between Moshe Dayan and Yigal Allon as his successor, and turned to Golda Meir as a compromise candidate.

At the age of 71, Mrs Meir became Israel's prime minister and began a round of talks at home and abroad with world leaders including Nicolai Ceausescu of Romania, Willy Brandt of West Germany, and Pope Paul VI in an effort to find a peaceful solution to the Mideast conflict. She had to give up her peace-making efforts in October 1973, however, to rally the Israeli people after Egypt and Syria attacked the country. The "Yom Kippur war" postponed Israeli elections, and when they were held in December, Labor lost five seats leaving it with 51 out of a total of 120. The losses were apparently due to charges that Israel had been unprepared for the Arab attack. After struggling for months to fashion a coalition government, Meir resigned on April 10, 1974.

After more than 50 difficult years devoted to Israel, Golda Meir finally retired and gained the time she had long sought to devote to her beloved grandchildren. She could be well satisfied with the outcome of her work. Through her efforts and those of other Israeli pioneers, the nation she wanted for the Jewish people had come into being, had survived despite the hostility of its neighbors, and had even thrived. But Israel has still to come to terms with its Arab neighbors. Only then will it live in peace.

Archbishop Makarios
1913 - 1977

Makarios, whose real name was Mikhail Kristodolou Mouskos, grew up at a time of increasing Greek nationalism in Cyprus. The son of a shepherd, he was born in the village of Ano Panayia in western Cyprus and attended the village school. At the age of 13, he was accepted as a novice at the Abbey of Kykkos. The Abbey sent him to secondary school in Nicosia, and then on to the Theological school at the University of Athens. Graduating in 1943, Makarios

Archbishop Makarios of Cyprus might be considered a colossal failure. He began his political career as Ethnarch, representative and protector of the Greek community in Cyprus when the island was a British colony. He set as his goal *enosis*, union of Cyprus with Greece. But when his career ended 27 years later, he was president of an independent Cyprus. Almost half its territory had been occupied by the Turkish army, which had invaded the island to protect the Turkish Cypriot minority there. But many Greek Cypriots still looked upon him as a hero, believed that someday his goal would be achieved.

The Greek Cypriots make up 80 per cent of the island's population. They base their kinship with Greece on their Greek culture which goes back to ancient times. Never a part of Greece, the island has been ruled by the Assyrians, Egyptians, Persians, Alexander the Great and the Ptolemies, the Romans and Byzantines, the British, and the Venetians. It became part of Turkey's Ottoman empire in 1571. The Turks continued to rule it until 1878 when they handed it over to Britain in return for military assistance against Russia. The British in turn offered the island to Greece for support in World War I. The offer was never taken up, but it led to widespread demands for *enosis* among Greek Cypriots.

Above: "Enosis" is scrawled on walls all over Cyprus. Eighty per cent of the islanders are Greek Cypriots. Union with Greece has been of passionate importance to many of them.

Above: Grivas demanding "Enosis."

Left: Archbishop Makarios, an inspiration to his people, he was regarded by western politicians as too "big" a man for a small island like Cyprus. One oft-quoted joke was that Cyprus was too small to be a world power, so decided to be a world of nuisance instead.

returned to the Abbey, joined the teaching staff there, and in 1946 was ordained. Later that year, he won a fellowship from the World Council of Churches to study theology at Boston University in the United States. His studies were interrupted in 1948 when he was called home to become a bishop, one of four in Cyprus. In 1950, the Archbishop died and Makarios was chosen to replace him.

As Archbishop, Makarios also assumed the role of Ethnarch. Traditionally, the Ottoman Turks had ruled their Christian subjects in Cyprus through the Archbishop. Archbishops continued to play this role under British rule. Makarios pledged to support the result of a plebiscite held earlier that year in which 95 percent of Greek Cypriots had voted for union with Greece. The British urged the Cypriots to accept independence while the Turkish Cypriots insisted upon partition of the island into two separate entities. Makarios fought for *enosis* for the next 10 years. He visited the United Nations, attended the Bandung conference of non-aligned nations in 1955, and persuaded the Greek government to support him. Meanwhile the EOKA, a terrorist group under the leadership of a Cyprus-born Greek general, George Grivas, conducted a reign of terror designed to drive out the British and effect *enosis*. The British suspected Makarios of cooperating with EOKA, and exiled him in 1956. In 1959, Makarios reluctantly agreed to independence under a constitution guaranteeing political rights to Turkish as well as to Greek Cypriots.

Independence came in August, 1960. Makarios was elected the new nation's first president. But the constitution failed almost immediately. The

Greek Cypriots accused the Turks of obstructionism, while the Turkish Cypriots accused the Greeks of prejudice and injustice. Fighting broke out. Makarios called upon General Grivas to return to Cyprus with Greek officers to lead the Cypriot National Guard. The Turks then withdrew into enclaves to protect themselves. A threatened Turkish invasion to help them was only averted when the United Nations intervened in 1965.

overthrow Makarios. Grivas died in early 1974. Makarios moved against the new EOKA. He also asked the Greek government to withdraw all Greek officers from the Cypriot National Guard. The Greek officers staged a coup against Makarios instead. He just managed to escape with his life, and with British help fled to Malta. The Turkish army then invaded the island, and took control of the northern 40 percent of its territory. About 180,000 Greek Cypriots were sent south as refugees. The invasion toppled both the Greek government and the new Cypriot government. Makarios returned to the island proclaiming "a long struggle" to oust the Turks and regain Greek lands. But the Turks would not be budged. Talks began but made little progress. The Turkish Cypriots wanted partition with a weak central government while the Greek Cypriots said they would only accept partition if it were accompanied by a strong, Greek-controlled central government. The strain of the coup, invasion, occupation, and stalled negotiations proved too much for Makarios. After two heart attacks, he died in 1977.

Makarios' death left Cyprus a rudderless ship in a storm. Some felt his removal from the scene might make resolution of the conflict between Cypriot Greeks and Turks easier. Others felt Makarios had been the only one strong enough

Below: Turkish troops patrolling the Mediterranean. The Turkish army invaded Cyprus in 1974 after an unsuccessful attempt at a coup organized by the Greek military junta.

In the mid-1960s, Makarios gave up *enosis* at least as an immediate goal. But a military junta, which took power in Greece in 1967, opposed him and declared its strong support for union of the two countries. When Makarios traveled to Moscow to order arms for his security forces, the strongly anti-communist Greek junta sent Grivas back to Cyprus to form a new EOKA to

Above right: a boat marina in Cyprus. Tourism is important to the Island's economy. Since 1974, the most profitable tourist regions – notably Famagusta – have been occupied by Turkish troops.

to gain and enforce a settlement, and that without him, the island faced a bleak future. But the Greek Cypriots found a temporary solution themselves. After a period of anger and mourning, they settled down to a new life in their half of the island. With foreign aid and hard work, they were soon riding the crest of an economic boom.

Abdul Ibn Saud
1880 - 1953

King Ibn Saud of Saudi Arabia fought his way to power. The son of an exiled former ruler, he returned to his homeland in 1901. Riding hard across the desert, Saud scaled the walls of the capital, Riyadh, and crept across its rooftops until he reached the governor's palace. When the governor came out for his morning walk, Saud leapt down and killed him. His followers stormed the city gates and overwhelmed the local garrison. When the sand settled, Saud controlled the city.

Over the next 30 years, he went on to win control of all central Arabia. He unified it under his rule, and renamed his kingdom Saudi Arabia. Later, he permitted exploration for oil. The resulting flood of oil revenue made him rich, but it also undermined the simple strict way of life

he believed in and was Islamic law.

In his drive to win control over the tribal people of Arabia, Saud fought under the banner of Wahabism, a strict, puritanical strain of Islam which his family had traditionally supported. Firing his followers with religious zeal, he sent them out to conquer believers and non-believers alike and bring them under his control. By the start of World War I in 1914, Saud controlled all

of the Arabian peninsula except a few small kingdoms in the south and the Hejaz – a region along the Red Sea which included the two holy cities of Mecca and Medina. It was ruled by Hussein Ibn Ali as part of the Ottoman empire.

During the war, Britain made alliances with both Hussein and Saud and paid them subsidies, but Saud sat on the sidelines while Hussein and his sons, with the aid of T E Lawrence of Arabia, led an Arab rebellion

Above: an oil rig in the Eastern Province of Saudi Arabia. The vast income from oil has transformed the country, provided it with some of the most modern facilities in the world. Ibn Saud proved a shrewd negotiator with the oil companies.

against the Ottoman Turks. After World War I, Hussein's son Abdullah became Emir of Transjordan and his son Faisal, King of Iraq. Both regions had been recovered from Turkish rule during the war and placed under British supervision on a mandate from the League of Nations. Saud, fearing encirclement by the Hussein family, unleashed his fanatical followers against the Hejaz while cabling Britain that they were acting against his orders. They defeated Hussein, sent him into exile, and brought the Hejaz under Saud's control. Then they turned to Iraq. When they refused to obey Saud's orders to stop fighting, he defeated them in the Battle of Sibilla in 1929.

With control of virtually all his family's ancestral lands, Saud concentrated on governing rather than fighting. He put his eldest son, Saud, in charge of the Nejd region around Riyadh and

Below: Bedouin tribesmen tend their flock. The Bedouin's primitive nomadic way of life is under threat from Saudi Arabia's rapid technological advance. Saudi Arabia has moved from being a backward feudal land to a sophisticated oil economy in only 30 years.

During his constant round of visits to all parts of his kingdom, Saud lived in a four-room silk-lined tent. Seated on luxurious cushions covered with oriental carpets, Saud sat surrounded by bodyguards armed with gold and silver daggers. He met local leaders and entertained visitors at lavish feasts which included whole roasted sheep or camels on the menu.

In the 1930s, Saud granted oil concessions to an American firm. Oil was discovered in vast quantities. But World War II intervened before it could be fully exploited. Officially neutral during the war, Saud provided a channel of communication between the Allies and Axis (Germany and Italy) powers. Following the end of hostilities oil revenue began to pour in. Under the highly favorable agreements Saud negotiated his oil income soared from about $60,000,000 in 1950 to $200,000,000 in 1952. The king spent a large part of the money on himself and his large family (approximately 140 children) and handed out vast sums to his subjects. He also drew up plans to build roads, railroads, ports, airfields, irrigation systems, schools, and hospitals.

The money provided many material benefits for the king and his people, but it also brought all the problems of sudden modernization and contact with alien ideas to a simple desert people. By the time of his death, Saud was said to be disheartened and confused to see so much

made his second son, Faisal administrator of the Hejaz as well as foreign minister. In traditional Arab fashion, Saud traveled his kingdom, visiting each area, listening to problems, judging crimes, and offering help. He persuaded many Bedouin nomads to settle down around wells and put a stop to the ancient practice of robbing pilgrims on their way to Mecca by making the crime punishable by the loss of a hand.

Above: the Saudi Arabian capital of Riyadh, indistinguishable from a prosperous western city.

Above right: a Saudi worker operates a keyboard on a computer terminal. Advanced technology and increasing westernization clashes head on with Saudi Arabia's rigid Islamic religious and legal code.

of what he believed in being swept away on a tide of oil. His sons, who succeeded him, inherited the problem. They looked for a middle road between the old way of life and the conveniences of the modern world. Saudi Arabia remains one of the richest of the Arab oil states, and continues to cling to the traditional and puritanical ideas around which Ibn Saud built the country. An anachronism in the modern world.

The Perons
Juan 1895-1974   Eva 1919-1952
Isabel born 1931

Juan Domingo Peron was elected president of Argentina after his beautiful mistress, actress Eva Duarte, organized a mass workers' demonstration in October, 1946 to demand his release from jail. The workers came to be known as "Peronistas." They kept him in office from 1947 to 1956, and returned him to the presidency again in 1973. With their support, he became one of the most remarkable populist and nationalist leaders in South American history.

Peron won the enthusiastic and loyal support of Argentina's workers while he was minister of labor, a post he chose after he and other army officers seized power in 1943. To win confidence for the new military government, Peron lavished benefits upon urban and rural labor. He raised wages, lengthened vacations, and provided retirement benefits and severance pay. As his popularity increased, he took on additional offices, minister of war and vice president. But some of his conservative military colleagues thought he was going too far. They removed him from office and sent him to jail in 1946.

Peron married "Evita" a few days after his release from prison. They governed jointly when he became president. Juan continued to improve the workers' lot. He also tried to reshape his country along nationalist lines. Argentina was a rich country compared to the rest of South

Above: Juan Domingo Peron. As populist dictator of Argentina he enjoyed enormous popularity among the Argentinian working class.

Right: the social conditions of the working class in Argentina was, and still is, appalling. Thousands of Buenos Aires workers live in filthy tenements like the one occupied by these dock workers.

Far right: General Jorge Videla (center) is sworn in as president of Argentina on March 29 1976. He and his junta have established a brutal anti-working class regime in Argentina.

America, and was populated mainly by Europeans. Since independence from Spain in 1916 it had been governed by a succession of strong, conservative governments. The economy had been largely agricultural until the 20th century. Large foreign investments brought industrial growth, and created a prosperous middle class propped up by a poor and unprotected labor force. Peron nationalized the British-owned railroads and some other public utilities. He speeded up industrialization to cut unemployment. Peron also attempted to make Argentina the leading political, financial, and military power in South America.

Peron could not tolerate opposition. He tried to ensure the success of his policies by muzzling criticism. He controlled the press, threw troublesome opponents in jail or exiled them, gerrymandered election districts to reduce the opposition's representation in Congress, and tried to force all interest groups including labor into government dominated organizations.

Eva made herself champion not only of labor but also of women, and especially of the poor. She held no official position, but dominated the ministries of health and labor. She established and ran a vast charitable organization called the "Eva Peron Social Aid Foundation" which handed out money to the needy. Eva visited hospitals and schools and electrified mass audiences with impassioned speeches. Her followers, called "descamisados" (shirtless ones) adored her. But the army distrusted her, and refused to permit her to run as vice-president to

leaders on the one hand, and a new left-wing revolutionary group on the other. Economic growth was nil and inflation was eating away wage increases and benefits. Political factions of both right and left were resorting to killing and kidnapping to try to defeat each other and win power.

Peron died less than a year after his return to power, leaving Isabel in charge. But Isabel was far from the strong and popular leader Eva had

her husband in the 1951 elections. Eva died of cancer in July, 1952.

After Eva's death, Juan cut back on help to the workers in an effort to stem inflation. But economic problems worsened and opposition grew. In September 1955, public discontent over Peron's opposition to the Roman Catholic Church and over inflation, corruption, and his demagoguery led to a military-civilian coup. Peron fled to Paraguay, Venezuela, Panama, and the Dominican Republic. He finally settled in a fashionable suburb of Madrid in Spain. Peron was vilified in Argentina. Peronism as a political movement was outlawed.

But Peron's political career was not over. In Spain, he married Isabel (Maria Estella Martinez), an Argentine dancer. He busied himself with writing, interviews, and taping messages for Peronistas in Argentina. They did not forget him. As military and civilian governments came and went in Argentina, the Peronistas remained aloof, uncommitted, and troublesome. Their power increased in the late 1960s and early 1970s as Argentina's economic problems grew worse and worse. Finally, the Argentine government, under General Alejandro Lanusse, decided to permit the Peronistas to run candidates in the March 1973 election. It hoped to restore political stability by including the Peronistas in the government. Peronista candidates captured the presidency and a majority of seats in the legislature. Peron returned to Argentina later that year. In new elections he and his vice-presidential running mate, Isabel, won overwhelmingly.

But Peron was an old man, and Argentina had changed. The peronistas were split between a more conservative faction made up of union

Above: Eva Peron – the friend of "the shirtless ones" – at a meeting held to fix a new wage rate for Buenos Aires municipal workers. Also present are Soto (center) head of the municipal workers' union and de Benedetti, Secretary for Public Works in Buenos Aires.

Right: Isabel Peron makes a public speech. A weak ruler, she was overthrown in March 1976.

been. She relied heavily on her advisers, and clung to power until March, 1976 when she was finally overthrown by a military junta which extinguished all workers' rights.

Ho Chi-Minh
1892 - 1969

States had over 700,000 troops fighting on the side of South Vietnam. They also dropped more bombs on North Vietnam than had been dropped by all sides in the whole of World War II. But Ho never wavered in his resolve to drive out the foreigners and reunite his country. The South Vietnamese government finally collapsed in 1975, six years after Ho's death. The Americans pulled out, and Vietnam was reunited under a communist government.

Ho Chi Minh began fighting for Vietnamese independence when he was nine years old. He carried messages for rebels struggling to force French colonial rulers from his country. But he did not gain prominence until 45 years later when Vietnam was occupied by the Japanese during World War II. Ho had become a communist as well as a nationalist. Determined to drive out the Japanese and prevent the return of the French after the war, he hid out in northern mountains and organized Vietnamese resistance. In 1945, Ho and his Viet Minh forces entered Hanoi, proclaimed Vietnam an independent republic, and set up an elected government there with Ho at its head.

But the French refused to give up their colony. They fought the Viet Minh for eight years before they finally surrendered after the 55-day siege of Dienbienphu in 1954.

The Geneva agreements ending the war with the French divided Vietnam in two. Ho and his communists were to rule in the north. The south was to be administered by a western-inclined government. The Vietnamese people were to vote on a government for the whole country within two years.

The election never took place because the South Vietnamese government and its American allies feared that Ho would win. He went to war again. This time he fought indirectly. He supplied arms and expertise to rebels in South Vietnam trying to topple the government there. At the height of their involvement, the United

Above: Ho Chi-Minh pictured on a propaganda poster calls on his countrymen to unite to defeat the United States aggressors.

Right: a makeshift armaments factory. Viet Cong boys and girls prepare ammunition for the liberation forces on March 1 1966.

Ho's struggle to free Vietnam of foreign rule stemmed from his belief that imperialism was a form of racism. He saw it as subjugation of non-white people by whites. He opposed it all over the world, not only in Vietnam. This conviction made him unpopular with the French authorities in Vietnam when he was young. He left for Europe in 1912, paying his way by working as a galley hand on a French steamer.

Ho visited Africa and America and lived for a time in London before settling in Paris in 1917. There he paid his way with odd jobs while he read, attended classes, met with other exiles from colonial territories, and tried to arouse western European opinion over the plight of colonial people. But he found little support for anti-colonialism except among socialists. He joined the French Socialist Party in 1919.

A year later, Ho became a founder-member of the French Communist Party when the Socialist Party split over the issue of colonialism. The left, anti-colonial wing formed the Communist Party.

The party sent Ho to Moscow to attend meetings in 1922 and 1923. He stayed on there for indoctrination and training in revolutionary techniques at the Toilers of the East University. In Moscow, Ho met Lenin, Trotsky, and Stalin.

He returned to Asia in 1925 in the service of two masters: international communism and anticolonialism. Ho was prepared to put his considerable talents to work for both. His gentle manner and sense of humor masked a shrewd and

calculating mind prepared to do whatever was necessary to achieve his goals. His love of mystery and frequent changes of name helped him cover his tracks and confuse the enemy.

The Russian government sent Ho to China ostensibly to serve as a translator at their consulate in Canton. Chiang Kai-shek and the nationalists then held power in China, but Chiang was on good terms with Mao's communists. Ho formed a Vietnamese Revolutionary Youth League, recruited young Vietnamese exiles in the area as members, and arranged to have Soviet instructors give them indoctrination and training. When Chiang broke with the communists in 1927, Ho fled to Moscow and then to Hong Kong. There he founded the Indochinese Communist Party in 1930.

For the next 10 years, Ho traveled Asia organizing revolutionary groups and coordinating their activities. When the Japanese conquered most of Asia in the early stages of World War II, he turned to southern China. There, on May 19,

Below: a United States Army tank in the Vietnamese jungle. All the United States firepower, napalm, defoliants and advanced technology failed to defeat the North Vietnamese liberation forces.

1941, Ho and his military aide, Nguyen Vo Giap, formed the Viet Minh, a nationalist organization led mainly by communists, to free Vietnam from foreign rule.

After more than 30 years in exile, Ho returned to Vietnam in December, 1944 to lead and inspire his people in what was to be the longest and costliest war of independence in Asia. Ho did not live to see the struggle end successfully. But his followers acknowledged their debt to him when they marched into Saigon, capital of South Vietnam, in 1975. One of their first acts was to rename the city. They called it Ho Chi Minh.

Mohammed Hatta
born 1902

Mohammed Hatta never wanted to take the leading role in Indonesia's fight for independence from the Netherlands. Known for his realism and administrative skills, this quiet man preferred to work behind the scenes while others enjoyed the limelight. But he is considered by many Dutch to have been the real power behind his country's nationalist movement. It was his organizational skill and persistence that finally persuaded the Dutch to give up the rich East Indies, and grant them independence as Indonesia.

Hatta first helped the nationalist cause while a student in the Netherlands. Born of an aristocratic family in Sumatra, he entered the University of Rotterdam in 1922. The economics courses he wanted were not offered at home. While earning two doctoral degrees there, he joined other East Indian students in the Indonesian Association, an organization dedicated to achieving Indonesian independence. Hatta edited the association's newspaper and served as its chairman from 1925 to 1930.

He went home in 1932 and joined forces with Sukarno, the founder of the Indonesian nationalist movement, and other nationalist leaders. With them, he began a campaign of open resistance to Dutch rule. Hatta's job was mainly

Right: Queen Juliana of the Netherlands attends a ceremony at the Hague to transfer sovereignty to Indonesia on December 27 1949. Mohammed Hatta is seated at Queen Juliana's left.

Far right: a street scene in the Indonesian capital of Jakarta.

propaganda. Within two years he had become a dangerous political agitator to the Dutch, and was jailed.

Hatta and other nationalist leaders remained in jail until 1942 when the Japanese invaded the East Indies, drove out the Dutch, and freed them. When the Japanese asked the nationalists to form a puppet government, Hatta and Sukarno agreed – apparently to protect other nationalists working underground for independence. Japan surrendered in August 1945. Sukarno and Hatta declared Indonesia independent. Their followers took over much of Java, Sumatra, and Madura before the Allies arrived to take control of the islands. The puppet government became the independent government of these areas which were combined and called the Republic of Indonesia.

With the end of World War II, the Dutch tried to retake power in the islands. But the nationalists were determined to hang on to what they held. For four years, the two sides fought, negotiated, agreed, and then fought again. Hatta played a leading role in the negotiations and the fighting. He also served as vice-president and later premier of the Republic's government. In December 1948, the Dutch bombed and invaded Jakarta, the Republic officials were captured. But Hatta still refused to agree to any settlement short of complete independence. Finally, in May 1949, the United Nations staged a roundtable conference at The Hague to end the struggle.

Hatta served as vice-chairman of the conference at The Hague. He insisted upon complete sovereignty for Indonesia including full control

Left: Mohammed Hatta pictured at his 70th birthday party on August 13 1972. President Sukarno presented him with the Star of the Indonesian Republic on the occasion.

was named premier and foreign minister.

Hatta's first job as premier was to help Sukarno lead the new nation through a difficult transition from the loose confederation formed before independence to a more strongly centralized state. Then, as vice president in the new government, he tackled the problem of reorganizing and developing the potentially rich economy. But by 1956 Hatta had become disillusioned with Sukarno's "guided democracy," in particular his opposition to the creation of Malaysia from areas formerly under British rule, and his anti-West stand. Hatta resigned and retired from political life.

Sukarno continued without Hatta. Under his rule Indonesia drifted away from democratic rule, and into economic chaos. Sukarno depended on the army and the nation's large Communist Party for support. When the Communists attacked the army in 1966, Sukarno fell between the two stools. The army under General Suharto suppressed the coup and went on to assume political power. Suharto set the restoration and development of the economy as one of his goals. Hatta briefly came out of retirement to help. By the 1970s conditions in Indonesia had improved, but many problems remained.

Sukarno, like so many successful nationalist leaders, found governing a new nation far more difficult than achieving its independence. He died in 1970 better known for his failures than his successes. But Hatta, who chose to play a less prominent role and resigned from government rather than compromise his principles, remains a national hero.

over finances; the Dutch finally agreed after 10 weeks argument. Indonesia officially gained independence from the Netherlands in December 1949. Sukarno became President and Hatta

Above: President Sukarno mourns at the graveside of slain general Ahmed Yani on October 18 1966.

Daniel Malan
1874 - 1959

Below: white supremacy in action. A sign bearing the legend "White Persons Only" warns the black man to stay off this beach. The black population has revolted against this naked racism on a number of occasions, and many people believe that it is only a matter of time before race war breaks out in South Africa. Meanwhile, western investment makes Apartheid possible.

Daniel Malan began his career as a minister in the Dutch Reformed Church. He spent ten years in relative obscurity preaching to his flock of Afrikaners in Transvaal and Cape Province in South Africa. Later, he entered politics, and as prime minister of South Africa, he secured passage of racial laws which established the legal framework of apartheid and white supremacy.

Apartheid, or separation of races, had been practiced in South Africa long before Malan took office. But under his leadership it became official government policy. Apartheid laws separated not only whites from blacks, but also blacks from other non-whites, and even blacks from other

blacks. Under Malan's laws, thousands of non-whites were forced out of their homes in the cities and moved out to townships from which they commuted to the jobs they continued to hold in the cities. They were barred from city streets at night, and had to carry passbooks to identify themselves. If found without them, they could be, and often were, arrested.

In a sense, apartheid was another in a long line of attempts by the Afrikaners of South Africa to maintain their separate identity and way of life. Descendants of early Dutch settlers in South Africa, they established prosperous

farms and vineyards on the Cape of Good Hope in the 17th and 18th centuries. They used slaves imported from east and west Africa as well as Malayans as laborers. To gain more land, they fought a long series of bloody wars with Africans of the Xhosa tribe in the southeastern part of the continent. In 1814, at the Congress of Vienna, the Afrikaner lands in South Africa were assigned to Great Britain as a colony. When British settlers arrived, they did not choose to adapt to

the Afrikaner way of thinking and living. After the British outlawed slavery in 1833, many Afrikaner farmers (Boers) moved inland to what is today Transvaal and the Orange Free State. They formed independent states and imported Indians as indentured laborers to work on their sugar plantations. But when diamonds and gold were discovered in Afrikaner territory, the British annexed one part of their land and tried to foment an uprising in another. Finally, the Boers declared war on the British in 1899 (the Boer War). But they lost, and in 1910 they and their lands were incorporated into the Union of South Africa, a British dominion.

Malan was born on a farm in the British-ruled Cape Colony at a time when many other Afrikaners lived in their own states in South Africa's interior. In his youth, he championed their struggles to maintain their independence. He became a life-long supporter of the Afrikaner language and way of life. After graduating from the University of Stellanbosch, he traveled to the Netherlands to pursue theological studies at the University of Utrecht. He returned just after the end of the Boer War to take up a career in the church.

At the beginning of World War I, when many Afrikaners were opposing the government's

Below: Jan Smuts, head of the United Party. Malan and Hertzog formed the Nationalist Party to oppose him.

decision to support the Allies, Malan left the ministry and became editor of a Capetown newspaper that backed the newly-formed Afrikaner Nationalist Party. He ran for Parliament as a Nationalist in 1918, and won. By 1924, he had proved to be an able politician and speaker. He was invited by the new Nationalist prime minister, James B M Hertzog, to join the cabinet as Minister of the Interior.

Malan remained in the cabinet until 1934

a policy of separate development in separate areas for different peoples. Each of the nine Bantu groups in the country was to become a separate nation with a separate homeland or Bantustan. Land in outlying areas, often unsuited for agriculture and undeveloped for any other type of economic activity, was allocated to the Bantustans. Most of the country including the cities and the gold and diamond mining regions were reserved for the white minority. In

when Hertzog merged the Nationalist Party with Jan C Smuts' South African Party to form the United Party. He refused to be part of the merger, and formed a new Purified Nationalist Party. This was to become the main opposition to the United Party government.

When World War II started, Smuts took over the leadership of the United Party after Hertzog opposed South African participation with the Allies. Hertzog and Malan then joined forces again to form a new Nationalist Party. The party, with Malan as its leader, took a stand in favor of apartheid, white supremacy, and the use of the Afrikaner language by high government officials. In 1948, the party won a majority of seats in Parliament. Malan became prime minister. The party increased its strength in the 1953 election. Malan resigned in 1954, but the party continues to hold power today.

The Nationalist prime ministers who followed Malan intensified apartheid. Under Henrik Verwoerd's government, apartheid evolved into

Above: a black shanty town outside Johannesburg. The Nationalist regime claims that the black population belong to various "independent" homelands, and are not citizens of South Africa at all. They are only in the country as migrant labor. Most of the blacks have lived in South Africa all their lives, and have never been near their alleged "homelands."

their homelands, blacks were supposed to have independence and freedom, even though their "nations" could hardly be anything but poverty-stricken. But in the white areas where many continued to work and live, the blacks were treated as aliens and subjected to severe restrictions.

Apartheid in South Africa has been condemned by nations and organizations around the world, as well as by protest movements within the country. As nearly all the rest of the African continent has come under black rule, South Africa has become increasingly isolated. Many believe that the policy followed by Daniel Malan and his Nationalist successors is not only unjust but also unrealistic in a world where different groups of people are learning to accept one another as equals and live together. But the Afrikaners still cling to apartheid as the right and best way for people in their country to live. Their attitude persists despite international pressure, and seems likely to provoke a racial war.

Antonio Salazar
1889 - 1970

Antonio Salazar tried to enter into the spirit of democratic government in Portugal as a young man. He gave up after one day. "The truth is that I am profoundly antiparliamentarian," he said. "I hate the speeches, . . . the flowery, meaningless interpolations, the way we waste passion, not around any great idea, but just around futilities, nothingness from the point of view of the national good." In the end, Salazar became a dictator and imposed his own austere, and highly moralistic ideas on the Portuguese people. Under his rule the people were denied civil rights, political freedom, and a free press. They also had the lowest income per head, and the highest illiteracy rate in Europe.

Salazar's ideas were formed during his early years in the church and in higher education. His peasant parents wanted a better life for their children. He was sent to literate neighbors for his early education and then attended a newly-built village school before qualifying for admission to

a Jesuit seminary at the age of 11. Graduating in 1908, Salazar took preliminary orders, and became prefect of students at the seminary's school. There he developed a liking for teaching. In 1910, he entered the University of Coimbra as a candidate for a degree in letters. He obtained a bachelor's degree in 1914, and joined the teaching staff at the university. But he continued studying and writing on economic subjects. By 1918, he had become a full professor and received a doctorate in law.

While Salazar continued his academic studies, Portugal was in the throes of political and economic upheaval. The king, Manuel II, was overthrown, and a republic was declared. A

Above: a parade held in the Colosseum in Lisbon to mark the reelection of President Carmona. A huge effigy of Carmona is being carried by his supporters. Salazar succeeded Carmona on the latter's death in 1951.

parliamentary government based on the British model was set up. But the government was weak and inefficient. Salazar came to believe it should be replaced with one based on principles set forth in the encyclical, *Rerum Novarum*, of Pope Leo XIII. To help put his views across, Salazar helped form the Portuguese Catholic Center Party. As its leader, he spoke and wrote widely. In 1921, Salazar was one of three party members to be elected to the Cortes (Parliament). He walked out in disgust after one debate and returned to his academic career.

The government was overthrown in a military coup in 1926. Generals Francisco Gonez da Costa and Antonio Carmona took power. They invited Salazar, now considered a leading young economist, to become finance minister. The capricious Salazar again resigned, this time after five days because he could not get his own way in attempting to straighten out the nation's economy. Later that year, General Carmona forced Gomes da Costa out of power, named himself premier and acting president, and again appointed Salazar finance minister – this time giving him full powers. Within a year, Salazar had balanced the budget and by 1932, had paid off Portugal's foreign debts.

In November of that year, Carmona, now the elected president, named Salazar premier. He set to work drafting a new constitution which was ratified in a plebiscite in 1933. Under the constitution, the president selected the premier, and the premier appointed a cabinet responsible only to him. The constitution also provided for a national assembly which was to represent national union, and a corporative chamber for the different interest groups such as labor and management. There were no political parties and the premier ruled by decree.

Carmona continued to be reelected as president until his death in 1951, and Salazar

remained his premier and finance minister. Salazar kept order with the aid of the army and the secret police. Unions and political parties were outlawed to prevent opposition groups from forming. For the benefit of rich and reactionary landowners and businessmen, he kept the masses poor and weak. "The Portuguese must be treated as children" he said. "Too much, too often would spoil them."

During the Spanish Civil War, Salazar sided with Franco against the republicans. The two men became friends. In World War II, he remained neutral, but he allowed the Allies to use bases in the Azores because of an old alliance between Portugal and Great Britain.

After the war, Britain and France gradually granted independence to their colonies, but Salazar clung to Portugal's empire in Asia and Africa. A guerrilla war for independence broke out in Angola in 1961. Salazar contained it with bombs and thousands of Portuguese troops. The cost in lives and money was enormous. Portugal could not accept African rule, he said, because it "could only lead to . . . the return to former states of backwardness that one might consider to have been surpassed."

In 1968, Salazar suffered a stroke and was replaced as premier by Marcello Caetano. But his doctors and associates decided against telling him of his loss of power. He died in 1970 at the age of 81 still believing he headed the Portuguese government.

Towards the end of his long rule, Salazar summed up his role in Portugal by saying: "Maybe my function has been to serve as a brake against too much acceleration." The description was apt for his death precipitated a rush of

Above: March 1976. Soldiers of the National Army of the People's Republic of Angola pictured on the occasion of the liberation of Huamba. When Portugal relinquished control of Angola after the revolution at home, the white supremacist regimes of Rhodesia and South Africa lost a valuable buffer.

change. All Portugal's African colonies gained independence while at home, civil liberties and political rights were restored, and a new democratic government established. But freedom led to political squabbles that undermined the government and held up economic development. The future remained uncertain.

Right: a calendar for the year 1975 entitled *Novo Portugal* (New Portugal) celebrates the overthrow of Salazar's successor Caetano in April 1974.

Jomo Kenyatta
c. 1889 - 1978

When he was a boy, Jomo Kenyatta rebelled against tribal life in his Kikuyu village near Mount Kenya. He ran away to take part in the glittering European life of Kenya's colonial rulers, the British. As a young man working in a lowly job for the British government, he rebelled again – this time against Britain's colonial rule in Kenya. He joined the nationalist movement and became the leader in a long struggle to win Kenya independence. When the country gained its freedom in 1963, Kenyatta gave up his rebelliousness. He became Kenya's first president and a father figure to the young nation.

Kenyatta was born shortly after the British arrived in East Africa but before white settlers had seized much rich tribal land for farming or affected the Africans' traditional ways. Like other boys of the Kikuyu tribe at that time, he learned tribal history and customs from his mother, while the skills of farming, herding, and hunting were instilled by the father. His first encounter with European ways apparently occurred while he was recovering from an operation in a British hospital. He was so fascinated by it that he later ran away from home to attend a mission school before going on to Nairobi to seek

his fortune. There he held a succession of minor jobs, ending as a water meter reader for the Nairobi local government.

Right: Kenyatta was a member of the Kikuyu tribe, who are mostly farming people. Picture shows typical Kikuyu farmland in the Ngong Hills.

Left: Jomo Kenyatta was leading figure in Kenya's struggle for independence from Britain. He became the first president of independent Kenya. In later life, Kenyatta was treated as a venerable elder statesman by Britain, although they had kept him in prison from 1953 to 1961.

During his early years in Nairobi, Kenyatta enjoyed city life and the material benefits his pay brought him. But he soon became interested in more serious matters. Other educated young Kikuyu in Nairobi, members of a discussion group called the East Africa Association (EAA), had begun to protest against the white-dominated government. In 1923, Kenyatta joined them secretly. As a government employee he was not allowed to take part in political activity.

The EAA disbanded in 1925, but its members founded a new and more overtly political organization, the Kikuyu Central Association (KCA). Kenyatta left his government job to become its full-time secretary and to found and edit its journal, *Maigivithania* (the Conciliator).

The KCA sent Kenyatta to London in 1929 to testify against a proposal to join the three British territories in East Africa – Kenya, Tanganyika, and Uganda – in a federation. White settlers in Kenya supported the idea because they thought it might bring them internal self-rule. But the Africans feared it would diminish or destroy any chance of African self-rule in Kenya. When the Colonial Secretary refused to meet Kenyatta, he made contact with other anti-colonial groups, visited Moscow, and wrote a letter published in the London *Times*. This spelt out KCA objectives and predicted trouble if they were ignored. The objectives consisted of recognition of African rights to the land, government-financed education, and African representation in the government.

Kenyatta returned to Kenya in 1930, but he was back in London the next year to renew his efforts to present the KCA's demands to the British government. This time he stayed for 15 years. While there, he studied anthropology at the London School of Economics and wrote a thesis which he later turned into a book called *Facing Mount Kenya*. The book described the Kikuyu culture with perception and pride and was one of the earliest analyses of an African

with responsibility for the Mau Mau. In a trial widely criticized as political, he was convicted and sentenced to seven years in prison followed by restriction to a remote area. But after the trial, the British government took the first steps to prepare Kenya for self-rule and independence. African participation in the government gradually increased until 1961 when a new party, the Kenya African National Union, campaigning on the slogan "Freedom and Kenyatta," won the

Right: two Mau Mau fighters under the command of Mau Mau leader Mwariama. Kenyatta offered generous amnesty terms to Mau Mau guerillas while he was prime minister during Kenya's transition period to full independence.

culture by an African. Kenyatta joined other African nationalists in discussions and plans and wrote radical pamphlets demanding complete self-rule. In 1945, he worked with Kwame Nkrumah of the Gold Coast (Ghana) and others to organize a Pan-African Congress in Manchester around the theme "Africa for the Africans."

Kenyatta's years in London isolated him from the usual splits and rivalries of the nationalist political groups at home. When he finally returned to Kenya in 1946, they chose him as their leader. As president of a newly formed intertribal political party, the Kenya Africa Union (KAU), Kenyatta built a mass movement based on three demands: the return of foreign-held land to Africans, the right to vote, and an end to racial discrimination.

Tension grew when British settlers refused to accede to these demands. In 1948 a terrorist organization, the Mau Mau, took shape and began to threaten and attack whites, especially the farmers in the rich highlands.

Kenyatta was arrested in 1952, and charged

largest number of seats in the Legislative Council, but refused to form a government without Kenyatta. Kenyatta was released in 1962, and Kenya moved rapidly to self-rule and then complete independence in December 1963. Kenyatta became prime minister. A year later, the nation became a republic with a strong one-party government, and with Kenyatta as president.

Under Kenyatta's leadership, Kenya became one of the most stable countries in Africa. Africans, Asians and those Europeans who remained lived in harmony despite a policy of gradual Africanization designed to bring Africans into positions of power and influence. Kenyatta kept tribal rivalries under control by including representatives of all tribes in his government. But many Kenyans felt less confident about the future. They believed that Kenya's success depended largely on Kenyatta and after 10 years of rule, "the grand old man" was over 80. He remained strong and active, but the day would come when Kenya would have to rule itself without him.

Mrs Bandaranaike
born 1916

the largely western-owned banks, insurance companies and tea, rubber, and cacao plantations.

In the 1956 general election, the SLFP allied itself with several left-wing parties and won. Mr Bandaranaike became prime minister and formed a government. But he made little progress in implementing his policies. Sri Lanka's large Tamil-speaking Hindu minority objected to his preferential treatment of the Singalese Buddhists. At the same time, the

Right: Mrs Bandaranaike's husband, the Oxford educated lawyer Solomon. While Solomon wielded political power Mrs Bandaranaike remained in the background. It was only after he was assassinated in 1959, that she was prevailed upon to enter active politics. Only a year later, she became the world's first prime minister.

Left: Mrs Bandaranaike arrives at 10 Downing Street for lunch with the British prime minister Mr Harold Wilson on 19 October 1964.

Below: detail from the dome of the Hindu temple at Kandy University, Sri Lanka.

Sirimavo Bandaranaike did not consider herself a revolutionary. Like most other women in Ceylon (now Sri Lanka), she married soon after she finished her education. She then settled down to manage a home, raise a family, and work as a volunteer in the community. Her husband, an Oxford-educated lawyer, followed a career in politics and eventually became prime minister. She remained quietly in the background. Even when he was assassinated and his supporters asked her to help them, she was reluctant. But when she did decide to fight elections she was so successful that her party won. In 1960, she became the world's first woman prime minister.

The party Mrs Bandaranaike led to victory, the Sri Lanka Freedom Party (SLFP), had been founded by her husband in 1951 in opposition to the moderate, pro-western United National Party (UNP) that had governed the country since independence from Britain in 1948. The SLFP was a nationalist party. Its main policies were to remain neutral in world affairs, to replace English with Singalese as the nation's official language, to increase the influence of the Buddhist religion and culture, and to nationalize

lower house of the legislature herself. She was appointed to the upper house which named her prime minister.

As head of the government, Bandaranaike pursued the nationalist and socialist policies formulated by her husband. In January 1961, her government made Singalese the country's official language. When the Tamils rioted in protest, she banned their separatist political party. The government nationalized a number of western-owned businesses, and moved to take over state-aided religious schools. Bandaranaike's radical policies and the country's continuing economic problems contributed to her party's defeat in 1965. The UNP returned but also failed to put the economy right. In 1970 the SLFP and its leftist allies were voted back into power and Bandaranaike again became prime minister.

During her second term in office, Bandaranaike carried out a pledge to institute a new constitution. This made the country a republic and changed its name from Ceylon to Sri Lanka. She also introduced such welfare benefits as rice subsidies. But her reforms did not satisfy the far left. In 1971, the Maoist Popular Liberation Front led a peasant uprising aimed at overthrowing the government. Government forces defeated the rebels after seven weeks of bloody fighting and heavy loss of life. The state of emergency declared during the uprising persisted until 1977, just before campaigning began for the 1977 general election.

In the 1977 campaign, the UNP blamed Bandaranaike for the country's 20 percent unemployment rate and growing inflation. It also accused her of corruption. They adopted a new economic policy which they called democratic socialism. The election gave the UNP 112 seats in the legislature to only eight for the SLFP.

country faced serious economic problems. The population was growing rapidly and the need to import food was combined with falling earnings from tea, rubber, and cacao.

After Mr Bandaranaike was shot and killed by a disgruntled Buddhist priest in 1959, the party talked his wife into running for his seat in the legislature. But before the by-election could be held, the legislature was dissolved and a new general election called in 1960. Mrs Bandaranaike toured the country campaigning for SLFP candidates. Largely through her efforts the party won 46 out of a total of 151 seats. But the UNP won 50 seats, and its leader formed a minority government. It fell within weeks and a new election was called. In this election Mrs Bandaranaike formed a coallition with leftist groups to make victory more certain. The SLFP alone won 75 seats giving it a majority in the legislature even without its allies' support. Mrs Bandaranaike had not run for a seat in the

Above: a market scene in the Sri Lankan capital of Colombo. Under Mrs Bandaranaike's rule the Sri Lankan economy has expanded – even though it is still a poor country.

Above right: a Sri Lankan tea picker at work. Tea is vital to the economy. Tea workers are poorly paid and housed, and there have been complaints that large British companies have been exploiting their tea workers.

Konrad Adenauer
1876 - 1967

"The Old Man" Konrad Adenauer was 73 when he became West German chancellor in 1949. He held the post until he was 87. But despite his age, he succeeded in rebuilding western Germany from the smoking ruin of the end of World War II to a sovereign nation, politically and economically strong, and respected as an important member of the western community.

For Adenauer, the post-war chancellorship was a second career after a long earlier one spent in local government in his home town of Cologne. After studying law and political science at the Universities of Freiburg, Munich, and Bonn, he joined a law firm headed by the leader of the Catholic Center Party in the Cologne City Council. The party had been formed by Catholics to protect their interests against the

Above: the shattered remains of the Hohenzollern bridge with the shell of Cologne Cathedral in the background. The climax of World War II reduced much of Germany to rubble. The first task that Adenauer and his ministers faced was to provide the conditions necessary for the rebuilding of West Germany.

Protestants in the government. Adenauer, a devout Catholic, became an active member. With the help of his employer, he secured a position as an administrative assistant to the chief mayor in 1906. Six years later, he was elected deputy chief mayor. Exempted from service in World War I by his civic position, he ran for and was elected chief mayor for a 12-year term in 1917.

As mayor, Adenauer presided over a period of unprecedented growth in the city and its surroundings. Under his administration its boundaries were extended, new suburbs built, the first autobahn laid out, the harbor rebuilt, and industry expanded. Reelected in 1929, he

Right: Konrad Adenauer signs the West German constitution in Bonn on May 23 1949.

planned to continue his work. But he publicly opposed the Nazis and was removed from office in 1933.

Adenauer spent much of the period of Hitler's rule quietly at home in Rhondorf near Cologne working in his rose garden. But the Nazis continued to suspect him. He once avoided arrest by taking a trip to Switzerland. Another time, he was arrested and released. In 1944, he narrowly escaped death when he was sent to a detention camp along with other suspects after Claus von Stauffenberg's attempt on Hitler's life in July. Moments before he was to be sent to an extermination camp, Adenauer was admitted to a hospital with a faked heart attack. He escaped, was caught by the Gestapo, and imprisoned. But the Allies were closing in by now. Adenauer's son, an army officer, intervened and secured his release. The Allies entered Cologne in March, 1945, and the American Commander asked Adenauer to return to his post as chief mayor. But the city was transferred to the British occupation zone, and the British dismissed him.

Adenauer's dismissal stung him, but it also released him to take part in national politics. He formed a new political party, the Christian Democratic Union (CDU) – a Christian party including both Catholics and Protestants dedicated to individuality protected by the rule of law. Its major opponent was the Social Democratic party. Adenauer's attitude was that socialism promoted egalitarianism which in turn prevented natural leaders from emerging.

The CDU gradually gained strength in local

elections. Adenauer became a well-known figure. The three western occupying powers, Britain, France and the United States, called a Parliamentary Council to draw up a provisional constitution in preparation for self-rule. Adenauer was included as a member and through adroit maneuvering became its chairman. The constitution was accepted in 1949. When elections were held for parliament later that year, the CDU won by a narrow margin, and Adenauer became chancellor.

From the start, Adenauer ruled with absolute confidence in himself and in his conviction that West Germany must be restored to an important place in a strong united western Europe. Within months he had persuaded the Allies to relax the strict occupation laws and to stop dismantling German factories. The occupation had ended by 1952 and West Germany had become a member of the western alliance. In 1955, West Germany regained its sovereignty and joined NATO, and in 1957, it signed the Treaty of Rome making it a member of the European Economic Community.

Adenauer was frequently criticized for not making a stronger effort to secure reunification of Germany. A bitter foe of the Soviet Union, he believed the Russians would demand German neutrality as the price. As he saw it, the western alliance backed by military strength was the deterrent holding back Soviet expansion in Europe, and he wanted Germany to be part of that deterrent for its own protection. He visited Moscow in 1952, but his talks there failed, and he did not try again.

Another 1952 meeting, with Nahum Goldmann, President of the World Zionist Organization, proved far more successful. Adopting a policy of atonement and conciliation, Adenauer agreed to pay reparations to Israel and to the world Jewish community for Nazi crimes against them. His action won wide acclaim and did more than anything else to restore confidence in the good will of the German people.

In another emotional and important reconciliation, Adenauer visited Paris in 1961 where he received a warm welcome from Germany's old adversary, General Charles de Gaulle. When de Gaulle returned the visit, he spoke in German and was greeted by huge cheering crowds.

Conciliation with de Gaulle was a fitting climax to Adenauer's long term as chancellor. Afterwards, he came under increasing pressure from other CDU leaders to resign. Many of his associates and others believed he had been in office too long – that advancing age had brought an inflexibility that shut out new ideas and blocked progress. In 1963, he gave in and resigned, but he continued as head of the party until 1966.

Below: Adenauer with the French president Charles De Gaulle. One of the lasting achievements of the Adenauer era was the friendship forged between France and Western Germany in the face of all that had gone before.

Martin Luther King
1929 - 1968

Rosa Parks, a black seamstress, boarded a bus in Montgomery, Alabama, in 1955 after an exhausting day of shopping. She sank into an empty seat for the ride home. When a white woman asked her to move, she refused. Her refusal and subsequent arrest sparked off a black bus boycott that ended segregation on Montgomery buses and launched its leader, a young minister named Martin Luther King, on a crusade to end segregation and ensure civil rights for blacks all over the United States. With non-violent protests and moving words, King won wide support among both blacks and whites. He was largely responsible for the passage of laws outlawing discrimination against blacks. He had embarked on a new campaign against economic and social inequality when he was shot dead at the age of 39.

Black leaders in Montgomery chose King to

Above: an anti-segregation demonstration in Birmingham Alabama on December 28 1956. Negro integration leader Rev R L Shuttlesworth sits next to the window with a young Negress sitting next to him. Even though the mayor of Birmingham had threatened that anyone breaking the city's segregation laws would be arrested, Negroes led by Shuttlesworth boarded the bus and sat with the white passengers without incident. Martin Luther King's long fight for racial equality began in 1955, when a black seamstress, Rosa Parks, was arrested when she refused to move for a white passenger on a segregated bus in Montgomery Alabama.

lead the bus boycott there partly because he was exceptionally well-qualified to get a job somewhere else if the boycott failed. The son of a well-known minister in Atlanta Georgia, King entered Morehouse College at the age of 15. He graduated at 19 with a BA. In his third year at Morehouse, King decided to become a minister

and was ordained in 1947. From Morehouse, he went on to Crozier Theological Seminary. There he was elected president of the student body, achieved the highest grades in his class, and won a scholarship for further education. He chose to go to Boston University and was awarded a doctorate of philosophy there in 1955 before returning to the South and becoming a pastor at the Dexter Avenue Church in Montgomery.

When the Montgomery bus boycott ended in victory, King and other black leaders vowed to fight discrimination in all its forms across the United States. In January 1957, they formed the Southern Christian Leadership Conference (SCLC) and named King as its president. SCLC arranged mass meetings in many southern cities to demand black voting rights. King traveled and spoke widely demanding justice for blacks. He visited Ghana in 1959, and went on to India at the invitation of Prime Minister Jawaharlal Nehru. There he met with some of Gandhi's followers and discussed his teaching on passive resistance.

Returning home, King found that many young blacks in the southern states were staging peaceful protests against segregation despite violent white opposition. He decided the time was right for a full-scale campaign for civil rights. To give himself more time and freedom to lead it, he resigned from his position in Montgomery, and moved to Atlanta to become an associate pastor in his father's church. From there, he launched the first and most successful phase of his civil rights campaign.

The campaign included sit-ins at segregated lunch counters by young blacks and increasing numbers of whites, protest marches, and later freedom rides. King often led these protests. Along with his followers, he was attacked and jailed. But the demonstrators' courage and control and their willingness to go peacefully to jail earned them admiration, and increasing support for their goals. The tide turned decisively in their favor when news photographs appeared all over the United States and the world showing police in Birmingham, Alabama using police dogs and fire hoses against civil rights marchers, including many children.

In 1963, King staged a march on Washington. More than 200,000 people, black and white, took part. The march ended with a speech by King in front of the Lincoln Memorial: "I have a dream that one day this nation will rise up and live out the true meaning of its creed; 'We hold these truths to be self-evident that all men are created equal'." The following year the Civil Rights Act of 1964 was passed. It empowered the government to enforce desegregation in employment and in public facilities. The Voting Rights Act of 1965 and the Civil Rights Act of 1968 followed. This last banned discrimination in housing and real estate.

But these new laws did not satisfy young blacks suffering from economic and social discrimination in northern cities. They accused King of being too cautious and humble and adopted the slogan "Black Power." To meet this new challenge, King moved his crusade north to Chicago, and led marches and demonstrations against discrimination there. When this achieved few visible results, he widened his campaign to include attacks on the Vietnam War and on poverty which he insisted was the root cause of the misery of many people including blacks. He was planning a poor people's march on Washington when he was called away to help striking sanitation workers in Memphis, Tennessee. At a rally of 2000 supporters there, he spoke prophetically and uncharacteristically: "I have been to the mountaintop and I've looked over and I've seen the promised land. I may not get there with you, but I want you to know tonight that we as a people will. . . ." The next day, he was shot dead by James Earl Ray as he stood on a balcony at his motel.

As King predicted, the civil rights movement continued without him. Through it many blacks gradually gained a sense of dignity, strength, and unity. But a lot of the real work of securing equality for blacks had already been done while King was alive through the passage of the civil rights laws of the 1960s. Though these were often not enforced with much vigor, they at least provided blacks with equal opportunity in education and employment, and gave them some of the tools they needed to fight discrimination. King deserves a large share of the credit for these laws. It was he who aroused most blacks and

Above: the massive civil rights march on Washington, August 30 1963, photographed from the top of the Lincoln Memorial.

encouraged them to fight for the human rights that had been so long denied them. With his persuasive oratory King gave the cause of racial equality a new dignity. He also enlightened many whites about inequality and persuaded them to support legislation to end it. But blacks are still fighting the racism endemic in white society.

293

Willi Brandt
born 1913

Willy Brandt first gained a reputation on the international stage by opposing the physical partition of Berlin. In 1961 the East German government built a wall across Berlin. Brandt, West Berlin's mayor, saw the wall as part of a larger effort to divide East and West Germany permanently, and he demanded that it be removed. The East Germans refused. Brandt led West Berliners in a stubborn and successful fight to survive and prosper as part of West Germany, even though the city was 100 miles east of the border with West Germany.

Less than 10 years later, as West Germany's foreign minister, Brandt took on a larger barrier – the Iron Curtain. He knocked much of it down. By improving West Germany's relations with Eastern Europe, recognizing existing boundaries including the one between East and West Germany, and establishing trade, he greatly reduced East–West tension. Brandt's "Ostpolitik" helped him to be elected West Germany's first Socialist Chancellor in 1969, and win the Nobel Peace prize in 1971.

Brandt's dislike of isolationist politics stemmed from his strong belief in a united Europe. The illegitimate son of a shopgirl and an unknown father, he grew up in Lubeck under the influence of his maternal grandfather, who was a

Right: the divided and occupied post-World War II Berlin. "Europe cannot afford this Germany." Brandt's most significant political achievement was the easing of tension between East and West Germany, and the building of greater understanding with the Communist bloc.

truck driver and a socialist. With his grandfather's encouragement, Brandt joined the Social Democratic Party's youth movement and began writing articles for the party newspaper. These so impressed the editor that he persuaded party leaders to accept Brandt as a full member at 16, two years younger than the usual minimum age for entry. When the Nazis came to power a few years later, Brandt left the country to avoid arrest because of his party affiliation. He settled

in Norway and worked as a journalist, while also studying history and philosophy at Oslo University and promoting the anti-Fascist cause throughout Europe. The Nazis invaded Norway in 1940. Brandt fled to Sweden where he continued his by now highly successful journalistic career, and his work with underground movements in occupied Europe.

In 1947, Brandt gave up the Norwegian citizenship he had acquired in 1940 and his journalistic career to return to Germany and work with the Social Democrats to rebuild the country. Settling in Berlin, he was elected in 1949 as West Berlin's representative in the Bundestag, the lower house of the German legislature – a seat he held until 1957. He also sat in the Berlin legislature, and was its chairman from 1955 to 1957. When he headed off a mob of angry constituents marching towards East Berlin to protest at the Soviet invasion of Hungary in 1956, he became a hero to many relieved West Berliners. He was elected mayor of the city in 1957.

As Berlin's Mayor, Brandt became a leading

member of the German Social Democratic party. He played an important part in a meeting of party leaders in 1959. They changed the party's policies by eliminating all remnants of Marxism and adopting instead support for a free market economy and private property. Brandt became chairman of the party in 1964. In 1966, he led it into a "grand coalition" with the majority Christian Democrats and was named foreign minister. In the 1969 elections, the

Above: sudden death at the Berlin Wall. Peter Fechter was shot in the back as he tried to flee over the wall from East Berlin. Fechter was just a few yards short of West Berlin territory when the East German border guards opened fire. This young man is by no means the only East German citizen to die in the attempt to flee to the West.

Social Democrats, with the support of the smaller Free Democratic Party, won a majority of seats in the Bundestag. Brandt became Chancellor.

During his first term in the chancellorship, Brandt continued the drive for European unity he had begun as foreign minister. He supported application for Britain's admission into the European Economic Community, which had been vetoed by French president Charles de Gaulle, and signed the multi-lateral nuclear non-proliferation treaty. Negotiations with Eastern European countries led to a treaty normalizing relations with Poland, a non-aggression pact with the Soviet Union including West German recognition of controversial German borders established at the end of World War II. The Berlin Accords providing for free access between West Germany and West Berlin were also signed. Finally a treaty was concluded normalizing relations between East and West Germany but leaving open the door for possible reunification in the future.

In the 1972 elections, the Social Democrats

again joined with the Free Democrats and the two won a large majority of seats in the Bundestag. As Chancellor for a second term, Brandt continued his Ostpolitik. He signed economic agreements with the Soviet Union and Romania, and became the first German chancellor to visit Israel. But he concentrated most of his efforts on domestic problems such as tax reform. He accomplished little in the domestic sphere, however, because of bickering within the party and the coalition. In May 1974, in a dramatic midnight announcement, Brandt resigned from office because one of his aides was accused of being an East German spy. He was succeeded a few days later by Helmut Schmidt.

Brandt's resignation shook the nation. Many people thought he could have survived the spy incident and encouraged him to withdraw his resignation. But he refused. By persuading the two Germanies and their allies to accept the status quo, he had finally ended the cold war in Europe, reduced the chances of another war, and freed Europeans to tackle their economic and social problems.

Elizabeth II
born 1926

When Elizabeth II took the throne in 1952, she was hailed as Queen of Great Britain and Northern Ireland and of her other realms and territories and Head of the Commonwealth of Nations. At that time, the British crown's realms were sizeable while the Commonwealth consisted of only nine countries, most of them predominantly European in population. By the time Elizabeth celebrated her silver jubilee in 1977, her role had changed. Many lands that were once part of her realm had gained independence leaving her as queen of a much diminished empire. But most of these former colonies had chosen to join the Commonwealth swelling its ranks to more than 30 members, bringing in large numbers of Africans, Asians, West Indians and others.

Few could have foreseen that Elizabeth would preside over so drastic a change in world organization when she was born in London in 1926. She was not even expected to become Queen. Her father, the Duke of York, was a younger son of the then king, George V. The

King's elder son, later Edward VIII, was heir to the throne. Edward did become king in 1936 but he abdicated 11 months later in order to marry the American divorcee Mrs Wallis Simpson. The Duke of York came to the throne as King George VI. George's eldest daughter, Elizabeth, was now the heir presumptive.

Elizabeth and her younger sister, Margaret Rose, had been brought up, as many upper-class children were at that time, in a highly restrictive

Above: Commonwealth heads of government pose with Elizabeth II before a dinner party on June 8 1977. Elizabeth's reign witnessed a drastic change in Britain's role in the world. Its once mighty empire has become a loosely linked Commonwealth of independent states.

manner. They had few friends and had only governesses and tutors to educate them. After her father became king, Elizabeth was gradually introduced to and trained for her future role. She delivered her first radio address, a short talk to the children of the empire, in 1940 when she was 14.

In 1942, she was named an honorary colonel

Left: the famous portrait of Elizabeth II by Pietro Annigoni. It is housed in the National Portrait Gallery, London.

of the Grenadier Guards and presided at a review. She became a member of the Council of State in 1944. This acted for the king during his absences from the country. In 1947, Elizabeth embarked on a goodwill trip to Africa with her parents and sister, her first trip outside Britain. In South Africa, she addressed the empire by radio dedicating her life to "the service of the great imperial family to which we all belong." On another tour early in 1952, she visited Africa

Her rule was largely symbolic, and her duties consisted mostly of attending and participating in ceremonies, holding honorary positions in a variety of charitable, cultural and other organizations, entertaining heads of state, and traveling to all parts of the world.

Gradually, the queen and her family also came to symbolize traditional family life in Britain. Married in November 1947, while still a princess, to Philip Mountbatten, a distant

Above: Elizabeth II meets the people on a walk-about tour in New Zealand. Although the British royal family remains aloof from the ordinary people, efforts have been made to make them more accessible. There is little doubt that Elizabeth II is very popular personally, even with those who disapprove of a hereditary monarchy.

Left: the British royal family wave to the crowds from the balcony of Buckingham Palace during the 1977 Silver Jubilee celebrations.

cousin, in a splendid ceremony in Westminster Abbey, she gave birth to her first child and heir, Prince Charles, on November 14, 1948. Charles was followed by Princess Anne in 1950, Prince Andrew in 1960, and Prince Edward in 1964. All of the children attended schools rather than be educated at home. Each took on a share of the royal duties as they grew up.

Sending her children to school has been one of the concessions the queen had made to the changed world. Others have included an end to royal receptions for debutantes, a television film showing the royal family in their everyday lives, and "walkabouts" in which she and other members of the royal family shake hands and chat with members of the huge crowds that turn out to see them wherever they go.

Some Britons say these changes are insufficient. The queen and her family not only place too heavy a financial burden on Britain, but they represent and encourage the continuation of an outmoded class system rather than reflecting the broader British society and multi-racial Commonwealth the queen heads. But there is no doubt that most British people admire Elizabeth personally and support the monarchy.

again, and planned to go on to Australia and New Zealand. But she was called home when her father died on February 6. She was formally proclaimed Queen two days later.

As monarch, Elizabeth became head of the British government and the Church of England as well as Queen of the Empire, and Head of the Commonwealth. But she had little real power.

Dag Hammarskjold
1905 - 1961

Dag Hammarskjold's predecessor, Trygve Lie, called it the most impossible job in the world and resigned under pressure from the Soviet Union. Soviet pressure was even greater on Hammarskjold but he coolly hung on. Through skill and determination he became the most powerful and effective secretary-general the United Nations has had so far. Under Hammarskjold's leadership, the UN gained prestige and influence in settling international disputes. Its secretary-general was an independent mediator more interested in peace, justice, and stability than in the national interests of any one country.

Hammarskjold actively involved himself in disputes all over the world. In 1955, for example, he provided a channel of communication for two nations which had no diplomatic relations with each other, the United States and Communist China. Traveling to Peking, he negotiated the release of 15 American fliers imprisoned there.

In 1956, Hammarskjold served as a discreet and trusted consultant to all sides after Egypt's

Above: the United Nations funded World Health Organization finances agricultural schemes around the world. The Sapu rice project which introduced swamp rice into the Gambia has been a great success. The rice is a valuable cushion against famine, and saves the Gambia valuable foreign exchange.

Left: Dag Hammarskjold, by common consent the most effective secretary general of the United Nations so far.

Opposite top: symbols of three of the most important organizations to be spawned by the United Nations. Left, the High Commissioner for Refugees; center, Food and Agricultural Organization; right, World Health Organization.

nationalization of the Suez Canal led to invasion by Israel, Britain, and France. With United States and UN backing, he persuaded the invaders to withdraw, and arranged for a UN peacekeeping force to patrol areas Israel returned to Egypt.

Hammarskjold traveled through Africa in 1960 meeting nationalist leaders and gathering information for the UN about the economic needs and problems of new nations there. The following year, he sent a UN military force to restore order in the Republic of the Congo at the request of Congolese Premier Patrice Lumumba. Among the Congo's problems was the secession of Katanga Province. Hammarskjold was on his way to a meeting with Katanga's president Moise Tshombe when he was killed in a plane crash.

The crash shocked the world. It took the life of a man many had come to rely on to defuse world crises. The chances of finding a successor as well suited to the job by training seemed remote. A member of an aristocratic Swedish family with a long history of government service, Hammarskjold was trained in law, economics, and political science at Uppsala University where he received a BA, an MA, and a law degree. The University of Stockholm later awarded him a doctorate in political economics.

He served in the Bank of Sweden as Secretary and later as Chairman of the Board, as a financial advisor to the Swedish Cabinet, and as an Under Secretary at the Department of Finance. He joined the Foreign Office in 1946 as a financial expert. In 1949, he became Assistant Foreign Minister. Two years later, he entered the Cabinet as Deputy Foreign Minister. As a member of the Swedish Foreign Office, Hammarskjold represented his country at many international meetings and in negotiations with other countries. He soon earned a reputation as a skilled negotiator who could speak several languages and get along well with all kinds of people. In 1952, he served as vice-chairman of the Swedish delegation to the UN and the following year was named chairman. The UN Security Council chose him as a dark horse to replace Trygve Lie as secretary-general thinking he would iron out administrative problems in the Secretariat, while avoiding the controversy that had surrounded Lie. He was accepted overwhelmingly by the General Assembly in April,

1953, and became its most effective secretary-general.

Hammarskjold took the UN post as the conflict over Korea was dying down. During the relative quiet of the next few years, he concentrated on reorganizing and strengthening the UN staff while quietly building confidence in himself and in the organization he headed. A remote, but relaxed man, he impressed both staff and UN members with his interest, integrity, and ability. Gradually, more powerful members trusted him with policy decisions they formerly reserved for themselves, while weaker members increasingly sought his advice and aid in solving their problems.

A few people criticized his aloofness and unwillingness to delegate – they said he had grown over-confident – but most thought him a brilliant diplomat thoroughly dedicated to the task of keeping peace and bettering the lot of the poorer nations. Only the Soviet Union demanded that he be replaced. They resented his power and independence, accused him of being pro-West,

Above: Hammarskjold's successor as secretary general of the United Nations, U Thant of Burma.

Below: United Nations troops sent to keep the peace between the Greek and Turkish communities of Cyprus.

and demanded that a three-man *troika*, made up of representatives of the West, the Communist nations, and the Third World could take over.

With Hammarskjold's death, the Soviet Union dropped its demand for a *troika*, and U Thant of Burma was chosen as the new secretary-general. Thant continued to deploy troops to trouble spots such as Cyprus, but he never achieved as much personal prestige and power as Hammarskjold. The reason was partly that Thant acted less independently than his predecessor. More importantly, the UN itself changed, and this change affected the role of the secretary-general. New members, most of them Asian and African nations, swelled the organization's ranks in the 1960s and they soon could and did outvote the big three western powers and their allies in the General Assembly. The West, first blocked in the Security Council by the Soviet veto and then in the General Assembly by a Third World majority, turned away from the UN. In such disputes as the Arab-Israeli wars of 1967 and 1973 and the India-Pakistan war of 1971 they dealt directly with the belligerents rather than rely on the UN secretary general. By the 1970s, the UN was increasingly effective in dealing with Third World economic and social problems, but the peacekeeping function once carried out so effectively by Dag Hammarskjold seemed to have taken second place. The UN increasingly stands helplessly by as wars are waged and blood shed. At least Hammarskjold employed considerable moral force to try to stop the fighting.

Fidel Castro
born 1927

Fidel Castro first tried to reform Cuban society by constitutional means. A young lawyer and liberal, he joined a reform party and campaigned for election to Congress. But the election, set for June, 1952, was never held. Fulgencio Batista overthrew the government and established a dictatorship. From then on, Castro resolved to

fight for revolution with armed force. At first, he failed. But eventually, he and a few loyal supporters, including his younger brother Raul and Ernesto "Ché" Guevara, an Argentine physician, established a secure base in the Sierra Maestra Mountains. From there they waged an increasingly successful guerrilla war. Batista was put to flight, and on January 2 1959 a victorious Castro marched into Havana and began setting up a Marxist-Leninist government there, the first in the western hemisphere.

Castro aimed to free Cuba from economic domination by its giant neighbor to the north, the United States. American businessmen owned hundreds of millions of dollars worth of business in Cuba ranging from oil refineries to gambling casinos. Organized crime had a field day under Batista. By early 1961, Castro had seized virtually all American property, paying far less than it was worth in compensation.

The United States retaliated by imposing a trade embargo and cutting off diplomatic rela-

tions. The embargo badly strained Cuba's economy. It had depended almost entirely on the United States to buy its major export, sugar. But the Soviet Union offered to buy Cuba's sugar instead. The two nations signed a trade agreement and established diplomatic relations. Russia also agreed to supply economic and military aid.

The spectre of a Communist-bloc nation right on its doorstep alarmed the United States. In April 1961, a group of Cuban exiles, organized and trained by the American Central Intelligence Agency (CIA) invaded Cuba at the Bay of Pigs.

Right: Cuban poster of Ché Guevara. Guevara was Castro's closest friend and able lieutenant. He was killed in Bolivia in 1967, while leading guerrilla fighters against the military regime. This poster was issued in Cuba to mark the "Day of the Heroic Guerrilla, October 8."

Left: civilians caught in the cross-fire between troops supporting the dictator Batista, and guerrillas under Castro's command in Havana in 1959.

accomplished the first two by appropriating land and distributing it to the landless or turning it into state farms, and by nationalizing almost every business in the country. He also extended the education system to include all children and provided literacy classes for adults.

Castro solved the corruption problem by running the country himself almost single-handedly in a day-to-day, pragmatic, and highly personal style. A big, burly man wearing a beard and fatigues, he traveled constantly around his country, visiting new schools and hospitals, listening to problems, admitting mistakes, and exhorting the people to be patient. He loved crowds and thought nothing of speaking to mass rallies for five or six hours at a stretch. Castro claimed he was governing by mass approval. Most Cubans did approve of Castro, and what he was doing.

Many of the Cubans who thought differently had left Cuba. More than 500,000 – most of them formerly members of the middle class – fled taking with them much-needed skills. Thousands of other dissenters were jailed without trial. Some, including most of Batista's associates, were tried and executed by firing squad.

Despite Castro's constant attention and aid from the Soviet Union, Cuba's economy remained depressed throughout the 1960s. Attempts to increase sugar exports failed, partly because of bad weather and partly because of a shortage of labor to cut the cane. Smaller exports meant fewer imports of consumer goods. Rationing became the norm. But what wealth there was was fairly evenly distributed. For most Cubans, living, health, working, and educational standards were higher than they had ever been.

By the 1970s, Castro evidently felt his revolution was secure enough for him to let go some of the strings. The first Congress of the Cuban Communist Party, meeting in 1975, drafted a constitution providing for a degree of self-rule through locally-elected assemblies. The constitution was approved in a plebiscite in February, 1976.

With more free time on his hands, Castro also began to dabble in new foreign adventures. He had tried to export his revolution from the beginning by training guerrillas to foment uprisings all over Latin America. But he met with little success. When his friend, Ché Guevara, was killed in Bolivia in 1967 while trying to implement a master plan, Castro seemed to lose interest. In the mid-1970s, Castro turned to Africa. He sent Cuban troops to support a Marxist faction in a civil war in Angola. Troops, advisers, and technicians were also despatched to help Marxist groups in many other African countries.

Some people in non-Communist countries felt that a few thousand Cubans in Africa were a minor irritant. Others felt that the Cubans were there to help the Soviet Union establish a foothold in Africa.

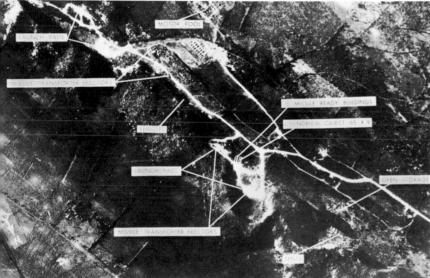

The invasion was a fiasco. President John F Kennedy had refused to allow air cover.

Relations between the United States and the island deteriorated still further when the Soviet Union installed long range missiles in Cuba. Kennedy demanded the removal of the missiles and threatened to attack the Soviet Union if they were used. Soviet leader Nikita Khruschev backed down. The missiles were shipped back to Russia. After that, the United States settled down to reluctant acceptance of Castro's rule in Cuba.

Castro had more in mind than an end to United States economic domination when he seized power in Cuba. He also wanted to free his country from the extremes of wealth and poverty, from discrimination based on color, and from corruption in the government. Castro largely

Above: a United States Air Force photograph reveals a base equipped with Russian medium range missiles on Cuban soil. The picture was taken during the Cuban crisis – October 24 1962.

Kwame Nkrumah
1909 - 1972

at Lincoln University and the University of Pennsylvania. He read the works of Karl Marx and Marcus Garvey, advocate of an autonomous black state in Africa free of white domination. Nkrumah also visited Harlem to see for himself the atrocious conditions in which New York urban blacks were forced to live. Nkrumah moved to London in 1945 and studied at the London School of Economics. While there, he served as vice-president of the West African

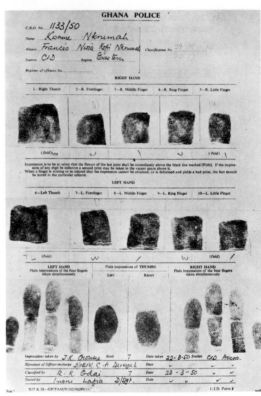

Kwame Nkrumah studied art at Lincoln University in Pennsylvania. In 1939, his classmates described this foreign student from the British colony of the Gold Coast, in these words: "Africa is the beloved of his dreams; philosopher, thinker, with forceful schemes." They must have watched with interest and some self-satisfaction as Nkrumah went on to become an influential theoretician for African nationalism, the leader of the successful independence movement through which the Gold Coast became the free nation of Ghana, and as Ghana's prime minister, the head of one of the first all-black governments on the continent. What they could not have foreseen was his downfall and exile after he had seized dictatorial power, made himself a cult figure, and led Ghana into corruption and debt.

Nkrumah's career began in a village in the Gold Coast where he attended local mission schools before entering Achimota College to be trained as a teacher. But teaching did not prove enough of a challenge, and in 1935, Nkrumah was persuaded by some local African nationalists to continue his studies in the United States. Over the next 10 years, he earned three degrees

Above: Nkrumah speaks at a party rally in 1957. He was an impassioned and effective orator.

Above right: a fingerprint record of Nkrumah issued after his fall from power. It was published in the "Police Gazette", Accra, Ghana by the National Central Bureau on May 20 1966.

Opposite top: considerable technical progress was achieved in Ghana during Nkrumah's rule. This bridge over the Volta river is one example. The massive Volta dam is another.

Opposite: the downfall of a dictator, a mutilated statue of Nkrumah lies decapitated on its side in the central police grounds, Accra, February 28 1966.

Students Union, and led "the Circle" – a group experimenting with the cell system of political organization. He also published his first book, *Toward Colonial Freedom*.

In 1947, after 12 years away, Nkrumah was called home to become the general secretary of the United Gold Coast Convention (UGCC), a nationalist party dedicated to winning self-government by constitutional means. Exploiting his skills as a speaker, learned from black preachers in the United States, he spoke all over the Gold Coast and attracted a wide following. But the impatient Nkrumah soon quarreled with the more conservative UGCC leaders. He formed the Convention People's Party (CPP) in 1949. Its goal was immediate self-government. In a program of "positive action" designed to cripple the "forces of imperialism," the CPP led disruptive strikes and boycotts all over the country. Nkrumah was arrested and sentenced to one years hard labor. Predictably, his imprisonment made him a hero and strengthened his cause.

Alarmed by the unrest in the Gold Coast and by the failure of the local colonial administration to concede to Africans any voice in the govern-

president and party leader for life. But few opposed him, as he used his power to develop the country with vast building programs including highways, schools, hospitals, a sports stadium, and the massive Volta Dam. At the same time he became a world figure writing books advocating African unity and traveling widely to such countries as the Soviet Union, China, and Egypt. In 1961, he conferred with United States President John F Kennedy and spoke at the United Nations. The following year, he attended the conference of non-aligned nations at Belgrade.

Ghana had accumulated debts of $600 million by the end of 1965. This was due partly to corruption in the government, the extravagant building program, and to a fall in the price of cacao, Ghana's main export. Nkrumah had dismissed the Supreme Court, rigged elections, and jailed thousands of opponents. Many Ghanaians had turned against him and several assassination attempts had been made. Nkrumah withdrew to his official residence which he turned into a fortress and became a "voice on the radio" to his people.

When Nkrumah left his fortress in February 1966 to travel to North Vietnam to discuss a Vietnamese peace plan with Ho Chi Minh, a group of army officers seized control of the government, outlawed CPP, and declared that "the myth of Kwame Nkrumah is ended forever." Nkrumah tried to rally support for a return to power but failed. He finally settled down to lonely exile in Guinea. He died of cancer in 1972, in Bucharest, Romania. Kwame Nkrumah had once only wished to see a free Ghana. He ended his career a suspicious and arrogant dictator.

ment, the British arranged for a new constitution to be written by Africans and scheduled elections for 1951. When the returns came in, the CPP had won 80 percent of the seats in the new Parliament. Nkrumah, was one of those elected, and was released from prison. He became prime minister in 1952, and appointed a cabinet including eight Africans. But the British retained three important portfolios, foreign affairs, defense, and finance. In 1954, Britain gave the Gold Coast full internal self-rule with the first all-African government in British colonial history. Three years later the Gold Coast gained full independence within the Commonwealth as Ghana. After a plebiscite in 1960, Ghana became a republic under a new constitution. Nkrumah as its president gained wide executive and legislative powers.

As early as 1958, when Nkrumah pushed through a law allowing security risks to be jailed without trial, some Ghanaians suspected that he would be an autocratic ruler. Their suspicions were confirmed in 1961 when he assumed absolute control over both the government and the CPP. In 1964, Ghana officially became a one-party state with Nkrumah as

Moise Tshombe
1919 - 1969

Moise Tshombe of the Congo (now Zaire) was never one to accept defeat. A failure in business when the Congo was a Belgian colony, he entered politics and by the time independence was declared in 1960, he headed Conakat, one of the new nation's leading political parties. When his party failed to win enough seats in the national assembly to make him premier, he declared his province, mineral-rich Katanga (now Shaba), independent and became its president. With the secession ended by United Nations troops, Tshombe became premier of the national government. Only when he began to have designs on the presidency was he ousted from power and sent into permanent exile.

Tshombe's appetite for power and prestige developed early in life. His father was one of the most successful African businessmen in the Congo. He owned several stores, a European hotel, and plantations in and around Elizabethville, capital of Katanga. He was also a leading member of the dominant Lunda tribe. Moise grew up basking in reflected glory. After attending Methodist missionary schools, he toured Europe before marrying the daughter of the Lunda tribal chief and joining his father in business. Upon his father's death, he inherited the business. But it failed under his direction and he had to declare bankruptcy three times.

In 1956, Tshombe became head of a Lunda

Right: a copper mine at Jadotville-Panda. The Jadotville area was the most important industrial complex in Katanga. Apart from copper mines, there are factories, pumping stations, and a hydro-electric power station. The region was vital if Katanga was to retain its independence.

tribal association. This had begun with Belgian encouragement as a discussion group and welfare organization, but became in 1959, as independence approached, a political party called Conakat. Conakat favored autonomy for Katanga in close association with Belgium. It had the support of the Lunda tribe, as well as most of the whites in the province.

As head of Conakat, Tshombe was called to Brussels in January 1960 along with other Congolese leaders to discuss plans for an independent Congo. Tshombe urged decentralization with strong provincial governments, but Patrice Lumumba, who favored strong central government, prevailed. In pre-independence elections in May, Lumumba's party won the largest number of seats in the national assembly and he became premier. But Tshombe's Conakat won a majority of seats in the Katanga provincial assembly. He was made provincial premier.

Independence on June 30 brought looting, murder, and rape. When the army mutinied against its Belgian officers, the central government was powerless to reestablish order. Tshombe took advantage of the chaos to lead Katanga into secession on July 11. He declared it an independent country and turned to Belgians to staff its government, run its businesses and services, and lead an army made up mostly of white mercenaries. In August, the Katanga assembly approved a new constitution. Tshombe was elected president. Only the Baluba tribe, traditional rivals of the Lunda in Katanga, opposed Tshombe. Their rebellion was brutally suppressed by Tshombe's army.

Left: Moise Tshombe at a press conference held to discuss the "destiny" of Katanga – July 25 1960. Katanga had been declared independent to weeks previously.

was released. He changed his mind as soon as he got home.

Katanga remained independent, with Tshombe as its president, for more than two years. United Nations troops sent to the Congo originally to reestablish order and evict Belgian troops there became increasingly involved in Katanga. In September 1961, they clashed with Tshombe's forces for the first time and suffered heavy losses before a temporary truce was declared. Not until January 1963 were they able to defeat Katanga forces and restore the province to the central government. Tshombe moved to Spain where he plotted a return to power.

As it turned out, Tshombe's plots were unnecessary. In June 1964, President Kasavubu invited him to return to the Congo to help fight an insurrection in the eastern part of the country. He was named premier and waged a successful struggle to hold together the country he had so recently tried to divide. Afterwards, in October 1965, when he began to vie with Kasavubu for the presidency, he was dismissed. But he refused to recognize Kasavubu until General Mobutu took power, and branded Tshombe a traitor. Back in Spain, he plotted again until he was kidnapped and delivered to Algeria. Algerian President Boumedienne re-

Below: Congolese president Joseph Kasavubu inspects an honor guard of Congolese army officers at Leopoldville airport after his return from the United Nations in New York – November 27 1961. Kasavubu is on the extreme left of the picture with Mobutu standing next to him.

In March 1961, Tshombe met with Congolese President Kasavubu and other Congolese leaders to discuss ways to counter an uprising led by followers of deposed premier Lumumba. He agreed to a confederation of autonomous states in the Congo. But he later walked out of a meeting in anger and was arrested and jailed. After promising to return Katanga to the Congo he

Left: mercenaries paid by the Congolese government during the war against Katanga go on patrol equipped with British mortars.

fused to turn him over to Mobutu and he remained there under house arrest until his death, apparently from natural causes, in June 1969.

In the years between 1960 when he led Katanga into secession and 1965 when he was ousted as Congolese premier, Tshombe often dominated the news and attracted worldwide attention. Some ridiculed his elegant dress and flamboyant manner, others raged against his use of white mercenaries to fight black Africans. Still others accused him of acting as a front man for European economic interests. Many blamed Tshombe for the chaos in the Congo after independence. In fact the causes of the trouble went much deeper. Tshombe simply took advantage of it to gain power and prestige. His death left behind little but dim memories of an African who stood briefly against the tide of black nationalism in Africa and was swept away by it.

Patrice Lumumba
1925 - 1961

The Belgians granted independence to the Congo (now Zaire) on June 30 1960. They held what had been planned as a dignified and friendly ceremony. King Baudouin I of the Belgians spoke and extended his good wishes to the new nation. But in his reply Congolese premier Patrice Lumumba threw away the script. "Slavery was imposed on us by force," he said. "We remember the blows we had to submit to morning, noon, and night because we were negroes." Lumumba's outburst embarrassed the Belgians. But many Africans were delighted at his honesty. When he was deposed and murdered by political opponents a few months later, they declared him an African hero. Lumumba said openly and fearlessly what many Africans felt. His death made him a martyr to the cause of African nationalism.

Lumumba had little time to transform his brave words into action in office. No sooner had independence been declared than Belgian administrators and professionals pulled out. The ill-prepared Congolese were left to run schools, hospitals, businesses, and government offices. Belgian military officers stayed, but their Congolese troops mutinied against them leaving the infant nation without a reliable army to keep order. Then the richest of the Congo's six provinces, Katanga (now Shaba), seceded under the leadership of Moise Tshombe. Belgium flew in troops, ostensibly to protect their remaining citizens. But most Belgian soldiers landed in

Above: independent Zaire under Mobutu. The banner advertises the virtues of the Daily Newspaper of Central Africa, and bears the legend "For a revolutionary country, a revolutionary press."

Left: Patrice Lumumba arrives in Brussels as president of the Congolese National Movement to participate in the conference on self-rule for the Congo – January 28 1960. He had just been released from Stanleyville prison where he had been incarcerated for allegedly fomenting revolt. At Brussels airport, Lumumba showed injuries to his wrists, suffered through ill-treatment at Stanleyville.

306

Katanga, and many Congolese suspected they had come to protect their interests in the province's copper mines.

Lumumba appealed to the United Nations for help in establishing order and evicting Belgian forces. They sent troops, but refused to help end Katanga's secession. When Lumumba asked the Soviet Union for planes to transport Congolese troops to Katanga to put down the rebellion, some western leaders accused him of being pro-Communist. Their fears were alleviated somewhat when he flew to the United Nations to ask for its support and acted with poise, confidence and good sense. But soon after his return home Lumumba reached deadlock in a power struggle with Congolese president, Joseph Kasavubu. Kasavubu removed the premier from office in September. Lumumba countered by firing Kasavubu from the presidency. But Army leader Joseph Mobutu sided with Kasavubu. Lumumba was jailed. He tried to escape, but was sent to hostile Katanga where he was murdered in February 1961.

Lumumba died at the age of 35 after a short and unconventional career. The son of an illiterate Batetelas tribesman, Lumumba was born in Katako Komba in northeastern Kasai province. He grew up hearing tales of Belgian atrocities against his tribe after it attempted to rebel. One of the punishments, dispersing the tribe across the Congo, later helped Lumumba by giving him a national power base which proved a distinct advantage in consolidating power.

Left: teaching in a makeshift classroom in Leopoldville in January 1959. The schools have just reopened after serious rioting in the city, during which at least 70 people were killed. Most of this school was completely destroyed, and this picture shows that the classrooms in use are only partially rebuilt.

Other Congolese leaders had to depend on tribes centered in one region. Lumumba attended both Protestant and Catholic mission schools before taking a job in the post office in Stanleyville (now Kisangi) at the age of 19. In his spare time, he wrote essays and poems for local publications and took part in the activities of a number of organizations including a union of government employees. He applied to enter the first Congolese university, which opened in 1954, but was turned down on the curious grounds that he was married. In 1956, after 11 years in the post office, he was convicted of embezzling $2500 in post office funds, and was sentenced to two years in prison. Released after a year, he moved to Leopoldville (now Kinshasa). Here he took a job as a salesman for a beer company and within a short time was promoted to commercial director.

In Leopoldville, Lumumba became increasingly involved in politics. In 1958, he formed the National Congolese Movement (MNC), the first national party in the Congo. As its leader he attended the first All Africa People's Conference in Accra, Ghana. There he met many African nationalist leaders and discussed such revolutionary ideas as pan-Africanism. After his return, the Belgians grew increasingly suspicious of him. In late 1959, they jailed him for inciting a riot in Mangobo where he had been speaking. But he was released four days later when his followers refused to take part without him in a conference the Belgians had arranged to discuss independence. Flown from jail to Brussels, Lumumba dominated the meeting. At his insistance, the conference decided that the Congo would have a strong central government rather than decentralization with strong provincial governments as many Congolese leaders wanted. The Belgians agreed to elections for a national and provincial assemblies on May 31, with independence to follow on June 30.

None of the many parties running in the May election won a majority of seats in the national assembly, but Lumumba and his MNC won the largest block and made a strong showing in the provinces as well. On the strength of the results Lumumba was named premier on June 23 and appointed an all-party cabinet. Kasavubu, the second runner, was given what was thought to be a largely ceremonial position, the presidency. A week later, independence was proclaimed.

Few new nations have faced such severe problems as soon after independence, and tried to solve them with a less-trained and experienced government. Lumumba's ousting and death solved nothing. The Congo continued to stagger from crisis to crisis until the mid-1960s when General Mobutu seized power and gradually imposed order. But the memory of Lumumba and his death lingered on, and even Mobutu may have been paying homage to it when he replaced European place names in the country with African ones, and even changed his own name to Mobutu Sese Seko.

Julius Nyerere
born 1922

Left: Julius Nyerere pictured at a press conference at the end of a state visit to Belgium.

Right: a member of the nomadic Masai tribe tends his cattle. The Masai have not taken part in any of the Tanzanian settled villages, and have remained nomads.

Tanzania (formerly Tanganyika) was probably the only country in Africa to win independence without the loss of a single life. Sir Richard Turnbull was the governor general of this United Nations Trust territory ruled by Great Britain. The mutual trust between him and the nationalist leader Julius K Nyerere helped a good deal in the peaceful handover to black rule. But even more important was the personality and character of Nyerere himself. An intelligent man, Nyerere never lost sight of his goal, but he fought for it with restraint, skill, and compromise. Once Tanzania was independent, he turned his abilities to building a new state. He soon gained a reputation as the most original political thinker and one of the most respected political leaders in Africa.

Many of Nyerere's ideas came from his background as a member of the small and rather poor Zanaki tribe, which lived on the eastern shore of Lake Victoria. Like other African tribes in the area, the Zanaki believed in the equality of all its members, and in cooperation and self-help. It had no tribal leaders until they were imposed by the Europeans. Nyerere, the son of one of these chiefs and his fifth wife, spent his early years living in a mud hut, herding goats, and learning his tribe's history, beliefs, and customs from his parents. Later, while a student at a government school in Tabora, he could not accept the privileges and status he gained as a prefect and fought to change the system. He was introduced to Roman Catholicism there and discovered its teachings on brotherhood. He was attracted and later converted.

From the school in Tabora, Nyerere went on to Makerere University in Uganda where he qualified as a teacher and later earned a degree at Edinburgh University. He returned to Tanganyika in 1952 to teach history at a Catholic secondary school near Dar es Salaam where he joined local nationalists in a discussion group called the Tanganyika Africa Association. Within months, Nyerere had been elected head of the group. Soon after he turned it into a political organization called the Tanganyika Africa National Union (TANU) dedicated to preparing the country for self-rule and independence under a predominantly African government.

At first Nyerere and TANU made little progress. The country lacked communications by which the message could be spread. Also, most educated Tanganyikans who might have helped worked as civil servants for the British, and were therefore forbidden to take part in political activities. But in 1954, a United Nations mission visited Tanganyika, and Nyerere presented TANU's case to it. Mission members were impressed by Nyerere's well-thought-out ideas, his determination, and charm. They criticized the British administration in this report, and proposed a timetable for independence. The report incensed the British governor general, Sir Edward Twining. But it bolstered Nyerere's cause and brought a flood of recruits to TANU. Following up his success. Nyerere went to New York in 1955 to address the UN Trusteeship Council. UN members again admired his carefully reasoned arguments and his restraint. But the British opposed independence and he returned empty-handed. The UN was powerless, because Britain had the right of veto.

Nyerere's political activities had begun to seriously interfere with his job. When he returned from New York, he gave up teaching to work full time for TANU. He toured the country seeking support, but as his support grew, the measures taken by Twining to hinder and

Below: the Tanganyikan Constitutional Conference of March 1961, held in Dar es Salaam. Nyerere (second right, front row) is next to the British Colonial Secretary Mr Iain Macleod.

fulness employed in the struggle for independence. Gradually he rejected many British ideas about government and society and returned to African sources for inspiration. In 1967, after much thought and experimentation, he spelled out his policies in the Arusha Declaration. The basic principle from which all others flowed was equality. To assure it, he proposed a form of African socialism in which all people including government leaders worked together for the

restrict him and the party increased. Nyerere was finally arrested in 1958, and brought to trial for criminal libel after he had criticized government officials for trying to undermine TANU. He expected to be jailed and feared his imprisonment would provoke the violent confrontation he had worked so hard to avoid.

The confrontation never came. During the course of the trial, Twining's term of office ended. He was replaced by Sir Richard Turnbull. Turnbull supported independence and majority rule for Tanganyika. He asked only that Nyerere accept the step-by-step procedure by which Britain granted independence to its colonies. Nyerere agreed.

In December 1961, less than four years after Turnbull's arrival, Tanganyika gained complete independence. TANU had won 70 of the 71 seats in the legislature in pre-independence elections, and Nyerere became prime minister. A year later, the new nation became a one-party republic within the British Commonwealth. Nyerere was elected president with 97 percent of the vote. Tanganyika was renamed Tanzania in 1964 after a coup in Zanzibar toppled the government there and the new regime agreed to a union with Nyerere's government.

With independence, Nyerere turned his attention to nation-building with the same thought-

Above: Nyerere has presided over an agricultural revolution in Tanzania. Women have been organized into cooperatives, to work together rather than individually at home. Picture shows women from the Makonde tribe winnowing rice in 1974.

community rather than for personal gain or prestige. Emphasis was to be on agricultural development rather than industry and farmers were to form villages, pool their land, and work together. Political decisions were to be arrived at within the party rather than in conflicts between parties, and the nation was to rely on its own resources and self-help rather than on foreign aid and investment.

Ian Smith
born 1919

Ian Smith of Rhodesia left University during World War II to join the British Royal Air Force. He was shot down twice and ended up fighting behind enemy lines for five months before walking over the Alps to rejoin Allied forces. Later, he went into politics and showed similar determination in fighting for Rhodesia's independence from Britain under a government dominated by the country's tiny white minority – a government deplored by Britain and most of the rest of the world. Only when black Rhodesian nationalists turned much of the country into a battlefield did Smith go some way toward conceding to demands for majority rule and accepting the inevitability of black domination in the country Africans call Zimbabwe.

The change in name from Rhodesia to Zimbabwe was almost as significant to both blacks and whites as the shift in political power. The old name commemorated the British arch-imperialist Cecil Rhodes who founded a colony there in the 1890s and invited whites to settle in it. Douglas Smith, Ian's father, took up the offer. He emigrated from Scotland and established a cattle farm at Selukwe, a small farming and mining town about 175 miles southwest of

Above: Joshua Nkomo, one of the leaders of the Patriotic Front forces. One of the Front's demands has always been that Smith be completely removed from power before any ceasefire in the guerrilla war.

the capital Salisbury. There Ian Smith was born, grew up, and attended school before going on to Rhodes University in South Africa. He left university in 1939 to enlist in the RAF and was shot down the first time in North Africa. Badly wounded, plastic surgeons had to rebuild much of his face leaving him with a drooping eyelid and a fixed expression. Returning to active duty, he was hit again, this time over Italy. He baled out, landed safely, and joined the partisans who rescued him.

After World War II, Smith returned to Rhodes University and earned a degree before entering politics in what was then called Southern Rhodesia. In 1948 he entered the Legislative Assembly as a member of the opposition. When Southern Rhodesia joined Northern Rhodesia and Nyasaland in a federation in 1953, Smith switched parties, and was elected to the federal parliament as a member of the ruling United Federal Party. By 1958, he had been named chief government whip by prime minister Sir Roy Welensky. But in 1961 he resigned from the party in protest against its support for a new constitution for Southern Rhodesia giving blacks token representation in the Legislative Assembly. Smith and other white supremacists formed a new party, the Rhodesian Front, and chose Winston Field, a respected farmer, to head it in the 1962 election for the Legislative Assembly. The party won a surprising victory. Field became

Left: white Rhodesia's war against the guerrilla forces of the Patriotic Front is hampered in rural border areas by an indigenous black population deeply sympathetic to the guerrilla's cause. Rhodesian troops' attempts at brute force have further alienated the black majority.

lock and on November 11, 1965 Smith issued a unilateral declaration of independence reminiscent of the one issued by the American colonies in 1776. British prime minister Harold Wilson ruled out armed force as a response, but he imposed economic sanctions. At Britain's request, the United Nations followed suit in December, 1966. But Rhodesia continued to receive oil and other necessities from its sympathetic neighbors, South Africa and Portuguese

prime minister of Southern Rhodesia with Smith as his deputy.

The Federation was dissolved in 1963 as Northern Rhodesia and Nyasaland moved toward independence as Zambia and Malawi under black-controlled-governments. Southern Rhodesia, now called Rhodesia, insisted that Britain relinquish the few powers it still held there as well. But Britain refused to take the final steps until the Rhodesian government provided more political and social rights for the country's 95 percent black majority. In the negotiations that followed, Field tried to formulate a compromise. But he was forced out of office by right-wing extremists in 1964. They thought he was not taking a strong enough line with Britain. On April 13, 1964, Smith became prime minister – the first native-born Rhodesian to hold the post.

He began by arresting and banishing Joshua Nkomo and other Rhodesian nationalist leaders. When the arrests provoked riots, he crushed them with police violence. In negotiations with Britain, he argued for independence under the 1961 constitution he had once rejected. The constitution provided for two voting roles. One had stiff economic and educational requirements that only whites could satisfy. But Britain insisted on constitutional change that would guarantee eventual black majority rule, or, one man one vote.

The negotiations did little to break the dead-

Above: surrounded by his Rhodesian Front cabinet, Ian Smith signs the Unilateral Declaration of Independence from Britain, November 11 1965. The illegal regime promptly set about enacting racialist laws withdrawing the few rights the black population possessed. Ian Smith's refusal to concede black majority rule, despite enormous pressure, has resulted in the situation where majority rule will be taken by force of arms.

Mozambique. The country prospered despite the sanctions. In 1970 with the backing of a referendum, Smith took Rhodesia out of the Commonwealth and severed all ties with Britain. But negotiations between the two continued, and in 1971 they reached agreement on a plan to give blacks power in 40 to 60 years. Blacks rioted against the plan, and by the mid-1970s a black nationalist-sponsored guerrilla war had forced many white Rhodesians to take up arms and was swallowing up a large percentage of the nation's income. In November 1977, Smith finally accepted the principle of universal adult suffrage.

Smith's acceptance of universal adult suffrage marked the beginning of the end of his battle to maintain white majority rule in Rhodesia. It was a battle many other white settlers in Africa had fought and lost – the French in Algeria, the Portuguese in Angola and Mozambique, the British in Kenya, and others. These whites had developed the countries where they settled and felt entitled to maintain their power there and reap the economic benefits. They lost just as Smith did because they faced a far more powerful adversary – the rising tide of black pride and African nationalism. Rhodesia is faced with violent civil war. By obstinately refusing majority rule for so long, Smith has turned the white population into an enemy to be defeated. They may not fare too well in a free Zimbabwe they had done so much to thwart.

Ferhat Abbas
born 1899

Algerian political leader Ferhat Abbas spent much of his life changing his mind. He was once a friend of the French colonial rulers of Algeria and advocated assimilation of Algerians into the French culture on a basis of equality with French settlers. When the French rejected this idea, Abbas shifted to coexistence with Algerians retaining their own culture and language alongside the French. But the French turned this down too. Finally, he called for autonomy in association with France. When the French refused again, he joined the FLN, a militant nationalist group battling for complete in-

Above: French troops patrolling in the region of the national fort in Algeria. This group is moving towards an encircled village in 1956.

Left: a worried looking Ferhat Abbas leaves the conference room at Casablanca.

dependence. After nearly eight years of bloody fighting, the French finally gave up Algeria. Abbas became the president of the newly independent country.

Abbas began his personal struggle for equality with the French as a boy in school. His father, an official in the Algerian civil service and a francophile, sent him to a French lycee. There he learned that the French firmly kept Algerians in a subservient position. Abbas began looking for ways to change things. After receiving his

baccalaureat, he served two years in the French army before studying pharmacy at the University of Algiers. Settling in Setif in the department of Constantine, he opened a pharmacy and began taking part in local affairs. He wrote editorials for the local newspaper and ran for and was elected to the municipal council and later to the council in Constantine. In 1930, he wrote a book attacking the injustices of French rule in Algeria. Three years later he helped organize the Algerian People's Union to fight for equal rights for Algerians.

During World War II, Abbas volunteered to serve in the French medical corps. He urged the French army to enlist other Algerians on an equal footing with the French in what they were calling a "war of liberation." Their refusal shocked him. In 1943, he issued the Manifesto of the Algerian People calling for self-determination. Later, he formed a political party to campaign for its support using non-violent means. But he continued to cooperate with the French, and served in the French Constituent Assembly in Paris in 1946 and in the Algerian Assembly from 1947 to 1955.

Unlike Abbas, many Algerians were growing impatient with French rule and in 1945, a nationalist uprising in Setif caused the deaths of 90 Europeans. A French reprisal took 1500 Algerian lives. The French government called for reforms to give the Algerians more say in their government. But the *colons*, French settlers in Algeria, refused to implement most of them and tried to supress the nationalist movement. Finally, in 1954, a group of radical nationalists formed the National Liberation Front (FLN), demanded complete independence under an Algerian-dominated government, and attacked government offices and police stations in northern Algeria to ensure that their message was heard. The revolt spread across the whole country and swallowed up almost all other nationalist groups.

Abbas at first held back from the FLN because he opposed violence. But in 1956 he met with its leaders in Cairo and became an active member. He traveled widely seeking support. In 1958 he was chosen to head a provisional Algerian government. Meanwhile, FLN forces had gained control of much of the Algerian countryside. They were kept out of the cities only by a French military force 500,000 strong. By 1960, the French government under the leadership of Charles de Gaulle had acknowledged that Algerian independence was inevitable. But the French Army and the colons refused to accept it. French-Algerian negotiations at Evian-les-Bains in France led to agreement early in 1962 and the agreement was overwhelmingly approved by the French people in a referendum in April. French army officers in Algiers refused to accept the position and formed a terrorist organization, the OAS, to oppose independence. The revolt

fizzled out in June after the OAS leader was captured. In July the Algerians voted almost unanimously to accept the agreement. Two days later, on July 3, de Gaulle transferred sovereignty to the new nation.

The Algerian National Assembly met in September and named Abbas as President and Ahmed Ben Bella, a radical leftist, as prime minister. They took over the administration of a

Above: French troops and *materiel* in the streets of Algiers as the FLN intensify their guerrilla campaign for Algerian independence.

Left: troops and checkpoint in the streets of Algiers. A massive security operation was launched, which included the brutal interrogation of suspects. But it failed to quell guerilla activity.

new nation exhausted by war and in economic ruin. Ben Bella sought socialist and revolutionary solutions to Algeria's problems, while Abbas urged parliamentary debate and decisions. In the end, Ben Bella won. Abbas resigned and retired from public life. Under a new constitution providing for a strong central government, Ben Bella nationalized industry and seized colon-owned land. But he moved too fast and neglected the army.

In 1965, he was ousted and replaced by Houari Boumedienne, his defense minister, who suspended the constitution and ruled through a revolutionary council.

Independence gave the Algerians the dignity and equality Abbas had sought for them most of his life. Under Boumedienne, their country also achieved stability and some economic growth. But the political power they might have had under the truly democratic government Abbas sought remained a distant goal.

Salvador Allende
1908 - 1973

earthquake in 1939 made him a popular figure. In 1945 he was elected to the Senate, the upper house of Congress. He remained in the Senate, becoming one of its leaders, until his election to the presidency in 1970.

From his earliest days in politics, Allende concentrated on Chile's economic and social problems. He blamed the country's wealthy ruling class and the free enterprise system that supported it for the poverty of the peasants and

On the eve of the 1970 presidential election in Chile Salvador Allende, the Popular Unity candidate backed by socialists, communists, radicals, and others, was talking to the press. He had run and lost three times before. Someone asked him what he would do if he was defeated again. "I'll just keep trying until the day I die," he said, "and if I don't make it, then my epitaph should read, 'Here lies Salvador Allende, a future president of Chile.'" The proposed epitaph proved unsuitable. Allende won the election and became the first freely elected Marxist head of state in the Western hemisphere, but the social and economic changes he introduced led to increased inflation, shortages, strikes, and widespread opposition. He was

overthrown in a military coup in 1973 and reportedly committed suicide before he could be taken captive.

The coup ended Allende's dream of a socialist Chile – a dream that went back to his student days. The son of a wealthy, upper middle-class, free-thinking family in Valparaiso, Allende became politically active while he was in medical school. He was jailed twice for his radical activities. After his graduation in 1932, he joined other student leaders and Marxists in forming the Chilean Socialist Party. After practicing medicine for five years, he ran for and won a seat in the House of Deputies, the lower house of the national Congress in 1937. The next year, he successfully managed the presidential campaign of Pedro Aguirre Cerdo and was rewarded with the position of Minister of Health in Aguirre's Popular Front cabinet. His management of relief efforts after a disastrous

Above left: Salvador Allende, the first democratically elected Marxist leader. Allende was dedicated to constitutional government. Many critics point to this as a major failing, and that his failure to mobilize the Chilean working class in support of his government facilitated his downfall. It is certainly true that the military junta which overthrew Allende had no respect for the constitution or any other legal niceties.

Above: when Allende won power the extremes of riches and poverty confronted him on every side. Chile was one of the richest countries in South America, yet grinding poverty was all around. Picture shows dwellers in Antofagasta.

workers, and he saw socialism as the solution. As Minister of Health, he wrote a book condemning capitalism and suggesting changes. As a legislator, he introduced more than 100 bills attacking such problems as low wages, poor health, bad housing, and discrimination. Visits to the Soviet Union, China, North Korea, and North Vietnam, and friendship with the Marxist leader of Cuba, Fidel Castro, strengthened his views.

Allende first stood for the presidency in 1952 and lost by a wide margin. The margin narrowed when he tried again in 1958 and 1964. In 1970, he won a plurality. This meant, under Chilean law, that Congress had to decide among the candidates. Right-wing conservatives in Congress opposed Allende, but liberal Christian Democrats gave him the necessary support for election after he guaranteed the freedom of political parties, the press, and unions and forbidding government interference in education.

Left: Araucanian Indians fire their guns into the air as they celebrated the seizure of a piece of land for cultivation. Such "unconstitutional" seizures were discouraged by the Allende government, and perpetrators were removed – by force if necessary.

Below: revolutionaries of the MIR and workers demonstrate demanding greater progress towards socialism.

palace. The battle last 20 minutes. When troops entered the building, they found Allende's body slumped over a sofa.

The military leaders announced that they were liberating Chile "from the Marxist yoke." They set up a four-man junta headed by army chief, General Augusto Pinochet Ugarte. Under Pinochet's leadership, Congress was dissolved and all political activity banned. One of the most brutal regimes of the modern world was established. Thousands of Chileans were arrested. The lucky ones were deported or were persuaded it would be safer to leave. The others were tortured and jailed or executed. The junta returned some nationalized industries to their former owners and compensated the owners of others. But the economy continued to deteriorate.

The coup turned Allende's dream of a socialist Chile into a nightmare of authoritarian repression. Chile, long considered the most democratic country in Latin America, took its place alongside many of its neighbors as a military dictatorship with a potentially rich but failing economy.

During his campaign, Allende pledged himself to introduce sweeping changes including social and economic planning, nationalization of the nation's rich copper mines and other industries, and redistribution of land. After he was elected he was as good as his word. Implementing legislation passed in the previous administration, he seized more than 2,500,000 acres of land from large landowners and gave it over to peasants as agricultural cooperatives. With Congressional support, he seized the copper mines and nationalized many other industries. When Congress balked at nationalization of the banks, Allende used government bonds to buy a controlling interest in them.

But his presidency created as many problems as it solved. His election was enough to frighten many wealthy Chileans. They fled the country taking their money with them. His land reform encouraged radical students and poor Chilean Indians to seize land illegally. He removed them by force. But inflation was the real culprit. Declines in agricultural and industrial production caused shortages, and prices for what was available rocketed. Gradually, many Chileans turned against Allende. By the autumn of 1973, doctors, professional workers, small business owners, shopkeepers, and housewives were demonstrating against him. A prolonged strike of truck drivers had almost halted transportation of freight in the country. Factory workers were forming private armies. The military, traditionally subservient to the elected government in Chile, bypassed Allende and acted independently to maintain some semblance of order.

In September, the commanders of the Army, Navy, Air Force and National Police issued an ultimatum demanding that Allende resign. When he refused, they attacked the presidential

Mrs Gandhi
born 1917

undisputed power on the Indian subcontinent.

In giving Gandhi two crushing election victories, the Indian people showed that they supported her package of reforms. But the country faced serious economic problems caused partly by drought and overpopulation, with corruption and inefficiency making things worse still. Both prices and unemployment were rising. Even with the largest parliamentary majority in Indian history, Gandhi failed to overcome these

Indian Congress Party leaders named Indira Gandhi prime minister in 1965, after the death of Lal Bahadur Shastri, partly because she was the daughter of Jawaharlal Nehru. Nehru, India's first prime minister, was one of the country's most respected leaders. They thought his daughter would win votes. But they also chose her because they thought she would be pliable and let them govern through her. They were wrong. She appealed to the people direct for support, and called for sweeping reforms to provide more economic and social justice for all Indians. Her leftish stance angered right-wing leaders of the party. They broke away and joined several small conservative parties in an opposition coalition. But the people backed Mrs Gandhi and her New Congress Party when she called a general election in 1971. Her sweeping election victory strengthened her position.

Mrs Gandhi consolidated her position in an even greater election triumph in state elections in 1972 after India defeated its old enemy Pakistan. India backed an uprising in East Pakistan (now Bangladesh) against the Pakistani forces trying to quash the rebellion. The split of Pakistan into two countries made India the

Above: the Indo-Pakistan war of 1971. An Indian soldier guards Pakistani prisoners of war as they clamber from a truck at Khulna, East Pakistan. They were captured during the battle of Khulna. The war split Pakistan. Mrs Gandhi had backed an uprising in East Pakistan. This region emerged from the war as the independent state of Bangladesh.

Left: Indira Gandhi, after her electoral disgrace in 1977, she is now making a determined come-back to active politics.

problems or to push through the reforms the people wanted. Many of her supporters defected, and the ranks of the opposition swelled.

In 1975, in a case pending since 1972, a local court convicted Mrs Gandhi of two minor election irregularities, and forbade her to sit in Parliament. Mrs Gandhi appealed against the decision to the Supreme Court. But before the case could be heard, she declared a State of Emergency. The Emergency was necessry, she said, because the opposition had embarked on a campaign of "internal subversion." It was calling for "country-wide defiance of laws and civil disobedience." Only strong measures could counter the threat it posed to the security of the state.

Under the emergency, civil liberties were suspended, the press muzzled, and police powers strengthened. Thousands of opposition leaders and their followers were jailed without trial. A new law was passed making Gandhi's election offenses legal. An atmosphere of fear pervaded the country.

Mrs Gandhi's son, Sanjay, emerged as her chief assistant. Sanjay took charge of a birth control program designed to arrest India's population growth. The program included forced sterilization. It became the most hated feature of the Emergency. Sanjay's own arrogance and ruthlessness provoked anger in many Indians.

The Emergency lasted 21 months and ended as abruptly and unexpectedly as it began. In parliamentary elections in March, 1977, Mrs Gandhi was defeated in her own election district and her New Congress Party was routed. Victory went to the Janata Party, a coalition of opposition groups "born in the prison cells where Indira sent us." Morarji Desai, formerly a conservative leader of the Congress Party and now leader of the Janata, became prime minister.

Desai lifted the Emergency. Within weeks India returned to normal. Newspapers freely criticized the new government. All political prisoners were released. Thousands of Indians filed cases in court alleging injustices during the Emergency.

Congress's defeat was a strange turn in the long political career of Nehru's proud and ambitious daughter. She entered politics as a

Below: sterilization operations being performed on men. Under the Emergency, Mrs Gandhi's son Sanjay was put in charge of India's sterilization. Widespread abuses occurred, and there were accusations of operations being performed on people recruited under duress, and sometimes by outright force. Nothing else under the Emergency caused such resentment.

Left: Mr Morarji Desai, leader of the Janata Party coalition. Desai became prime minister after Janata routed the Congress Party in the March 1977 elections. Mrs Gandhi even lost her own seat, where she had a seemingly impregnable majority.

child when she worked with her father for independence. After graduating from Oxford University, she married Feroze Gandhi, in 1942. On their return from their honeymoon they were both locked up for nationalist activities. After independence, Nehru became prime minister and Indira Gandhi served as his official hostess and aide until his death in 1964. She also served on the powerful 11-member central election board of the Congress Party, and was elected the party's president in 1959. In 1964, Shastri, her father's successor, brought her into his cabinet with the post of Minister of Information and Broadcasting.

Indira Gandhi's downfall saddened many Indians who did not like to see Nehru's daughter in disgrace. They said the Emergency and her support for her son, Sanjay, had brought her down – not her overall policies or any personal wrong doing. Some were not ready to consider her finished.

Makers of History

Index

Opposite: one maker of history honors another. General Dwight D Eisenhower is decorated by General Charles de Gaulle. The Allied Expeditionary Force, under Eisenhower's command, liberated France from the Nazi yoke in 1944. Both men moved from a military career into politics. De Gaulle, leader of the Free French Forces during World War II, became president of France's Fifth Republic in 1958. General Eisenhower was elected the 34th president of the United States in 1952.

Boer War, *188*, 189, *189*, 194, 222, 282
Boers, 188–9, *188*, 190, 191, 282
Bogart, Humphrey, *253*
Boleslav I (King of Bohemia), 48
Boleslav II (King of Bohemia), 49
Boleyn, Anne, 78, 79, 95
Bolingbroke, Henry St John, 1st Viscount, 119
Bolívar, Simon, 164–5, *164*, *164–5*, 167
Bolivia, 164, 165
Bolshevism, 208–9, 210–11, 228, 245
Bonaparte, Hortense, 182
Bonaparte, Louis, 182
Bonizo, Hildebrand (Pope Gregory VII), 56–7, *56*, *57*
Bonn University, 290
Booth, John Wilkes, 181, *181*
Bordeaux University, 146
Boston University, 272, 292
Boumedienne, Houari, 305, 313
Bourbon, Duke of, 65
Bourbons, 100–1
bourgeoisie, 187, 209
Boyne, battle of the, 117, *117*
Braddock, General Edward, 138
Brandeis, Louis, 239
Brandt, Willy, 271, 294–5, *294*
Braun, Eva, 219
Brest Litovsk, Treaty of, 209, 210
Brezhnev, Leonid, 265, *265*
Brietenfeld, battle of, 105
Britain
    Cyprus and, 272, 273
    Ghanaian problems, 302–3
    Hitler and, 219
    Indian problems, 258–9, 260–1, 262–3
    Irish problems, 169, 195, 204–5
    Israel and, 207, 239, 240, 241, 270
    Kenya and, 286–7
    Rhodesia and, 311
    South Africa and, 188–9, 190–1, 282
British Gazette, 222
British Museum Library, 186
British South Africa Company, 191
British Zionist Federation, 239
Brooke, Geraldine, *253*
Brutus, 34
Buchenwald, *221*
Buckingham, George Villiers, 1st Duke of, 106
Buckingham Palace, *296–7*
Buda, fortress captured at, *175*
Buddhism, 28, 29, 62, 63, 288, 289
Bulganin, Nicholai, 265
Bulow, Prince Bernhard von, 203
Burgh, Hendrick van der, 98
Burke, Edmund, 154
Bury St Edmunds monastery, 51
Bute, John Stuart, 3rd Earl of, 129
Byzantine empire, 39, 40–1, 42, 43, 47, 68, 69, 90

C

Caesar family, *32*
Caetano, Marcello, 285
Cairo, 268, *269*
    Conference, *207*
Cajetan, Cardinal, 82
Calais, French capture of, 92
Calvin, John, 84–5, *84*, *85*
Calvinism, 84–5, 92, 97, 99, 100, 142
Cambridge University, 154, 160, 168, 260
Cambyses, 18
cameos, *32*, *35*, *39*
Campo Formio, Treaty of, 152
Canaan, 6–7, 8
Canakya, 28
Canning, George, 159

Canossa, 57, *58–9*, 59
Canute (King of England and Denmark), 50–1, *50*, *51*
Cape Bojador, 66
Cape Colony, 190–1, 282
Capital, 186, 208
capitalism, 187, 193, 208, 209, 250
Caprera, 178, 179
Carchemish, battle of, 16
Carinus, 36
Carloman, 46
Carlsbad Decrees, 163
Carlos, Don Juan (King of Spain), 215
Carmona, Antonio, 284–5, *284*
Carnatic, the, 126
Carthage, 30, 31, *31*
Casimir, John II (King of Poland), 114
Casimir, Marie, 114
Cassander, 26
Cassius, 34
Castle Doorn, 203
Castlereagh, Robert Stewart, Viscount, 156
Castro, Fidel, 142, 267, 300–1, *300*, 314
Castro, Raul, 300
Catharine (wife of Matthias Corvinus), 76
Catherine I (Empress of Russia), 121
Catherine II (Catherine the Great, Empress of Russia), 134–5, *134*, *135*
Catherine de Medici (Queen of Italy), 100
Catherine of Aragon (Queen of England), 72, 78, 79
Catholic Center Party, 290
Catholic Emancipation Bill, 157
Catholicism, *see* Roman Catholic Church
Cavaliers (Royalists), 107, *107*, 108
cavalry, Polish, *114–15*, *115*
Cavour, Count Camillo Benso di, 176–7, *176*, 178
Ceausescu, Nicolai, 271
Cecil, Robert, 1st Earl of Salisbury, *94*
Cecil, William, 1st baron Burghley, 94
centaurs, *39*
Central Intelligence Agency (CIA), 300
Cerdo, Pedro Aguirre, 314
Ceuta, capture of, 66
Ceylon (Sri Lanka), 288–9
Chains of Slavery, The, 146
Chamberlain, Neville, 222, 243, *243*
Champaigne, Philippe de, 103
Chander, Douglas, 224
Chandragupta Maurya (King of Magadha), 28–9
Charlemagne (Holy Roman Emperor), 46–7, *46*, *46–7*
Charles I (King of Britain), 106–7, *106*, *107*, 108, 109
Charles II (King of Britain), 116
Charles II (King of Spain), 113
Charles V (Holy Roman Emperor), 72, *74*, 75, 78, 82, 83, 88–9, *88*, *89*, 92
Charles VI (Holy Roman Emperor), 132
Charles VI (King of France), 64
Charles VII (Holy Roman Emperor), 132
Charles VII (King of France), 65
Charles VIII (King of France), 75
Charles IX (King of France), 100
Charles IX (King of Sweden), 104
Charles XII (King of Sweden), 121
Charles, Prince (of Wales), 297
Charles, Prince (Regent of Belgium), 257
Charles Albert (King of Piedmont-Sardinia), 176, 178
Charles the Bond (Duke of Burgundy), 64, 74
Charleston Mercury, 180
Charlotte (Empress of Mexico), 171, 173
Charlotte, Princess (wife of Leopold I), 170, *170*
Checa, 42

Chiang Ching, 249
Chiang K'ai-shek, 227, 244, 245, 246–7, *246*, *247*, 248, 251, 255, 279
Chigi vase, *21*
Chile
    Allende and, 314–15
    independence for, 166–7
China
    Chiang K'ai-shek and, 246–7, 255, 279
    Genghis Khan and, 60–1
    Japan and, 246–7
    Kubilai Khan and, 62–3
    Mao Tse-tung and, 227, 248–9, *248*, 255
    Russia and, 248–9, 264
    Sun Yat-sen and, 244–5
Chinchow, storming of, *249*
Chocim, battle of, 115
Chotin, battle of, *134*
Chou En-lai, 245, 246, 248
Christian Democratic Union (CDU), 290–1, 295
Christian Democrats (Chile), 314
Christianity
    Canute and, 50–1
    growth of, 38–9
    Hébertists and, 149
    in China, 62, 63
    Mohammed II and, 67
    persecution by Diocletian, 37, 38
    Southern Slav, 232
    Wilberforce and, 160, 161
    see also Protestantism, Roman Catholic Church, Russian Orthodox Church
Chroniques de Hainault, 65
Chuh Teh, 248
Church of England, 78–9, 106, 169
churches, 8, 9, 38, 40, 41, *40–1*, 47, *74*, 78–9, *85*, *105*
    see also monasteries, mosques
Churchill, John Strange, *222*
Churchill, Lady Randolph (Jenny Jerome), 222, *222*
Churchill, Lord Randolph, 222
Churchill, Sir Winston, 196, *207*, 222–3, *222*, *223*, 225, *225*, 229, 230, 240–1, 254, *256*
city-states
    Greek, 19, 20–1, 22–3, 24
    Phoenician, 30, 31, *31*
Civil Constitution of the Clergy, 145
civil rights, 253, 258, 259, 266, 267, 292–3
civil wars
    American, 173, 181, *181*
    English, 107, 108–9
    Spanish, 214, 285
    see also revolutions
Clapham Sect, 160–1
Clark, *141*
Clarkson, Thomas, 160
Clemenceau, Georges, *194–5*, 195, 196–7, *196*, *197*
Cleopatra, 27, 33, 34–5
"Cleopatra's Needle", *12*
Clinton, General Sir Henry, 139
Clive, Margaret, 126
Clive, Robert (Clive of India), 126–7, *126*, *127*
Clovis (Frankish king), 46
Cluny, Abbot of, *59*
Cluysenaar, J. A., 59
Cochrane, Admiral Lord Thomas, 167, *167*
Coimbra University, 284
coins, *see* currencies
Colbert, Jean-Baptiste, 113
Cold War, 227, 253
Colijn, Hendrik, 234
collaborators with Germans, French, *201*
Cologne
    American tanks enter, *219*
    Cathedral, *290*

Picture Credits

334

152(L)	Musée de la Legion d'Honneur/Photo Bulloz
152(BR)	Giraudon
153(T)	Service de Documentations Photographiques
153(C)	Rudolph Britto © Aldus Books
153(B)	The Slide Center
154(L)	Mary Evans Picture Library
154(R)	*Radio Times* Hulton Picture Library
155	Mary Evans Picture Library
156–157(TC), 156(B)	The Wellington Museum/Photos Eileen Tweedy © Aldus Books
157(C)	Mary Evans Picture Library
157(TR)	*Radio Times* Hulton Picture Library
157(B)	Picturepoint, London
158(L)	Photri
158(R)	Collection of the Louisiana Historical Society. Courtesy of the Louisiana State Museum
159(T)	Museum of Fine Arts, Boston
159(B)	The Bettmann Archive
160(T)(BR)	American Historical Picture Library
160(BL)	National Portrait Gallery, London
161(L)	American Historical Picture Library
161(TR)	Photri
161(BR)	*Radio Times* Hulton Picture Library
162(L)	Bildarchiv Preussischer Kulturbesitz
162–163(CB)	Giraudon
163(TL)	Bernard Richardson © Aldus Books
163(TR)	Bildarchiv Preussischer Kulturbesitz
163(BR)	© Aldus Books
164(L)	The Bettmann Archive
164–165(TC)	The Mansell Collection, London
165(R)	Photri
166(L)	Courtesy The Hispanic Council, London/Photo John Freeman © Aldus Books
166–167(TC)	Bildarchiv Preussischer Kulturbesitz
166–167(CB)	The Bettmann Archive
167(TR)	The Mansell Collection, London
167(BR)	Photo Laird Parker, Oban, Courtesy The Earl of Dundonald
168(C)	National Portrait Gallery, London
168(B)	Mary Evans Picture Library
169(TL)	Victoria & Albert Museum/Photo John Freeman © Aldus Books
169(TC)	Reproduced by permission of *Punch*
169(TR)	Mary Evans Picture Library
169(B)	*Radio Times* Hulton Picture Library
170(TL)	Snark International
170(TR)	National Portrait Gallery, London
170(B)	*Radio Times* Hulton Picture Library
171(T)	Photo J.-L. Charmet
171(B)	Kunsthalle, Hamburg/Photo Ralph Kleinhempel
172(L)	Snark International
172(C)	San Jacinto Museum of History Association
172–173(T)	Stadtische Kunsthall Mannheim/Photo Hans Bergerhausen
173(B)	Photri
174(L)	Hungarian News Agency
174(R), 175(T)	Photos J.-L. Charmet
175(B)	*Radio Times* Hulton Picture Library
176(T)	The Mansell Collection, London
176(B)	Bavaria Verlag
177(T)	Scala
177(B)	Gordon Cramp © Aldus Books
178(T)	Mary Evans Picture Library
178(BL)	I.B.A.
178(BR)	Scala
179(T)	Mary Evans Picture Library
179(B)	Scala
180(T)	Aldus Archives
180(C)	The New York Public Library (Rare Book Division)
180–181(TC)	Chicago Historical Society
180–181(CB)	Roy Meredith
181(TR)	Aldus Archives
181(BR)	Meserve Collection, New York
182(TL)(B)	Photos J.-L. Charmet
182(TR)	Roger-Viollet
183(L)	Süddeutscher Verlag
183(R)	Goldner/Edimages
184(L)	The Mansell Collection, London
184–185(C)	Archiv für Kunst und Geschichte
185(T)	Archiv Gerstenberg
185(BR)	Jochen Blume
186(TL)	David Paramor, Newmarket
186(TR)	International Institute of Social History, Amsterdam
186(B)	Archiv für Kunst und Geschichte
187(TL)	The Mansell Collection, London
187(TR)	Snark International
187(BR)	Aldus Archives
188(T)	Jean Forest/Edimages
188(B), 189(T)	*Radio Times* Hulton Picture Library
189(B)	Bildarchiv Preussischer Kulturbesitz
190(L)	*Radio Times* Hulton Picture Library
190–191(TC)	Snark International
190–191(CB)	The Mansell Collection, London
191(R)	Mary Evans Picture Library
192(L)	American History Picture Library
192(C)	Archiv Gerstenberg
192–193(TC)	The Bettmann Archive
193(TR)(B)	Photri
194(L), 194–195(CB), 195(R)	*Radio Times* Hulton Picture Library
194(BL)	Mary Evans Picture Library
194–195(TC)	Imperial War Museum, London/Photo John Freeman © Aldus Books
196(L)	Bulloz
196(R)	Snark International
197(T)	Roger-Viollet
197(B)	Snark International
198(T)	Photri
198(BL)(CB)	Mary Evans Picture Library
198–199(CB)	© Aldus Books
199(T)	Photri
199(CR)	American History Picture Library
200(L)	Photo J.-L. Charmet
200(R), 201(R)	Roger-Viollet
201(T)	Imperial War Museum, London/Photo Eileen Tweedy © Aldus Books
202(L)	Mary Evans Picture Library
203(T)	Bildarchiv Preussischer Kulturbesitz
203(CL)	Imperial War Museum, London
203(B)	I.B.A.
204(T)	Mary Evans Picture Library
204(BL)	Fabian Bachrach/Camera Press
204(BR)	The Mansell Collection, London
205(L)(B)	John Topham Picture Library
205(TR)	*Radio Times* Hulton Picture Library
206(TL)	Imperial War Museum, London/Robert Harding Associates
206(TR)	The Mansell Collection, London
206(B)	Historical Pictures Service
207(T)	Imperial War Museum, London
207(B)	*Radio Times* Hulton Picture Library
208(B)	William Klein
208–209(T)	Popperfoto
209(CL)	Aldus Archives
209(CR)	Society for Cultural Relations with the U.S.S.R.
209(B)	Novosti Press Agency
210(L)	Süddeutscher Verlag
210(R)	Snark International
211(TR)(B)	Archiv Gerstenberg
211(CL)	Süddeutscher Verlag
211(CR)	Bildarchiv Preussischer Kulturbesitz
212(TL)	Photo J.-L. Charmet
212(TC)(TR)(BL)	*Radio Times* Hulton Picture Library
212–213(CB)	Snark International
213(R)	Ullstein Bilderdienst
214(L)	Rex Features
214(R)	Museo de Arte Moderno, Madrid/Photo Ventura
215(T)	Fitzroy Collection
215(B)	Giraudon
216	Popperfoto
217(L)	© Roy Illingworth
217(R), 218(T)	Popperfoto
218(B)	Institute of Contemporary History and Wiener Library
219(T)	Popperfoto
219(B), 220(T)	Fitzroy Collection
220(BL)	U.S. Army photo
220(BR)	Jack Pia
221(TL)	Institute of Contemporary History and Wiener Library
221(TR)(B)	John Topham Picture Library
222(L)	John Frost
222(R)	Syndication International Ltd.
223(T)	*Radio Times* Hulton Picture Library
223(B)	Rex Features
224(L)	National Portrait Gallery, Smithsonian Institution, Washington, D.C.
225(T)	Courtesy Office of the Assistant Secretary of Defense, Washington, D.C.
225(B)	Keystone

226(L)	Imperial War Museum, London
226(R)	Rex Features
227(T)	Popperfoto
227(BR)	Keystone
228(L)	Pictorial Press
228–229(C)	John Topham Picture Library
229(R)	*Radio Times* Hulton Picture Library
230(L)	Keystone
230–231(TC)	Imperial War Museum, London
231(TR)	Camera Press
231(B)	Rex Features
232(L)	Camera Press
232–233(C), 233(R)	Imperial War Museum, London
234(L)	Aldus Archives
234(R)	I.B.A.
235	ANP Foto
236(L)	Courtesy Finnish Embassy
236(TR)	Triangle Photo Service
236(B)	SOVfoto
237(L)	John Topham Picture Library
237(R), 238(T)	*Radio Times* Hulton Picture Library
238(BL)	The Mansell Collection, London
238(BR)	Fitzroy Collection
239(TL)	The Mansell Collection, London
239(TC)	Aldus Archives
239(TR)	Central Zionist Archives, Jerusalem
239(B)	Israel Labour Archives, Tel Aviv
240(T)	Central Zionist Archives, Jerusalem
240(BL)	Popperfoto
240(BR)	Photo Meyer Levin
241(TL)	Jerry Cooke/Magnum
241(B)	Israel Government Press Office
242(T)(BL)	John Frost
242(BR)	John Topham Picture Library
243(T)	Archiv Gerstenberg
243(B)	Alan Fox
244(T)	*Radio Times* Hulton Picture Library
244(B)	Mary Evans Picture Library
245	Archiv Gerstenberg
246(L)	Popperfoto
246(R)	Süddeutscher Verlag
247(T)	John Topham Picture Library
247(B)	Camera Press
248	John Frost
249(T)(BR)	Rex Features
249(BL)	Archiv für Kunst und Geschichte
250(T)(BL)	Popperfoto
250(BR)	I.B.A.
251(T)	*Radio Times* Hulton Picture Library
251(B)	Rex Features
252(L)	Photo Research Int.
252(C)	Popperfoto
252–253(CB)	Photri
253(T)	John Topham Picture Library
253(BR)	Popperfoto
254(L)	Photo Research Int.
254(B)	Fitzroy Collection
254–255(TC)	John Topham Picture Library
255(B)	I.B.A.
256(L)	Rex Features
256(B)	John Topham Picture Library
256–257(TC)	I.B.A.
257(TR)	*Radio Times* Hulton Picture Library
257(BR)	Rex Features
258(L)	*Radio Times* Nulton Picture Library
258(R), 259	John Topham Picture Library
260(L)	Government of India
260(R)	I.B.A.
261, 262, 263(T)	John Topham Picture Library
263(B)	The MacQuitty Collection
264(L)	SOVfoto
264(R)	John Topham Picture Library
265(L)	Camera Press
265(R), 266(L)	Rex Features
266(C)	Popperfoto
266(R)	NASA
267	Popperfoto
268(T)	Rex Features
268–269(CB)	The MacQuitty Collection
269(T)	John Topham Picture Library
269(B)	Associated Press
270	Camera Press
271(TR)	John Topham Picture Library
271(B)	Alan Fox
272(T)	*Radio Times* Hulton Picture Library
272(BL)	Rex Features
273, 274(L)	Rex Features
274(R)	Camera Press
275(T)	John Topham Picture Library
275(B)	Photos Alan Hutchison
276(T)	Rex Features
276(B), 277(TL)	*Radio Times* Hulton Picture Library
277(TR)(B)	Rex Features
278	John Topham Picture Library
279(R)	Rex Features
280(B)	ANP Foto
281(TL)(B)	John Topham Picture Library
281(TR)	Photo Alan Hutchison
282(L)(B)	John Topham Picture Library
282(TR)	Camera Press
283	*Radio Times* Hulton Picture Library
284(L)	Rex Features
284(R)	I.B.A.
285(T)	Tass from SOVfoto
285(B)	Fitzroy Collection
286(L)	Associated Press
286–287(C)	Photo Alan Hutchison
287(R), 288(T)	John Topham Picture Library
288(B)	Rex Features
289(L)	The MacQuitty Collection
289(R)	Ceylon Tea Center
290(T)	Bundesbildstelle, Bonn
290(B)	Popperfoto
291	Stern Archiv
292(T)	Popperfoto
292(B)	Photri
293	Popperfoto
294(L)	Bundesbildstelle, Bonn
295(L)	*Radio Times* Hulton Picture Library
295(R)	John Topham Picture Library
296(BL)	Camera Press
296(T)	Press Association
296–297(CB), 297(TR)	Rex Features
298(T)	Photo Alan Hutchison
298(B)	John Topham Picture Library
299(T)	United Nations
299(C)(B)	Rex Features
300(L)	John Frost
300(B)	Fitzroy Collection
300–301(TC)	John Topham Picture Library
301(B), 302(L)	Popperfoto
302(R)	John Frost
303(T)	Camera Press
303(B), 304(B)	John Topham Picture Library
304–305(T)	I.B.A.
305(BL)	Camera Press
305(BR)	John Topham Picture Library
306(T)	Camera Press
306(BL)	Popperfoto
307	John Topham Picture Library
308(L)	Rex Features
308(R), 309(B)	Photos Alan Hutchison
309(TR)	John Topham Picture Library
310(T)	Camera Press
310(BL)	Rex Features
310(BR)	Popperfoto
311(R)	I.B.A.
312(L)	Rex Features
312(R)	Keystone
313(L)	Rex Features
313(R)	Camera Press
314(L)	Rex Features
314(R)	Camera Press
315(T)	Eastfoto
315(B), 316(B)	Rex Features
316(T)	Popperfoto
317(T)	Transworld
317(B)	Rex Features